Fodor's

ROME

FODOR'S
TRAVEL PUBLICATIONS

NEW YORK • TORONTO
LONDON • SYDNEY • AUCKLAND

WWW.FODORS.COM

113

CONTENTS

KEY TO SYMBOLS

✚ Map reference
✉ Address
☎ Telephone number
◷ Opening times
Ⓙ Admission prices
Ⓜ Underground station
🚌 Bus number
🚉 Train station
⛴ Ferry/boat
🚗 Driving directions
ℹ Tourist office
🎫 Tours
📖 Guidebook
🍴 Restaurant
☕ Café
🍷 Bar
🏬 Shop
Ⓘ Number of rooms
Ⓢ Air conditioning
🏊 Swimming pool
🏋 Gym
❓ Other useful information
▷ Cross reference
★ Walk/drive start point

150

74

214

UNDERSTANDING ROME

Understanding Rome is an introduction to the city and its economy, its
history and people, giving a real insight into Italy's capital. Living Rome
gets under the skin of the city today, while The Story of Rome takes you
through its past.

Rome is the world's greatest historical city, its staggering monuments, museums, galleries and architectural treasures spanning almost 3,000 years. Nowhere else will you find such a surfeit of artistic riches, from the grandiose ruins of Imperial Rome to the glories of the Vatican, and from sculptural masterpieces of the golden age of the Renaissance to the baroque. However, although history has left a considerable legacy, it is not the legacy of a modern capital city and Rome sometimes strains to live up to its contemporary role. Traffic and pollution can be a problem, as can the pressure imposed by many millions of visitors on an already overburdened infrastructure. But Rome has survived three millennia, and today, as monuments are restored and problems confronted, its time-worn face is slowly adapting to the needs of one more in a long line of new centuries.

LAYOUT OF THE CITY

Rome belongs to no single historical period, but is a patchwork of ancient, medieval and modern sights. At the same time, the city is small enough to explore on foot, with all but a handful of its main sights being in, or close to, the place where it all started—the Foro Romano (Roman Forum). To the north of the Forum lies Piazza Venezia, heart of the more modern city, linked by roads that strike off to the four points of the compass: Via dei Fori Imperiali leads south, back past the Forum to the Colosseum; Via IV Novembre heads east towards a mostly newer 19th-century quarter; Via del Corso strikes north to Piazza del Popolo, passing close to Piazza di Spagna and the shopping streets around Via Condotti; and Via Corso Vittorio Emanuele II runs west towards St. Peter's and Vatican City. This last street also bisects the *centro storico,* or historic heart, the area where most of the key sights are situated, including Piazza Campo dei Fiori and Piazza Navona, two of the city's most captivating squares. This area is bounded to the west by the curve of the River Tiber, across which lies St. Peter's, and, to the south, the more traditional Trastevere area, known for its restaurants and nightlife. Farther south still is the nightlife district of Testaccio.

CLIMATE

Rome has a marked Mediterranean climate, characterized by summers that are hot and dry, with possible thunderstorms (especially in July and August) and temperatures up to 40°C (105°F). Many Romans take their annual holiday at this time, so shops and businesses can close for several weeks. Winters are short and mild, with temperatures that average 14°C (58°F) and rarely fall below freezing. Spring (late March to May) is usually brief and autumn (September to November) long: Both can be prone to spells of heavy rain or humid weather. October and November are usually the wettest months.

THE ECONOMY

Rome may be the Italian capital, but it is far from being its economic fulcrum. It lacks the financial clout of Milan, the heavy manufacturing base of Turin or the international maritime reach of Genoa. Most jobs are in the service sector, in particular those parts of it that provide for the city's millions of visitors. The state is also a big employer, with many jobs in local and national government. Office workers outnumber industrial workers by about six to one. Manufacturing firms are mainly small-scale family concerns, economic mainstays that help counter what might otherwise be a debilitating unemployment problem.

POLITICS

Italy's politics are largely Rome's politics, the city having been a political hub for millennia: head of an empire that once covered much of the known world, the headquarters of the Roman Catholic Church for almost 2,000 years, and—more recently—the seat of Italy's national government. It has been capital of a united Italy since 1870 and of the present Italian republic since 1946, when the monarchy was abolished by popular referendum. The two houses of the Italian parliament are here, the Senate (in the Palazzo Madama) and Chamber of Deputies (in the Palazzo Montecitorio); members of both houses are elected for five years. The city's Palazzo del Quirinale is home to the Italian president, elected by both houses and regional representatives for seven years. Most power, however, is wielded by the prime minister, who is usually the leader of the party with a majority of seats in the Chamber of Deputies. Much of the day-to-day administrative business in the city is carried out by the Comune di Roma, or city council, whose headquarters is in the Palazzo Senatorio in Piazza del Campidoglio on the Capitoline Hill.

SOCIETY

Rome sits on a social and economic faultline, with the more prosperous and dynamic Italy to the north and the more traditional and generally less wealthy Italy to the south. As such, its inhabitants exhibit a variety of traits, from the lingering Mediterranean habits of the siesta and a generally laid-back attitude to life, to a more northern European sensibility that is expressed through obvious displays of material well-being and the increased all-day opening of shops and offices. Rome's inhabitants also share the largely liberal values of Italians as a whole, values that can come as a surprise to those who still see Italy as a country constrained by religion and history. Divorce and abortion, for example, have been legal for decades, while one of Europe's lowest birth rates belies the notion of Italians in thrall to the Church. Indeed, while most Romans are Catholics, fewer than 10 per cent regularly attend church. To speak of Romans these days, however, is not only to speak of the familiar Fellini-esque stereotypes, as the last decade has seen the arrival of thousands of immigrants, notably from the Philippines and Eastern Europe, an influx that is changing the face of the city.

THE SEVEN HILLS OF ROME

According to tradition, Rome was built on seven hills, but 3,000 years of history means that it is difficult to see the contours of the ancient city. Look closely, however, and you can still see them.

Legend has it that the **Palatine Hill** was the site of Romulus' ancient city. In the middle of the group, it became the seat of power and the residential district of choice, and gave us the word 'palace' after the elegant houses of the patrician classes who built on its summit. Today, you can see the remains of temples and palaces on the hill, as well as the Orti Farnesiani—the 16th-century gardens of the Farnese family. To the northwest is the **Capitoline Hill**, once a fortified stronghold and later, following the building of the Temple of Jupiter, a religious hub. The Capitoline has two summits: the Arx, where a temple to Juno was built, and where the church of Santa Maria in Aracoeli stands today; and the Asylum, where Romulus allowed refugees from other towns to stay, and which is now Piazza del Campidoglio. North of the Capitoline is the **Quirinal Hill**, which, during the imperial age, was the largest residential area. Here is the Palazzo del Quirinale, home of the popes from 1573, then the official residence of the king until Italy's unification in 1870. It is now the seat of the president of the republic. Just to the south lies the **Viminal Hill**, the smallest of the seven, running towards Termini station. Farther south again is the largest of all the hills, the **Esquiline Hill**, where Nero built his Domus Aurea, the Golden House. Below this and to the east of the Palatine is the **Caelian Hill**, stretching across the city from the Colosseum to San Giovanni in Laterano. The **Aventine Hill**, the most southerly of all the seven hills, is divided from the Palatine by the Circo Massimo. It was traditionally the home of the working classes.

Opposite *Ancient ruins on the Palatine Hill*
Below *The Piazza del Campidoglio on the Capitoline Hill*

THE TREVI FOUNTAIN TO VILLA BORGHESE

Bernini's *St. Teresa* (▷ 78) This statue, in Santa Maria della Vittoria, has been called one of the most erotic in Italy.

Colonna di Marco Aurelio (▷ 61) Magnificent third-century AD bas-reliefs cover this massive column.

Frette (▷ 85) For fine Italian linens and sleepwear, head to this renowned shop on Piazza di Spagna.

Gilda (▷ 88) If you want to see and be seen, this long-established club is the place to come in central Rome. There is live music on weekends.

Giorgio Sermoneta (▷ 85) Gloves, gloves and more gloves are sold in this small shop on Piazza di Spagna.

Hassler (▷ 95) Join visiting film stars and other VIPs at their traditional luxury hotel of choice.

Hotel de Russie (▷ 96) This is by far the best of Rome's modern hotels, a successful blend of the classic and the contemporary.

***Paolina Borghese* (▷ 65)** Canova's masterful statue of Napoleon's sister, Paolina, in the Museo e Galleria Borghese is his most famous work.

Piper Club (▷ 88) Piper was trendy before the word was coined, and decades later it's still popular.

CENTRAL ROME

Antico Caffè della Pace (▷ 126) One of Rome's prettiest bars, this is a lovely place to sit, indoors or out.

La Città del Sole (▷ 121) This long-established store is crammed with educational and high-quality toys.

Il Convivio (▷ 127) Enjoy creative regional cuisine served in Il Convivio's spacious modern surroundings.

Dai Tre Amici (▷ 128) Savour the bustle and old-fashioned fittings of this traditional Roman restaurant.

Der Pallaro (▷ 128) This trattoria near the Campo dei Fiori seems to have been around forever, and offers reliable Roman home cooking.

***Gaul and His Wife Committing Suicide* (▷ 109)** Head to the Palazzo Altemps to see one of the most dramatic statues of the Classical age.

Grand Hotel de la Minerve (▷ 133) This historic hotel enjoys an excellent position close to the Pantheon.

Jonathan's Angels (▷ 124) Quirky to a fault, this eccentrically decorated bar is popular with locals and visitors alike.

Pizzeria La Montecarlo (▷ 130) Enjoy simple, inexpensive food with good service at this typical Roman pizzeria.

Raphael (▷ 133) More intimate than many of the city's luxury hotels, the Raphael offers romantic rooms behind an ivy-covered facade.

San Luigi dei Francesi (▷ 116) This otherwise modest church is made exceptional by a trio of paintings by Caravaggio.

Sant'Eustachio il Caffè (▷ 131) This café rivals the nearby Tazza d'Oro (see below) for the quality of its coffee, and has the bonus of somewhere to sit.

Spazio Sette (▷ 122) A vast range of furnishings, gadgets and other items for the home.

Tazza d'Oro (▷ 131) Join the crowds at this bustling café for what many Romans consider the city's ultimate cup of coffee.

Volpetti (▷ 123) Rome's best deli is worth a trip if you want to buy food to take home.

Above *The imposing Castel Sant'Angelo on the banks of the Tiber now houses part of the Museo Nazionale Romano*

THE ANCIENT CITY AND EASTERN ROME

Bar Capitolina (▷ 180) This bar has few rivals when it comes to views of ancient Rome.

Coin (▷ 176) A popular department store, Coin is a great place for one-stop shopping.

Colosseo (▷ 142–144) Its partially ruined state hardly dents the impact of this vast amphitheatre. Visit again at night to see the floodlit exterior in all its glory.

Equestrian statue of Marcus Aurelius (▷ 157, 160) Be sure to see either the original statue in the Museo del Palazzo dei Conservatori or the replica in Piazza del Campidoglio.

Foro Romano (▷ 146–151) The focal point of the Roman Empire, the Forum is not to be missed, particularly at night, when the ruins are floodlit.

TRASTEVERE

Asino Cotto (▷ 201) Enjoy superb seasonal Roman cooking with a 21st-century twist.

Da Agusto (▷ 202) This is the best of Trastevere's surviving traditional trattoria.

Café di Marzio (▷ 202) The popular café is one of two good places in Piazza Santa Maria in Trastevere (the other is Café dell'Arancia).

Right *Da Agusto, a traditional Trastevere trattoria*
Below *Statues by Bernini, dubbed the 'Breezy Maniacs', once lined the Ponte Sant'Angelo. Today copies stand in their place*

Pizzeria Popi Popi (▷ 203) This long-established pizzeria in Trastevere has outside tables in summer.

Villa Farnesina (▷ 193) Surprisingly few people visit this Trastevere villa, which has an exceptional series of frescoes by Raphael and Baldassare Peruzzi.

VATICAN CITY AND AROUND

Castel Sant'Angelo (▷ 216–217) This imperial mausoleum sits grandly by the banks of the Tiber.

Castroni (▷ 226) Selling all manner of delicacies from around the world, this shop stands out even in Rome, which has more than its share of good delicatessens.

Laocöon (▷ 222) This virtuoso Classical sculpture is the highlight of the Musei Vaticani's sculpture collection.

Michelangelo's *Pietà* (▷ 213) Now behind glass, Michelangelo's masterpiece is one of the treasures in St. Peter's.

Raphael's *Transfiguration* (▷ 221) In the Vatican's Pinacoteca, this painting has long considered the most sublime in the city.

Roof Garden 'Les Etoiles' (▷ 227) Fine food, with a sensational view of St. Peter's.

Stanze di Raffaello (▷ 220) Four rooms in the Musei Vaticani with stunning allegorical frescoes by Raphael.

TOP EXPERIENCES

Don't miss the Palatine Hill when you visit the Foro Romano. It's a leafy retreat with pretty gardens and sweeping views of the ancient city (▷ 160).

Walk up the Gianicolo Hill, and stroll along the ridge (Passeggiata del Gianicolo) that overlooks Rome (▷ 191).

Visit Campo dei Fiori in the morning, partly to take in one of the city's quainter squares, but also to enjoy the sights, smells and sounds of one of Rome's best markets (▷ 104–105).

When it starts to rain, don't dive for just any available cover, but head for the Pantheon, where the water pouring through the hole deliberately left in the dome is one of the city's most evocative sights (▷ 112–114).

Drink coffee in the Piazza Navona (▷ 111). Although you pay a premium to sit at a café table in the square, it's worth it to watch the constant parade of people, and to admire Bernini's famous central fountain.

Climb to the top of the dome at Basilica di San Pietro (▷ 214). The views from the top, over the Vatican Gardens and back into the city, are stunning.

Eat ice cream in Piazza Navona (▷ 111). Tre Scalini (▷ 131) makes Rome's best *tartufo*—rich chocolate ice cream topped with cream. Or try a poison apple—ice cream, coated in chocolate, with an alcoholic filling.

Throw a coin into the Fontana di Trevi (▷ 62). Throw a coin backwards, over your shoulder, into the fountain and make a wish to come back to Rome; throw a second coin to make the wish come true.

The Villa Borghese (▷ 79) is popular on weekends with families. If you want to do more than relax, take a walk through the park (▷ 82–83) or visit the Museo Nazionale Etrusco at Villa Giulia (▷ 80–81).

Mingle with the *bel mondo* on the world-famous shopping avenue, Via Condotti (▷ 118), where you'll find all the top fashion names: Armani, Fendi, Gucci, Max Mara, Valentino, Versace and (on Via Bocca di Leone, cutting across Via Condotti) Yves Saint Laurent.

View the outside of the Colosseo and Foro Romano on a summer evening, when they're floodlit (▷ 142–144 and 146–151).

Below *An evening visit to the Colosseum is not to be missed*

LIVING ROME

It's not always easy living with 3,000 years of history. Monuments tend to get in the way, and the Forum occupies a prime piece of *centro storico* (historic centre) real estate. But Romans have grown used to the challenge. Writer and historian Georgina Masson summed up the way Rome lives with its past when she called the city a palimpsest: a sheet of parchment used over and over again, with the new text written over the faded original or squeezed in between the lines. Rome is just such a sheet of parchment, except that it has many more overwritings than other cities, and far fewer rubbings-out. This reuse is seen in single buildings—as in the Teatro di Marcello, a Renaissance palace grafted onto a first-century BC theatre—but it is also seen in the ground plan of the city: Piazza Navona curves to follow an ancient racetrack, and public parks mark out the boundaries of former private estates.

AUDITORIUM MOVED

At its inauguration in December 2002, the Auditorium was the biggest new building project to have been unveiled in Rome for a number of years. Designed by Italian architectural superstar Renzo Piano—whose career was launched as Richard Rogers' partner on the Centre Georges Pompidou in Paris—this three-hall city of music is the home of Rome's premier Santa Cecilia Classical music academy and orchestra. But the €140-million complex risked not being built at all when the remains of a huge Roman villa were discovered on the site. In the end, the whole project was simply shifted around on its axis to create room for the archaeological area, which has now become an added visitor attraction, complete with a small museum.

Clockwise from above *Detail of Giacomo della Porta's 1575 Fontana del Pantheon, Piazza della Rotonda;*
Piazza Navona was built on the ruins of Domitian's stadium and clearly follows the line of the original
racetrack; modern Romans live life in the shadow of their ancestors at the Musei Capitolini

ROME'S ARCHAEOLOGY

A celebrated scene from Fellini's classic 1972 film *Roma* shows workers who are drilling a new metro line in the city suddenly breaking through into a room decorated with Classical frescoes, which begin to fade as soon as they come into contact with the atmosphere. The wealth of archaeological remains is one of the main reasons why Rome has only three metro lines. Planners have made the most of the city's underground wealth in developing the new C metro line and once fully open its stations will allow access to previously hidden archaeological sites, like the Teatro di Pompeo, and some tunnels may be lined with clear acrylic sheets to allow passengers glimpses of the illuminated ruins.

ROMANS EN MASSE

Romans are good at high-density living. It breeds habits that may appear rude to those from more sedate cultures, but that are often determined by sheer force of numbers. Queuing three or four abreast is often the only way not to spill out of the door and down the street, but you can be sure that everyone in the queue knows exactly who came in after them (in doctors' waiting rooms, new arrivals will always ask, *'Chi è l'ultimo?'* — 'Who's last?'). The same goes for parking, which is all to do with making the most of the available space—even if this means parking facing into the edge of the road (a feat that the archetypal Roman car, the tiny Fiat 500, is uniquely designed to perform).

ACQUA POTABILE

Between 312BC and AD206, 11 aqueducts were built to provide Classical Rome with fresh water. These feats of engineering passed both overland (well-preserved sections of the Acquedotto Claudio can still be seen on the road to Ciampino airport) and underground, bringing more than a million cubic metres (35 million cubic feet) of water a day into the city. Despite the fact that most of Rome's modern water supply is guaranteed by a huge underground reservoir called the Peschiera, inaugurated in 1949, three of the old aqueducts (the Acqua Marcia, the Appio–Alessandrino and the Vergine) are still in use, though the routes they follow are slightly different now. Many older Romans can still be seen filling up bottles from certain single-aqueduct fountains: They swear it tastes better than water out of the taps.

LIVING LATIN

There have been a number of attempts by Roman politicians and power brokers down through the ages to co-opt the Glory That Was Rome. In 1347, rabble-rouser Cola da Rienzo persuaded the citizens to revolt against their aristocratic bosses and establish the Senate once more on the Capitoline (this new republic lasted precisely six months). Even the popes got in on the act, giving themselves the high-sounding Latin title Pontifex Maximus (chief priest). And Mussolini pushed the Roman parallels for all he was worth, adopting the Roman *fascio littorio* (a ceremonial bundle of sticks) as the symbol of the Italian Fascist party. Today, Rome's city council continues the tradition, inscribing its motto SPQR *(senatus populusque romanus*—the Senate and the Roman people) on everything from trams to drain covers.

News of the death of Pope John Paul II in April 2005 (▷ 40) was broadcast to the crowds of devoted followers that had gathered in Piazza San Pietro. The strong sense of the Pope's final hours being an experience shared by Romans and people around the world, as well as those inside the Vatican walls, owed a great deal to his personal qualities and achievements. It showed that Romans were far from indifferent to the mini-state in their midst. Similarly, the Vatican went out of its way to keep the devoted informed. The Holy See is a well-oiled para-governmental organization, whose 4,000 employees serve an estimated 1.1 billion Catholics worldwide. Like any such organization, it has public areas—such as the Basilica di San Pietro and the Musei Vaticani—and strictly private sections, hidden behind the imposing Leonine Walls. This is where the various ministries of the Vatican State are housed; but there are also more mundane necessities, like the tax-free Vatican supermarket and filling station.

THE CONCLAVE

The conclave, or the election of a new pope, is one of the world's most mysterious ballots. It's strictly one cardinal, one vote. Following the pontiff's death, the cardinals are locked into the conclave area, which comprises the Sistine Chapel and some adjoining rooms. Voting, in which the cardinals are guided by the Holy Spirit, takes place twice a day until a successful candidate emerges. At the end of each session, the voting slips are burned. In the event of a deadlock, the slips are mixed with wet straw to produce a plume of black smoke. When a pope is finally chosen—usually after several days—a plume of white smoke (la fumata bianca) rises from the chapel to signal the end of voting.

Clockwise from above *Pope Benedict XVI meets with his cardinals in the Vatican; following his election in 2005, Pope Benedict XVI greets the crowd in Piazza San Pietro; Mother Teresa of Calcutta, a modern-day candidate for canonization*

WORKING FOR GOD

The Holy See's 600 clerical staff and 3,300 lay workers may not be paid global corporate rates, but staff loyalty is boosted by a range of tax breaks and other perks, which include free health care and subsidized rents. Vatican workers pay around a third less for fuel than they would across the border in overpriced Italy—which explains the popularity of Vatican City's two fuel pumps. The employees-only Vatican supermarket also offers substantial savings, though the patchy selection of items available can recall Eastern Europe before the fall of the Berlin Wall. The only part of the complex that is open to outsiders is the Vatican pharmacy, which stocks certain medicines that are unavailable in Italy (a doctor's prescription is required to buy these).

JOHN PAUL II—THE SAINTMAKER

Pope John Paul II (1920–2005) created more saints than any other pope in history, and more than all the popes of the previous four centuries. He also smoothed the road to sainthood, reducing the interval between the candidate's death and the initiation of the process from 30 to just 5 years. The first step, beatification, is a courtroom-style 'cause' in which the prosecuting attorney—the original 'devil's advocate'—argues against the person's holiness. Full canonization requires two proven miracles after beatification, following direct appeals to the purported saint through prayer. Even for those on the 'fast track' to sainthood, like Mother Teresa of Calcutta, the process will take at least 15 years.

THE PAPAL PAPER

The Vatican's daily newspaper, *L'Osservatore Romano*, is distributed in the Vatican City and 129 other countries worldwide. First published on 1 July 1861, the paper's original objective was to bolster and defend the Papal States, which had lost power and territory following the proclamation of the Kingdom of Italy. One of its founding articles declared its intention 'to reveal and to refute the calumnies unleashed against Rome and the Roman pontificate'. For years, many articles were written in Latin. The first weekly edition in English appeared in 1968. Ultra-serious in tone and content, the paper has been called 'the pope's own paper'. A recent issue promised a photo story on 'A day in the "vacation life" of Pope Benedict XVI' and a feature on St. Alphonsus and the Eucharist.

THE VATICAN ONLINE

The Vatican may be a male-dominated organization, but one branch at least is in female hands. Sister Judith Zoebelein, an American Franciscan nun, is the mind behind the Holy See's website. Brought over in 1991 to expand the Vatican's rudimentary computer network, she soon became involved in setting up the website (www.vatican.va), which was launched in earnest over Easter 1997. The three computers that initially handled the internet traffic were called Michael, Gabriel and Raphael, after the three archangels. After a million hits in the first three days, contacts settled to their present average of 50,000 per day. Available in six languages, the Vatican website gives access to over 25,000 Holy See documents, including some in the Vatican Secret Archives.

INSIDER'S ROME

Sometimes it's not the obvious things that strike you about a city. It might be a detail, such as the scent of cherry blossom in spring, the leisurely walking pace, or the way Italian banks seem geared towards keeping people out. In Rome, for example, visiting the Colosseum is a top tourist priority—but so is crossing the road in one piece. At first this might seem a vain hope, as cars and Vespas are often reluctant to stop even for those waiting at crossings. The local technique seems to be to stride out purposefully, all the while staring the oncoming driver or motorcyclist firmly in the eye. Roman drivers, after all, have no desire to mow down pedestrians: It messes up their car and makes them late (or, rather, later) for appointments. A little inside knowledge also helps make sense of other local stimuli, from football graffiti to stray cats; and mastering Roman habits, such as not drinking cappuccino after lunch and not leaving tips of more than five per cent, will do wonders for your self-esteem, though hard-up waiters may be less impressed.

CAFFÈ CULTURE

Coffee is a serious business in Rome and has little to do with the Americanized genre peddled in London or Seattle by lookalike chains. To do *caffè* as the Romans do, a few rules are in order. First, opt for tradition over variety: Mochacchino is unheard of, as is any form of flavoured coffee. Second, respect the time of day: Cappuccino is a breakfast drink, and no Roman would dream of ordering it after lunch or dinner. Third, learn the terminology: If you want an espresso, just ask for *un caffè*; if you want a little more water, it's *un caffè lungo*; if you just want an extra-strong espresso, ask for *un caffè ristretto*.

Clockwise from above *Scooters, the quickest way to travel through the city's crowded streets, are extemely popular; the stray cats that roam around the city's ancient sites are cared for by* gattare (*cat ladies*); Sant'Eustachio il Caffè *serves some of the best coffee in the city*

GIALLOROSSI OR BIANCOCELESTI?

Rome has two Serie A football teams: Roma and Lazio. They share the 85,000-capacity Stadio Olimpico, scheduling home matches on alternate Sundays (stadium timeshares are common in Italian soccer: AC Milan and Inter have the same arrangement in Milan, Juventus and Torino in Turin). Roma have traditionally fared better, but in 2011 Lazio finished just ahead of Roma, in fifth place in Serie A. Both teams are often referred to by the colours they wear: Roma are the *giallorossi* (yellow-and-reds), while Lazio are the *biancocelesti* (white-and-light-blues). Roma supporters are concentrated in the city itself, and tend to be more leftist (football, like everything else in Italy, is politicized), while Lazio supporters hail more from the hinterland, and mostly veer to the right.

THE CAT LADIES

Visitors to Rome are often surprised, and sometimes shocked, by the number of stray cats that roam around the city's archaeological sites. There are large communities in the Forum, in the sunken Area Sacra in the middle of busy Largo di Torre Argentina, around Caius Cestius' Pyramid and in the adjacent Cimitero Acattolico, where Keats and Shelley are buried. You will also find them stretched out in sunny spots in any sleepy square and prowling the city's parks, especially the Colle Oppio near the Colosseum. Although they are not as well groomed as pampered apartment cats, these strays are in fact quite well looked after. An army of voluntary *gattare* (cat ladies) ensure that the cats are fed regularly, report illnesses or deaths to the city council vet, and provide additional comforts such as wooden cat houses.

THE MOTORINI INVASION

As anyone who has tried to cross Piazza Venezia during the rush hour can testify, central Rome has been invaded by motorcycles and *motorini* (light, 50cc mopeds and scooters). It now has a staggering 600,000 motorized two-wheelers: that's one for every five inhabitants, more than almost any other city in the world. Rome's balmy climate is one reason for their popularity, but it's also connected to the fact that going by scooter can more than halve journey times across the city, and it makes it a lot easier to find a parking space. All two-wheelers are now supposed to have catalytic exhausts, though there are still plenty of unmodified Vespas buzzing around.

FAITH IN THE FUTURE

It was not only ancient Romans who put their faith in soothsayers and augurs. Around 100,000 citizens visit one of the capital's estimated 1,700 *maghi*, or magicians, every year. Some come for help with affairs of the heart, others because they believe that enemies have put the *malocchio* (evil eye) on them. With names like Zorzi and Osiris, these modern soothsayers have websites and advertise their services. Their customers come from all sections of society, and range from professionals to housewives; even Fellini used to consult a Turinese *mago* called Rol. In the Lazio region as a whole, the annual turnover of these tarot-readers, palm-readers and crystal-ball-gazers is estimated at over €75 million (US$100 million).

Romans are quick to complain whenever the city's place as the nation's capital—and as the spiritual home of one of the world's largest religions—causes them any grief. Hold-ups resulting from anti-government demonstrations or motorcades ferrying heads of state to and from the airport are frequent, and are part of any self-respecting *romano's* repertoire of excuses for being late. Benefits from its special status included funds supporting the 1990 World Cup and the Jubilee Year in 2000, but in recent years Rome, like the rest of Italy, has been hit by the economic downturn and new large-scale projects have been put on hold. In 2012, with the unelected bureaucrat Mario Monti in charge as Italy entered its worst economic crisis since World War II, Rome's diversified economy, which had hitherto played in its favour, ceased to mean much. Tourism and IT remain important sectors and help protect the Eternal City from some of the worst effects of the downturn, and it has been less hard hit than industrial cities such as Milan and Turin. On the political front, Rome is often split—acrimoniously at times—between the generally centre-left loyalties of the city and provincial councils, and the sometimes centre-right orientation of both the Lazio region (of which Rome is the capital) and the national government, to which the city plays host.

Clockwise from above *Palazzo di Montecitorio houses the Chamber of Deputies, the lower house; tradition holds that if you make a wish and throw two coins over your shoulder into the Trevi Fountain you will return to Rome and your wish will come true; controversial Italian prime minister Silvio Berlusconi, who resigned in 2011*

SILVIO BERLUSCONI

In a country where politicians often have a short shelf life, former prime minister Silvio Berlusconi has proved to be a remarkable exception. He began his career in property in 1962, moving into television in the 1980s, and buying the football team AC Milan in 1986. In 1993, he founded the centre-right Forza Italia party, the springboard from which he became prime minister a year later. His first term lasted just seven months, and opponents highlighted the potential conflicts of interest arising from his business interests. The criticisms didn't prevent him becoming prime minister for a second term in May 2001, and a third term in 2008. In 2011, amid an acute debt crisis that threatened the whole Eurozone, and after losing his parliamentary majority, Berlusconi resigned as prime minister. He was succeeded by Mario Monti.

A MODERN-DAY MELTING POT

It was only in 1976 that Italy became a net importer of people. For over a century, Italians were more used to being immigrants than receiving them. Romans have had plenty of experience with outsiders. In the 25 years following Italian unification in 1870, the city's population doubled. Today's immigrants, though, come not from Abruzzo or Campania but from the Philippines, Romania and Poland (in that order), plus a host of other developing and developed countries. There are established African and Asian communities around Piazza Vittorio, near the station, where it is not unusual to see impromptu cricket matches in the park in the summer. Integration, however, has been slow; most Romans still use *la filippina* as a synonym for the cleaning lady.

THE ROMAN ART OF GETTING BY

The *arte di arrangiarsi* — the old Roman knack of muddling through and of turning even the least promising situation to some advantage — extends to matters of finance and employment. The classic example is the *portiere condominiale*, the porter who, in the more well-heeled areas of the city, sits in a tiny booth at the entrance to an apartment block, screening visitors and taking messages. The *portiere*, who generally lives with his family in the basement apartment, earns a subsistence wage, collected via a tax levied on the apartments' owners. However, this basic income is supplemented by a whole range of other activities: procuring documents, doing the shopping, watering plants, taking calls from lovers — all of which carry extra fees.

MAMMA'S CHILDREN

These days, the image of a prosperous, pasta-serving mamma surrounded by dozens of children is a long way off the mark. Italy has one of the world's lowest birth rates, at 9.1 per 1,000 inhabitants, and one of the lowest fertility rates, with 1.2 children born per adult woman (compared with 1.7 for the UK and 2.0 for the US). However, *mamma* still exercises a strong influence on the few children she does have: At the last count, 56 per cent of 25- to 29-year-olds still lived at home, and the number is increasing. According to the Italian statistical institute Eurispes, the two figures are connected: 'Young people are getting married less, and until they do marry they prefer to live at home.'

WALTER VELTRONI

Roman mayor Walter Veltroni took over city hall in May 2001. His main achievement was to persuade the national government to channel €300 million into city funds. He also attempted to push through the new *piano regolatore*, the first Rome town-planning blueprint for 40 years. Veltroni was re-elected in May 2006, with a commanding 61.4 per cent of the vote. He turned his back on city politics, however, when he became leader of the Democratic Party, resigning as mayor in February 2008. He has since also resigned from this role. There's now a sense of regrouping, and although the direction his political career will take still seems uncertain, Veltroni remains a force to be reckoned with.

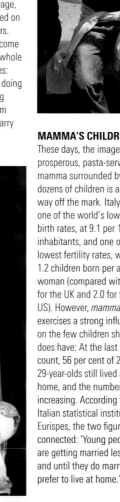

Rome is too full of life and noise and theatre to allow itself to become a museum. But this is all to the benefit of the tuned-in visitor. Caravaggio's striking *chiaroscuro* canvases in the churches of San Luigi dei Francesi or Santa Maria del Popolo are likely to seem forced and artificial until, emerging into a Roman summer evening, you see how the golden light really does slant in sideways, leaving dark pools of shadow. Bernini's baroque creations, like the Four Rivers fountain in Piazza Navona, translate the city's love of theatre and spectacle into a concerto of stone and water. To uncover Rome's artistic jewels, a little patience is needed. Alongside top attractions like the Sistine Chapel are lesser-known treats such as the church of Santi Quattro Coronati, with its medieval cloister, and that of Santa Prassede, with its Byzantine mosaics. There are quirky architectural one-offs, such as Bramante's *tempietto* (miniature temple) in the church of San Pietro in Montorio, and a few unexpected modern classics, including Mazzoni's Termini station and Libera's Marmorata post office.

PIETRO CAVALLINI

Few visitors realize that one of Italy's great medieval frescoes is not in Tuscany but in Rome. In its nascent realism, Pietro Cavallini's late 13th-century *Last Judgement* in the church of Santa Cecilia is a clear anticipation of the Renaissance. Late, great Italian art critic Federico Zeri (1921–98) went so far as to suggest that Cavallini, rather than Giotto, may have been responsible for the St. Francis cycle in the Upper Basilica at Assisi; and a recent book by Zeri disciple Bruno Zanardi lends support to the claim by demonstrating the clear stylistic analogies between the Santa Cecilia frescoes and the Upper Basilica cycle. The jury is still out — so catch Cavallini before he becomes a household name.

Clockwise from above *Carvings depicting a Roman victory decorate a small second-century AD sarcophagus at the Palazzo Altemps; the Palazzo dei Congressi, designed by Modernist architect Adalberto Libera as part of the EUR (Esposizione Universale di Roma) complex, was completed in 1954; the Fontana dei Fiumi, Bernini's baroque masterpiece, is the centrepiece of the Piazza Navona*

THE PERFECT BLUE

Renaissance painters, and their patrons, observed a rigid hierarchy of hues. It is easy today to appreciate the value of the silver and gold pigments that enriched the altarpieces of the Middle Ages, and that derived directly from the precious metals themselves. But few modern observers realize that ultramarine blue was just as valuable. Extracted from lapis lazuli, it was a costly Arabian import. Contracts would stipulate the grade to be used, in order to prevent its replacement with the inferior German blue (a copper carbonate). Without lapis lazuli, the deep blue firmament that provides the luminous backdrop of Michelangelo's *Last Judgement*, on the altar wall of the Sistine Chapel, would have faded to grey long ago.

FASCIST ARCHITECTURE

Mussolini may have made those trains run on time, but it was architecture, rather than punctuality, that he bequeathed to the Romans. Fascism is kept alive today only by a fringe of far-right nostalgics, but the clean, sharp, marble-faced buildings that encapsulated the regime's dreams of a Brave New World are still standing, in silent reproach to the lack of identity and vision of their post-war counterparts. Leading examples are the Foro Italico, built between 1928 and 1935 to host the Olympic Games; the model suburb of EUR to the south of the city, which includes Adalberto Libera's groundbreaking Palazzo dei Congressi; and Termini station, with its soaring cantilevered roof, completed after the war to a 1930s design by Angiolo Mazzoni.

PRIVATE WEALTH MAKES PUBLIC ART

In terms of masterpieces per square metre, Rome does not have a gallery to compare with the Ufizzi in Florence or the Accademia in Venice. What it does have, however, is a wealth of private collections that have remained substantially intact. The Museo e Galleria Borghese, the Palazzo-Galleria Doria Pamphilj and the Ludovisi collection in the Palazzo Altemps are fascinating because of the personalities that lie behind them and the way they illuminate the history of taste. The Ludovisis, for instance, thought nothing of asking baroque sculptors such as Alessandro Algardi to 'improve' the Classical statues they owned. Meanwhile, Scipione Borghese's mixture of hedonism and seriousness comes through in his eclectic collection, which veers from the religious piety of Raphael's *Deposition* to the worldly eroticism of Correggio's *Danaë*.

THE RARITY OF NEW BUILDINGS

Compared to cities such as London, Paris or Berlin, Rome has little contemporary architecture of any breadth or vision. Red tape is one problem; so is the sheer lack of sites in a city where nothing is ever knocked down. Well, almost nothing. Of the handful of new projects that represent central Rome's long-awaited architectural reawakening, the most controversial is the new casing for the ancient Ara Pacis (Altar of Peace) monument, designed by American architect Richard Meier. Until recently this graceful Classical altar, brought to light in the 1930s, was housed in a fascist-era pavilion, which was demolished to prepare the ground for Meier's boxy white Ara Pacis Museum. The ensuing political row blocked work on the project for a time, but this Roman masterpiece—enclosed in Meier's controversial pavilion—was reopened in 2006.

Rome has always seen itself as one big movie set. Much of the city's theatre is spontaneous: Rows erupt, jokes are cracked—Romans love playing to the gallery. It's no surprise, then, if this talent for spectacle should take more organized forms, and the natural medium for this instinct is cinema. The golden age of Roman film was in the 1950s and 1960s, when low-budget swords-and-sandals movies, many shot in the historic Cinecittà studios, alternated with intense neo-realist classics such as De Sica's *Umberto D* or Pasolini's *Accattone,* shot on location in the depressed inner suburbs. And then there were the Americans, attracted by low labour costs. Today, you can rent a Vespa to re-enact *Roman Holiday* (though helmets are now compulsory) or mime the chariot race from *Ben Hur* in the Circo Massimo. But don't attempt a *Dolce Vita*-style dip in the Trevi Fountain: The resident policeman's main job these days is to foil any would-be Anitas and Marcellos.

ALBERTONE

When actor Alberto Sordi died in February 2003, a quarter of a million Romans turned out for his funeral. In almost 200 films, 'Albertone' (Big Alberto) had become a screen icon. But Sordi was no action hero. With his *faccia da mammone* (Mamma's-boy face), he embodied a new type of Italian of the post-war generation: Outwardly modern and besotted with American values (as in *Un Americano a Roma*, 1954) but in reality profoundly Italian; outwardly the Don Giovanni (as in Fellini's *I Vitelloni,* 1953) but in reality ill at ease with women. Later in life, Sordi became an unofficial Roman elder statesman; he was even made mayor for a day on his 80th birthday.

Clockwise from above *Martin Scorsese's 2002 film the* Gangs of New York *was shot in a Cinecittà backlot; Anita Ekberg famously takes a dip in the Trevi Fountain in Fellini's 1960 film* La Dolce Vita; *Audrey Hepburn and Gregory Peck starred in the iconic 1950s film* Roman Holiday

CINECITTÀ

It was not until the 1930s that Rome emerged as the capital of Italian cinema ahead of rivals Turin and Florence. Inaugurated by Mussolini in 1937, the Cinecittà studios were built on a huge area of farmland on the Via Tuscolana. The studios worked flat out until the wartime lull, then returned to health in the 1950s on the back of a string of American productions, from *Roman Holiday* (1952) to *Cleopatra* (1963). Meanwhile, director Federico Fellini, who claimed that the real world never matched the heightened reality of a studio set, was weaving his cinematic fantasies in Studio 5. The 1970s and 1980s saw a drastic decline in Cinecittà's fortunes, with TV productions far outnumbering films.

THE NOT-SO-SWEET LIFE

Perhaps the most iconic Italian film of all time, Federico Fellini's *La Dolce Vita* was shot in Rome between March and September 1959. It was not an easy birth: The film's original producer, Dino De Laurentiis, pulled out at the last moment, alarmed by the 'chaotic' script and Fellini's refusal to replace Marcello Mastroianni with Paul Newman. Shooting was equally eventful. The famous Trevi Fountain sequence was shot on a freezing night in March, with Anita Ekberg shivering in her evening dress. Ever the entertainer, Fellini turned his megaphone to the crowd and said: 'Where would you find another like her? I've made her do things a circus horse wouldn't do. And now I'm throwing her into the water.'

THE RETURN OF THE AMERICANS

Although the days when Rome was known as 'Hollywood on the Tiber' are long gone, the 1990s saw a return of big-budget international productions to the competitively priced Cinecittà studios. First came two Sylvester Stallone vehicles, *Cliffhanger* and *Daylight*; interior scenes of *The Portrait of a Lady* and *The Talented Mr Ripley* were also shot here. Then, in the autumn of 2000, the heavy artillery moved in, when Martin Scorsese built a replica of 1860s New York on the studio backlot for *Gangs of New York*. With Hollywood A-listers like Leonardo DiCaprio and Cameron Diaz in town, it was paparazzi paradise. The city continues to be a popular setting for movies; the 2009 adaptation of Dan Brown's novel *Angels and Demons* and *The American* (2010), starring George Clooney, were shot here.

ITALIAN CINEMA

It's not quite true that nothing has happened in Italian cinema since the days of Fellini, Pasolini, Antonioni and Bertolucci, but it's an understandable assumption, as few contemporary Italian films are distributed abroad, and those that are tend to languish in arthouse cinemas. The exception is the 1997 Oscar-winning film *La Vita è Bella (Life Is Beautiful)*, directed and co-written by Roberto Benigni, and in which he played a lead role. The film, which tells the story of Jewish Italian Guido Orefice and his family before and during World War II, was a huge international hit, but not really representative of the new Italian cinema, which is at its most incisive in the films of Nanni Moretti *(The Son's Room*, 2001*)*, veteran political filmmaker Marco Bellocchio *(The Divinity Lesson*, 2002*)*, and Ferzan Ozpetek *(Ignorant Fairies*, 2002*)*.

LA BELLA FIGURA

If style is all about care for your appearance, an instinct for what looks good and the ability to project self-confidence, most Romans have it in abundance. These personal qualities can be observed during the evening *passeggiata*. Though not as strong a tradition as it is in other towns further south, the custom of walking up and down observing others who are also walking up and down reaches critical mass along Via del Corso on Fridays and Saturdays between 5pm and 8pm. But if style is interpreted in the more Northern European sense of originality and standing out from the crowd, many Romans would fail to qualify. Roman style tends to be fairly conformist, opting for the prevailing designer uniform rather than going out on a customized limb. In fashion terms, Rome is more provincial, but also more relaxed, than Milan, Italy's *capitale della moda* (fashion capital). The only big designer to have made his power base in the city is Valentino, though the Fendi siblings and a few mavericks such as Roberto Cappucci are strong supporting acts.

VALENTINO

Though he hails from Voghera in the north of Italy, Valentino long ago adopted the Eternal City as the hub of his fashion empire. Valentino Garavani, as he was christened in 1932, moved to Rome in 1959 after a stint as an apprentice in the couture houses of Paris. It was the White Collection in 1967 that really made his name and before long he was dressing such divas as Jackie Kennedy and Elizabeth Taylor. His Roman headquarters is at Rampa Mignanelli, just behind the Spanish Steps, where the *alta moda* (haute couture) collections are presented in January and July.

ROMAN STYLE

Understand *bella figura* and you're halfway to understanding the Romans. *Bella figura* is a little bit presence, a little bit self-respect and a little bit being careful not to let your team down. It's what *carabinieri* motorcycle cops are communicating when they lean against their Moto Guzzis in jodhpurs and wraparound shades; it's what makes kids from the financially depressed outer suburbs dress up on Saturday night as if they were in Beverly Hills. The opposite is *brutta figura,* to show oneself up. In Rome, it's not so much what you've got, it's what you project.

Above *The early evening* passeggiata *in Trastevere*

THE STORY OF ROME

All civilizations have their creation myths, like the tale of Romulus and Remus. We know for certain that tribes had colonized the Seven Hills of Rome by 1000BC, between the Etruscans to the north and the Greeks to the south. The Etruscans soon dominated the city and brought with them much of what we regard as typically Roman: irrigation, temple-building, gladiatorial displays and togas. Their aristocratic rule was oppressive, and the last of the kings was driven out in 509BC. The following republic was a system of power-sharing among noble families, but rights for commoners were gradually won, set out in the Twelve Tables in 450BC and displayed in the Forum. Over the next two centuries the Romans conquered Italy and moved inexorably beyond. They defeated the Carthaginians so, by the end of the Third Punic War in 146BC, the Roman Empire comprised Italy, the western Mediterranean and Asia Minor. Strict warrior values had created it, but the aristocracy appropriated land and wealth, leaving soldiers and peasants almost nothing. Attempts at reform from the top, led by the Gracchi brothers, and from the bottom in the form of slave revolts, achieved nothing. By 100BC the rulers of Rome had become violent, selfish and dictatorial.

ROMULUS AND REMUS

The legend goes that Romulus and Remus were the twin sons of Mars and a Vestal Virgin. Left to die on the banks of the Tiber, they were cared for by a she-wolf and fed by a woodpecker. The brothers grew up to be robbers and wandered with a band of men. Romulus took possession of the Palatine Hill and founded Rome on 21 April 753BC. Remus set up his rival kingdom on the Aventino. Eventually, Romulus killed Remus and his power grew. The legend rings true in one respect: the gaining of imperial power through violence and murder within the family, which was to become a familiar pattern in Roman history.

Clockwise from above *A sixth-century Etruscan bronze of the she-wolf feeding Romulus and Remus, legendary founders of Rome, on display in the Palazzo dei Conservatori; the Via Appia Antica was built in 312BC and is still paved with its original basalt cobbles; Giambologna's powerful statue* Rape of the Sabine Women

THE RAPE OF LUCRETIA

According to tradition, in 509BC Sextus Tarquinius, the son of the Etruscan king, went to visit Lucretia and her husband, Collatinus, one night, and they fell to discussing virtuous wives. Lucretia, a true Roman matron, was strict and irreproachable, and Tarquinius, aroused by this, determined to seduce her. He came back when she was alone, threatened her and then raped her. With her honour gone, Lucretia committed suicide after telling her husband what had happened. This act represented everything that was wrong with the corrupt Etruscan monarchy, which was plundering the country and trampling on Roman virtues, so Collatinus and his powerful friends rose up in revolt. The people of Rome supported them, the King was forced into exile and the Republic was established.

THE CAPITOLINE GEESE

In 390BC, an army of Gauls surrounded Rome. The smaller Roman army withdrew and evacuated the city except for the Capitoline Hill, where the soldiers were besieged. The hill had long been a place of refuge, home to two important temples, including that of Juno Moneta. One night a former consul, Marcus Manlius, woke to hear the honking of geese, which the starving soldiers had not eaten because they were sacred to Juno. Manlius looked over the wall in time to see the shield of a Gaulish soldier who was about to climb over. He knocked him back, and a volley of stones and javelins from the other soldiers sent the Gauls to their deaths. The Capitoline Hill was never taken, but the Gauls stayed in Rome for seven more months, and left only when they received a hefty ransom.

THE THEFT OF THE SABINE WOMEN

Romulus' fledgling state needed women, so he decided to steal some. In 750BC, he invited the nearby Sabine tribe to attend a ceremony in honour of a newly discovered holy altar to the god Concus. The Sabines came peacefully, and Romulus and his armed men simply ran away with their women, 683 of them if legend is true. Strangely enough, after a few skirmishes both sides agreed to avoid a ruinous war and cooperate. Romulus, with typical Roman pragmatism, then ruled over the Seven Hills jointly with the Sabine chief, Titus Tatius. This joint-rule system entered Roman government: Consuls often worked in pairs, as did many of the other officers of state.

THE GRACCHI BROTHERS

The tribune Tiberius Gracchus attempted to break up the great estates of the rich and distribute the land to the poor, especially former soldiers, who were wandering the country. The Senate, composed of the owners of great estates, was horrified to see the growing public support for Tiberius and hired a band of thugs to kill him. He was beaten to death with a chair leg outside the Capitoline temple, and 300 supporters were thrown into the Tiber. In 120BC his brother Sempronius met the same fate over the same issue, and 3,000 followers were murdered. These acts of shocking violence by the very men supposed to uphold the law set the scene for the fall of the Republic.

Riot, unrest and civil war in the first century BC led to the emergence of the army and the rise of ruthless dictators as the guarantors of public order, gladly supported by the Senate. The brutal rule of Sulla was followed by the first triumvirate in 70BC, composed of Pompey, Crassus and Julius Caesar. They resisted all attempts by the Senate, somewhat belatedly, to regain democratic power. The triumvirs eventually turned on each other. In 49BC Julius Caesar crossed the Rubicon from his territories of Gaul and took control of Rome; by the following year he was sole ruler of the Empire. Caesar was an autocrat who demanded total obedience: The Republic was finally at an end. The Senate nevertheless rallied its forces, albeit for the last time, and a group of conspirators murdered the dictator in 44BC. What followed was a contest for power between the impulsive, emotional Mark Antony and the icy, calculating Octavian. Antony was absent from Rome for long periods during his spectacular love affair with the queen of Egypt, Cleopatra, while Octavian built up his military base in the western part of the Empire. After moving against Antony and defeating him at the Battle of Actium in 31BC, Octavian secured the Empire for himself to become the first emperor, Augustus.

MARIUS AND SULLA

Gaius Marius, the son of a farmer, and Lucius Cornelius Sulla, an aristocrat, played out the murderous rivalry that Romulus and Remus had set as the Roman pattern. The men had once been comrades, but, as the Republic was about to collapse, Marius, seven times consul, wanted to break the power of the Senate; Sulla was determined to oppose him. Marius massacred the Senate and thousands of aristocrats in 87BC. After Marius' death, Sulla murdered his foe's army. He formed a dictatorship and paraded through the streets protected by a vicious force of 10,000 slaves, the Cornelii. When Sulla abruptly stepped down and retired to the country, he left Rome brutalized and the Senate ripe for overthrow.

Clockwise from above *Built in 62BC, Ponte Fabricio is the oldest bridge in the city; Julius Caesar was murdered in the Senate on the Ides of March (15 March) 44BC; a bust of Julius Caesar*

SPARTACUS

There were three slave revolts between 140BC and 70BC. Life rested on the caprice of the master: 'Lighten a ship by throwing out the slaves, not the horses,' Cicero said, while the philosopher Seneca thought slavery the worst shame of the Empire. Spartacus, possibly a deserter, was a slave in the gladiator barracks in Capua in 73BC, when he escaped with 70 other gladiators and weapons from the kitchens. They hid on the slopes of Vesuvius and were soon joined by other escaped slaves and gladiators. Spartacus wanted to lead his men to freedom across the Alps, but his followers sought to plunder the surrounding countryside, attracting punitive action from Rome. For two years Spartacus' army (120,000 strong at its peak) managed to defeat all the forces the Roman Senate sent to deal with it. Eventually, in 71BC, his forces were defeated at Brindisi, and 6,000 slaves were crucified along the Appian Way. Spartacus died in battle and his body was never found.

CICERO

Cicero (106BC–43BC) was Rome's best lawyer, a respected author with political skills that made him consul in 63BC, a position usually reserved for members of the aristocracy. These were violent times — killing was state policy — and he spent much time on murder trials. In 80BC the young Cicero made his reputation defending Sextius Roscius for the murder of his father. In a barnstorming speech he described the horrible punishment for this: being tied up in a sack and thrown into the sea. Then Cicero dared to suggest that a servant of Sulla, the dictator of Rome, was the real murderer. This was a brave challenge to Sulla's authority and could easily have resulted in the young, unknown lawyer being murdered. Sensationally, however, the jury believed him and Roscius was acquitted of patricide. Cicero's career as a lawyer was launched. In time his versatile mind ensured that he became equally celebrated as an orator, philosopher, statesman, writer and political theorist.

THE ASSASSINATION OF JULIUS CAESAR

Julius Caesar was dictator of Rome. 'Regard what I say as law,' he declared. When the Senate, gritting its teeth, knelt before him, Caesar stayed seated. In the atmosphere of brutality and murder that he had used himself, Caesar's fate was sealed. A group of conspirators planned his murder for 15 March 44BC in the Senate. Caesar seemed not to fear assassination, and the night before he died said he wanted a quick and unexpected death. He ignored all warnings. The conspirators stabbed him 23 times, and a strange detail is recorded: He put his toga around his head, then drew the bottom around his thighs to preserve his modesty. He knew he was going to fall.

ANTONY AND CLEOPATRA

In 41BC Mark Antony, joint ruler of the Empire, became captivated by Cleopatra during her spectacular entrance to Tarsus, on a bejewelled ship with silver oars, dressed in cloth of gold. Antony left his wife, and he and Cleopatra were crowned as semi-divine rulers of Egypt. Rome was outraged: Antony had abandoned his country and ideals. His co-ruler, Octavian, declared war and met Antony's navy at Actium in 31BC. The battle was won by Octavian, and Cleopatra sailed away. Antony had to choose. He still had his armies and his wealth: Rome might still be his. Nevertheless, he decided to sail after Cleopatra and lost everything. They committed suicide together the next year.

C. JULIUS CÆSAR.

EX:NUM:MUS:GUL:HUNTERI.

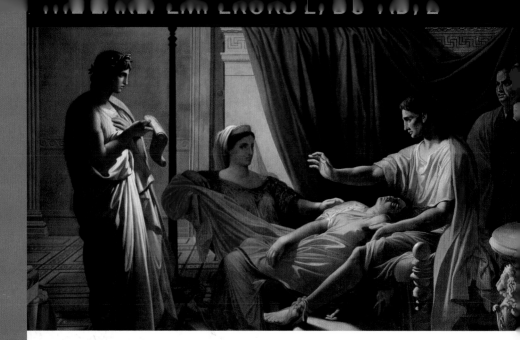

The 41 years of Emperor Augustus's rule (27BC–AD14) were looked back on as the Golden Age by the Romans. He halted expansionist wars, set up a government bureaucracy and transformed the face of Rome itself. Too shrewd to accept the title of emperor—he was called 'First Citizen'—Augustus held all major posts in government, the army and religion for life, while leaving the forms of the Republic intact. The glory of his reign notwithstanding, it set the scene for the breathtaking excesses that followed: Tiberius, Caligula and Nero were known for lust, perversion and cruelty. A well-ordered bureaucracy ensured the Empire almost ran itself: Germanicus easily suppressed revolts in Germany (AD14–16), and great public buildings rose throughout Italy. However, Tiberius (AD14–37), fearing conspiracy, invoked laws to suppress any opposition; Caligula (AD37–41) despised the Senate so much that he planned to turn the Empire into an autocracy. Fear and oppression seeped into government, and the emperors depended on the Praetorian Guard to terrorize opponents. Claudius (AD41–54) bribed the Praetorians well, but the reckless actions of his successor, Nero (AD54–68), antagonized the Senate and lost him the army's support. Nero fled the city and committed suicide in AD68.

AUGUSTUS

The first emperor, Augustus (previously known as Octavian; ruled 27BC–AD14), lived in a modest villa by the Palatine, but he made the city splendid, saying, 'I found Rome built of brick; I leave it clothed in marble.' This was not personal vanity; Rome had to be grand in the eyes of the world and orderly for its citizens. A hundred public buildings were raised; *insulae*, tenements for the poor, were limited in height to 25m (80ft). The city was divided into 250 precincts, each with its own police force and fire brigade—the poor made do with wood, not marble, and Rome was forever in flames. To deal with this, Augustus's architect, Agrippa, created a remarkable system of six aqueducts, which brought in more than a billion litres (220 million gallons) of water a day.

Clockwise from above *A 19th-century depiction of the Emperor Augustus by Jean-Auguste-Dominique Ingres; Emperor Nero, best remembered for his debauchery and extravagance; the reign of Augustus was a Golden Age, in which the arts flourished*

CALIGULA

The notorious Caligula (ruled AD37–41) endured a traumatic childhood and probably suffered from some kind of mental illness. His appearance—tall, thin, bald and hollow-eyed—was truly frightening. Stories about his depraved private life are outdone only by accounts of his amazing extravagance. He sailed along the coast in jewel-studded galleys fitted with baths and dining rooms. He offered dinner guests victuals made of gold. Mountains were levelled and plains raised for his public buildings, all at high speed since everything was done under threat of death. He showered people in the streets with gold and liked rolling around on heaps of it. The coffers were soon empty. In just one year, it is estimated, he spent 3 billion sesterces, a sum equivalent to the entire revenue of Tiberius's 23-year reign.

NERO

Nero (ruled AD54–68) wanted to be a great actor and athlete. Progressing from private theatricals, he made his debut in Naples during an earthquake, warbling to his lyre and dressed in garish wig and robes. He entered competitions and, naturally, won. During a tour of Greece, he won 1,808 prizes, including one for a race when he'd fallen out of his chariot and been knocked senseless. Contemporaries giggled over his awful acting, but he was probably just mediocre. The doors were locked when he performed and the audience, bored to tears, endured endless applause and encores. More seriously, the Senate abhorred Nero's neglect of government business and rose against him. Deluded to the end, he fled Rome crying, 'What a loss I shall be to the arts!'

CLAUDIUS

It was easy to make fun of Claudius (ruled AD41–54) in his lifetime. He stammered and trembled, gave way to screaming anger, and stuffed himself with so much food and drink he frequently fell asleep in the middle of a banquet. His mother called him a monster whom Nature had begun but failed to complete, and he was regularly the object of practical jokes. As often happens, the embittered, humiliated man retreated to the world of books and learning. He made himself a formidable scholar. Pliny regarded Claudius as one of the greatest minds in the Roman Empire. Claudius wrote a treatise on dicing, a study of the Roman alphabet and a 20-volume Etruscan history whose loss is a tragedy for historians.

ST. PETER IN ROME

Peter probably visited Rome in the AD50s and it's almost certain that he died there during the persecution of the Christians begun by Nero around AD64. Some of those martyrs were torn to pieces by animals, others smeared with pitch and burned as human torches in the Circus of Nero to illuminate night-time races. According to early Christian tradition, Peter was crucified upside-down at his own request, feeling unworthy to be killed in the same way as Christ. In AD324, Constantine built a church on the site of the Circus of Nero, which was subsequently replaced by Pope Julius II's 16th-century basilica that we see today. In the crypt of the great basilica is a place that tradition glorifies as St. Peter's grave.

For nearly two centuries, the citizens of Rome enjoyed peace and wealth. The five 'good emperors' of the Antonine dynasty—Nerva, Trajan, Hadrian, Antoninus and Marcus Aurelius (ruled AD81–180)—worked with the Senate, and the Empire expanded to its greatest limits. Soon, though, its very size proved its undoing. A huge army of approximately half a million men, composed of many different nationalities, could not easily be controlled. The army started to dictate policy, and local commanders were often made emperor without ever seeing Rome. In AD193 the Praetorian Guard put the Empire up for sale—the winner lasted 66 days in power. In all, some 50 emperors came and went in the period up to the beginning of the rule of Diocletian in AD286. The enormous territories in the east meant Rome no longer occupied its central role. Recognizing that the Empire was ready to collapse under its own weight, Diocletian divided it into the Western and Eastern empires, under two rulers, which brought some respite from political tension. Diocletian then tackled a much greater force for change, the Christians. He persecuted them ruthlessly, but the conversions went on and Christianity continued to grow and develop, with converts increasingly coming from all ranks of society.

THE COLOSSEUM

The ruins of the Colosseum, built AD72–96, dominate the city today, much as the games once held within dominated Roman life. Their equivalent today is the hugely expensive blockbuster movie with its pampered stars, but there the similarity ends. A successful gladiator might be adored by the whole city, but, as Seneca said, 'this was a serious business— pure murder.' The games themselves probably evolved from Etruscan funeral games, and this echo of the underworld never left them. At the games of Trajan in AD107, for example, 80,000 people watched 10,000 men fight to the death over a period of four months. As they became an instrument of social control, more frequent games with greater cruelty kept the populace in line.

Clockwise from above *Construction of the Colosseum began in AD72 and was completed in AD96. Serious conservation of its ruins started in the 19th century; a detail of the Colonna Traiana in Trajan's Forum, whose exquisite bas reliefs depict scenes from the Dacian wars; a bust of the Emperor Hadrian (ruled AD117–138)*

THE FEASTS OF ELEGABALUS

Even by Roman standards, Elegabalus (ruled AD218–221) is astonishing. He was a teenage Syrian covered in makeup, jewels and silk, and the tales of his luxury are astounding. He liked to swim in pools stained yellow with saffron, and to walk on roses and lilies. At his feasts guests lay on couches of solid silver; one evening the food was blue, the next it was green. He liked to eat peacocks' tongues, then suddenly would demand nightingales' tongues instead. Once, 600 ostrich heads were served and guests ate their brains. Not surprisingly, the guests often fell asleep in a stupor. Elegabalus would then lock them in the hall, and send in tame bears and lions to wake them up.

ROME WITHOUT AN EMPEROR

In AD300, more than 1,000 years after Romulus occupied the Palatine Hill, the emperors left Rome. The vast city was a rich brew of contrasting nationalities, from Arabs to Britons and Turks. The emperor himself might be African or Spanish, but he had always respected Rome as the focal point of the Roman world: Diocletian had no such scruples. He came from Dalmatia, toured the Empire as all the emperors had done, and it's probable that he did not even see Rome until he was almost 60. He didn't like the excess and corruption, and found Milan to the north and Nicomedia to the east far more practical as capitals. They were built up swiftly and soon became as grand as the Eternal City itself.

TRAJAN

During Trajan's reign (ruled AD98–117) the *Pax Romana* (Roman Peace) extended over a huge empire, from Scotland to Portugal, over the Sahara to the borders of Persia, and into Germany. Trajan expanded the Empire to its limits, his armies following the routes of Alexander the Great. Trajan was a typical mixture of Roman brutality and magnanimity. The Dacians (modern-day Transylvanians) were completely subdued by him. Their gold was taken to Rome and thousands of men and women brought there as slaves and gladiators. Yet Trajan forbade the persecution of Christians, causing the governor of Bithynia, worried about that troublesome group, to write that 'they create the worst kind of precedent and are out of keeping with the spirit of the age.'

HADRIAN

Hadrian (ruled AD117–138) spent most of his time journeying through the Empire and usually left a building or two behind him. In Britain, he constructed a wall across the north to keep out marauding tribes. In Egypt, an entire city, Antinopolis, was raised in memory of his friend, Antinous. Two buildings in Rome express the opposites in his personality, the cool-headed administrator and the imperial master. The Pantheon is a masterpiece of design — classical, deceptively simple, perfectly symmetrical, the work of the man who revised the codes of tax and the law. On the other hand, his tomb — renamed Castel Sant'Angelo in the sixth century — turned out to be an immense piece of unsubtle grandeur, so vast that medieval Romans used it as a fortress.

Christianity became the state religion under Diocletian's successor, Constantine (AD306–37). Although he moved the capital to Byzantium, Rome became the Empire's spiritual hub. Increasingly, the western borders were under threat from Goths and Vandals. The city was sacked several times and in AD476 the last Roman emperor, Romulus Augustulus, was deposed. During centuries of war between the Byzantine Empire and the Goths, the popes acquired territory known as the Papal States and the authority to crown the Holy Roman Emperor. The Emperor of Germany claimed rights over the election of the pope, and only under Innocent III (1198–1216) did papal power finally become independent. Throughout this turmoil Rome shrank to a provincial town. In AD546, reduced to rubble by the Goths, it was deserted for weeks. The papacy alone ensured Rome's survival, but its very wealth and power sparked such feuding that the popes fled to France from 1307 to 1377. The demagogue Cola di Rienzo set up a republic based on ancient principles during this period, but it soon collapsed. The return of the papacy was marred by the Great Schism of the West, when popes and antipopes fought for control of the Church, each backed by half of Europe. Only in 1417 did Rome gain its position as the residence of the true pope.

THE CONVERSION OF CONSTANTINE

No one is sure when Constantine converted to Christianity. Was it at the vision of a flaming cross in the sky in AD312, or at his deathbed baptism in AD337? Despite being the son of St. Helena, who found the True Cross, did he genuinely convert at all? What mattered was that a spirit of Christianity began to pervade the Empire. A master who mistreated his slaves was punished, children were protected from abusive parents, prisoners no longer fought in gladiatorial displays, which were denounced by Constantine as 'bloody spectacles'. Much money was spent on erecting churches, many at sites linked with events of the New Testament. Constantine himself gave up imperial power, and the honour of being high priest of the state religion now went to the Bishop of Rome.

Clockwise from above *The 12th-century Byzantine mosaic in the church of San Clemente; Charlemagne was crowned Holy Roman Emperor in AD800, an event which marked a turning point in the fortunes of the Western Empire; Pope Gregory the Great was canonized after his death*

THE SACK OF ROME

The Goths, being driven out of their own lands by invading Huns in AD370, moved south into Greece and then, in AD400, under their leader Alaric, attacked Italy. The Italians begged Alaric to stop, but he told them of a voice urging him on: 'It says to me, "Go to Rome and make that city desolate."' The day came when he besieged the city itself. Alaric told Roman ambassadors to give him all their gold, silver and slaves. Horrified, they asked what he would leave them. 'Your lives,' he replied. The Goths stripped Rome in four days and left behind a traumatized city. Rome had been inviolate for 800 years and the sack of the city sent shock waves through the civilized world. Although the Empire survived a little longer, the attack heralded the end of the Imperial era.

POPE GREGORY THE GREAT

Gregory I combined the grandeur of his position with the simplicity of a true Christian, eating sparingly and giving money to the poor. His revision of the Mass introduced Gregorian chant. He sent St. Augustine to England to convert the Anglo-Saxons ('not Angles but angels'). Gregory became pope in AD590, a testing time: Rome was gripped by plague. He arranged penitential processions in Rome to ask for God's mercy. On his procession near the Tiber, he had a vision of an angel in the sky sheathing a bloody sword; from that moment the plague ended. The building beneath the vision, Hadrian's Tomb, was renamed the Castel Sant'Angelo. On his death, Gregory was made a saint by popular acclamation.

CHARLEMAGNE, HOLY ROMAN EMPEROR

Pope Leo III was attacked by jealous rivals who wanted the wealth of the papacy for themselves; he also needed to separate the Church from the influence of the Byzantine Empire. He was fortunate to find his saviour in Charlemagne, king of the Franks, a truly great leader, enlightened and energetic. Charlemagne arrived in Rome and Leo was reconciled with his enemies. They then played out a little charade: Charlemagne, who happened to be wearing splendid robes, went to St. Peter's on Christmas Day AD800 to attend Mass. Suddenly, the Pope drew out a crown, put it on the amazed King's head and declared him Holy Roman Emperor. Rome now had a worthy successor to the likes of Trajan and Hadrian.

THE POPES LEAVE ROME

The medieval Church was cursed by its wealth and power. Everyday corruption was so great, and papal elections themselves so violent, that the popes were driven out of the city. For almost 70 years from the beginning of the 14th century, the papacy resided in Avignon, in the south of France. For a while the popes were safe, but the greed of King Philip of France (which lay behind his original invitation) soon infected the Court of Avignon. The poet Petrarch, a man of immense public influence, pleaded with the popes to come back to their traditional home in the city. Finally, it was a young mystic, Catherine of Siena, who is said to have convinced Pope Gregory XI to leave France and return to Rome in 1377.

The papacy dominated Rome completely. Clement VII, trying to lessen the power of the Habsburg Emperor by a treaty with France, drew down on himself the terrifying Sack of Rome in 1527. After this, the energy of the papacy was taken up with the Counter-Reformation. Paul III (1534–39) approved a new order, the Jesuits, whose members pledged their services to the pope and tackled heresy. Papal wealth continued to attract the Roman nobility. Some were monsters, like Roderigo Borgia (Pope Alexander VI, 1492–1503); others were great patrons of the arts, such as Urban VIII (Maffeo Barberini, 1623–44), who issued a directive for public building.

Rome's glory was the baroque. Even so, Julius II (1503–13) brought the Renaissance masters to the city and commissioned Bramante to rebuild St. Peter's in 1503. In the 17th century the flamboyant baroque architecture of Bernini and Borromini filled the city, and much of the Gothic and Romanesque disappeared. Sometimes, building materials from ancient monuments were used. The papal coffers were emptying fast, and Rome's influence and importance all but vanished in the 18th century. As the century ended, Napoleon annexed the Papal States to the French Empire and forced Pope Pius VII to come to France as a virtual prisoner.

THE SISTINE CHAPEL

Julius II and Michelangelo were both strong-willed men who secretly enjoyed their tempestuous relationship. When Julius sent envoys to arrest the artist, who had left Rome in a huff, Michelangelo returned with a rope around his neck, a childish symbol of imprisonment. In 1508 Julius commissioned Michelangelo to decorate the ceiling of the Sistine Chapel. He wanted a pattern of circles and squares bordered by the Twelve Apostles. Michelangelo retorted he would paint anything he liked. Wisely, Julius let him alone, fully understanding the nature of his genius. However, after four years of painting, it was only when Julius threatened to hurl the man off his scaffold that Michelangelo showed off his masterpiece, one of the most magnificent frescoes in the world.

Clockwise from above *Michelangelo's frescoes on the ceiling of the Sistine Chapel are an artistic tour de force; the Fontana dei Fiumi, in Piazza Navona, typical of Bernini's flamboyant baroque style; the 17th-century philosopher and scientist Galileo, who fell foul of the Inquisition*

CHARLES V AND THE SACK OF ROME

The armies of the Charles V, Habsburg Emperor, in his war against the French, fought on Italian soil and entered Rome in May 1527. It was the last of the sackings of the city and in some ways the worst: 20,000 German, Spanish and Italian soldiers occupied Rome and stayed for nearly a year. Their leader died in the assault, and the troops ran out of control, raping, murdering and burning every day. The Pope escaped into Castel Sant'Angelo. Many of the Germans were Protestants and delighted in smashing all evidence of Catholicism, including countless artworks. Rome was left in ruins and the population fell to 30,000. This catastrophe could well have brought about the end of the Renaissance.

THE TRIAL OF GALILEO

In 1633 Galileo was charged with 'grave suspicion of heresy' and summoned to Rome for trial by the Inquisition. His bold advocacy of Copernican theory—that the earth revolved around the sun—provoked Church authorities, who interpreted Scripture as saying the opposite. Because the 69-year-old Galileo was ill, his patrons, the Medicis, attempted to have the trial held in Florence, but the Pope insisted on Rome. Galileo was interrogated four times, finally under threat of torture, and recanted. He was found guilty and sentenced to unlimited imprisonment. However, the Church was not harsh. The Pope, once Galileo's patron, let him leave Rome for house arrest, and many in the Church secretly supported him. He was allowed to work and write for the rest of his life. He died in 1642.

ROMAN BAROQUE: BORROMINI VS BERNINI

If the Renaissance belonged to Florence, then the baroque belonged to Rome. Its two greatest practitioners, Gian Lorenzo Bernini (1598–1680) and Francesco Borromini (1599–1667), loathed each other with that ancient Roman fratricidal passion. Bernini, aristocratic and urbane, produced sophisticated work; Borromini, working class and hot-tempered, was wild and untamed. Borromini's genius led him to create beautiful churches in the cramped spaces of Rome, among them the masterful Sant'Ivo alla Sapienza. Bernini, never a trained architect, produced flamboyant sculptures of angels, tritons and saints. It ended tragically. Old and frustrated, Borromini committed suicide; Bernini went smoothly on, blackening his rival's name.

THE GRAND TOUR

Wealthy young Englishmen of the 18th century were expected to travel to France and Italy as clumsy youths and to come back as polished gentlemen. The tours could last four years, and Rome was the high point, for various reasons: 'Look, listen, learn—and buy' was one of them. Young lords with money to burn returned with an abundance of paintings, sculptures, coins and anything else the dealers could sell. More tellingly, Britain was conscious of her growing empire, and where better to educate her young men in ruling it than Rome, the blueprint of all empires? The young John Northall, an 18th-century traveller, wrote in 1752: 'One is confronted by emperors, consuls, generals…a cast of almost 2,000 years backwards, and the past becomes present.'

For centuries, Italy had been a collection of states under the control of foreign nations. The shock of Napoleon's occupations was felt not only by the Papal States, annexed by the French between 1797 and 1814, but right across Europe. A wave of nationalism swept the continent; Germany was unified, as was Italy eventually. Rome kept out of the great movement of this Risorgimento (resurgence). The papacy was unwilling to give up its political power. Even when Garibaldi and Cavour united the country in 1860, the Pope held off until he was forced to join in 1870. Rome became the capital and administrative hub of the new country. Immense government buildings went up and boulevards cut through the city. Papal political power vanished completely and the popes withdrew until the onset of fascism in the 1920s, when Mussolini finally recognized the Vatican State. The fascists had great dreams for Rome as the capital of a new empire, but many of these had to be postponed with the onset of the war. Mussolini was overthrown in 1943 and Rome was ruled directly by the Germans. As the war ended, Rome was threatened with massive destruction during the Allies' battle for control. Then the Germans suddenly left—Hitler had declared Rome an 'open city'.

NAPOLEON AND PIUS VII
'Being master of Italy, I considered myself master of Rome,' Napoleon announced in his memoirs. He didn't like opposition and decided that the Pope should cease to have any political power. Moreover, since France ruled most of Europe, it made sense to the Emperor for the Pope to establish himself in Paris. Pius VII was told to come to Paris for Napoleon's coronation in 1804. He was treated rudely by the Emperor, and the Romans, outraged, felt a new affection for a pope they previously hadn't much liked. Napoleon consolidated his power ruthlessly; Rome was declared second capital of the Empire and his son was made king of Rome in 1811.

Clockwise from above *Mussolini's Blackshirts marched on Rome in October 1922 in a successful bid for power; an equestrian statue of Vittorio Emanuele II, first king of unified Italy, in Piazza Venezia; a bust of Giuseppe Garibaldi (1807–82), father of Italian unification, in the Villa Borghese*

REVOLUTION IN ROME

A year of revolution came in 1848 as people across Europe called for more freedoms. For a few months Rome experienced a social experiment, a kind of welfare state that anticipated modern systems by a hundred years. Republicans drove Pope Pius IX out in the autumn. Pius allowed a free press and granted amnesty to all political opponents, but would not support a war for the unification of Italy. The romantic revolutionary Giuseppe Mazzini formed a triumvirate with Carlo Armellini and Aurelio Saffi to govern the new Republic of Rome, and for three months ruled as an idealist socialist. He pardoned his enemies, introduced progressive taxation and rehoused the poor. It was not to last. French forces restored the Pope in 1849, and Mazzini fled the country.

THE CAPITAL OF ITALY

After 1860, when Italy was united, it lacked its true capital. The new king of Italy, Vittorio Emanuele II, had been king of Piedmont and lived in Turin. The Pope refused to recognize unification and was protected by French troops. In 1870, when Garibaldi finally occupied Rome, the Pope, like the emperors of the collapsing Empire, fled from his territories into St. Peter's, declaring himself 'the prisoner of the Vatican'. Garibaldi passed the Law of Guarantees, promising to defend the Pope and granting him a pension. The Pope retaliated with *Non Expedit,* forbidding Italians from participating in the new state. This had little effect, and the King occupied the Pope's residence, the Quirinale Palace, when Rome was declared the official capital in 1871.

THE MARCH ON ROME

Italy could not be ruled without Rome, and in Mussolini's bid for power, his dramatic march on the city in 1922 was more a piece of theatre than political warfare. Although Mussolini controlled large forces throughout Italy and reviewed 40,000 soldiers in Naples on 24 October, he could not have fought a civil war. Four days later a fascist army of 16,000 surrounded Rome. Since most of them had arrived by train and were poorly organized, they presented no great threat to the city. The royal army was well run and equipped, and up until the evening of 27 October the King seemed determined to resist Mussolini. However, fearing civil war, the King relented and the fascists entered Rome. Mussolini was soon declared prime minister.

THE LATERAN PACT

Almost 60 years had passed since Garibaldi had occupied the papal territories. The Lateran Pact of 1929, which became part of the constitution of the republic, settled the differences between the Vatican and the kingdom of Italy. The Pope became head of an independent state measuring 43ha (106 acres) and received 2 billion lire compensation for the loss of all lands in 1870. The pact established Catholicism as the state religion of Italy and made it a required subject in all schools. In return, the papacy recognized the unification of the country. At the time, public imagery showed the pope, the monarch and the dictator as the three pillars of the Italian state: The papacy is the only one of the three to have survived today.

G. Garibaldi

The new Republic of Italy enjoyed a post-war boom. For a few years in the 1950s, Rome became the hub of fashion and hedonism, summed up in Fellini's film *La Dolce Vita*, made in 1960, the same year Rome hosted the Olympics. The 1970s were marred by terrorism from both extreme Right and Left. One of the worst acts, the kidnap and murder of Prime Minister Aldo Moro, took place in Rome in 1978. Protests and demonstrations eventually led to the election of a communist city government in 1976, which did much to improve housing and a chronic transportation problem. Further to this, plans for the new millennium, *Roma Capitale*, extended the metro and improved the bus system.

THE TREATY OF ROME

The Treaty of Rome was signed on 25 March 1957 by six European nations, thereby creating what would become the European Union (EU). Echoes down the centuries are strong: Much of the EU today comprises the vassal states of the former Roman Empire, and the inclusion of Turkey would see the ancient territories reunited after a split of some 1,700 years.

A NEW CONSTITUTION

A referendum in 1946 voted against the monarchy. The King's ties with Mussolini and his flight from Rome when German troops attacked after the fall of the fascists made him unpopular. The new constitution aimed to prevent a return of either the monarchy or fascism. Parliament elects a president, who then nominates a prime minister for parliament's approval. In 1946, Luigi Einaudi was elected as the first president. He took up residence in the Quirinale Palace, home of popes and then the monarch, almost 2,000 years after Julius Caesar destroyed the Republic of Rome.

A NEW POPE

On 2 April 2005, Pope John Paul II died after serving 26 years as head of the world's 1.1 billion Roman Catholics. The news was received by huge crowds keeping vigil in Piazza San Pietro. His successor, Cardinal Joseph Ratzinger, a 78-year-old German, was elected on 24 April and took the name Pope Benedict XVI. He was installed as the new pontiff in an open-air Mass in Piazza San Pietro. One of the overriding concerns of Pope Benedict's papacy has been Christian unity and the reinforcement of Catholicism. This was underlined by the apostolic constitution of October 2009, which was designed to make it easier for disaffected Anglicans to join the Catholic church.

Above left *The opening ceremony of the 1960 Olympic Games*
Above right *The signing of the Treaty of Rome in 1957, the first step towards the creation of the European Union*

ON THE MOVE

On the Move gives you detailed advice and information about the various options for travelling to Rome, then explains the best ways to get around the city once you are there. Handy tips help you with everything from buying tickets to renting a scooter.

BY AIR

Rome has two airports: Fiumicino (officially Aeroporto Leonardo da Vinci) and Ciampino (Aeroporto G. B. Pastine).

AIRPORTS
Arriving at Fiumicino
Fiumicino, 36km (22 miles) southwest of the city, has been the main gateway to the city since 1961, and has been extended to become the Mediterranean's largest airport. Most scheduled international and domestic flights to Rome arrive here and it is served by Air Canada, Alitalia, British Airways, Cathay Pacific, Continental Airlines, Delta, Japan Airlines, Lufthansa and Qantas, among others. The airport has three terminals, plus a satellite, which is linked by an automated shuttle, the Sky Bridge. **Terminal 1** handles domestic flights, **Terminal 2** handles international and some domestic flights and **Terminal 3** (including the satellite) handles international flights only. The airport is open 24 hours.

In the arrivals areas *(arrivi)* of terminals 2 and 3 there are ATMs *(bancomats)*, foreign exchange facilities *(cambio)*, toilets and public phones. Light refreshments are available, as is limited shopping (newspapers, magazines and sweets/candy). Not all of these facilities are open 24 hours.

The best way to get to the city centre from Fiumicino is by fast train. The Leonardo Express runs from just outside the airport to Termini station *(stazione)*. The service runs every 30 minutes between 6.36am and 11.36pm, takes around half an hour and costs €14 one way. There are other, more frequent trains *(treni)* that stop at Tiburtina, Tuscolana, Ostiense and Trastevere (but not Termini). These smaller stations are usually not as convenient for visitors as Termini. These services operate from 5.57am to 11.27pm and cost €8 one way. Outside of these times, a night bus runs between the airport, Termini station and Tiburtina station. There are four buses through the night (1.15, 2.15, 3.30 and 5am), which leave from near the international arrivals area. The journey costs €4.50 one way, and you can buy your ticket *(biglietto)* on the bus.

Traffic congestion means that the 36km (22-mile) taxi ride into the city can take anything from 30 minutes to 2 hours. There is a fixed charge of €48 to points in the city centre, but prices to non-central destinations vary. If you have small children or heavy luggage, taxis are convenient, but there are surcharges for trips to and from the airport, for each item of luggage, on Sundays and public holidays, and between 10pm and 7am.

Returning to Fiumicino
The Leonardo Express takes about 30 minutes to reach the airport. The ticket costs €14 one way, and the service runs from 5.52am to 11.52pm. If you are using the stopping train from Tiburtina,

Tuscolana, Ostiense or Trastevere, journeys take around 50 minutes, and trains run from 5.36am until 11.36pm. A one-way ticket costs €8. When arriving by train, allow at least an extra 15 minutes to get from the station to the check-in desk.

Arriving at Ciampino

Ciampino is Rome's second airport and, at 16km (10 miles) to the southeast, it is closer to the city. It is primarily a military airport, but also handles charter flights and some no-frills airlines, such as easyJet and Ryanair. It is much smaller than Fiumicino, which means it has fewer facilities. However, there are ATMs, a foreign currency exchange, public phones and toilets.

Bus companies Cotral (www. cotralspa.it), SIT (www.sitbusshuttle. it), Schiaffini (www.schiaffini.com) and Terravision (www.terravision. eu) operate 24-hour services daily to Stazione Termini in central Rome. All have ticket desks in the arrivals hall or you can buy tickets online in advance. Terravision (tel 06 9761 0632) also sells its tickets on easyJet flights to Ciampino. Note that tickets are only valid for services operated by the issuing company, so check the bus stops outside the terminal to see which company has the first departure before buying your ticket. Tickets cost between €4 and €6 one way, depending on the operator.

If you decide to take a taxi, you can find taxi stands on the right as you exit the terminal. The journey into central Rome takes approximately 35 minutes if the traffic is light and fares start at €35, but there are surcharges for journeys between 10pm and 7am, on Sundays and public holidays, and for each item of luggage. Journey times in rush hour will be longer.

Returning to Ciampino

Airport buses operated by Cotral, SIT, Schiaffini and Terravision all leave from Via Marsala outside Stazione Termini in central Rome 24 hours daily. Tickets cost between €4 and €6. Services are less frequent during the night so check departure times if you need to arrive very early at the airport. Allow extra time to get to the check-in desk.

At both airports, smoking is permitted only outside the airport buildings. Both of Rome's airports have wheelchair access to all facilities (▷ 54 for more details).

TIPS

» Avoid people who approach you at the airport offering taxi services or hotel rooms. Use only licensed (yellow or white) taxis.
» Buy a ticket for your return journey from central Rome to Fiumicino when you arrive. The queues are much longer at Termini, and the ticket will not become valid until you stamp it on your return journey.
» Suitcases with wheels are a godsend at Fiumicino, where it is some distance between baggage reclaim and the exit and there are some stretches where you cannot use a baggage trolley.

USEFUL TELEPHONE NUMBERS AND WEBSITES

FIUMICINO	CIAMPINO
» ☎ 06 6595 9515 (flight information; daily 5am–midnight)	» ☎ 06 6595 9515 (flight information; daily 5am–midnight)
06 65951 (central line; daily 24 hours)	06 65951 (central line; daily 24 hours)
» ☎ 06 6595 9327 (items lost in airport, *ufficio oggetti rinvenuti*; Mon–Fri 9–1, 3–8)	» ☎ 06 6595 9327 (items lost in airport, *ufficio oggetti rinvenuti*; Mon–Fri 9–1, 3–8)
» ☎ 06 6505 9275 (taxis)	» ☎ 06 6505 9275 (taxis)
» ☎ 06 6595 9225 (flight care; daily 24 hours)	» ☎ 06 6595 9225 (flight care; daily 24 hours)
» www.adr.it	» www.adr.it
» Tourist office (www.romaturismo.it) at International Arrivals, Terminal 3. Open daily 8am–7pm	

GETTING TO CENTRAL ROME FROM THE AIRPORT

AIRPORT	FIUMICINO (FCO)	CIAMPINO (CIA)
	Aeroporto Leonardo da Vinci (Fiumicino) Via dell'Aeroporto di Fiumicino 320, 00054 Fiumicino (Roma). Tel 06 65951 (switchboard)	Aeroporto G.B. Pastine (Ciampino) Via Appia Nuova 1651, 00040 Tel 06 65951
Taxi	€48–€60	€35 plus
Trains	Fast train, around 30 minutes—€14 Stopping train, 50 minutes—€8	
Bus	Terravision Fiumicino (tel 06 6595 8646, www.terravision.eu) To Stazione Termini—about every 30 minutes from 8.30am to 10pm. From Stazione Termini (Via Marsala)—about every 30 minutes from 6.30am to 10pm. Less frequently at night. One hour 10 minutes, €6 one way, €11 round trip	Terravision Ciampino (tel 06 7949 4572, www.terravision.eu). To Stazione Termini–regularly from 8.40am to 0.20am. From Stazione Termini—regularly from 4.30am to 7.30pm. 40 minutes, €6 one way, €12 round trip (€4/€8 when booked online)

BY CAR

If you are arriving by car and staying in central Rome, you will need a permit to drive in the city. If you are staying in a hotel, the staff can arrange this (▷ 53), otherwise you will need to contact STA (tel 06 679 4129) to obtain one.

In the days of the Empire, all roads led to Rome, but in these modern times, all roads lead to the Gran Raccordo Anulare, known as the GRA. This 70km (43-mile) road completely encircles the city, and is always busy. Its 30 exits can make the GRA seem confusing, but there are only a few intersections that you need to worry about.

From Fiumicino airport, take the Autostrada Roma Fiumicino, which leads to the GRA. If you are coming from Ciampino you will need to follow the Via Appia Nuova. From Florence or Pisa, take the A1, also known as the Autostrada del Sole. Visitors arriving from Naples should also use the A1, while those coming from Abruzzo or the Adriatic coast should follow the A24.

Wherever you join the GRA, make sure you know which exit you need; your hotel can tell you which one is best. Also ensure staff at your hotel know that you will be arriving by car so that you have somewhere to park. (See also Driving, ▷ 52–53.)

If you are arriving by car, but don't want to use your car in Rome, you can leave it in the long-term parking area *(lungo sosta parcheggio)* at Fiumicino airport and take the train into the city. Parking costs from €18 daily when booked online at www.adr.it.

BY TRAIN

There are rail connections between Rome and many other European cities, most of which end at Termini station and are operated by Trenitalia, still often referred to as FS (Ferrovie dello Stato), the state-run railway. Contact RailEurope for more information (tel 1-800/622-8600 in the US or 1-800-361-RAIL in Canada, or www.raileurope.com; tel 08448 484064 in the UK, or www.raileurope.co.uk).

For trips to or from smaller stations, you will need to use a *locale* train, which is a stopping service, but if you are coming from another major Italian city, your best option is a faster Intercity train. There is also the Eurostar Italia (ES) service, which runs from Milan, Turin, Genoa, Bari, Naples, Florence and Venice. This service is faster than the Intercity, but you need to reserve your ticket in advance, particularly if you intend to travel on the weekend (www.trenitalia.com).

Termini is Rome's main rail station. It is a large, busy station on the edge of the *centro storico*, with a tourist office, banks and ATMs, shops, bars, a post office, telephones, newspaper shops, a pharmacy, foreign exchange and left luggage. The area is a popular haunt for pickpockets, so keep a careful eye on your valuables at all times.

BY BUS

Most long-distance buses terminate at Tiburtina, Rome's second-largest rail station, to the northeast of the city. Although the station is some way out of the city, it is well served by the metro (line C) and by numerous bus services (for example, No. 492).

Eurolines runs buses from more than 100 European cities. For further information about routes and ticket prices, visit the company's website (www.eurolines.com).

CAR RENTAL

All major rental firms, and some local ones, have desks at both airports and also in town. However, car rental is expensive in Italy and you can often get a better deal if you arrange it before you leave home. The minimum age for renting a car is between 21 and 25 (depending on which company you use), and you will need to have held a driver's licence for at least a year. Most firms require a credit card as a deposit. Accident rates are high in Rome, so check that you have adequate insurance coverage. Most car rental contracts include breakdown coverage. Make sure you know who to call.

RENTAL COMPANY	AT FIUMICINO	AT CIAMPINO
Avis	06 6595 7885	06 7934 0195
Budget	06 6595 4074	06 7934 1429
Europcar	06 6576 1211	06 7934 0387
Hertz	06 6595 5842	06 7934 0095
Maggiore	06 6504 7568	06 7934 0368
Sixt	06 6595 3547	06 7934 0718

Once in the city, you will find that central Rome is actually quite compact—it is only 4km (2.5 miles) west–east as the crow flies from the Basilica di San Pietro to Stazione Termini. Exploring the city on foot gives you the opportunity to cut through side streets, stop for coffee or a snack in one of the many bars or cafés, or explore some of the wonderful shops, and generally slow the pace. If walking is not your thing, however, or if the distance is too great, your best option is to make use of the city's efficient public transport service, particularly its comprehensive bus network.

LA METROPOLITANA
The metro system *(la metropolitana)* has been designed primarily to bring commuters into the city and the network is not as comprehensive as similar systems in other countries. However, its two lines can be useful for getting across town, and avoiding Rome's congested streets. The first sections of a third line, construction of which was stalled by archaeological excavations, are due to open in 2012–13 and will be extended over the next few years.

BUSES
Rome's bus service is more useful for visitors than the metro system, as it can often get you closer to the sights. By using a combination of standard buses and electric minibuses, you can get within striking distance of most of the city's key sights. You can change buses as often as you need, within the time constraints of your ticket.

TRAMS
The tram system is much less comprehensive than the bus service, usually operating on the outskirts of the city.

For metro, bus and tram information, call ATAC (tel 06 57003; www.atac.roma.it). Phone lines are open Mon–Sat 8–8.

TAXIS
Taxis are useful for late-night travel around the city, but because of traffic congestion will not necessarily save you much time. And remember, while you are stuck in Rome's busy streets, the meter is still running, making this an expensive way to travel. Licensed taxis are yellow or white.

ON TWO WHEELS
Scooters can be a good way to see the city, but only if you are already used to handling two-wheeled vehicles. Bicycles are ideal for getting around traffic-free areas, such as Villa Borghese, but traffic fumes and Rome's hilly terrain make cycling on the city's streets a less attractive prospect.

BY CAR
The advice to anyone wishing to drive in Rome is quite simple—don't! Restricted access, busy, narrow streets, congestion, bad driving and inadequate parking can mean this is a stressful way to spend your holiday. If you really must drive, stay alert and remember that pedestrians have right of way (▷ 52–53 for more information on driving in Rome).

DISCOUNTS
Children under 10 travel free on public transport if they are accompanied by an adult; discounts are also available to students. Other discounted fares are available only to residents.

Rome's public transport service, run by ATAC (tel 06 57003 or 06 4782 4044), is inexpensive, frequent and reliable. There are around 282 bus routes in the city, plus 6 tram routes and 3 metro lines, but don't be daunted as you will find you only need a select few to get to where you want to go. At an ATAC kiosk you can pick up a transport map—Mappa dei Trasporti Pubblici. This is free, and gives details of buses, trams, the metro and the night buses, with transport and ticket information in both English and Italian. You can also find information panels at metro stations. There is an ATAC kiosk just outside Termini, in Piazza dei Cinquecento. Information is also available online at www.atac.roma.it.

TICKETS

Apart from the night bus (▷ 49), you must have a ticket before boarding buses, trains or the metro. There are ticket machines in the metro stations, and tickets are also sold in most tobacconists *(tabacchi)* and in some bars—look for the ATAC sticker displayed in the window. An increasing number of bus stops now have automated ticket machines.

The cheapest ticket is the integrated time ticket *(biglietto integrato a tempo—BIT)*, usually just referred to as *un biglietto* (a ticket). It costs €1, and can be used for 75 minutes from validation for any number of bus or tram trips, plus one metro journey.

One-day passes *(biglietto integrato giornaliero—BIG)* are also available. These are valid for unlimited use on buses, trams and the metro, and on trains operated by both Cotral—which runs services to other major cities—and Trenitalia (FS)—the state-run railway—until midnight on the day they are first used, and cost €4. They are not valid on ATAC sightseeing routes (▷ 246) or the non-stop Leonardo Express service to Fiumicino airport (▷ 42).

Multiday passes *(plurigiornalieri)* are available for 3, 7 or 30 days at €11, €16 or €30. They are valid on the same modes of transport as the BIG. You must write your name and the dates for which it is valid on the front of the ticket.

VALIDATING YOUR TICKET

Whichever ticket you choose, it must be validated the first time you use it. At metro stations the validation machines are located just before the escalators, where you descend to the trains. Buses and trams have machines on board. If you are using a BIT ticket, you must stamp it when you use it on the metro, too. Other than this, you do not need to stamp your ticket every time you change vehicles.

It is illegal to travel without a validated ticket. Ticket inspectors make regular checks, and you will be fined if you do not have a ticket with a valid stamp. The fixed-rate fine is €55 plus the price of your ticket, and ignorance is not an acceptable excuse.

BUSES

Rome has two types of bus: standard, single-decker buses and small electric minibuses. Most routes are covered by the standard buses, but minibuses operate on routes 116, 117 and 119. They are not very comfortable, even if you manage to get one of the eight hard plastic seats, but they are the only buses small enough to cope with Rome's narrow streets.

Bus Stops

At every bus stop there is a board showing the route number, the headstop (or *capolinea*—where the

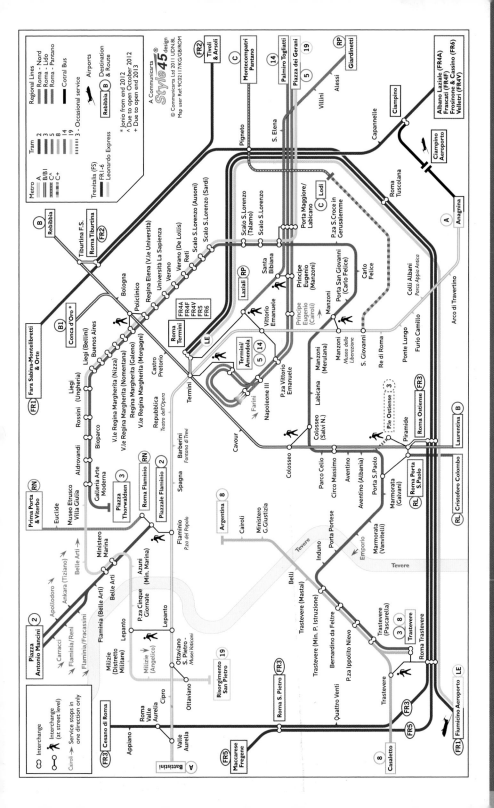

route starts) and a list of the main intermediate stops for each bus that uses the stop. The bus stop you are at will be circled. The last journey of the day will usually start from the headstop at around midnight, after which it will be replaced by a night bus (▷ 49).

Boarding the Bus
You usually board the bus through the rear doors *(salita)*. Make sure you validate your ticket on the way in—the fine for travelling without a validated ticket is €55. If you have already validated your ticket you may enter by the front *(entrata)* or rear doors. Use the middle doors, marked *uscita*, to leave the bus. Try to use the correct doors, but if the bus is busy you can leave by the front or rear doors. Minibuses have only one door.

TIPS
» To find out how to get around by public transport contact ATAC (tel 06 57003).

» If you have internet access, you can check your route online at www.atac.roma.it.

METRO
Rome's metro *(metropolitana)* system has two lines (A and B), which make roughly a cross shape, intersecting only at Termini. A third line, running northwest to southeast, is due to open in 2012–13; its construction has been delayed for many years while archaeological discoveries along its route were assessed (▷ 13).

Entrances to metro stations are marked with signs showing a large white 'M' on a red background, and there is usually more than one entrance—for example, on either side of a busy street. Just below street level are the ticket machines—remember to buy and stamp your ticket before you go down to the trains. Boards at the bottom of the escalator show you the route direction to help you identify your platform.

Although primarily a commuter service, the metro provides a good cross-city service, and is always very busy—there is usually standing room only. This makes it very hot, particularly in summer, and the crowds are also a good cover for pickpockets. Look for the route map inside the metro carriage (car)—it shows you on which side of the carriage the doors will open at each stop, giving you a fighting chance of getting there before the train pulls away from the station. Most services run between 5.10am and 11.30pm (12.30am on Saturdays), after which you will have to use the night bus service.

TRAMS
Rome's six tram routes operate mostly on the outskirts of the city and are not as useful to visitors as the buses or the metro. However, route 19 will take you to Piazza del Risorgimento, the closest public transport point to the Basilica di San Pietro and the Musei Vaticani. From

---

UNDERSTANDING THE TRANSPORT MAP

ONE-WAY STOPS
The tram will only call at the stop in the direction indicated by the arrow.

CONNECTION AT STREET LEVEL ONLY
Some connections can be made only at street level.

STATION STOP
A simple notch indicates a station with no interchanges.

INTERCHANGES
Interchanges are marked with one, two or more circles.

TERMINUS STATION
A boxed station name means that the line ends here.

COLOUR-CODED LINES
Each line is colour coded to make your navigation easy.

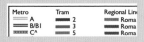

Metro lines intersect only at Termini station, but you can change onto a tram or suburban or regional train at lots of other places along your route.

The information above will help you understand the transport map on page 47 and the inside back cover.

here, it runs around the northern edge of Villa Borghese, close to Villa Giulia and the Museo Nazionale Etrusco, the Galleria Nazionale d'Arte Moderna and Bioparco, as does route C3. Route C3 also runs through the south of the city, ending up in Trastevere. Route 8 goes to Trastevere (and beyond), starting at Via di Torre Argentina, not far from Piazza Venezia.

NIGHT BUSES

From around midnight, Rome's public transport system is replaced with night buses. The only exception to this is tram line 8, which runs until 2am. On the bus stops the night bus routes are easily recognizable by the dark blue owl logo, and on the bus the letter 'n' will precede the route number. A night bus also follows as close as possible to each of the metro lines: Bus n1 follows line A, and buses n2 and n11 follow line B.

Night buses have conductors, and you can buy a BIT ticket on board for €1. Don't forget that BIG (one-day) tickets expire at midnight.

DISCOUNTS

Children under 10 travel free if accompanied by an adult. There are no discounts for seniors (unless resident).

To qualify for discounts, students should contact their students' union to get an ISIC (International Student Identification Card) before leaving home. Cards can also be issued by CTS (Centro Turistico Studentesco), as can Euro<26 cards for non-students aged under 26 (contact www.cts.it in Italy, www.isiccard.com in the UK or www.myisic.com in the US).

TIPS

» Charta Roma: The Official CityMap includes an up-to-date metro map. It is free from tourist information points. A free bus and tram map is available from ATAC (▷ 46).
» If the bus or tram is busy, pass your ticket through the crowd so someone can stamp it for you.
» Watch out for pickpockets.

MAIN TOURIST BUS ROUTES

Certain bus routes link a number of places of interest. Below are four routes of particular interest to visitors.

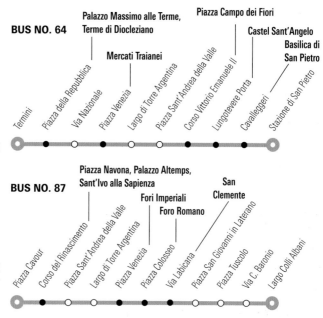

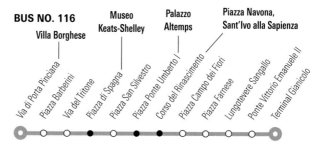

Because of Rome's one-way system, some buses, like route 116, follow different roads on their outward and return journeys

BICYCLES AND SCOOTERS

Seeing the city on two wheels has its advantages: Traffic jams and parking restrictions are not the problem they are for visitors in cars. However, Rome's busy streets are definitely not for the uninitiated, and if you've never ridden a scooter or bicycle in a busy city, Rome is not the place to start. Bicycles are best reserved for exploring the quieter parts of the city, but don't forget—Rome is built on seven hills.

To rent a scooter you must be over 21 and hold a full driver's licence. You will usually need to leave your passport and/or a credit card as a deposit. Crash helmets are compulsory, and you should also wear gloves, shoes that enclose your feet, trousers and long sleeves.

It is compulsory to wear a helmet when riding a bicycle. When renting a bike, you will be asked to leave your passport or similar ID as a deposit. Rome also has a bike-sharing scheme, with 29 pick-up points across the city centre; hop on and go, then leave the bike at the pick-up point nearest to your destination. Go to www.roma-n-bike.com for more information.

Avoid the busy main streets, where traffic and exhaust fumes make cycling unpleasant. Instead, make for the quieter cobbled streets west of Campo dei Fiori or south of Via dei Coronari.

SAFE CYCLING TIPS

» Wear bright clothing in the day, and fluorescent clothing and lights at night.
» Always wear a helmet.
» Wear gloves, and cover your knees and elbows.
» Make sure other road-users are aware of your movements. Indicate your intentions clearly and in advance.
» Watch out for people opening doors of stopped or parked cars.
» Don't cycle down the inside of traffic when there is a right turning ahead.
» Always lock your bicycle to a fixed object when parking.

WHERE TO RENT A BICYCLE OR SCOOTER IN ROME

BARBERINI SCOOTERS FOR RENT
www.rentscooter.it
✉ Via della Purificazione 84
☎ 06 488 5485
🕐 Daily 9–7

BICI E BACI
www.bicibaci.com
✉ Via del Viminale 5
☎ 06 482 8443
🕐 Daily 8–7

NEW SCOOTER FOR RENT (Scooters only)
✉ Via Quattro Novembre 96a/b
☎ 06 679 0300
🕐 Daily 9–8

ON ROAD
www.onroad.it, www.scoooterhire.it
✉ Via Cavour 80/a
☎ 06 481 5669
🕐 Daily 9–7

ROMA RENT
✉ Vicolo de' Bovari 7/a
☎ 06 689 6555
🕐 Daily 9–7

ROMA IN SCOOTER
✉ Corso Vittorio Emanuele II 204
☎ 06 687 6922
🕐 Daily 9–7

RONCONI
www.ronconibiciclette.it
✉ Via San Leo 54–56
☎ 06 881 0219
🕐 Daily 9–dusk

RONCONI-VILLA BORGHESE
✉ Viale delle Belle Arti/Via dei Monti Parioli (in front of the Galleria Nazionale d'Arte Moderna)
☎ 06 881 0219
🕐 Daily 9–dusk

SCOOT-A-LONG
✉ Via Cavour 302
☎ 06 678 0206
🕐 Daily 9.30–7.30

SCOOTER RENT JOY RIDE
✉ Via Cavour 199
☎ 06 481 5926
🕐 Daily 9–7

TRENO E SCOOTER (TERMINI STATION)
www.trenoescooter.com
✉ Piazza dei Cinquecento
☎ 06 4890 5823
🕐 Daily 9–2, 4–7

TAXIS

Rome's busy streets and one-way systems mean that taxis are not the most economical way of getting from one part of the city to another, but there may be times when they are your best bet.

Always use official, licensed taxis, which are either yellow or white, and have an illuminated 'taxi' sign on the roof. You should avoid the many unlicensed taxis operating in Rome, as you have no way of knowing if they are adequately insured.

Taxis can be hailed on the street, but it is easier to get one from the *fermata dei taxi* (taxi stand) at Termini, Piazza Venezia, Largo di Torre Argentina, Piazza San Silvestro, Piazza di Spagna or Piazza Sidney Sonnino (in Trastevere).

If you want to be sure of a taxi, or you need to be collected from your hotel to get to the airport, it is best to telephone for a radio taxi. You cannot book a radio taxi in advance, so factor in enough time for the taxi to reach you. The taxi company gives you a reference, plus the timeframe within which the taxi is expected to arrive. Radio taxis start charging from the time they leave to pick you up, so the meter will not be at zero.

RADIO TAXIS

The following numbers are recommended by the tourist office for calling a radio taxi:

☎ 06 6645

☎ 06 5551

☎ 06 4994

☎ 06 8822

☎ 06 4157

☎ 06 3570

☎ 06 550 0036

TAXI FARES

All taxi fares are controlled by the meter, and a list of charges, in several languages, should be displayed inside the taxi. Fixed rates apply from Fiumicino and Ciampino airports to points in central Rome (€48 and €35 respectively).

For journeys within the city, the charges are as follows:

Fixed charge: €4 between 7am and 10pm (€6 on Sundays and public holidays between 7am and 10pm, €7 between 10pm and 7am).

Increments: 10¢ every 141m (154 yards).

Stationary/slow-moving traffic: 10¢ every 19.2 seconds; €0.92/km.

Surcharges for: each item of luggage after the first piece: €1; trips to and from the airports and outside the Gran Raccordo Anulare (GRA).

TIPS

» Use only licensed cabs.

» Except in radio taxis, make sure the meter is set to zero at the start of your journey.

» The meter still runs when the taxi is stationary (eg, in traffic jams).

DRIVING

What with restricted access, busy, narrow streets, bad road skills and poor parking, driving in Rome can be a stressful experience. However, if you decide you can't do without your car, here are some points to bear in mind when driving:

Do carry your registration and insurance documents and driver's licence. You will need to produce them if you are stopped.

Don't dazzle oncoming traffic. Cars manufactured to drive on the left should adjust their headlights—kits are widely available.

Don't drive too fast. The speed limit in built-up areas is 50kph/31mph; outside built-up areas, 110kph/68mph; motorways *(autostrade)*, 130kph/81mph.

Do carry a warning triangle and a fluorescent vest for emergencies, and display a nationality sticker (unless you have Euro-plates).

Do carry a first-aid kit, a fire extinguisher and headlight bulbs.

Don't use undipped (high-beam) headlights in towns or cities.

Do use dipped (dimmed) headlights when driving in tunnels, even if they are well lit.

Don't drink and drive—penalties are severe. The legal level is below 0.05 per cent of alcohol in the bloodstream.

Don't allow children under four years old to travel without a suitable restraint system. Children under 12 years old cannot travel in the front of the car without an adapted restraint system.

Do wear a seatbelt. They are compulsory in the front and rear of the vehicle (where fitted).

Don't use a mobile (cell) phone when driving.

Don't drive in shoes that do not fully enclose the foot.

DRIVER'S LICENCES

Both UK and US driver's licences are valid in Italy, but it is recommended that you also carry a translation. In the UK, photo licences and the pink, EU-style ones include a translation, but if you hold an older, green licence, you should either update the licence or apply for an International Driving Permit. Holders of US driver's licences should also apply for an International Driving Permit. These permits are not compulsory, but are easier to understand. They also act as another form of identification. Permits can be obtained from the Italian state tourist offices or many national motoring (auto) organizations (including the AA and AAA).

Drivers must be at least 18 years old and hold a full driver's licence.

ACCIDENTS

If you are involved in an accident, call the police (tel 112) and ask any witness to stay and make a statement. Do not admit liability. Exchange details (name, address, car details, insurance company's name and address) with the other drivers involved.

BREAKDOWNS

If you break down, turn on your hazard warning lights, place the warning triangle 50m (164ft) behind the vehicle, and put on your fluorescent vest.

The Automobile Club d'Italia (ACI) provides a free service to foreign drivers who are members of national automobile clubs affiliated with ACI (for more information visit www.aci.it). If they cannot repair your car at the roadside, they will tow you to a garage. You can contact ACI 24 hours a day (tel 116). They will need to know where you are, your vehicle registration (licence plate) number and the make of the vehicle.

FUEL

Petrol (gas) stations in Rome are small, and generally keep shop hours, closing all day Sunday. Lead-free fuel is called *benzina senza piombo* or *benzina verde*; leaded fuel is still available in some places. Some petrol (gas) stations, particularly those on the GRA, are open 24 hours.

TRAFFIC RESTRICTIONS

Most of the *centro storico* is covered by the Limited Traffic Zone, which restricts access to permit holders from 6.30am to 6pm Monday to Friday, and 2 to 6pm on Saturdays. Electronic systems are in place to record the number plates of unregistered vehicles and to issue fines. If you need to drive in the restricted area, fax details of your registration number and length of stay to STA (fax 06 5711 8259). If you are staying in a hotel, the staff will usually do this for you. For more details visit www.sta.roma.it.

TIPS

» If your vehicle is causing an obstruction, it might be towed away. Contact Vigili Urbani (tel 06 67691 or 06 6769 6000/1) to find out where it has been taken.

» At night, traffic lights are switched to flashing amber. This means it is up to you to decide whether or not it is safe to go.

» When drivers flash their headlights they are asserting their right of way, rather than ceding it to you.

PARKING

Parking in the *centro storico* is limited and expensive. Street parking is indicated by blue lines and costs €1 per hour—buy your ticket from the nearby vending machines (which only take coins) or at tobacconists or news-stands. The most convenient parking areas in central Rome are:

PARK SÌ (VILLA BORGHESE)

- ✉ Viale del Galoppatoio 33
- ☎ 06 322 5934
- ⏰ 24 hours
- 🖐 €1.30 per hour for up to three hours, then €1 for 4th to 15th hour; €22 per day if pre-paid

TERMINAL PARK (TERMINI)

- ✉ Via Marsala 30–32
- ☎ 06 444 1067
- ⏰ 6am–1am
- 🖐 €5 for one hour, €2 for 2nd hour, €1.50 per hour for 3rd to 12th hours; €26 per day for the second day

PARK SÌ (STAZIONE ROMA-OSTIA)

- ✉ Piazzale dei Partigiani
- ☎ 06 574 5942
- ⏰ 24 hours
- 🖐 €1 per hour; €5 per day

TERMINAL GIANICOLO
VIA DI PORTA CAVALLEGGERI

- ☎ 06 684 0331
- ⏰ 7am–1.30am
- 🖐 €27.60 per day, €55 for 50 hours, €66 for 3 days

PARKING DELL'AUDITORIUM,

- ✉ Viale M. Pilsudski 21
- ☎ 06 808 1646
- ⏰ 7am–12.30am
- 🖐 €1 per hour; €4 per day; €1.50 per night

AUTOSILO VIA MANTOVA,

- ✉ Via Mantova 24
- ☎ 06 841 3853
- ⏰ 24 hours
- 🖐 €3 per hour for first hour, then €2 per hour up to 10 hours; €25 per day

PARKING LUDOVISI

- ✉ Via Ludovisi 60
- ☎ 06 474 0632
- ⏰ 5.30am–1.30am
- 🖐 €2 per hour for first five hours, then €1 per hour; €20 per day

Rome is a very difficult city for people with physical impairments to get around without able-bodied help. There has been a gradual improvement to accessibility in recent years, but some areas can still cause problems.

BY AIR
Contact your airline in advance of your date of travel to let them know what assistance you will need. Both Fiumicino and Ciampino have wheelchair access to all airport services, and many signposts are in braille. At Fiumicino, there are also paths with textured surfaces to guide people with visual impairments to key places in the airport. The airports have a courtesy hotel shuttle for visitors with disabilities; contact your airline 24 hours in advance to book.

BY BUS AND TRAM
Many of Rome's buses and trams have been, or are being, adapted for wheelchair access, with a view to replacing the whole network. The newer buses have lower access platforms. For the most up-to-date information, contact ATAC's services for visitors with disabilities (tel 800 154 451; open daily 8–2.30).

BY METRO
The metro system is also being upgraded. Most stations on line B have elevators and toilets suitable for people with disabilities. The exceptions are Circo Massimo, Colosseo and the southbound platform of Cavour. On line A, only Cipro and Valle Aurelia have wheelchair access, but bus No. 590 follows the same route and is, on the whole, wheelchair accessible. Ten stations on line A have textured paths for people with visual impairments, although only Cipro is useful for the main attractions. The new line C will be accessible to travellers with disabilities, with elevators and disabled toilets.

BY TRAIN
Some of Rome's trains have wheelchair access, and this is indicated on the timetable with a wheelchair symbol. You can also get this information from Termini station (tel 06 488 1726) — tell them where you want to start and end your journey. If you will need assistance, call the Ufficio Disabili (tel 199 30 30 60 from inside Italy) 12 hours before the start of your journey. Someone else can do this on your behalf.

BY TAXI
Most taxis can take wheelchairs, but they will need to be folded and stored in the boot (trunk).

For general information about access in Rome, ▷ 255.

USEFUL CONTACTS

CO.IN SOCIALE
www.coinsociale.it
✉ Via Enrico Giglioli 54a, 00169 Rome
☎ 06 2326 9231
Has useful information on accessible sights in Rome and Lazio. Publishes guides, organizes guided tours, and has a minibus available for excursions and transfers.

ROMA PER TUTTI
www.romapertutti.it
☎ 06 5717 7094
Helps visitors with special needs. Also organizes guided tours (reservations essential), but in Italian only.

ASSOTAXI
www.assotaxi.it
✉ Viale Aldo Ballarin 138
☎ Bookings 199 414041 (in Italy only),
Runs taxis specially fitted with seat elevators for wheelchair access. Booking 24 hours ahead is recommended.

NATIONAL DISABILITY SERVICES
www.nds.org.au
✉ 33 Thesiger Court, Deakin, ACT 2600, Australia
☎ 02 6283 3200
Responds to the needs of people with disabilities.

TOURISM FOR ALL
www.tourismforall.org.uk
✉ c/o Vitalise, Shap Road Industrial Estate, Shap Road, Kendal, Cumbria LA9 6NZ
☎ 0845 124 9971 (UK only)
Produces publications and information on accessibility.

SATH (Society for Accessible Travel & Hospitality)
www.sath.org
✉ 347 Fifth Avenue, Suite 605, New York NY10016, USA
☎ 212/447-7284, fax 212/447-1928
Lots of tips on how to travel with mobility or vision impairment

REGIONS

This chapter is divided into five regions of Rome. Region names are for the purposes of this book only and places of interest are listed alphabetically in each region.

REGIONS | ROME

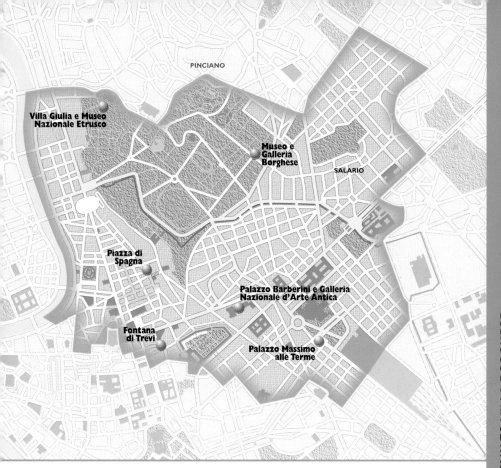

PINCIANO

Villa Giulia e Museo
Nazionale Etrusco

Museo e
Galleria
Borghese

SALARIO

Piazza di
Spagna

Palazzo Barberini e Galleria
Nazionale d'Arte Antica

Fontana
di Trevi

Palazzo Massimo
alle Terme

THE TREVI FOUNTAIN
TO VILLA BORGHESE

Northern Rome embraces several very different parts of the city, ancient and modern, from chic shopping streets and open green spaces to stately squares and the cluttered streets around Termini, the main railway station.

The area's southeast corner—along either side of Via del Corso, the street that bisects the district—contains the same mixture of Roman monuments, picturesque streets and baroque churches found in the city's adjacent historic core. This corner is home to famous sights such as the Fontana di Trevi and Spanish Steps, along with ancient monuments such as the Ara Pacis Augustae and Colonna di Marco Aurelio.

Via del Corso is also one of the city's main shopping streets, though Rome's most prestigious designer and other names are found in the grid of streets close by, centred on Via Condotti and Via Frattina. To the east, closer to Termini, streets such as Via Nazionale, Via XX Settembre and Via Barberini are more modern and less attractive (the same can be said of the famous Via Vittorio Veneto, now a shadow of its former self), though there are sights here that should not be missed, including the museums of the Palazzo Barberini and Palazzo Massimo alle Terme.

Other major museums—the Museo e Galleria Borghese, full of art and sculpture, and the Villa Giulia, devoted to the Etruscans—are tucked away in the vast Villa Borghese, Rome's main, if rather marginal park, which stretches across most of northern Rome.

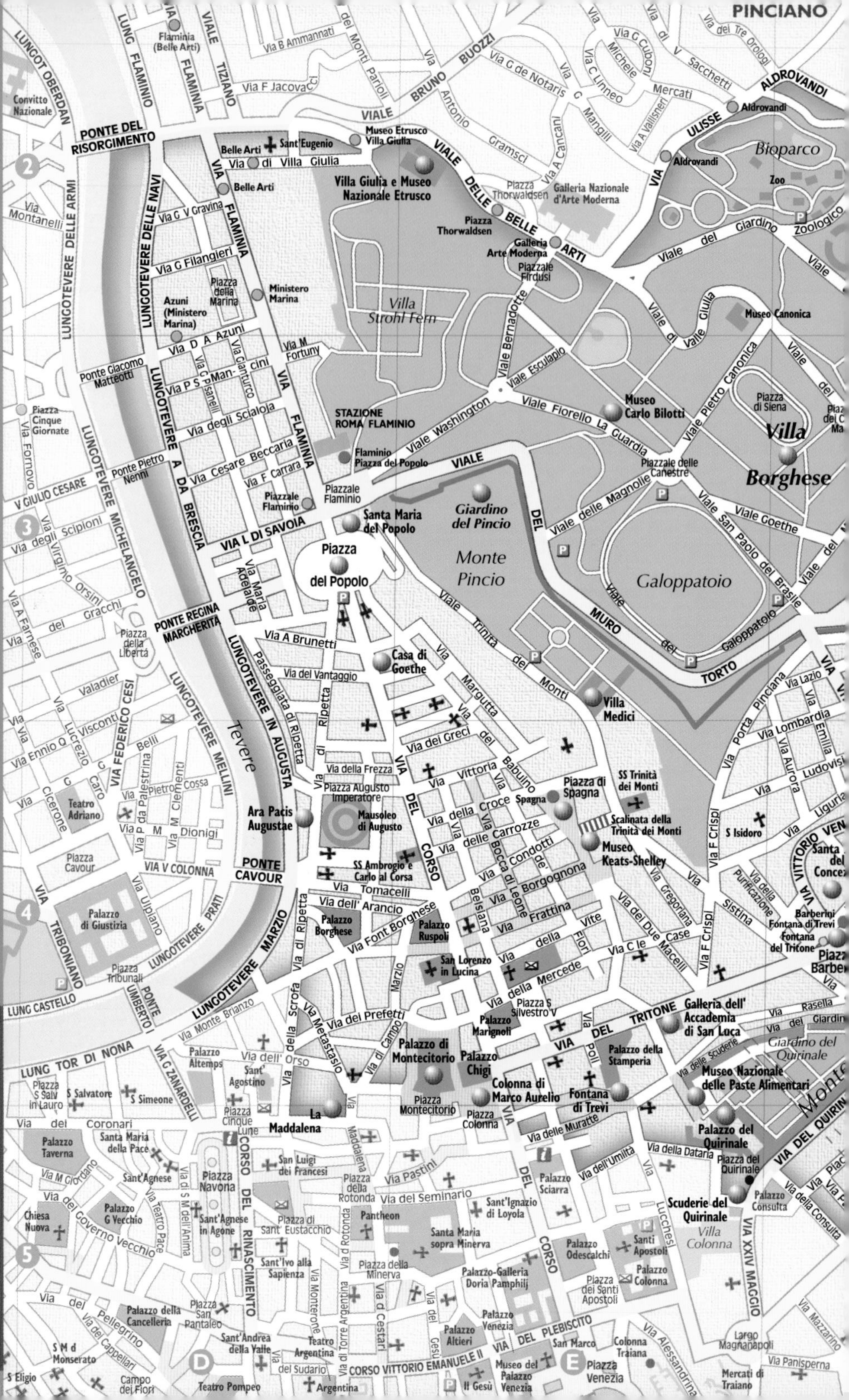

Villa Giulia e Museo Nazionale Etrusco

Museo Etrusco Villa Giulia

Galleria Nazionale d'Arte Moderna

Galleria Arte Moderna

Villa Borghese

Museo Canonica

Bioparco
Zoo

Museo Carlo Bilotti

Piazza di Siena

Santa Maria del Popolo

Piazza del Popolo

Giardino del Pincio

Monte Pincio

Galoppatoio

Casa di Goethe

Villa Medici

Piazza di Spagna

SS Trinità dei Monti

Scalinata della Trinità dei Monti

Museo Keats-Shelley

Ara Pacis Augustae

Mausoleo di Augusto

SS Ambrogio e Carlo al Corso

Palazzo Borghese

Palazzo Ruspoli

San Lorenzo in Lucina

Galleria dell' Accademia di San Luca

Barberini Fontana di Trevi
Fontana del Tritone

Palazzo di Montecitorio

Palazzo Chigi

Colonna di Marco Aurelio

Fontana di Trevi

Museo Nazionale delle Paste Alimentari

Palazzo del Quirinale

Giardino del Quirinale

La Maddalena

Palazzo Altemps

Sant' Agostino

San Luigi dei Francesi

Santa Maria sopra Minerva

Sant'Ignazio di Loyola

Scuderie del Quirinale

Piazza Navona

Sant'Agnese in Agone

Pantheon

Palazzo-Galleria Doria Pamphilj

Santi Apostoli

Palazzo della Cancelleria

Sant'Ivo alla Sapienza

Teatro Argentina

Museo del Palazzo Venezia

Il Gesù

Piazza Venezia

Mercati di Traiano

CORSO VITTORIO EMANUELE II

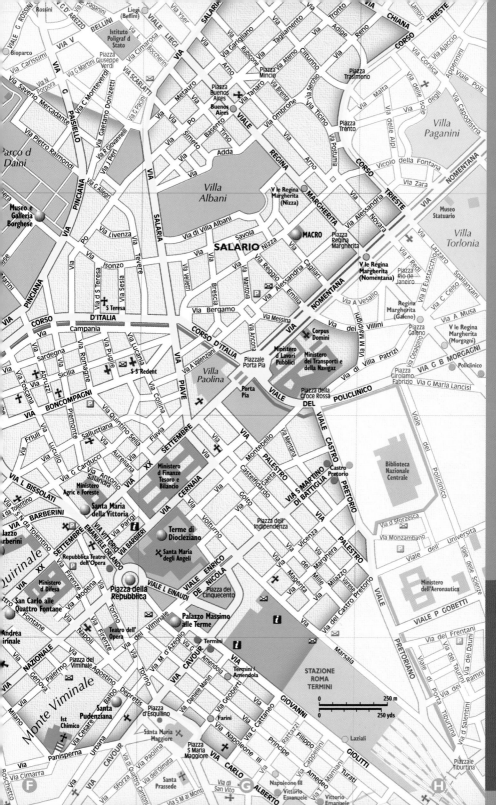

ARA PACIS AUGUSTAE

www.arapacis.it

The Altar of Peace is the best example of Augustan monumental sculpture in Rome. The altar, decorated with bas-reliefs carved in 9BC, was built to celebrate Augustus' triumphal return to Rome after campaigns in Spain and Gaul, and to commemorate the peace he had established throughout the Roman world. Over the centuries the altar became buried, and was lost until the first fragments were rediscovered in 1568. It was not until 1938 that the monument recovered its ancient beauty, when the Fascist regime sponsored its reconstruction.

The outside of the enclosure is decorated with mythological scenes and processional friezes in which life-size figures portray Augustus, the imperial family, officials and other notables. The monument is enclosed in a modern glass structure designed by American architect Richard Meier.

🚩 58 D4 ✉ Lungotevere in Augusta, 00100 ☎ 06 0608 🕐 Tue–Sun 9–7. Ticket office closes 6pm 🎫 Adult €9 🚇 Spagna 🚌 30, 70, 81, 91, 186, 204, 224, 492, 590, 628, 913

CASA DI GOETHE

www.casadigoethe.it

Casa Moscatelli was just a small boarding house when German poet and dramatist Johann Wolfgang von Goethe lived here from 1786 to 1788, and it has changed little since that time.

In the 1990s, the second floor of the house, where Goethe spent one of the happiest and most productive periods of his life, was purchased and renovated to house the Goethe Museum, the only Goethe museum outside Germany, and it has developed into a lively cultural meeting place. The museum has a permanent exhibition, Goethe in Rome, which documents the poet's time in Italy and the influence this had on his work, and includes pictures, drawings, manuscripts, prints and books.

Above *Carvings on the Colonna di Marco Aurelio run in a continuous spiral*
Opposite *A detail of one of the bas-reliefs on the Ara Pacis Augustae, dating from 9BC*

The German painter J. H. W. Tischbein (1751–1829), who also lived in this house, portrayed Goethe in a famous work known as *Goethe in the Roman Countryside*; you can see Andy Warhol's modern interpretation of it at the entrance to the exhibition.

🚩 58 D3 ✉ Via del Corso 18, 00186 ☎ 06 3265 0412 🕐 Tue–Sun 10–6 🎫 Adult €4, child (under 18) €3 🚇 Flaminio 🚌 52, 53, 61, 71, 80, 85, 117, 119, 160, 590, 850

COLONNA DI MARCO AURELIO

The Column of Marcus Aurelius stands in the paved and pedestrianized Piazza Colonna, an area that has always been the hub of political power and is now home to the Italian government.

It is made from Luni marble, is 29.5m (96ft) high and 3.5m (11ft) wide, and was erected between AD180 and AD193. A frieze runs in a continuous spiral round the column, with beautiful bas-reliefs depicting significant episodes in the wars conducted by the Emperor Marcus Aurelius against various Danubian tribes in the second century AD. The frieze gives a wealth of information about military and social history for this period.

A statue of Marcus Aurelius and his wife, Faustina, once stood on top of the column, but was lost; in its place, Pope Sixtus V erected a bronze statue of St. Paul (1589) by Domenico Fontana. A spiral staircase of some 200 steps inside the shaft of the column leads up to a little terrace on the top, but it is no longer possible for visitors to go inside.

🚩 58 E4 ✉ Piazza Colonna, 00186 🚇 Spagna 🚌 52, 53, 61, 85, 117, 119, 160, 175, 492, 628, 630, 850

INFORMATION

✚ 58 E4 ✉ Piazza di Trevi, 00187
🚇 Barberini 🚌 52, 53, 61, 62, 63, 71, 80, 116, 119, 175, 204, 492, 590, 630, 850 stopping at Piazza San Silvestro
📖 Available in souvenir shops
🏪 Many souvenir shops

FONTANA DI TREVI

The Trevi Fountain is one of Rome's most familiar sights, yet as you step out of the shadows of the surrounding narrow streets into the small Piazza di Trevi, the fountain, with its theatrical setting, baroque architecture, cascading water, weathered rocks and wide basin, cannot fail to impress.

Long before the fountain was built, water was brought to central Rome from the hills surrounding the city along the aqueduct designed by General Agrippa, Augustus' adviser and friend, in 19BC. Part of the original underground channel still supplies the fountain, one of the few original Roman waterways still in use in the city.

The present fountain dates from 1732, when Pope Clement XII held a competition to design a new fountain as part of his plans to revive the splendour of ancient Rome. Nicola Salvi emerged the winner and was given the delicate task of carrying out this ambitious project. The fountain was completed after Salvi's death and finally inaugurated in 1762 by Clement XIII. A thorough restoration project was completed in 1991, returning the fountain to its original grandeur.

THE BACKDROP

The story of the fountain is told in two bas-reliefs, above the two figures flanking the large central statue of Neptune. On the right, a young girl shows Agrippa's thirsty soldiers the way to a freshwater spring (by G. B. Grossi), and on the left, a panel by Andrea Bergondi shows Agrippa approving the plans for the 19km (12-mile) aqueduct from the Salone Spring to Rome.

THE FOUNTAIN

The imposing figure of Neptune, with his fluttering mantle, sits in the middle of this compelling stage, riding in his shell-shaped chariot pulled by two spirited sea horses that are steered by giant tritons. The tall niche that he stands in gives balance and symmetry to the composition. There are various animals, both mythological and real, in the basin, which represents the sea. In the niches to the right and left are the statues of Plenty (left) and Health (right) carved by Filippo della Valle.

THE RITUAL

There is one very important ritual to complete before leaving this magnificent scene behind. Legend has it that visitors should make a wish and toss two coins over their shoulder into the fountain; the first coin ensures a return to Rome and the other makes the wish come true. The huge number of coins thrown into the fountain are collected daily and given to CARITAS, an Italian religious charity.

Above *The sculptures on the Trevi Fountain are full of symbolism. The figure of Triton blowing a conch shell represents a calm sea*

GALLERIA DELL'ACCADEMIA DI SAN LUCA

www.accademiasanluca.it

This gallery, one of Rome's most prestigious, was founded to promote the training of artists in Renaissance techniques. From 1633, every artist member of the academy had to donate a work of art, resulting in a wonderful collection that includes paintings by Raphael, Antonio Canova, Sir Anthony van Dyck, Titian, Peter Paul Rubens, Il Guercino, Il Sassoferrato, Guido Reni and Pietro da Cortona.

When its original home was demolished in the 1930s to make way for the Via dei Fori Imperiali, the academy moved to Giacomo della Porta's 16th-century palazzo.

Works of particular interest include *Portrait of Clement IX* by Baciccia, *St. Luke Painting the Virgin*, attributed to Raphael, *Judith and Holophernes* by Piazzetta, and the *Virgin and Angels* by Van Dyck. There are almost 400 portraits of all the artists of the academy, spanning the 400 years from its inception to the 20th century (although not all are on display). Look out for the spiral staircase leading to the upper floors, based on a design by the 17th-century architect Francesco Borromini.

✠ 58 E4 ✉ Piazza dell'Accademia di San Luca 77, 00186 ☎ 06 679 8850 🕓 Sep–Jun Mon–Sat 10–2 🖐 Free 🚇 Barberini 🚌 52, 53, 60, 61, 62, 63, 71, 80, 85, 160, 850 stopping at Piazza San Silvestro

GIARDINO DEL PINCIO

The gardens on the Pincio Hill are Rome's first and most famous public gardens. Designed around 1810 by Giuseppe Valadier, they stretch from Trinità dei Monti to Piazza del Popolo, adjoining Villa Borghese park.

The fashionable gardens occupied part of the area where the Horti Luculliani once stood. This was the villa and terraced gardens built by the politician (and epicure) Lucullus in the first century BC, and which extended for about 20ha

(50 acres) between Trinità dei Monti and Villa Medici. After the sack of Rome, in the fifth century AD, the Pincii family bought the estate, along with most of the hill, and the gardens still bear their name.

If you climb the Rampa del Pincio from Piazza del Popolo, you reach the Pincio Terrace, dedicated to Napoleon I, from where there are spectacular views of the city. Nearby is the lovely Casina Valadier, built by architect Giuseppe Valadier between 1813 and 1817 as a coffee house. Inside are some noteworthy frescoes and tempera decorations discovered during recent restorations. A fashionable café, the building is still a meeting place for Roman aristocrats.

✠ 58 E3 🕓 Closes at sunset 🚇 Spagna or Flaminio 🚌 88, 95, 117, 119, 204, 231, 490, 491, 495

MACRO

www.macro.roma.museum

As late as 1999 Rome had no exhibition space dedicated to contemporary art, an anomaly in such an art-rich city. The conversion and extension of the old Peroni brewery, under the guidance of French architect Odile Decq, into the Museo d'Arte Contemporanea di Roma (MACRO) has finally provided space for large-scale contemporary works and installations in every medium, attracting both the modern art scene's biggest names and up-and-coming young artists. The permanent collection concentrates on Italian contemporary artists

working from the 1960s to the present day, while the changing exhibitions highlight the work of Italian and international artists. MACRO has an off-shoot, the Mattatoio, in an old slaughterhouse in the outlying Testaccio district.

✠ 59 G3 ✉ Via Nizza 131 (corner of Via Cagliari), 00198 ☎ 06 6710 70400 🕓 Tue–Sun 11–11 🖐 Adult €11; EU citizens under 25 and over 65 €9 🚌 38, 90

LA MADDALENA

Just a stone's throw away from the Pantheon is the church of La Maddalena, a typical example of the baroque style, sumptuously decorated and furnished according to 18th-century Roman taste.

The church is the work of various 17th- and 18th-century artists: Carlo Fontana was responsible for the dome and the vault, while Giulio Quadrio completed the church in 1699, except for the facade. The latter was finished in 1735 and influenced by the baroque master Francesco Borromini; it is made of plaster and stucco, which are more ductile and cheaper than traditional travertine. The interior is rich in stucco and fresco decoration, with a magnificent organ, inlaid wood confessionals, exquisite side chapels and an 18th-century sacristy.

✠ 58 D5 ✉ Piazza della Maddalena 53, 00184 ☎ 06 899 281 🕓 Mon–Fri 7–12, 5–8, Sat 9.30–12, 5–8, Sun 9–12.30, 5–8 🖐 Free, audioguide €2.50 🚌 40, 46, 62, 64, 70, 81, 492, 628, 630, 780, 787, 916; tram 8 to Largo di Torre Argentina or 116 to Via della Palombella

Below *Superstar architect Odile Decq designed the new extension at MACRO*

MUSEO E GALLERIA BORGHESE

INFORMATION

www.galleriaborghese.it

59 F3 Piazzale del Museo Borghese 5 (entrance on Via Pinciana), 00187 06 3996 7800; 06 32810 Tue–Sun 8.30–7.30. Advance booking essential, ticket must be collected 30 min before time slot (www.ticketeria.it; tel 06 32810; Mon–Fri 9–6, Sat 9–1) Adult €8.50 (plus €2 booking fee), concessions €5.25, EU citizens under 18 and over 65 free (€2 booking fee) Flaminio or Spagna 52, 53, 910 Guided tours every 2 hours in Italian and English (2 hours duration); audiotours €5, Italian, English, Spanish, French, German (2 hours duration) Italian, English, French, German guide to Galleria Borghese €13, TCI guidebook €19 Café with bar Shop with good selection of guides, postcards and souvenirs

INTRODUCTION

The Museo e Galleria Borghese, one of Rome's most exquisite collections of paintings and sculpture, is housed in a 17th-century villa standing in parkland on the eastern edge of the Pincio Hill. Built in 1612–13, it was designed to be the focal point of the Rome estate of the immensely rich Borghese family.

Cardinal Scipione Borghese chose Flaminio Ponzio as his architect, commissioning a building modelled on the villas of ancient Rome and suitable to house his collections of paintings, sculpture and other artefacts. Besides being a passionate and unscrupulous collector, the Cardinal had interests ranging through music, geology and natural history, and the villa had its own farm, vineyard and zoo. The sculpture and pictures were in place by 1620 and they still form the museum's core collection.

The Borgheses were forced to sell up at the end of the 19th century, and both park and villa were acquired by the Italian state in 1902. Restoration in the 1990s returned both the exterior and interior to their original appearance.

The entrance leads into the lower ground floor, where you will find the ticket office, shop, café and other services. The gallery and museum, a series of interconnecting rooms set around a central hall, occupy the next two floors. The sculptural highlights are in the first rooms on the lower floor, as are Caravaggio's paintings. The Pinacoteca, the main picture gallery, is on the upper floor. The museum is relatively small, so you are unlikely to run out of time to see everything. Remember tickets must be booked ahead of a visit.

WHAT TO SEE

PAOLINA BORGHESE POSING AS VENUS

Antonio Canova (1757–1822), the most famous of all neoclassical sculptors, sculpted this portrait of Napoleon's sister Paolina in 1805. Dominating room 1, it is acknowledged to be his masterpiece and is certainly his most famous work. It shows the beautiful 25-year-old reclining semi-naked on a couch, posing as Venus, with an apple in her hand. The other hand supports her head, her hair is scooped up to show her delicate neck and profile, and the line of her body combines Classical tranquillity with more than a hint of suggestiveness. It was Paolina's own idea to commission this openly erotic piece from Canova. She already had a reputation for beauty and bad conduct when she was married off to the much older Prince Borghese, and she visualized her elderly, dull husband using the statue to flaunt the charms of his young wife in front of his friends. Once unveiled, Venus caused an immediate scandal—how could Paolina have brought herself to pose naked? 'There was a stove in the studio,' she replied. Years later, separated from the prince, Paolina regretted her nudity, and forgetting her original motives for posing, begged that the statue remain private. 'It was created only to afford you pleasure,' she wrote. The statue is carved from finest white Carrara marble; the sheen on the skin was achieved with candlewax.

TIPS

» Entrance is limited to 360 people every 2 hours, so reserve well ahead whatever the time of year.
» Leave plenty of time for the Pinacoteca.
» If you're into Italian gardens, visit the palazzo's secret garden (tours Sat–Sun 10 and 11; free).

Opposite *Bernini's powerful* David
Below *Cavona's sculpture of Paolina Borghese posing as Venus caused a scandal when it was unveiled*

65

CARAVAGGIO

Caravaggio's life was as dramatic as his work, full of feuds, plots and flight. In 1606 he was charged with murder and fled Rome to Naples. Pursued again, he fled to Malta, where he was made a knight of the Order of Malta. He subsequently fell foul of the knights, who arrested and jailed him in 1608. He escaped and reached Sicily, from where, still in fear for his life, he moved on again to Tuscany, all the time hoping that word of his pardon would come from Rome. But no word came; he was arrested again, contracted a fever, and died on the beach at Porto Ercole.

THE BERNINI SCULPTURES

Cardinal Scipione Borghese, enthused by the vitality of Gian Lorenzo Bernini's work, commissioned three works from the sculptor: *The Rape of Proserpine* (1621–22), *David* (1623) and *Apollo and Daphne* (1624). With his dynamic compositions and mastery of marble as a medium, Bernini was by far the greatest Italian exponent of the baroque style.

Apollo and Daphne is a perfect example of Bernini's genius. The myth tells the story of how the pure and chaste nymph Daphne was pursued by Apollo, the god of light. Desperate to escape, Daphne implored the other gods to save her. Her wish was granted and she was turned into a laurel tree, saved from Apollo's clutches by protective bark. Bernini's life-size sculpture shows the moment of her change, bark creeping over her body and her fingers sprouting leaves. When it was in its original position, the group was seen first from the back left, and there is no doubt that this is the best viewing point.

Bernini's virtuosity shines again in the Sala degli Imperatori with *The Rape of Proserpine*, also inspired by pagan legend. Proserpine, the daughter of Ceres, goddess of the harvest, attracted the attention of Pluto, ruler of the underworld. He seized the girl, taking her to Hades, but when her mother intervened Pluto agreed to return her to earth for six months of each year. Pagans believed that during Proserpine's months in Hades, Ceres mourned, winter reigned, and the world was cold and barren. On her return, the earth welcomed Proserpine with a carpet of flowers, and crops grew once more. Bernini shows the moment of abduction: From the left we see Pluto grasping Proserpine, his fingers sinking into her flesh, while she claws at his face. Viewing the group from various angles reveals different aspects of the myth.

Clockwise from below *Bernini's dramatic* Apollo and Daphne *is one of the collection's treasures;* The Return of the Prodigal Son *by Guercino (1627–28);* The Ecstacy of St. Catherine *by Carracci (c.1590)*

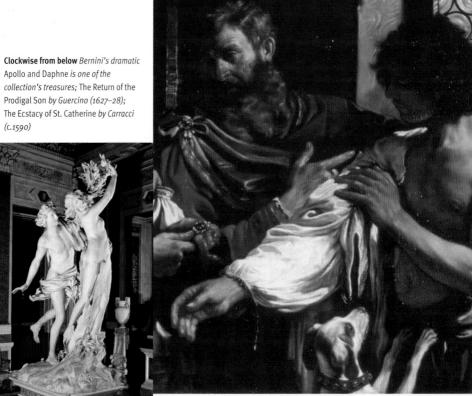

THE CARAVAGGIO MASTERPIECES

Michelangelo Merisi, known as Caravaggio (1573–1610), is represented by six dramatic paintings in room 8. This artist is recognized for the extraordinary realism and detail found in his work, but he is known above all for his use of *chiaroscuro*, the balance of light and shade in a painting. The device is judged by the skill with which the artist handles shadows, and the best such artists tend to paint dark pictures illuminated by brilliant shafts of light. You can see this beautifully in Caravaggio's *Madonna dei Palafreni*, painted in 1606. The Virgin holding the child Jesus stands on the left, with her mother, St. Anne, to the right. All three figures are gazing downwards, their attention riveted on a writhing snake about to strike. Jesus' foot is on the serpent, symbol of sin and heresy, as his mother teaches him how to crush it. Caravaggio painted the picture for the Confraternity of the Palafreni, who hung it in their chapel in St. Peter's Basilica. It was there just a month before the reactionary Vatican clique ordered its removal on the grounds of its realism and lack of decorum. Caravaggio had his revenge when the painting was bought by Cardinal Scipione Borghese, preferred nephew of Pope Paul V, and hung in pride of place in his collection.

The artist's triumph was short-lived, for in the same year, 1606, he was accused of murder and fled Rome, escaping to Malta. It was here that he painted *David with the Head of Goliath*, which he sent to the Papal Court in the hope of pardon. The subject is simple: the boy David holding the head of the slaughtered giant. It is the superb play of light on skin and drapery that makes the painting shine; Caravaggio portrayed himself as Goliath.

GALLERY GUIDE
GROUND FLOOR
Entrance hall Stunning mix of marble, frescoes and sculpture
Room 1 *Paolina Borghese*
Room 2 *David*
Room 3 *Apollo and Daphne*
Room 4 Sala degli Imperatori, decorated with busts of Roman emperors and *The Rape of Proserpine*
Room 5 *Sleeping Hermaphrodite*
Room 6 *Aeneas and Anchises*
Room 7 Decorated in Egyptian style with Classical sculpture
Room 8 The Room of the Faun, with Caravaggio's paintings

GALLERY GUIDE
FIRST FLOOR
Room 9 Umbrian school

Room 10 Italian Mannerism, including *Venus* by Cranach, *Danae* by Corregio, *Madonna and Child* by Andrea del Sarto, *St. John the Baptist* by Bronzino

Room 11 Ferrara school, including *Tobias and the Angel* by Girolamo Savoldo

Room 12 Schools of Siena, Lombardy and Veneto

Room 13 Florentine school

Room 14 Gallery of Lanfranco, including *Diana* by Domenichino and portraits of Cardinal Scipione Borghese by Bernini

Room 15 Schools of Ferrara, Veneto and Brescia, including *Deposition* by Peter Paul Rubens

Room 16 Florentine Mannerism

Room 17 17th- and 18th-century art

Room 18 17th-century art

Room 19 17th-century art

Room 20 Veneto school, including *The Education of Cupid* and other works by Titian

Opposite *Bernini's masterful work* The Rape of Proserpine

Below *Titian's* The Education of Cupid *(c.1565)*

THE UMBRIAN SCHOOL
Room 9 is crammed with some of the best paintings in the gallery, mainly by Umbrian artists. Perugino and Pinturicchio are both represented, but it is the three works by Raphael that shine, in particular the *Deposition*, a picture inspired as much by Classical art as religion. It was commissioned in 1507 by Atlanta Baglioni, in memory of her son Grifonetto. The Baglioni were one of the most important families in Perugia, a city where feuds were a way of life. The image of a young man's dead body was the perfect subject to commemorate the dead boy. It hung for a century in Perugia, but, with the connivance of the local priest, was spirited away in 1608 and sent to Pope Paul V, who passed it on to his nephew Scipione to adorn the Villa Borghese. Raphael used a relief on a Roman sarcophagus as his inspiration, and the whole composition echoes Michelangelo's *Pietà* in St. Peter's (▷ 213).

TITIAN'S SACRED AND PROFANE LOVE
Of the four paintings by Titian in room 20, *Sacred and Profane Love* stands apart, transfused with warm light and soft hues. It was painted in 1514 to celebrate the marriage of the Venetians Nicolò Aurelio and Laura Baragotto. The meaning of the picture has been hotly debated down the years. It portrays two beautiful women seated on a sarcophagus, which also serves as a fountain; while one woman is clothed in white, the other is naked except for a few light draperies. Between them, a putto leans over the water in the fountain; behind, the tranquil landscape is washed with light. This is probably a picture about married love, the woman in white representing the bride, assisted by Venus and Cupid. Venus, with her burning flame, stands for the durability of married love. The picture's present title, coined in the late 18th century, reflects later thinking, and adds a moral dimension that was never intended. In 1899 the Rothschild family offered 4 million lire for the painting, almost half a million lire more than the total value of the rest of the collection and the villa together. The offer was promptly refused.

MUSEO CARLO BILOTTI

www.museocarlobilotti.it

The converted 17th-century *arancieria* (orangery) in the Villa Borghese opened in 2006 as a showcase for Italian-American billionaire Carlo Bilotti's collection of modern art. Bilotti's passion was the surrealist artist De Chirico, who lived in Rome for 30 years until his death in 1978. Twenty-two works by this artist are displayed in the museum's permanent collection, along with a Larry Rivers portrait of Mr Bilotti, a 1981 Warhol of his wife and daughter, and works by other late 20th-century luminaries. The ground floor shows changing exhibitions, featuring works by big-name contemporary artists.

✚ 58 E3 ✉ Viale Fiorello La Guardian ☎ 06 0608 🕐 Tue–Sun 9–7 💷 Adult €6, concessions €4; museum and exhibition adult €8, concessions €7 🚍 52, 53, 95, 910

MUSEO E GALLERIA BORGHESE

▷ 64–69.

MUSEO KEATS-SHELLEY

www.keats-shelley-house.org

At the foot of the Spanish Steps lies the Casina Rossa, where poet John Keats spent the last few months of his life from 1820 to 1821.

Since 1903 the house has been owned by the Keats-Shelley Memorial Foundation. The museum documents the life and works of the Romantic poets, including Byron, Leigh Hunt, Shelley and Keats, with a collection of letters, manuscripts and documents. In particular, it is a memorial to the last two, both of whom died in Italy.

✚ 58 E4 ✉ Piazza di Spagna 26, 00187 ☎ 06 678 4235 🕐 Mon–Fri 10–1, 2–6, Sat 11–2, 3–6 💷 €4.50, concessions €3.50 🚇 Spagna 🚍 117, 119, 530, 590 💷 🏛

MUSEO NAZIONALE DELLE PASTE ALIMENTARI

www.museodellapasta.it

Not far from the Trevi Fountain is this museum dedicated to pasta. It traces the history and evolution of pasta and of the manufacturing processes, from early grindstones to modern industrial machinery. Visitors also discover how pasta is dried, a process that dates from the 12th century.

✚ 58 E4 ✉ Piazza Scanderberg 117, 00184 ☎ 06 699 1119 🕐 Currently closed for restoration 💷 €10 🚇 Barberini 🚍 52, 53, 61, 62, 63, 71, 80, 85, 160, 850 stopping at Piazza San Silvestro

PALAZZO BARBERINI E GALLERIA NAZIONALE D'ARTE ANTICA

▷ 71.

PALAZZO MASSIMO ALLE TERME

▷ 72–73.

PALAZZO DI MONTECITORIO

Pope Innocent X commissioned parts of this vast palace from Bernini in 1653, notably the clock tower, central facade and columns, but much of the present structure dates from after 1871, when the building was given over to the Camera dei Deputati, the lower house of the Italian parliament. The interior (usually open only once a month, depending on when parliament is in session) is distinguished by Ernesto Basile's exceptional wooden ceilings (1903–27) in the main hall.

The 22m (72ft) Egyptian obelisk (594BC) in Piazza Montecitorio stood in nearby Campo Marzio, serving as the pointer for a vast, but inaccurate, sundial until the 11th century, when it collapsed. It was restored and raised in its current position in the late 18th century.

✚ 58 E4 ✉ Piazza Montecitorio, 00186 ☎ 06 67061 🕐 First Sun of each month (except Aug) 10–6; guided tours in Italian only 💷 Free 🚇 Spagna 🚍 62, 63 and all other services to Via del Corso

PALAZZO DEL QUIRINALE

www.quirinale.it

This luxurious palace looking out over the city stands on the Quirinale and is the seat of the presidency of the Italian Republic.

From 1592 the palace became the popes' summer home. Later, it was used by the kings of Italy, who decorated the rooms with expensive tapestries.

Domenico Fontana, Carlo Maderno and Gian Lorenzo Bernini all worked on the palace. It has a cycle of frescoes by Guido Reni in the Chapel of the Annunciation, while the Pauline Chapel is decorated with fine stuccowork by Martino Ferrabosco. The courtyard inside, once the reception area for heads of state, is guarded by very tall guards called Corrazzieri and leads to the magnificent staircase of honour built by Flaminio Ponzio. Across from the palace are the papal stables *(scuderie)*, where important exhibitions are held (▷ 78). The palace gardens are open to visitors only on 2 June, the anniversary of the Italian Republic.

✚ 58 E5 ✉ Piazza del Quirinale, 00184 ☎ Segreteria Generale Presidenza della Repubblica, for guided tours: 06 46991 🕐 Sun 8.30–12. Gardens open on Republic Day 2 Jun 💷 Adult €5, child (under 18) free 🚇 Barberini 🚍 H, 40, 60, 64, 70, 71, 117, 170

Below *The Museo Carlo Bilotti, in the Villa Borghese park, showcases a superb collection of modern art*

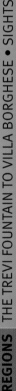

PALAZZO BARBERINI
E GALLERIA NAZIONALE D'ARTE ANTICA

This imposing baroque palace bears witness to the importance of the Barberini family, and highlights the innovative genius of three great artists: Gian Lorenzo Bernini, his great rival Francesco Borromini, and the painter Pietro da Cortona. The building was commissioned in 1623 by Pope Urban VIII to provide a prestigious dwelling for his family. Carlo Maderno was the original architect, but Bernini and Borromini completed the work in 1633. The palace is now home to one of the city's principal art galleries.

INSIDE THE PALACE

On entering you see two remarkable staircases: the small, spiral staircase by Borromini on the right and a wide, monumental structure by Bernini on the left. Take the Bernini one to reach the gallery. You can also take a tour of the 18th-century private apartments of the Barberini family on the second floor.

GALLERIA NAZIONALE D'ARTE ANTICA

Since 1949, the palace has housed the Galleria Nazionale d'Arte Antica (National Gallery of Ancient Art; shared with the Palazzo Corsini, ▷ 192). The impressive collection of works from the 12th to 18th centuries represents private collections of some of the aristocratic families of Rome. In the small antechamber to the gallery are displayed a marble bust of Urban VIII, carved by Bernini between 1637 and 1638, and a Virgin Mary with Christ, dating back to the second half of the 12th century. Other works to look for include the lovely *Virgin Mary with the Christ Child* by Filippo Lippi, *Narcissus* and *Judith and Holofernes*, both by Caravaggio, and Titian's *Venus and Adonis*. The gallery's best-known painting is Raphael's portrait of *La Fornarina (The Baker's Daughter)*, believed to be the artist's mistress, painted in the year of his death.

Pietro da Cortona painted his finest work, *The Triumph of Divine Providence*, on the vault of the Gran Salone between 1633 and 1639. It is a masterpiece of baroque art, admired for its powerful portrayal of light and shade *(chiaroscuro)*. The painting exalts the glory of the Barberinis; Divine Providence, holding a sceptre, stands above the clouds.

INFORMATION

www.galleriaborghese.it

🔢 59 F4 ✉ Via Barberini 18/Via delle Quattro Fontane 13, 00184 ☎ 06 32810, 06 482 4184 (for groups only) 🕐 Tue–Sun 8.30–7 💷 Adult €5, EU citizens aged 18–25 €2.50, EU citizens under 18 and over 65 free 🚇 Barberini 🚌 61, 62, 175, 492, 530 to Piazza Barberini; 52, 53, 63, 80, 95 116, 119, 204, 590, 630 to Via Veneto 📖 *Capolavori Galleria Nazionale Arte Antica Palazzo Barberini* in Italian and English €12.50, available in gallery bookshop 🎫 Guided tours of apartments every 45 min; booking recommended (tel 06 855 5952); €5. Tours run only for a minimum group size of 10 people 🍴 Beautiful café with panoramic view of Via Barberini 📚 Arts bookshop, very well stocked

TIP

» While you are here, buy tickets in advance for the Borghese Gallery (▷ 64–69), which is always very crowded.

Above *Paintings adorn the walls of the Sala delle Battaglie in the Barberini apartments*

SCOPRI IL MASSIMO

INFORMATION

www.archeoroma.beniculturali.it
www.pierreci.it (for online reservations)
🚇 59 G4 ✉ Largo di Villa Peretti
1, 00187 ☎ Information: 06 480
201. Advance tickets: 06 3996 7700
🕐 Tue–Sun 9–7.45 💷 Adult €7, EU
citizens 18–24 €3.50, EU citizens under
18 and over 65 free. For details of the
Roma Archeologica Card and Museum
Card, ▷ 259 🚇 Repubblica or Termini
🚌 40, 64, 84, 86, 90, 170, 175, 492, 910
to Piazza della Repubblica; 14, 36, 38,
64, 86, 90, 92, 105, 217, 310, 714 or tram
5 to Piazza dei Cinquecento or Termini
station 🚶 Sat–Sun 10.30, 3.30 in Italian
only, free. Audiotours: Italian, English, €4
📖 Available from museum shop: brief
guide €8.20, catalogue €49 🏪 Open 9–7

Above *The 19th-century Palazzo Massimo
has been beautifully restored*

INTRODUCTION

This beautifully restored and well-organized museum forms part of the Museo
Nazionale Romano (with the Palazzo Altemps, the Terme di Diocleziano and
Crypta Balbi) and is housed in a palace designed by Camillo Pistrucci in the
late 19th century for the Massimo family, replacing an earlier one demolished
to make way for the Termini station. In 1981 the palace was acquired by the
state, and in the 1990s it was transformed into one of Rome's most attractive
museums.

The palace has four floors of museum space, a modern library, a
conference room and a computer-based documentation area. The Classical art
collection is on the first three floors, and includes works of art from the end of
the Republican age (second–first century BC) to the late Imperial age (fourth
century AD), with some original Greek works from the fifth century BC.

WHAT TO SEE
GROUND FLOOR
Niobid from the Hortus Sallustiani (Room VII)

This superb Greek statue dates from 440BC, and was found on the site of
gardens once belonging to Julius Caesar; it was almost certainly once his
property. The statue portrays one of Niobe's daughters falling as she tries to
remove an arrow embedded in her back—she and her siblings were killed
by the gods Apollo and Artemis. The piece probably came from a group
decorating the pediment of a Greek temple, later collected by Caesar.

FIRST FLOOR

The Lancellotti Discobolus (Room VI)

One of the most famous copies of the great fifth-century BC works, this statue, discovered in the 18th century, was sent to Germany during World War II and returned in 1948. It reproduces an original bronze, showing an athlete throwing a discus, that was probably the work of Myron, a Greek sculptor renowned for his portraits of athletes. This very fine marble copy dates from the mid-second century AD.

The Sleeping Hermaphrodite (Room VII)

Dionysian cult statues were popular with both Greeks and Romans—with the Greeks for their religious symbolism, the Romans for their refined sensuality. This lovely example is a second-century AD copy of a second-century BC Hellenistic original. Endowed with the attributes of both sexes, the figure reclines languidly on drapery, the slick polished finish adding to its eroticism.

SECOND FLOOR

The House of Livia (Room II)

Crammed with realistic details, these lovely decorative wall paintings come from a villa belonging to Livia Drusilla, wife of the Emperor Augustus. The panels, moved from the excavations in 1951, decorated the walls of a summer triclinium, a large and airy outside living room, set partially below ground. Look out for the different trees, flowers, fruit and birds, as fresh now as when they were painted between 20 and 10BC.

The Villa Farnesina (Gallery II, Rooms III–V)

This complete set of frescoes was discovered in 1879 near the Renaissance Villa Farnesina; they can be dated to around 20BC and may have been commissioned to celebrate the wedding of Augustus' daughter Julia. The frescoes are immensely varied, embracing themes such as landscapes, architecture and Egyptian motifs. There are scenes portraying myths, battles and garlands of flowers and leaves: a superb example of the lavishness of upper-class Roman interior decoration.

GALLERY GUIDE

The galleries are arranged thematically.
Basement Coins and jewellery.
Ground floor Power in Republican and early Imperial times. Portrait busts, full statues, mosaics, urns and basins.
First floor Development of different iconographic trends, and copies and reworkings of Hellenistic statuary. Portrait heads, sculpture and bronzes.
Second floor Wall paintings, paintings, frescoes, mosaics and stuccoes of exceptional importance and quality.

Below *The mid-second century* AD *marble* Lancellotti Discobolus

REGIONS   THE TREVI FOUNTAIN TO VILLA BORGHESE • SIGHTS

PIAZZA DI SPAGNA

Piazza di Spagna gained its name when the Spanish ambassador took up residence here, but the section towards Via del Babuino—to the left as you look up at the Trinità dei Monti—used to be called Piazza di Francia, as the French claimed the right to pass through the square to reach their church. This resulted in fierce rivalry between the two nations. You can see another sign of diplomatic strife on the steps, this time between the French and the Italians, in the confrontation of Conti eagles (from the coat of arms of Pope Innocent XIII) and the fleur-de-lis of France.

During the 18th and 19th centuries, so many English visitors came to Rome and stayed in the numerous hotels and lodging houses scattered around the piazza that it eventually came to be known as the English ghetto. Poet John Keats was just one of the illustrious visitors to stay near here. He died in the Casina Rossa at the foot of the Spanish Steps (at the bottom on the right as you look up the steps), now the Museo Keats-Shelley (▷ 70). Babington's English Tea Rooms, opposite, on the left-hand corner of the steps, founded in 1896 by the Misses Babington, is another sign of the square's 19th-century popularity with the English. Today, it is one of the most sophisticated, refined and expensive tea rooms in Rome.

Start your explorations in the piazza itself, pausing on the far side of the fountain to take in the full sweep of the magnificent Scalinata della Trinità dei Monti (Spanish Steps). Walk round the square, with its shops and buildings, before tackling the steps. As you climb, pause to admire the changing view. At the top, from the church of Trinità dei Monti, there's a superb view of Rome, with the cupola of St. Peter's in the distance—wonderful at sunset.

THE PIAZZA

The butterfly-shaped Piazza di Spagna contains one of Rome's most unusual fountains, the boat-shaped Fontana della Barcaccia, commissioned by Pope Urban VIII to commemorate the great flood of 1598. It was designed by father and son Bernini to represent a boat that was stranded in the piazza during the flood, and was finished in 1629. Pietro Bernini exploited the low water pressure of the Aqua Virgo at this point to achieve the 'sinking' effect.

At the piazza's southern end is a Roman column topped by a statue of the Virgin Mary, erected in 1856 to commemorate the establishment of the doctrine of the Immaculate Conception. On 8 December a procession, led by the Pope, terminates here to crown the statue with wreaths.

THE SPANISH STEPS

The Scalinata della Trinità dei Monti, designed by Francesco de Sanctis, were built between 1723 and 1726. Prior to this, the church was separated from the piazza by a wood, a popular hideout for criminals. There are three flights of steps, 138 in all, of various widths and configurations, along with benches from which you can enjoy the increasingly lovely views. The final flight of two symmetrical staircases brings you to the Piazza della Trinità dei Monti.

THE CHURCH OF TRINITÀ DEI MONTI

King Charles VIII of France commissioned this church in 1495 on the request of St. Francis of Paola, who lived in the nearby convent. It was consecrated by Pope Sixtus V in 1585 and restored in 1816 by Louis XVIII after it was looted by Napoleon. The church of Trinità dei Monti is still owned by the French.

AT ITS BEST

If you're visiting Rome in the spring you'll see the Spanish Steps at their loveliest, when every level, including the balustrades, is decorated with giant tubs of multicoloured azaleas. The display is normally in place for around a month, starting sometime in April, depending on when flowering starts.

INFORMATION

✚ 58 E4 🚇 Spagna 🚌 116, 117, 119, 590 📖 Available from souvenir shops on the square ☕ Plenty in the area

THE TREVI FOUNTAIN TO VILLA BORGHESE • SIGHTS

REGIONS

Opposite *From Piazza di Spagna, a series of steps, the famed Spanish Steps, ascend to the church of Trinità dei Monti, with increasingly lovely views*

PIAZZA BARBERINI

This beautiful piazza, named after the powerful Barberini family, showcases the work of Bernini, who contributed to the family's imposing residential palace (▷ 71) and designed the two fountains on the square.

In the heart of the square is the Fontana del Tritone, commissioned in 1643 by Pope Urban VIII: Four dolphins support a huge scallop shell on which sits a triton blowing a jet of water through a conch. Look for the Barberini coat of arms (the bees) and the papal arms (St. Peter's keys and the papal tiara).

On the corner of Via Veneto is the other Bernini fountain, the Fontana delle Api. The Fountain of the Bees was commissioned to celebrate the 21st anniversary in August 1644 of Urban VIII's accession to the papacy. The fact that Bernini finished it before the actual date was considered a bad omen, borne out when the Pope died eight days before the anniversary. In 1865, the fountain was dismantled and removed from its original site, at the corner with Via Sistina. It was reassembled in its present position in 1916; the only surviving original pieces are the central part of a shell and three bees drinking the water.
✚ 58 F4 🚇 Barberini 🚌 61, 62, 175, 492, 630 to Piazza Barberini; 52, 53, 63, 80, 95 116, 119, 204, 590 to Via Veneto

PIAZZA DEL POPOLO

When approaching Piazza del Popolo from Via del Corso, pause for a moment to admire the square from a distance. Its charm lies in the complete harmony of all the distinct architectural styles within it.

Each end of the oval piazza is adorned with a fountain, with sphinxes and statues depicting the four seasons. At the end of the 16th century, Pope Sixtus V erected an Egyptian obelisk of the Pharaoh Rameses II in the middle of the square, and in 1823, Giuseppe Valadier added the rounded basins and four water-spitting marble lions to the base of the obelisk.

Above *One of Valadier's water-spitting lions at the base of the obelisk in Piazza del Popolo*

The 17th-century twin churches of Santa Maria dei Miracoli and Santa Maria di Monte Santo stand on either side of Via del Corso. Both churches were started by Carlo Rainaldi and completed by Carlo Fontana (work on Santa Maria di Monte Santo was supervised by Bernini). Inside Santa Maria di Monte Santo are frescoes by Baciccia and a 15th-century painting of the Virgin Mary on the high altar.

On the north side of the square is its grand entrance, Porta del Popolo, erected in 1561. The orginal structure was reworked by Bernini in 1655 to mark the entry to Rome of Queen Christina of Sweden after her conversion to Roman Catholicism. The adjoining church of Santa Maria del Popolo contains exceptional works of art by Caravaggio, Raphael, Bernini and Pinturicchio, among others.
✚ 58 D3 🚇 Flaminio 🚌 95, 117, 119, 491, 495, 590, 628, 926; tram 2

PIAZZA DELLA REPUBBLICA

Piazza della Repubblica, one of Rome's busiest spots, has a theatrical fountain at its heart and two semicircular porticoed buildings at the sides. The massive, but somewhat unappealing church of Santa Maria degli Angeli is the dominant building.

The square was created in the late 19th century to follow the curved line of the *exedra* (a recess with raised seating) of the nearby Terme di Diocleziano (▷ 79), hence its popular name—Piazza Esedra.

The central fountain, the Fontana delle Naiadi (1901), gets its name from the four water nymphs (naiads) that decorate it, the work of Sicilian artist Mario Rutelli. The naked nymphs and the allegorical marine animals represent water in various forms: rivers, lakes, oceans and underground streams. The city authorities thought the figures too erotic when they were first revealed, and ordered a fence (later removed) to be built to hide them from sight. The original central decoration of the fountain—three tritons, a dolphin and an octopus—was nicknamed the 'fish fry', and was moved to the gardens of Piazza Vittorio Emanuele. The present central figure is the minor god Glaucus in combat with a fish.
✚ 59 F4 🚇 Repubblica 🚌 H, 40, 64, 84, 86, 90, 170, 175, 492, 910

PIAZZA DI SPAGNA
▷ 74–75.

SANT'ANDREA AL QUIRINALE

Often called the baroque pearl, this church is one of Bernini's best works, and was closest to his own heart. It was here that he asked to be taken towards the end of his life to admire the effect of the light streaming through the windows, illuminating the rich and beautiful marble, gold and stucco he had used to embellish it.

The design is very unusual. The facade is on the shorter side of the building and is highlighted by elegant steps and a portico. Inside is an elliptical central hall with eight deep rectangular chapels off it, each one lit by a window over the altar. The dome above the altar is richly decorated with gilded stuccowork, marble and stucco angels and cherubs. The sacristy has a beautiful frescoed vault. In the adjacent convent are the rooms of St. Stanislaus, where the 17-year-old Jesuit novice died in 1568; the statue of the saint is by the 17th-century French sculptor Pierre Legros. Ask in the sacristy for access to these rooms.

✚ 58 F5 ✉ Via del Quirinale 29, 00184 ☎ 06 474 0807 🕐 Mon–Sat 8.30–12, 3.30–7, Sun 9–12, 4–7 ✋ Free 🚇 Barberini 🚌 H, 40, 60, 64, 70, 116T, 170 to Via Nazionale

SAN CARLO ALLE QUATTRO FONTANE

This minuscule church, also known as San Carlino, is famously smaller than a single one of the piers supporting the dome of St. Peter's.

Designed in 1638, the church was Francesco Borromini's first work; it was also his last, as the new facade he began in 1665 was unfinished when he committed suicide two years later. The architecture of San Carlino reflects the artist's tormented and contradictory state of mind: Every curve has its counter-curve, and concave and convex sections form complicated patterns. A statue of the Counter-Reformation saint, St. Charles Borromeo, is the main focus of the curved facade.

The church's interior is very simple, an oval shape with stuccoed niches. The intricately designed coffered dome adds to the elegant effect the artist managed to create in such a small space.

Borromini's cloister, with two rows of Doric columns and slightly convex corners, is beautifully proportioned.

Outside are four fountains *(quattro fontane)*, one on each corner of the street. They are the work of Domenico Fontana, and date from 1589.

✚ 59 F4 ✉ Via del Quirinale 23, 00184 ☎ 06 488 3109 🕐 Mon–Fri 10–1, 3–6, Sat–Sun 10–1 ✋ Free 🚇 Barberini 🚌 H, 40, 60, 64, 70, 116T, 170 to Via Nazionale

SANTA MARIA DELLA CONCEZIONE

www.cappucciniviaveneto.it

The original setting of this majestic structure, the church of a Capuchin convent, has been spoiled by the construction of Via Veneto, but even so it attracts many visitors.

The church's rather austere exterior gives no clue to the extraordinary sight it contains within—its macabre Capuchin cemetery.

The church was built around 1626, commissioned by Cardinal Antonio Barberini (brother of Pope Urban VIII). His tombstone is on the floor in front of the main altar, with the inscription: *'Hic jacet pulvis, cinis et nihil'* ('Here lie dust, ashes and nothing more').

On the right-hand side of the front steps is the entrance to the cemetery in the crypt. Here, the walls and ceilings of five chapels are gruesomely decorated with the skeletons (some of them clothed) and loose bones of about 4,000 Capuchin monks who died between 1528 and 1870. The floor is scattered with earth brought from the holy sites in Palestine.

✚ 58 F4 ✉ Via Vittorio Veneto 27, 00187 ☎ 06 487 1185 🕐 Church: daily 7–12, 3–6. Cemetery: Wed–Mon 9–12, 3–6 ✋ Free (donation for cemetery) 🚇 Barberini 🚌 C3, 52, 53, 63, 80, 95, 116, 116T, 119, 150, 630 to Piazza Barberini

Below *Gruesome decoration in the crypt of Santa Maria della Concezione*

SANTA MARIA DEL POPOLO

The church of Santa Maria del Popolo is unmissable for art lovers, with works by some of the great names from the 16th and 17th centuries, including Raphael, Caravaggio and Bernini.

According to legend, Nero's tomb once stood under a walnut tree on the site of this church and his ghost used to haunt the place. Pope Paschal II had the tree cut down and built a small chapel in its place. The name, St. Mary of the People, recalls the fact that the Pope asked the people of Rome to pay for the building of the chapel. In 1472, Sixtus IV commissioned the present church to be built by Andrea Bregno. It was later reworked in the baroque style, largely by Bernini.

The sumptuously decorated Chigi Chapel in the left aisle was designed by Raphael for the wealthy Sienese banker Agostino Chigi, its plain exterior a sharp contrast to the richly decorated interior; Bernini completed the chapel after Raphael's death. The bright red travertine marble Cerasi Chapel, at the end of the same aisle, contains two of Caravaggio's masterpieces: *The Conversion of St. Paul* and *The Crucifixion of St. Peter*.

➕ 58 D3 ✉ Piazza del Popolo 12, 00186 ☎ 06 361 0836 🕐 Mon–Sat 7–12, 4–7, Sun 7.30–1.30, 4.30–7.30 ✋ Free 🚇 Flaminio or Spagna 🚌 117, 119, 628, 926 🎧 Audioguide €1 in Italian, English, German, French and Spanish

SANTA MARIA DELLA VITTORIA

This rich, harmonious and beautiful baroque church was commissioned by Cardinal Scipione Borghese to celebrate the Catholic victory over the Protestants at the Battle of White Mountain near Prague in 1620; a victory attributed to the image of the Virgin taken into battle.

The vault and ceiling are frescoed by Perugino and the Orazi brothers, but the star attraction is Bernini's Cornaro Chapel, the last chapel on the left-hand side, designed in 1646. It is dominated by Bernini's superb marble *Ecstasy of St. Teresa of Avila* over the altar. Showing the moment she was pierced by an arrow, the sculpture has been described as one of the most erotic religious works of art ever produced.

➕ 59 F4 ✉ Via XX Settembre 17, 00184 ☎ 06 482 5705 🕐 Daily 9–12, 3.30–6.30 ✋ Free 🚇 Repubblica or Barberini 🚌 MA1, MA2, 36, 60, 61, 62, 84, 90, 150, 175, 492, 590, 910 to Via XX Settembre

Below *Bernini's* Ecstasy of St. Teresa of Avila, *in Santa Maria della Vittoria*

SANTA PUDENZIANA

This historic church is said to stand on the site of the house of Senator Pudens, father of saints Prassede and Pudenziana. The building was transformed into a church in the late fourth century, making it one of the oldest sites of Christian worship in the city.

The bell tower dates from the 12th century, as does the elegant door with its fluted columns. The dome was added in the 16th century and the facade was restored in 1870.

The interior of the church was transformed into one nave in 1588 by Francesco da Volterra. He also designed the dome, which was frescoed by Nicolò Circignani.

The apse mosaic portrays Christ sitting on a throne surrounded by the Apostles and two female figures, who may be Pudenziana and Prassede, or who may represent the Church of the Jews and the Church of the Gentiles.

➕ 59 F5 ✉ Via Urbana 60, 00184 ☎ 06 481 4622 🕐 Daily 8.30–12, 3–6. Closed to visitors during Mass ✋ Free 🚇 Cavour, Termini or Vittorio Emanuele 🚌 71 to Via Panisperna or C3, 16, 70, 71, 75 and other services to Santa Maria Maggiore

SCUDERIE DEL QUIRINALE

www.scuderiequirinale.it
Once the stables of the Quirinale Palace, the Scuderie was stunningly transformed by architect Gae Aulenti in the 1990s to become Rome's most prestigious exhibition space. Since opening, the gallery has staged major temporary loan exhibitions of works of art from all over the world in its airy, modern rooms. The Scuderie is worth visiting as a building in its own right, and has an excellent bookshop and an attractive café and restaurant.

➕ 58 E5 ✉ Via XXIV Maggio 16, 00184 ☎ 06 678 0842 🕐 Open during exhibitions only, Sun–Thu 10–8, Fri–Sat 10am–10.30pm ✋ Scuderie and Palazzo delle Esposizioni: adult €18, under 26 and over 65 €15. Exhibitions: adult €10, under 26 and over 65 €7.50 🚇 Repubblica, Cavour 🚌 40, 60, 64, 117, 170

Above *The Temple of Esculapio in the Villa Borghese*

della Meridiana. The most romantic part of the park is the artificial lake, with a little island in the middle dominated by the 18th-century temple to Esculapio, erected in Ionian style and adorned with a statue of the Greek god of medicine.

The Piazza di Siena, where in the early 19th century Prince Camillo Borghese allowed people to gather for the *Festa delle Ottobrate* revelries during October, is now the venue for Rome's annual International Horse Show *(Concorso Ippico Internazionale,* ▷ 89*)*. There is also a zoo, Bioparco, which was established in 1911 within the rambling parkland (▷ 89).

✚ 58 F3 🕐 Daily sunrise–sunset 🚇 Flaminio or Spagna 🚌 52, 53, 88, 95, 116, 117, 119, 490, 491, 495, 910

TERME DI DIOCLEZIANO

www.archeoroma.beniculturali.it
This grand baths complex was the largest to be built in Rome—it could accommodate 3,000 people. Today, it incorporates the church of Santa Maria degli Angeli and part of the Museo Nazionale Romano, and is the underlying structure of Piazza della Repubblica (▷ 76).

In AD298 the Emperor Diocletian commissioned Maximian, who ruled the Western Empire under him, to build the most luxurious baths in the city. At the height of their popularity they included libraries, concert halls, gardens, galleries and exercise rooms. Like the Terme di Caracalla, Diocletian's baths complex was abandoned in the sixth century.

In the 16th century, Pius IV commissioned Michelangelo to convert the grand central hall of the baths into a church, Santa Maria degli Angeli. His not particularly successful adaptation was not improved by Luigi Vanvitelli's later alterations. In the early 20th century the facade was removed to reveal the unadorned curved wall of the caldarium (hot room) of the baths, while the present atrium of the church corresponds to the tepidarium (warm room). The Octagonal Hall, next to the church, houses part of the Museo Nazionale Romano, including sarcophagi, decorations from the Aurelian temple. There is also a cloister by Michelangelo, enclosed by a portico of 100 columns and 100 arcades.

✚ 59 G4 ✉ Viale Enrico de Nicola 78, 00184 ☎ 06 3996 7700 🕐 Museum: Tue–Sun 9–7.45. Octagonal Hall: closed for restoration 🎟 Adult €7, EU citizens 18–24 €3.50, EU citizens under 18 and over 65 free. For details of the Roma Archeologica Card and Museum Card, ▷ 259. Audioguide €4 in English and Italian. 🚇 Termini or Repubblica 🚌 C2, C3, M, 16, 38, 75, 86, 90, 92, 217, 310, 360, 649 to Viale Enrico de Nicola

VILLA BORGHESE

In the early 17th century, Cardinal Scipione Borghese created a country estate, the Villa Borghese, the grounds of which now form one of Rome's most important parks.

The Cardinal kept his rich art collection in the imposing Villa Pinciana or Casino Borghese (now Museo e Galleria Borghese, ▷ 64–69), but there is still much to see here, including the Museo Carlo Bilotti (▷ 70) and the Casino

VILLA GIULIA E MUSEO NAZIONALE ETRUSCO
▷ 80–81.

VILLA MEDICI

www.villamedici.it
The grounds of the Villa Medici are one of the best examples of an Italian Renaissance garden, with elegantly placed fountains and sculptures, and rare plants growing amid the pine trees. The house is not open to the public. In 1576, Cardinal Ferdinando Medici (later Grand Duke of Tuscany) bought the building as a villa-museum, incorporating ancient Roman bas-reliefs in the facade. Look for the round fountain, topped with a cannonball fired, so the legend goes, from Castel Sant'Angelo by eccentric 17th-century Swedish queen Christina to announce to her hosts that she would be arriving for dinner.

Between 1961 and 1977, the villa was restored to its past glory: Statues were placed in the gardens, excavation works unveiled 16th-century frescoes, and an exhibition space was created.

✚ 58 E3 ✉ Viale Trinità dei Monti 1, 00187 ☎ 06 67611 🕐 Gardens only: guided tours Sep–Jun daily at 9.45, 11, 12.15 and 3 🎟 €7 🚇 Spagna 🚌 117, 119, 590

INFORMATION

http://villagiulia.beniculturali.it

⊞ 58 E2 ✉ Piazzale di Villa Giulia 9, 00187 ☎ 06 322 6571. Advance tickets: 06 320 1706 🕐 Tue–Sun 8.30–7.30 🏛 Adult €8, child (under 18) free 🚇 Flaminio 🚊 Tram 19 🎧 Audioguide €3 📖 Available in the bookshop, *Museo Etrusco Villa Giulia* in English and Italian, €13 ☕ Caffè dell'Aranceria: beautiful café in the Giardino dell'Aranceria 📚 Art bookshop, well stocked

TIPS

» Stroll among the orange trees in the Giardino dell'Aranceria, and pause for a coffee in the cafeteria.

» Combine the Villa Giulia with the nearby Galleria d'Arte Moderna, worth visiting for the quality of art it displays in a magnificent setting.

VILLA GIULIA E MUSEO NAZIONALE ETRUSCO

Splendidly housed in the 16th-century Villa Giulia is the National Etruscan Museum, the world's greatest collection of Etruscan art. The museum's wonderful collection introduces the way of life—and death—of the mysterious Etruscan civilization.

THE VILLA

Commissioned by Pope Julius III, the villa was built between 1551 and 1555 after a design by Giacomo da Vignola. It is set among a series of courtyards, with a beautiful loggia by Bartolomeo Ammannati, and is surrounded by pleasant gardens. The courtyard leads down to an enchanting nymphaeum with false grottoes and a Vasari fountain. The Etruscan museum was founded here in 1889.

THE SARCOPHAGUS OF THE SPOUSES

The most famous piece of Etruscan art is kept in the halls displaying the finds from Cerveteri. The terracotta Sarcophagus of the Spouses represents a husband and wife reclining in an affectionate pose, and vividly demonstrates that the Etruscans believed in the afterlife. It has become an emblem of the Etruscan civilization.

THE COLLECTION

Among the rest of the collection, the Tomb of the Warrior, from the sixth century BC, is of particular interest. A reconstruction beneath hall 5 shows what the funeral chambers of the tombs in Cerveteri would have looked like. Halls 11 to 18 contain a rich collection of bronze and terracotta domestic objects, including mirrors, statuettes, cinerary urns and, in particular, the bronze Chigi Vase, an exquisitely decorated wine pitcher dating from around 640–625BC (hall 15). In this room is another vase dating from the sixth century BC, decorated with the Etruscan alphabet, revealing its Latin and Greek influences and helping experts to unravel further the Etruscan language.

AN ENIGMATIC PEOPLE

The origins of the Etruscan people are shrouded in mystery. They arrived in Italy in the eighth century BC—from where, nobody knows, although there are several theories—and settled in Etruria (the area of present-day Tuscany and parts of Umbria and Lazio). They were rulers of Italy, with an empire extending from Corsica in the west to the Adriatic, and from Bologna in the north to Capua in the south, until they were conquered by the Romans in the first century BC. Little trace of the Etruscan civilization remains, except for what has been found and pieced together from the tombs.

Above *Mosaic detail, Villa Giulia*
Opposite *From Ammannati's beautiful loggia at the rear of the building there are views of a series of courtyards leading to the gardens*

VILLA BORGHESE

An leisurely walk through this popular park, once the private country estate of Cardinal Scipione Borghese, provides the perfect antidote to the turmoil of Rome's busy streets.

THE WALK

Distance: 2km (1.2 miles)
Allow: 2 hours
Start at: Piazza del Popolo
End at: Piazzale Flaminio

HOW TO GET THERE

The most convenient metro stations are Flaminio or Spagna. Alternatively, take a bus: Nos. 117, 119, 628 and 926 all serve the area.

★ Piazza del Popolo was the city's northern focal point (▷ 76). Two important Roman roads, the Via Cassia and Via Flaminia, entered the city through the Porta del Popolo before making their way to the Capitoline Hill and the fora. Today's traffic-free square is the site of the churches of Santa Maria dei Miracoli and Santa Maria di Monte Santo, which stand on either side of Via del Corso.

❶ The churches were designed by Carlo Rainaldi (and others) in 1679. His goal was to build identical churches, but the land available was not of equal size. What he built is an optical illusion: When viewed from the piazza, the churches appear the same, but Santa Maria di Monte Santo, on the left, has an oval dome while that of Santa Maria dei Miracoli, on the right, is round.

With your back to the churches, take Viale G. d'Annunzio, on the right-hand side of the square. Follow the road as it snakes up, turning left onto Viale Mickievicz for the Giardino del Pincio (▷ 63).

❷ In the Giardino del Pincio head to Piazzale Napoleone I for panoramic city views. Retrace your steps as far as Viale dell'Obelisco and turn left. Don't miss the Casina Valadier restaurant on your right.

Carry straight on, crossing Viale dell'Orologio, with its fascinating water-clock, and Viale del Muro Torto to reach the Villa Borghese park (▷ 79). Continue on, along Viale delle Magnolie, until you reach Via della Casina di Raffaello, the first right after busy Piazzale delle Canestre. Just ahead is the Casina di Raffaello, the small house said to have belonged to Raphael. Follow this road to the Tempietto di Diana.

❸ This 18th-century Classical temple is dedicated to Diana, goddess of hunting. The ceiling is decorated with blue medallions: The central motif is of Diana, accompanied by one of her hunting dogs; the rest are all hunting motifs.

Turn left at the temple, onto Viale dei Pupazzi. To the left is a good view of the Piazza di Siena, where Rome's International Horse Show is held in April/May. When you reach Piazzale dei Cavalli Marini, continue straight on to the end of the path. To your right is the Museo e Galleria Borghese (▷ 64–69).

Above *Views from the Piazzale Napoleone I in the Giardino del Pincio are spectacular*

4 The Museo e Galleria Borghese is one of the city's best-loved museums. Entrance is limited: tickets must be reserved in advance (▷ 64 for details).

Turn left down Viale dell'Uccelliera towards the Bioparco.

5 There has been a zoo on this site since 1911. Updated in 1997, Bioparco now concentrates on conservation. The zoo arranges many activities for children.

Keep left, walking down Viale del Giardino Zoologico until you reach Largo P. Picasso. Climb the steps up to the Tempio di Esculapio, which is almost surrounded by a lake where rowing boats can be hired. Take the next lane on the right (at the side of the temple) to emerge onto Piazzale Paolina Borghese. From here it is just a short walk to the Galleria Nazionale d'Arte Moderna.

6 The Galleria Nazionale d'Arte Moderna displays work by Italian and foreign artists, from 1800 to the present day. It is also used for major exhibitions.

Continue along Viale delle Belle Arti to the Villa Giulia e Museo Nazionale Etrusco (▷ 80–81).

7 The Museo Nazionale Etrusco houses the world's greatest collection of Etruscan art.

To leave the park, retrace your steps to Piazzale Paolina Borghese and take the road in front of you, Via Bernadotte, which leads you down to Piazzale dei Fiocco and the Esculapio Fountain. Continue straight down to Viale Washington, which ends with the spectacular gate in Piazzale Flaminio. On your left is the gate leading back to Piazza del Popolo.

WHEN TO GO
Villa Borghese is open from dawn to dusk. It is popular with Roman families on Saturdays and Sundays.

Above *A peaceful tree-lined avenue in the Villa Borghese*

WHERE TO EAT
CASINA VALADIER
www.casinavaladier.it
Enjoy light refreshments or a special meal and truly spectacular views.
✉ Piazza Bucharest, 00187 ☎ 06 6992 2090 🕐 Bar: Mar–Nov Tue–Sat 11.30–11, Sun 11.30–2.30; restaurant: Mar–Nov daily 12.30–3, 8–11

LA CASINA DELL'OROLOGIO
Stop for coffee or ice cream at this traditional café in the Villa Borghese.
✉ Viale dei Bambini, 00187 ☎ 06 679 8515 🕐 Thu–Tue 8am–9pm

PLACES TO VISIT
BIOPARCO
www.bioparco.it
✉ Piazzale de Giardino Zoologico, 00187 ☎ 06 360 8211 🕐 Apr–Sep Mon–Fri 9.30–6, Sat–Sun and public hols 9.30–7; Oct–Mar daily 9.30–5 💶 Adult €12.50, child €10.50

GALLERIA NAZIONALE D'ARTE MODERNA
www.gnam.beniculturali.it
✉ Viale delle Belle Arti 131, 00187 ☎ 06 3229 8221 🕐 Tue–Sun 8.30–7.30. Closed 1 May 💶 Adult €8, child €4, EU citizens under 18 and over 65 free

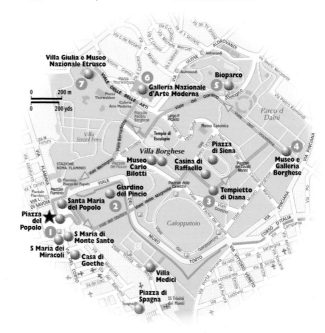

SHOPPING

ABITART
www.abitartworld.com
Rome designer Vanessa Foglia
makes vivid, flowing separates and
dresses, which look like works of art
both on and off the body. Unusual
shapes, forms and combinations of
patterns and hues, combined with
some quirky accessories, ensure an
individual look.
✚ 98 E4 ✉ Via della Croce 46–47,
00187 ☎ 06 6992 4077 ⏰ Daily 10–7.30
🚇 Spagna 🚌 81, 117, 119, 590, 628

ANGLO AMERICAN BOOK CO.
www.aab.it
Housed in a 19th-century building
a short distance from the Spanish
Steps, this is one of the better
English bookshops in the city. The
wide-ranging stock includes books
on music, cinema, philosophy,
religion and science, as well as a
good choice of fiction and children's
books. It also sells a wide range of
travel guides.
✚ 98 E4 ✉ Via della Vite 102, 00187
☎ 06 679 5222 ⏰ Jul–first week in Aug
Mon–Fri 10.30–7.30, Sat 10.30–2.30; Sep–
Jun Tue–Sat 10.30–7.30, Mon 3.30–7.30.
Closed 3 weeks in Aug 🚌 40, 62, 64, 116

ANTICA PESCHERIA GALLUZZI 1894
This most noble of fishmongers
has been supplying Romans for
well over 100 years. In a lovely old
palace with brick arches, you'll find
quality fish and shellfish caught
from all over the Mediterranean.
Their anchovies are said to be the
best in town.
✚ 99 F5 ✉ Via Venezia 26/28, 00184
☎ 06 474 4444 ⏰ Sep to mid-Aug Tue–
Sat 7–1.30 🚇 Repubblica 🚌 64, 70

BARRILÀ BOUTIQUE
In the best Italian tradition, the
women's shoes and boots sold here
are classic in style. Each model is
available in at least 26 colours—
something to match any bag, which
you can also buy here. Prices range
from around €50 to €150.
✚ 98 E3 ✉ Via del Babuino 31, 00187
☎ 06 3254 2348 ⏰ Mon–Sat 9.30–8, Sun
10–7.30 🚇 Popolo or Spagna 🚌 117

IL BIANCO DI ELLEPI
At this delightful shop in a 16th-
century building on the north side
of Piazza di Spagna, just across
from the Spanish Steps, you will
find all sorts of towels, bathrobes
and bathmats, which can be
personalized. A shipping service is
available to anywhere in the world.
Prices start at €15.
✚ 98 E4 ✉ Via della Croce 3/4, 00187
☎ 06 679 6835 ⏰ Mon–Sat 10–7.30
🚇 Spagna 🚌 116, 117

BRIONI
www.brioniroma.com
Brioni has dressed royalty and
celebrities since 1945, and has
a reputation as one of Italy's top
tailors. Leave your measurements
and you can call up for a suit
anytime, anywhere. This Via
Barberini branch, the oldest and
largest Brioni store, also stocks
women's ready-to-wear items. There
are other branches at Via Condotti
21a and Via Vittorio Veneto 129.
✚ 99 F4 ✉ Via Barberini 79, 00187 ☎ 06
484517 ⏰ Mon–Sat 10–7.30 🚇 Barberini
🚌 63, 116, 175, 492, 590, 630

CIR
Beautifully hand-embroidered table
and bed linens are the specialty
here, some appliquéd and others
with drawn thread work—truly
heirloom pieces. There are also
some beautiful embroidered silk

Opposite Abitart sells creations by Rome designer Vanessa Foglia

women's blouses and smocked children's clothes.

➕ 98 F4 ✉ Piazza Barberini 11, 00187 ☎ 06 488 3433 🕐 Summer Mon–Fri 9.30–7.30, Sat 10–1; winter Tue–Sat 9.30–7.30, Mon 3.30–7.30 🚇 Barberini 🚌 61, 62, 175

C.U.C.I.N.A.

www.cucinastore.com

With more than 20,000 items in stock, this is still the place to come for kitchen utensils in steel, porcelain and wood. With prices to suit all budgets, it's culinary heaven for cooks of all levels.

➕ 98 E4 ✉ Via Mario de' Fiori 65, 00187 ☎ 06 679 1275 🕐 Tue–Fri 10–7.30, Sat 10.30–7.30, Mon 3.30–7.30 🚇 Spagna 🚌 81, 117, 119, 590, 628

DAVIDE CENCI

www.davidecenci.com

Davide Cenci is the sophisticated preserve of those who prefer old-fashioned class over ephemeral fashion, with labels such as Burberry, Ralph Lauren, Tod's, Hogan, Ballantyne, Brooks Brothers and Church's. Everything required to dress both men and women for work and play, with an emphasis on timeless, unprovocative style.

➕ 98 E4 ✉ Via di Campo Marzio 1–7, 00186 ☎ 06 699 0681 🕐 Tue–Fri 9.30–1.30, 3.30–7.30, Sat 9.30–7.30, Mon 4–7.30 🚌 116, or any bus to Largo di Torre Argentina

IL DISCOUNT DELL'ALTA MODA

These two shops are tucked away in a little side street opposite Rome's Anglican church. One sells menswear, the other women's clothes. They both have a good selection of top designer labels (end of stock) at knock-down prices. They don't exactly advertise themselves, but the shops are bright, neat and compact inside.

➕ 98 E3 ✉ Via Gesù e Maria 14 and 16a, 00187 ☎ 06 361 3796 🕐 Tue–Sat 10.30–7.30, Mon 2.30–7.30 🚇 Spagna or Popolo

FABRIANO

www.fabrianoboutique.com

Minimalist in design, this store sells stacks of paper goods and stationery such as notepads and address books, laid out tantalizingly from the brightest to the most muted. The paper is of the highest quality and has been made by the same technique for 800 years, and prices are high. Pens and briefcases are also sold.

➕ 98 E3 ✉ Via del Babuino 173, 00187 ☎ 06 3260 0361 🕐 May–Dec Mon–Sat 10–7.30, Sun 2.30–7.30; Jan–Apr Mon–Sat 10–7.30 🚇 Spagna or Flaminio 🚌 81, 117, 119, 590, 628

FELTRINELLI INTERNATIONAL

www.lafeltrinelli.it

Come here for novels and books in English, French, Spanish, Portuguese, German and Japanese, including probably the widest selection of travel guides in English. There's also a good section dedicated to learning Italian. Feltrinelli has more than 100,000 books, at generally more competitive prices than most other bookstores selling foreign books.

➕ 99 F4 ✉ Via V. E. Orlando 84, 00184 ☎ 06 482 7878; 06 487 0999 🕐 Mon–Sat 9–8, Sun 10–1.30, 4–7.30 🚇 Repubblica 🚌 H, 40, 64, 170

FRETTE

www.frette.it

Beautiful sleepwear and household linens in stylish designs are what Frette is all about. You'll find only the best fabrics—cottons, linens, cashmeres and silks—as well as a range of beautiful accessories and lingerie. The goods deliver old-style glamour that is in step with modern design.

➕ 98 E4 ✉ Piazza di Spagna 11, 00187 ☎ 06 679 0673 🕐 Tue–Sat 10–7.30, Mon 3–7.30 🚇 Spagna 🚌 116, 117, 119, 590

FURLA

www.furla.it

Furla sells chic bags and practical totes in cheerful tones, along with scarves, shoes and jewellery. Prices are moderate compared with other

big-name accessory designers. Wild combinations and original touches add a twist. The company has several other branches in Rome.

➕ 98 E4 ✉ Via Nazionale 54, 00184 ☎ 06 487 0127 🕐 Mon–Sat 10–8, Sun 10.30–8 🚇 Spagna 🚌 116, 117, 119, 590

GABELLINI

Fine-quality, hand-painted pottery and porcelain are on display as you enter the shop and in the room behind you see a cheerful group of artisans at work. In summer they sit in the shady courtyard at the back. They are delighted to take special orders, and goods can be shipped worldwide. They also run courses on pottery-making and painting.

➕ 98 D4 ✉ Via di Monte Brianzo 76–77, 00186 ☎ 06 686 1075 🕐 Mon–Fri 9.30–1, 3–7 🚇 Spagna 🚌 70, 87, 492

GIORGIO SERMONETA

www.sermonetagloves.com

The shop front is fairly small and it may feel cramped, but there's a surprise in store—just look up. The gloves are the real decor of this shop, literally thousands of them, women's and men's, in a terrific array of shades and styles. Gloves are top quality and prices range from around €25–€120.

➕ 98 E4 ✉ Piazza di Spagna 61, 00187 ☎ 06 679 1960 🕐 Jun–Aug Mon–Sat 9.30–8; Sep–May Mon–Sat 9.30–8, Sun 10.30–7 🚇 Spagna 🚌 116, 117

GRAN CAFFÈ DAGNINO

www.pasticceriadagnino.com

This is a restaurant, café and bar in the unremarkable Galleria Esedra. However, once inside this Sicilian emporium of all things gastronomic, all else will be forgotten: mouth-watering ricotta, candied fruit-filled Sicilian sweets and other succulent delicacies. There are also plenty of attractive foodstuffs you might want to take back with you as gifts, ranging from jams and cakes to wines, sauces and preserves.

➕ 99 F4 ✉ Via V. E. Orlando 75 (Galleria Esedra), 00185 ☎ 06 481 8660 🕐 Daily 7am–11pm 🚇 Repubblica 🚌 H, 40, 60, 64, 70, 117, 170 to last stop on Via Nazionale

MARMI

www.marmiline.com

Floor mosaics here continue the city's 2,000-year-old tradition of using different colours and types of stone. Inviting trays of fruit made of painted alabaster and bowls, boxes and chess sets made from travertine and onyx are sold. They can arrange shipping worldwide.

✚ 98 E4 ✉ Via del Lavatore 28, 00187 ☎ 06 678 6347 🕐 Apr–Oct daily 10–midnight; Nov–Mar 10–10 🚇 Barberini 🚌 62, 63, 81, 85, 95, 175, 204

MEL BOOKSTORE

www.melbookstore.it

Mel Bookstore takes up two floors of a spacious art deco interior with wide marble staircases. Sofas are dotted everywhere, allowing you to peruse the books in comfort before buying. Other highlights include a small but interesting selection of second-hand books and CDs, a good number of English paperbacks, guides relating to current and recent art exhibitions in Rome, and a café.

✚ 99 F4 ✉ Via Nazionale 254–255, 00184 ☎ 06 488 5405 🕐 Jun–Aug Mon–Sat 9–8, Sun 10–1.30, 4.30–8.30; Sep–May Mon–Sat 9–8, Sun 10–1.30, 4–8 🚇 Repubblica 🚌 H, 40, 60, 64, 70, 117, 170

MESSI UNA VOLTA

Messi Una Volta sells an exceptional mix of new and second-hand clothes for kids. Used jeans by Levi and dungarees by OshKosh B'Gosh look brand new. It also stocks new clothes and shoes from Converse, Gap, Kookai and more.

✚ 99 G3 ✉ Via Salaria 91, 00198 ☎ 06 841 1374 🕐 Tue–Sat 9.30–7.30, Mon 3.30–7.30 🚌 38, 53, 63, 86, 92, 217, 360, 630, or any bus to Piazza Fiume or Via Salaria

MITSUKOSHI

www.mitsukoshi.it

Prices are given in euros and yen, and most of the customers here are Japanese: You may wonder if you are still in Rome, but all the goods are Italian. Accessories and some clothes from the major Italian names are sold here, plus, in the bazaar-style basement, food, wine and kitchenware.

✚ 99 F4 ✉ Via Nazionale 259, 00184 ☎ 06 482 7828 🕐 Daily 10.30–7 🚇 Repubblica 🚌 H, 40, 60, 64, 70, 117, 170

MUZIO

Every kind of shaving implement, manicure set, mirror, hair accessory and penknife under the sun can be found in this traditional store with

old-fashioned service. The goods are of high quality, and they stock lesser-known aftershaves, shaving creams, toothpastes and soaps. There is another branch at Via del Tritone 50 (same hours).

✚ 99 F4 ✉ Via Vittorio Emanuele Orlando 77, 00185 ☎ 06 4891 9798 🕐 Mon–Sat 9.30–8 🚇 Repubblica 🚌 H, 40, 60, 64, 70, 117, 170 to last stop on Via Nazionale

OLFATTORIO

www.olfattorio.it

This delightful store, one of a small chain, is a repository for scents and cosmetics from some of the world's most original *parfumiers*, including Diptyque, Piver, Coudray, Détaille, Parfums de Rosine and Compagnie de Provence. A fun novelty is the Bar à Parfums, where you can sample a variety of scents, in the manner of a drink, standing at a bar.

✚ 98 D3 ✉ Via di Ripetta 34, 00186 ☎ 06 361 2325 🕐 Nov–Sep Tue–Sat 11–2.30, 3.30–7.30 🚇 Spagna

OXUS

This Milan-based designer creates striking, hand-sewn bags, some inspired by artists such as Joan Miró, and also makes items under licence for designers, including Sonia Rykiel, Laura Biagiotti and the eccentrically brilliant Castelbajac. All bags are well finished, with inspired touches, such as zips that button shut once closed.

✚ 99 G3 ✉ Via Bergamo 14, 00198 ☎ 06 8535 6310 🕐 Mon–Fri 9.30–7.30, Sat 9.30–1, 3.30–7.30. Closed Sat pm Jul–Aug 🚌 38, 53, 63, 86, 92, 217, 360, 630, or any bus to Piazza Fiume

RAPHAEL JUNIOR

Helpful and knowledgeable staff will show you all the latest trends in garments and shoes for children. The range of 40 designers includes Armani, Versace, Byblos, Les Copains and Blumarine. Customers are the sort who don't bat an eyelash at the price tag.

✚ 98 F3 ✉ Via Vittorio Veneto 96–98, 00187 ☎ 06 4201 2058 🕐 Mon–Sat 10–7 🚇 Barberini 🚌 52, 53, 63, 95, 116, 119, 204, 630

LA RINASCENTE

www.larinascente.it

This six-floor department store, more modern and with a better selection than the original Via del Corso branch, sells upmarket cosmetics and accessories, designer diffusion lines such as Versace Classic and Trussardi Sport, and mid-range brands like Esprit, Diesel and Calvin Klein. It also has a good line for teenagers. There is a restaurant/café and a hairdresser on the top floor.

✚ 99 G3 ✉ Piazza Fiume, 00198 ☎ 06 884 1231 🕐 Mon–Sat 9.30–9.30, Sun 10–9 🚌 38, 53, 63, 86, 92, 217, 360, 630, or any bus to Piazza Fiume

SCHOSTAL

www.schostalroma.com

A family-run, friendly and reasonably priced shop, Schostal has a long tradition of selling good-quality lingerie. You can also find shirts, ties and socks for both sexes. The shop is remembered for giving every client a free shirt when it reopened after World War II, and photographs from its long history adorn the walls.

✚ 98 E4 ✉ Via del Corso 158, 00186 ☎ 06 679 1240 🕐 Sep–Jul Mon–Sat 9.30–7.30, Sun 10–7; Aug Mon–Sat 9.30–1, 3.30–7.30 🚇 Spagna or Popolo

SOFFITTA SOTTO I PORTICI

The focus of this monthly market is on antiques and rare items, and the setting—under the porticoes around the piazza—is very pleasant, especially in the summer. Credit cards are not accepted.

✚ 98 D4 ✉ Piazza Augusto Imperatore, 00186 ☎ 06 0606 🕐 3rd Sun of month 9–8. Closed Aug 🚌 71, 81, 117, 119, 224, 913

TAD

www.wetad.it

This smart store sells a bit of anything as long as it's cool, exotic and expensive. Beautiful flowers, magazines and books, fabrics, candles, furniture, tableware, clothing, shoes, cosmetics—you name it and (if it's the latest thing)

it's here. There is also an exclusive hair salon and café/restaurant.

✚ 98 E3 ✉ Via del Babuino 155a, 00187 ☎ 06 3269 5122 🕐 Mon 12–7.30, Tue–Fri 10.30–7.30, Sat 10.30–8 (also Oct–May Sun 12–8) 🚇 Spagna or Flaminio 🚌 81, 117, 119, 590, 628

TINA

www.tinalingerie.it

All you can dream of in luscious silks, laces and embroidery for special nightdresses or underclothes. There are also exquisite children's and baby clothes, all made in Italy. Special orders can be made as well.

✚ 98 E4 ✉ Via Bocca del Leone 9, 00187 ☎ 06 678 4076 🕐 Tue–Sat 10–8, Mon 3.30–7.30 🚇 Spagna 🚌 62, 63, 81, 85, 95, 175, 204

VALLI

Famous throughout Italy, Valli's Rome shop displays beautiful materials used by all the big names in French and Italian fashion, from Armani to Valentino. Sales offer incredible bargains.

✚ 98 F4 ✉ Via del Tritone 126, 00187 ☎ 06 488 2931 🕐 Jul–Sep Mon–Fri 9.30–7.30, Sat 9.30–1; Oct–Nov Mon–Sat 9.30–7.30; Dec daily 9.30–7.30; Jan–Jun Mon–Sat 9.30–7.30 🚇 Barberini 🚌 71, 117

ENTERTAINMENT AND NIGHTLIFE

ACCADEMIA NAZIONALE DI SANTA CECILIA

www.santacecilia.it

The Music Academy of Rome attracts the best professors and students. A beautifully put together menu of musical events is staged in different locations throughout the city. The official season means that it is closed in July, but the Accademia stages a number of outdoor concerts. Check the website for more details.

✚ 98 E4 ✉ Via Vittoria 6, 00187 ☎ 06 8024 2501. Box office: Biglieteria Auditorium, Parco della Musica, Largo Luciano Berio 3. Tickets available online from website 🕐 Oct–Jun Thu–Tue 11–6 🚌 Bus to Piazza del Popolo

Above *La Rinascente department store*
Opposite *Traditionally bound books make a fine gift to take home*

AGIMUS

www.agimus.it

Organized by the Associazione Giovanile Musicale, Rome's biggest youth choir stages performances at a variety of venues in the city.

✚ 98 E4 ✉ Via dei Greci 18, 00187 ☎ 06 3211 1001 🕐 Sep–Jul Mon–Sat 3–7 💶 €10 🚇 Termini 🚌 53, 217, 231, 910

ANTICA ENOTECA DI VIA DELLA CROCE

www.anticaenoteca.com

Expect old-fashioned style at its most enticing at this *enoteca* (wine bar). Sample its wines by the glass, with cheese or light snacks, before buying a bottle.

✚ 98 E4 ✉ Via della Croce 76b, 00187 ☎ 06 679 0896 🕐 Daily 11am–1am 💶 Free 🚇 Spagna 🚌 116, 117, 119

AUDITORIUM PARCO DELLA MUSICA

www.auditorium.com

This superb complex of concert and exhibition spaces, designed by Renzo Piano, offers a programme of extraordinary scope, with everything from symphony to jazz. It's worth a visit for the architecture alone.

✚ 289 D1 ✉ Viale Pietro de Coubertin 30, 00196 ☎ 06 0608, 892 982, 06 370 0106, 06 802411. Infoline: 06 80243 1281 🕐 Box office: Mon–Sat 11–8, Sun 10–6 💶 Tickets from €10 🚇 Flaminio 🚌 2, 910, 53, 217

Above Enjoy live jazz at some of the city's jazz clubs

PIPER CLUB

www.piperclub.it

High-tech effects complement the playlist at this popular club. Intimate seating areas allow you to see but not be seen. It is well north of central Rome.

✚ Off map 99 H2 ✉ Via Tagliamento 9, 00198 ☎ 06 841 4459 ⏰ Thu–Fri, Sun 11pm–3am, Sat 4pm–3am ✋ Prices vary from around €15 🚇 53, 63, 86, 92, 168, 630; tram 3, 19

SHAKI

This ultra-cool bar is in the chic Tridente area. The food is tantalizingly fresh, the wine expensive.

✚ 98 E4 ✉ Via Mario de' Fiori 29a, 00187 ☎ 06 679 1694 ⏰ Daily 10am–midnight ✋ Free 🚇 Spagna 🚌 116, 117, 119

THE SPACE CINEMA

www.thespacecinema.it

This venue is large, airy and high-tech, and its comfortable seats have plenty of legroom. The schedule is commercial, but one of the five screens shows blockbusters in their original language.

✚ 99 F4 ✉ Piazza della Repubblica 45, 00184 ☎ Reservations: 892 111 ✋ From €5 🚇 Repubblica 🚌 H, 40, 64, 170, 492

STAVINSKY

Prices may be high in this hotel courtyard bar, but they are worth paying at least once on a summer evening simply to enjoy the glorious gardens of the De Russie (▷ 96), one of Rome's leading luxury hotels.

✚ 98 D3 ✉ Via del Babuino 9, 00187 ☎ 06 3288 8874 ⏰ Daily 9am–1am 🚇 Flaminio or Spagna 🚌 117

TEATRO DELL'OPERA DI ROMA

www.operaroma.it

One of Italy's top opera houses, this is also a venue for ballet. The interior of the theatre is adorned with all the ornate trimmings expected of a true opera house, including opulent velvet boxes. When closed in summer, performances are sometimes run through Opera alla Terme di Caracalla.

GILDA

www.gildabar.it

Gilda is the place to see and be seen: It's all about attitude and who you know. A night here is an absolute must if you want to see Rome's people of the moment. There is live music on weekends.

✚ 98 E4 ✉ Via Mario de' Fiori 97, 00187 ☎ 06 678 4838 ⏰ Oct–May daily 11.30pm–4.30am ✋ €15 🚇 Spagna

GREGORY'S

www.gregorysjazzclub.com

John Bull and Guinness are washed down to the sound of live jazz at this nightspot. There is a Wednesday jam session and the fans who come here take their jazz very seriously.

✚ 98 E4 ✉ Via Gregoriana 54d, 00186 ☎ 06 679 6386 ⏰ Sep–Jul Tue–Sun 8pm–3.30am ✋ Free 🚇 Barberini 🚌 52, 53, 61, 62, 63, 80, 95, 116, 117

GUSTO

▷ 91.

METROPOLITAN MULTISALA

Enjoy maximum comfort at this four-screen cinema with a bar and air conditioning. From September to June one screen is dedicated to showing films in their original language.

✚ 98 D3 ✉ Via del Corso 7, 00187 ☎ 06 320 0933 ⏰ Daily screenings from 4pm ✋ From €5 🚇 Spagna 🚌 81, 117, 119, 590, 628

NEW CHAMBER SINGERS

www.newchambersingers.it

This amateur choir, previously directed by members of Rome's Episcopalian church, is now run by All Saints Anglican church. It stages a number of performances throughout the year.

✚ 98 E4 ✉ All Saints Church, Via del Babuino 153, 00187 ☎ 06 502 2624 ⏰ All year ✋ Free 🚇 Repubblica 🚌 H, 40, 64, 70, 71, 170

NUOVO OLIMPIA

www.circuitocinema.com

This two-screen cinema shows an interesting selection of art-house and more mainstream Italian and foreign-language films, most of which are not dubbed. It is often the only cinema in the city to screen certain films.

✚ 98 E4 ✉ Via in Lucina 16, 00186 ☎ 06 686 1068 ⏰ Sep–Jul daily ✋ From €5 🚌 81, 628 to Via del Corso

PALATIUM

On one of Rome's smartest shopping streets, Palatium serves reasonably priced snacks and light meals. It stays open late if you want a nightcap or light evening meal. The cheeses, wines and much of the produce come from Lazio, the region around Rome.

✚ 98 E4 ✉ Via Frattina 94, 00187 ☎ 06 6920 2132 ⏰ Sep–Jul Mon–Sat 11–11. 🚇 Spagna 🚌 To Piazza di Spagna

🏛 99 F4 ✉ Via Beniamo Gigli 1, 00186
☎ Information: 06 481 601; 892 982
🎭 Opera: €17–€130. Ballet: €11–€65
🚌 30X, 64

SPORTS AND ACTIVITIES
CAMPIONATO INTERNAZIONALE DI TENNIS
www.internazionalibnlditalia.it
Every May, Rome hosts the Italian Open tennis tournament, Europe's most important tennis event outside the Grand Slam. There are events for both men and women.
🏛 Off map 98 D2 ✉ Campionato Internazionale di Tennis Foro Italico, Viale dei Gladiatori, 00194 ☎ 800-622662 🕐 1–15 May ✋ €5–€195 🚌 32, 168, 186, 280 to Piazza Mancini, then cross river

CONCORSO IPPICO INTERNAZIONALE
www.piazzadisiena.org
Rome's International Horse Show, an important equestrian event, takes place annually in the Villa Borghese (▷ 79), with show-jumping at the heart of the action.
🏛 98 E3 ✉ Piazza di Siena, Villa Borghese 00186 ☎ 06 3685 8068 🕐 Apr or May ✋ Adult from €12, child from €7 🚌 116, 231, 491, 495

ROMAN SPORT CENTER
www.romansportcenter.com
Rome's finest sports venue is just a stone's throw from the Spanish Steps. Visit any one of the facility's three aerobics rooms, saunas, two weight rooms or the Olympic-sized swimming pool. Day membership is available.
🏛 98 E3 ✉ Villa Borghese, Viale del Galoppatoio 33, 00186 ☎ 06 320 1667; 06 321 8096 🕐 Mon–Fri 7am–10.30pm, Sat 7am–8.30pm, Sun 9–3 ✋ Check website for rates 🚌 95, 116, 119, 204, 490, 491, 495

STADIO FLAMINIO
www.federugby.it
Rugby enjoys great popularity in Italy, with the national team competing in the Six Nations tournament (with England, France, Ireland, Scotland and Wales). The country has 24 rugby clubs, and the best games are in the capital when RDS Roma hits the field. Credit cards are not accepted.
🏛 Off map 98 D2 ✉ Stadio Flaminio, Viale Tiziano, 00196 ☎ 06 3685 7832 🕐 Season: Oct–May ✋ From €10 🚌 204, 231, 910; tram 2

STADIO OLIMPICO
No spectator sport is more important to Romans than football. The city has two rival teams that share the Stadio Olimpico stadium and play at home on alternate Sundays. When Roma fans are in, they sit on the south side of the stadium; when Lazio is playing, the fans sit on the north side.
🏛 Off map 98 D2 ✉ Viale dello Stadio Olimpico, 00194 ☎ 06 36851 🕐 Aug–early Jun Sun ✋ From €18 🚌 32, 168, 186, 280 to Piazza Mancini, then cross river

VILLA BORGHESE
If you want to rent in-line skates or bicycles, or take out a rowing boat on a tree-lined lake, the Villa Borghese is the place to head. A green oasis in the heart of the city, the park is a popular weekend retreat with locals.
🏛 98 F3 ✉ Villa Borghese, 00186 🕐 Daily 24 hours ✋ Free 🚌 95, 116, 119, 204, 490, 491, 495

HEALTH AND BEAUTY
AROMA BEAUTY CENTER
www.aromabeautycenter.com
This is the salon of Aveda, Europe's leading potions and lotions brand. You can try plant steam inhalation, skin hydration or mild aromatherapy, plus facial treatments, manicures, pedicures and waxing. Aveda beauty products are on sale.
🏛 98 E4 ✉ Rampa Mignanelli 9, 00187 ☎ 06 6992 4886 🕐 Tue–Sat 10–8, Mon 3.30–7.30 ✋ Manicure: €25, facial: €80 🚇 Spagna 🚌 64, 117

BOSCOLO EXEDRA
www.boscolohotels.com
If you're in the mood for pampering, a wealth of treatments are on offer at the spa of the luxurious Boscolo Exedra hotel (▷ 94). There's a beautiful swimming pool, plus a solarium, a giant Turkish bath and a jacuzzi. Massages last for over an hour. There's also a manicure salon and fitness centre.
🏛 99 F4 ✉ Piazza della Repubblica 47, 00187 ☎ 06 489 381 🕐 Sep–Jul Mon–Sat 10–8; Aug Tue–Fri 11–7; ✋ Massage: from €65; facial: from €60 🚇 Barberini

HOTEL DE RUSSIE
www.hotelderussie.it
A huge range of holistic techniques are on offer at the exclusive Hotel de Russie (▷ 96), including shiatsu, reflexology and aromatherapy, as well as massage, saunas and facials. Masks, body wraps and personal training are also available.
🏛 98 D3 ✉ Via del Babuino 9, 00187 ☎ 06 328 881 🕐 Daily 9–8 ✋ Aromatherapy session: from €90 🚇 Spagna

FOR CHILDREN
EXPLORA—IL MUSEO DEI BAMBINI
www.mdbr.it
Rome's first and only children's museum is particularly good for children aged up to eight. Themes are humankind, the environment, communications and society. Reservations are required; tours last 1 hour 45 minutes.
🏛 98 D3 ✉ Via Flaminia 82–86, 00192 ☎ 06 361 3776 🕐 Sep–Jul Tue–Sun 10–6.45; Aug 12–6.45 ✋ Adult €7, child (3–12) €7, under-3s free 🚇 Flaminio 🚌 6, 88, 92, 231, 490, 495; tram 2, 19

VILLA BORGHESE/BIOPARCO
www.bioparco.it
The rambling parkland of the Villa Borghese, which extends for 6.5km (4 miles) through the heart of the city, is a great place for children to let off steam. You can rent bikes or row boats, ride a trolley train, hop on an old-fashioned carousel or visit the Bioparco zoo. The park is popular with locals at weekends.
🏛 98 F3 ✉ Viale del Giardino Zoologico, Porta Pinciana, 00187 ☎ 06 360 8211 🕐 Bioparco: Apr–Sep daily 9.30–7; Oct–Mar 9.30–5 ✋ Park: free. Bioparco: adult €12.50, child (6–12) €10.50 🚇 Flaminio or Spagna 🚌 95, 116, 119, 204, 495

PRICES AND SYMBOLS

The restaurants are listed alphabetically (excluding La, Il, Le and I). The prices given are the average for a two-course lunch (L) and a three-course dinner (D) for one person, without drinks. The wine price is for the least expensive bottle. All the restaurants listed accept credit cards unless otherwise stated.

For a key to the symbols, ▷ 2.

AL 34 (TRENTAQUATTRO)

www.ristoranteal34t.it
This comfortable, intimate restaurant produces Roman and southern Italian meat and fish dishes using seasonal vegetables and herbs. The service is fast and efficient—great for those in a hurry. Reservations are essential.
✚ 98 E4 ✉ Via Mario de'Fiori 34, 00187 ☎ 06 679 5091 ◷ Sep–Jul Tue–Sun 12.30–3, 7.30–10.30 ♨ L €22, D €40, Wine €12.50 ⊕ Spagna 🚌 116, 119

THE ALBERT

www.thealbert.it
This well-established English pub between the Spanish Steps and the Trevi Fountain is ideal for a break from sightseeing. Family run and with friendly service, it provides a step back in time: The furniture is Victorian, and there is a fireplace and stained-glass ceilings. Well worth the stop for a proper pint or a lunch buffet at good prices. Afternoon tea is served, too. Credit cards are not accepted.
✚ 98 E4 ✉ Via del Traforo 132, 00187 ☎ 06 481 8795 ◷ Daily noon–2am ♨ Salad bar €6, pint €5, spirits €4.50 ⊕ Barberini 🚌 71, 116, 117 or any bus to Piazza San Silvestro

ANTICO BOTTARO

This sophisticated restaurant near Piazza del Popolo serves creative cuisine with a French twist. The baroque decor contributes to the atmosphere of refined elegance, and although it is very formal the staff are friendly. It also has one of Rome's best selections of Italian and international wine.
✚ 98 D3 ✉ Passeggiata di Ripetta 15, 00186 ☎ 06 323 6763 ◷ Tue–Sun 8pm–11.30pm ♨ D €75, Wine €25 ⊕ Flaminio 🚌 95, 117, 119

ANTICO CAFFÈ GRECO

www.anticocaffegreco.eu
This famous old café was founded in 1767 by a Greek, hence the name. It has always been popular with the rich and famous, and numbered Keats, Byron and Goethe among its clientele. Look for pictures of some of the café's well-known past customers in the back room.
✚ 98 E4 ✉ Via Condotti 86, 00186 ☎ 06 679 1700 ◷ Daily 9–8 ♨ Coffee from €4.75, cake €6.20 (table service only) ⊕ Spagna 🚌 119 to Piazza di Spagna, or 52, 58, 61, 71, 85, 160 to Piazza San Silvestro

BABINGTON'S TEA ROOMS

www.babingtons.net
This very British tea room was opened in 1896 to cater for British visitors on the Grand Tour. Today, you can still enjoy a pot of Earl Grey with your afternoon tea, but you will also see American food, such as pancakes with maple syrup. Brunch is served all day.
✚ 98 E4 ✉ Piazza di Spagna 23, 00186 ☎ 06 678 6027 ◷ Daily 9–8.15 ♨ Brunch €34 ⊕ Spagna 🚌 116, 119

Opposite *Il Gelato di San Crispino serves some of the best ice cream in the city*

IL BACARO
www.ilbacaro.com
Near the Pantheon, Il Bacaro is ideal for a romantic dinner, especially in summer when you can dine outdoors under a roof of ivy vines. The creative cuisine is strongly based on seasonal products, including rigatoni pasta with blue Stilton and Brussels sprouts, and beef fillet cooked with Merlot wine. Among the home-made pastries, the flaky, creamy *millefoglie sbriciolato con crema pasticcera* (millefeuille crumble with a creamy sauce) is sublime. The wine and cheese lists are excellent. Reservations are recommended.
✚ 98 F4 ✉ Via degli Spagnoli 27, 00186 ☎ 06 687 2554 ⏰ Mon–Sat 8pm–11pm. Closed 1 week in Aug ✋ D €45, Wine €14 🚌 64, 87, 492 to Largo di Torre Argentina; tram 8

IL BRILLO PARLANTE
www.ilbrilloparlante.com
The downstairs restaurant, with vaulted ceilings and five small rooms, is popular among the locals, serving excellent grilled Danish meat and also fish. The pizzas are good but not memorable. Among the home-made desserts, the chocolate tart and tiramisù are great, but it's worth coming for the pear mousse alone. There's an excellent wine list and tables outside during the summer. Upstairs a wine bar serves a selection of cheeses and salami.
✚ 98 D3 ✉ Via della Fontanella 12, 00187 ☎ 06 324 3334 ⏰ Tue–Sun 12–5, 7–1, Mon 7.30pm–1am. Closed 1 week in Aug ✋ L €20, D €35, Wine €16 🚇 Flaminio 🚌 117, 119

BRUSCHETTERIA NONNA PAPERA
In a tiny alley behind the Trevi Fountain is this eatery, with country-style wooden furniture, cherry tomatoes hanging from the ceiling, and ceramic decorative tiles. The huge *bruschette*, which come with a variety of toppings, and the savoury crêpes make a good light lunch.
✚ 98 E4 ✉ Via dei Modelli 60, 00186 ☎ 06 678 3510 ⏰ Wed–Mon 10.30–3.30, 6.30–10.30 ✋ *Bruschette* €7.50, D €35, Wine €11 🚌 40, 64, 87, 628 to Piazza Venezia, or any bus through Via del Corso

EST! EST! EST!
Over 100 years old, this is one of Rome's longest-established pizzerias. It stays with the tried-and-tested combination of excellent pizza and Italian wines, served in a simple room with wooden tables.
✚ 99 F5 ✉ Via Genova 32, 00185 ☎ 06 488 1107 ⏰ Tue–Sun 7pm–midnight ✋ Pizza €9, Wine €10 🚇 Repubblica 🚌 H, 64, 170

FIASCHETTERIA BELTRAMME
Known to locals as Cesaretto, and very easy to miss in the narrow Via della Croce, this traditional trattoria is wonderfully understated. Locals, artists and shopkeepers, together with a few visitors in the know, sit down to simple but well-prepared food, including pasta and salads. They do not accept bookings, so arrive early for the chance of a shared table in this popular eatery. Credit cards are not accepted.
✚ 98 E4 ✉ Via della Croce 39, 00187 ⏰ Mon–Sat 12–3, 7.30–10.30 ✋ L €25, D €40, Wine €8 🚇 Spagna 🚌 117, 119

GELATERIA DELLA PALMA
Close to the Pantheon, this *gelateria* offers a huge variety of ice creams, including no less than 20 different kinds of chocolate, plus mousses and ice cream with meringues. For those who prefer the taste of fruit, the raspberry ice cream is simply unforgettable. There are two wooden benches inside, but the place gets extremely crowded. The best idea is to buy your ice cream, then stroll down to Piazza della Rotonda in front of the Pantheon. Credit cards are not accepted.
✚ 98 D5 ✉ Via Maddalena 20, 00186 ☎ 06 6880 6752 ⏰ Daily 8am–1am ✋ Ice cream from €1.80 🚌 64, 87, 492 to Largo di Torre Argentina; tram 8

IL GELATO DI SAN CRISPINO
www.ilgelatodisancrispino.com
This has to be the best ice cream shop in Rome—its attention to detail makes others pale in comparison. The ice creams are rich, creamy and additive-free, and the signature *gelato di San Crispino* is made with wild Sardinian honey. It can be hard to find as it has a very discreet entrance without a real sign. Facing the Trevi Fountain, head right down Via Lavatore, then take the second left down Via della Panetteria; San Crispino is halfway down on your right.
✚ 98 E4 ✉ Via della Panetteria 42, 00187 ☎ 06 679 3924 ⏰ Mon, Wed–Thu, Sun 12pm–12.30am, Fri–Sat 12pm–1.30am ✋ Ice cream €1.70–€6 per cup 🚌 61, 62, 116, 175, 492, 630

GUSTO
www.gusto.it
Inside this state-of-the-art restaurant, pizzeria and wine bar, behind the Mausoleum of Augustus, you'll find exposed brickwork and industrial lighting. Pizzas (from €6) and salads are decent, with a slight twist given to some traditional recipes. With somewhat inflated prices, you won't find many locals here. However, this place is about ambience and there's plenty of that. There's live jazz on Tuesday and Thursday at 11pm. There's also a kitchen shop.
✚ 98 D4 ✉ Piazza Augusto Imperatore 9, 00186 ☎ 06 322 6273 ⏰ Daily 12.45–3, 7.30–12 ✋ L €11 (buffet), D €16, Wine €18 🚇 Spagna 🚌 81, 116, 117, 628, 913

HARD ROCK CAFÉ
www.hardrock.com
Yes, there's a Hard Rock Café in Rome, and on the exclusive Via Vittorio Veneto. The interior is standard Hard Rock: wooden floors and a litter of 1950s paraphernalia, the only exception being the frescoed angels on the ceiling. The restaurant seats more than 260, with plenty of nooks and crannies to hide in. The menu is the same as always, with burgers and french fries. And there's a shop where you

can add another 'Hard Rock' T-shirt to your collection.

✠ 99 F4 ✉ Via Vittorio Veneto 62a, 00187 ☎ 06 420 3051 🕐 Sun–Thu 12–12, Fri–Sat noon–1am 🍴 L €28, D €48, Wine €9 Ⓜ Barberini 🚌 52, 53, 56, 58b, 95, 116

LOWENHAUS

Why eat Bavarian food in Rome? For the answer, try Lowenhaus's superb *stinco di maiale al forno* (roast pork shin with roast potatoes and cabbage). It's a great place if you like German beer; the list is extensive and includes some idiosyncratic choices. Cakes include strudel and *Sachertorte* (chocolate cake). The restaurant is divided into several rooms, with outside tables in summer.

✠ 98 D3 ✉ Via della Fontanella 16B, 000186 ☎ 06 323 0410 🕐 Daily 11am–2am 🍴 L €15, D €35, Wine €10 Ⓜ Flaminio 🚌 116, 117

IL MARGUTTA

www.ilmargutta.it
Il Margutta, the only real vegetarian restaurant in the city, is in this artists' street featured in the film *Roman Holiday*. It's a large, futuristic space with traditional touches and art exhibited on the walls. There is a buffet at lunchtime, but it is more intimate in the evening. More than 40 vegetarian dishes (mostly organic) are available. There are 120 wines on offer, some organic, all at reasonable prices. The dessert wine list is also very good.

✠ 98 E4 ✉ Via Margutta 118, 00187 ☎ 06 3265 0577 🕐 Daily 12.30–3.30, 7.30–11. Closed 2 weeks in Aug 🍴 L €20, D €35, Wine €15 Ⓜ Flaminio or Spagna 🚌 116, 117

OBIKA

www.obika.it
Traditional ingredients contrast with the cool, minimalist decor in this bustling wine bar/restaurant. The young staff care passionately about sourcing the best suppliers to create intensely flavoured dishes. Their specialty is *mozzarella di buffalo*, served in a variety of ways, as well as a range of organic salads and

pasta. Get there early to get a table outside in the little square.

✠ 98 D4 ✉ Piazza di Firenze, Angolo Via dei Prefetti 00186 ☎ 06 683 2630 🕐 Daily 10am–midnight 🍴 L €22, D €40, Wine €8 🚌 116

OTELLO ALLA CONCORDIA

www.otelloallaconcordia.it
Take refuge from the shopping madness of Via del Corso in this plant-laden 18th-century courtyard. Family-run for over 50 years, the restaurant serves typically Roman fare. Try the *antipasto* of meats and salamis to start, and the baked aubergine (eggplant) *parmigiana* is divine. Try a local Castelli Romani (Frascati) wine with your meal.

✠ 98 E4 ✉ Via della Croce 81, 00187 ☎ 06 679 1178 🕐 Mon–Sat 12.30–3, 7.30–11. Closed 3 weeks in Jan 🍴 L €11, D €23, Wine €16 Ⓜ Spagna 🚌 116, 117, 492

LE PAIN QUOTIDIEN

Rustic wooden tables and contemporary paintings make a pleasing setting for a light lunch or coffee break, with a selection of salads, sandwiches and cakes. Sit round a large table, either inside or on the roof terrace. Brunch is served on Saturday and Sunday.

✠ 98 D4 ✉ Via Tomacelli 24–25, 00186 ☎ 06 6880 7727 🕐 Daily 7.30am–11.30pm 🍴 L and D €18 Ⓜ Spagna 🚌 95, 117, 119

PIZZA CIRO

Behind Piazza San Silvestro and not too far from Piazza Navona, Pizza Ciro serves Neapolitan-style pizzas (large and thick), but you can also ask for a thinner Roman one. The starters are exceptional, especially the *antipasto sfizioso* of typical Neapolitan fried savouries. *Pizza bufalina doc*, with buffalo mozzarella, is the most popular. The patio at the back is just perfect on a warm summer night.

✠ 98 E4 ✉ Via della Mercede 43–45, 00186 ☎ 06 678 6015 🕐 Mon–Sat 9am–10pm 🍴 Pizza €9, L €11, D €20, Wine €14 🚌 117, 119, 175, 492, or any bus to Piazza San Silvestro

PIZZARÈ

www.pizzare.it
In a 1920s-style building surrounded by palm trees, just a short walk from Via Vittorio Veneto, this is probably the most popular pizzeria in the heart of Rome. They serve real Neapolitan pizza with buffalo mozzarella, bought fresh daily. Try *ripieno fritto*, a folded and fried pizza with a tomato, mozzarella, ham and ricotta filling, or *pizza re*, with tomato sauce, fresh Sicilian cherry tomatoes and buffalo mozzarella. The home-made traditional Neapolitan cakes, including the famous *pastiera* (filled with ricotta, egg yolks and candied peel) make a fitting end to the meal. Reservations are essential.

✠ 99 F4 ✉ Via Lucullo 22, 00199 ☎ 06 4201 3075 🕐 Daily 12.30–3.30, 7.30–1am 🍴 L €10, D €14, Wine €10; lunch specials €9 Ⓜ Barberini

IL POMODORINO

www.ilpomodorino.org
Part of a national chain of pizzerias, Il Pomodorino provides excellent value in the otherwise extortionately priced Via Veneto. There is indoor and outdoor seating for up to 400 people. Inside is Neapolitan terracotta with a white, beamed ceiling, pastel-coloured walls and red-and-white table linen. The huge central buffet is packed with tempting vegetables. Pizza chefs work on one side of the room, and the other chefs in the open kitchen. Try the veal *millefoglie*, a superb dish with a mountain of thinly sliced meat layered with crisply fried artichokes.

✠ 99 F3 ✉ Via Campania 45, 00187 ☎ 06 4201 1356 🕐 Sun–Fri 12–3, 7.30–12, Sat 7.30pm–midnight 🍴 Pizza €9, L €10, D €20, Wine €10 Ⓜ Veneto 🚌 52, 53, 56, 58, 58b, 95, 116

RISTORANTE GIOVANNI

www.ristorantegiovanni.net
The dining room of this family-run restaurant close to Via Veneto has terracotta floor tiles, beams, pristine white walls and traditional wooden chairs. Home-made gnocchi with

pheasant sauce makes a satisfying, if heavy, starter. The *osso buco* (veal stew in tomato sauce) with rice is a house recommendation, as is the fresh squid cooked on an open fire. The wine cellar contains 175 labels; the house wine is a crisp white Verdicchio from the Marche region.

🕀 98 F3 ✉ Via Marche 64, 00187 ☎ 06 482 1834 🕓 Sep–Jul Sun–Thu 12.30–3, 7.30–11, Fri 12.30pm–3pm 🖐 L €15, D €35, Wine €12 🚇 Veneto 🚌 52, 53, 56, 58, 58b, 95, 116

RISTORANTE NUOVA STELLA

www.nuovastella.it

This is an unpretentious place between Termini and Santa Maria Maggiore. The two large dining areas have white linen tablecloths and an eye-catching buffet; fresh fish is available Tuesday and Friday. Specials include spaghetti with prawns, courgettes (zucchini) and tomato sauce, fettuccine with hare, and the classic *saltimbocca romana* (veal with ham, cooked in white wine and butter), served with delicious rosemary roast potatoes. In warmer weather the tables spill out onto the pavement.

🕀 99 G5 ✉ Via Manin 54, 00184 ☎ 06 487 5390 🕓 Mon–Sat 12–3, 6.30–11; occasional Sun opening 🖐 L €18, D €30, Wine €10 🚇 Termini 🚌 40, 64

T-BONE STATION

www.t-bone.it

Between Piazza di Spagna and Piazza Barberini, this is the trendiest steakhouse in Rome. The decor is based around black-and-white movie stills and high-tech design. Steaks are the obvious choice, but the salads are huge and appetizing, especially the fresh crispy spinach and the classic chicken Caesar salad with Parmesan topping (make sure the cheese is slivered, *a scaglie*, rather than grated). The cocktails are also excellent. There are branches throughout the city.

🕀 98 E4 ✉ Via Francesco Crispi 29–31, 00186 ☎ 06 678 7650 🕓 Daily 12.30–3, 7–11.30 🖐 L €35, D €52, Wine €12 🚇 Barberini 🚌 52, 53, 61, 62, 63, 80, 95, 116, 117, 119, 175, 492, 590

LA TERRAZZA

www.edenroma.com/en/laterrazzadelleden

The formal atmosphere in the Michelin-starred restaurant of the Hotel Eden (▷ 95) provides the perfect excuse to dress up. The food here is predominantly modern Mediterranean, and is always excellent—try smoked scallops with asparagus, or sea bass with black olives and oregano. And as if the wonderful food wasn't enough, the view is fantastic.

🕀 98 E4 ✉ Via Ludovisi 49, 00187 ☎ 06 4781 2752 🕓 Daily 12.30–3, 7.45–10.30 🖐 L €110, D €165, Wine €30 🚇 Spagna or Barberini 🚌 116, 119

EL TOULÀ

www.toula.it

Considered one of Rome's best restaurants, El Toulà is a great place to look for the rich and famous. The service is exceptional, the Venetian and international cuisine divine and the wine list superb. Reservations are advised.

🕀 98 D4 ✉ Via della Lupa 29b, 00186 ☎ 06 687 3498 🕓 Sep–Jul Tue–Fri 1–3, 8–11, Sat, Mon 8pm–11pm 🖐 L €75, D €100, Wine €45 🚇 Spagna 🚌 81, 117, 119, 492 to Via del Corso or Largo Carlo Goldini

TRATTORIA ABRUZZESE

After passing through an entrance shrouded with plants, you find yourself in this welcoming trattoria spread over four rooms. Photographs of rich and famous patrons cover the walls. It specializes in the cuisine of Abruzzo, the mountainous region to the east of Lazio, which is famous for its wild boar and rich, heavy pasta. Try the *pasta all'amatriciana* (with bacon, tomato and onion) or one of their divine chargrilled veal chops.

🕀 99 F5 ✉ Via Napoli 3, 00184 ☎ 06 482 5556 🕓 Mon–Sat 12–3, 7–11.30 🖐 L €15, D €30, Wine €6 🚇 Repubblica 🚌 64, 70, 117

TRATTORIA DA NAZZARENO

This great-value restaurant in the busy Termini station area offers an especially good *antipasto* buffet

for vegetarians, and a fish buffet as well. The interior, which is dominated by the enticing central buffet table, is large, with white walls, stone floors and wooden chairs. *Bucatini* pasta with tomatoes and pancetta, and *osso buco* (veal stew in tomato sauce) are popular with the locals. Try the local Castelli Romani house wine.

🕀 99 G4 ✉ Via Magenta 35, 00185 ☎ 06 495 7782 🕓 Thu–Tue 12–3.30, 6.30–11 🖐 L €18, D €25, Wine €7 🚇 Termini 🚌 40, 64

TRIMANI 'IL WINEBAR'

This great wine bar/restaurant lies just along from Termini station in a leafy piazza. The original, 120-year-old Carrara marble counter has survived renovations, and the plain wooden tables and striking basaltic slab floor harmonize perfectly with the bottles lining the walls. All dishes have a wine suggestion—for instance, the wine recommended to accompany *bresaola* (thinly sliced dried fillet of beef) with Gorgonzola, walnuts and pear, or pâté de foie gras, is the Schiaffo Colacicci Anagni 2000. It's one of more than 600 wines, all of which are served by the glass. The platter of Italian cheeses is easily shared. The bar is open all day.

🕀 99 G4 ✉ Via Cernaia 37b, 00185 ☎ 06 446 9630 🕓 Mon–Sat 11.30–3, 7–12 🖐 L €25, D €58, Wine €10 🚇 Repubblica or Castro Pretorio

VITTI

Long-established Vitti has been making ice creams to special Sicilian recipes since 1898, and has now extended its range to include mouth-watering cakes and pastries. The bar inside is finished in welcoming warm dark wood, perfect for cooler winter days, or when it's fine weather you can linger in the large outside seating area on the charming square.

🕀 98 E4 ✉ Piazza S. Lorenzo in Lucina 33, 00186 ☎ 06 687 6304 🕓 Apr–Sep daily 7am–2am; Oct–Mar 7am–10pm 🖐 Ice cream €2–€3.50 takeaway, €7 at table 🚇 Spagna 🚌 81, 117, 119, 590, 628

PRICES AND SYMBOLS

Prices are the lowest and highest for a double room for one night. Breakfast is included unless noted otherwise. All the hotels listed accept credit cards unless otherwise stated. Note that rates vary widely throughout the year.

For a key to the symbols, ▷ 2.

ANGLO AMERICANO

www.hotelangloamericano.it
The distinguished Anglo Americano hotel has a genteel, belle époque atmosphere, from the cool, blue-and-white striped wallpaper in the lounge to the solemn busts guarding the door. The 18th-century palazzo has well-appointed rooms furnished in a contemporary style, all with private bath, satellite TV and internet connection. The hotel is near the Piazza di Spagna, Trevi Fountain and the exclusive shops on Via Vittorio Veneto. Its proximity to the Italian parliament makes it popular with politicians.
✚ 98 F4 ✉ Via delle Quattro Fontane 12, 00184 ☎ 06 472 941 ✋ €200–€340 ① 122 🅂 🅠 Spagna

BAROCCO

www.hotelbarocco.com
Three historic buildings have been merged to form this intimate, elegant hotel. The newer wing has jacuzzi tubs in some rooms, while the older part is rich with opulent drapes and precious marble. Although it overlooks Piazza Barberini, the hotel is well soundproofed, muting Rome's constant roar. Visitors praise the Barocco's fresh flowers, extra towels, courtesy kits and efficient staff. Guests in the suites also get bath robes.
✚ 98 F4 ✉ Via della Purificazione 4, 00187 ☎ 06 487 2001 ✋ €150–€420 ① 37 rooms, 5 suites 🅂 🅠 Barberini

BERNINI BRISTOL

www.berninibristol.com
www.sinahotels.it
This hotel has always been popular with aristocrats and royalty. The 1874 palazzo is refurbished, but antiques and vintage tapestries maintain the tone. Both of the hotel's restaurants are renowned, especially the rooftop L'Olimpo, with its panoramic views. Once the heart of *la dolce vita*, the Bernini's nightclub and lounges remain chic. Facilities include babysitting, car rental, valet parking, private garage, secretarial service, sauna and hot tub. Pets are welcome.
✚ 98 F4 ✉ Piazza Barberini 23, 00187 ☎ 06 488 931 ✋ €580, excluding breakfast ① 127 🅂 🅥 🅠 Barberini 🚌 61, 62, 116, 119, 175, 492, 590

BOSCOLO EXEDRA

www.boscolohotels.com
Built over the remains of Diocletian's third-century baths, on Piazza della Repubblica, the hotel is truly luxurious. Carrara marble and Venetian glass are used to stunning effect in the lobby. Guest rooms are equally lush, in Regency style with marble bathrooms, satellite TV and a safe. There is contemporary artwork throughout. This hotel also has two restaurants, a solarium, spa and roof terrace with a pool and bar.
✚ 99 F4 ✉ Piazza della Repubblica 47, 00185 ☎ 06 489 381 ✋ €660–€880, excluding breakfast ① 241 🅂 ✉ 🅥 🅠 Repubblica 🚌 40, 64 to Via Nazionale

Opposite *The luxurious interior of the Boscolo Exedra hotel*

CASA HOWARD
www.casahoward.com
Staying in this very central little hotel feels like staying as a guest in a private apartment. Care has been taken with the decorations and furnishings to create a warm, soft ambience, and each room is unique. The hotel is on the first floor, reached either by a marble staircase or an elevator. Breakfast can be served in your room on request.
✚ 98 E4 ✉ Via Capo le Case 18, 00187 ☎ 06 6992 4555 🖐 €150–€300 🕐 5, plus 5 in nearby annexe 🆒
🚇 Spagna, Barberini 🚌 52, 53, 63, 95, 116, 204

COLUMBIA
www.hotelcolumbia.com
This charming hotel is just a stone's throw away from Termini station, just around the corner from Teatro dell'Opera, and its friendly, efficient staff are always happy to help guests. All the rooms are simply furnished and have satellite TV. Breakfast is served on the roof terrace—a great way to start the day—and as the day wears on, you can relax in the bar or lounge. Ask for a quiet room, as those near the road can be noisy.
✚ 99 F4 ✉ Via del Viminale 15, 00184 ☎ 06 488 3509 🖐 €250 🕐 45 🆒
🚇 Termini 🚌 40, 64 or any bus to Termini

FAWLTY TOWERS HOTEL AND HOSTEL
www.fawltytowers.org
This hotel/hostel provides decent inexpensive accommodation near Termini station, with both private and shared rooms. When you arrive, take the elevator up to the fifth floor. This isn't dormitory bunk-bed accommodation; instead, you get a bed for the night in a four-person room. The place has a clubby feel; there are wood floors and a theme of cheerful orange and zany stripes, with bouquets of sunflowers and an odd papier-mâché puppet head.

It is slightly eccentric in a fun and functional way. There is a communal kitchen and free internet access, and no curfew. Credit cards are not accepted.
✚ 99 G4 ✉ Via Magenta 39, 00187 ☎ 06 445 4802 🖐 €26–€155 🕐 16 🆒 6 rooms 🚇 Termini 🚌 40, 64 or any bus to Termini

GABRIELLA
www.gabriellahotel.it
This first-floor hotel with elevator is near Termini station and the main bus terminal. There is a comfortable feel about the place: It has a welcoming lobby and small reading/TV lounge with sofas and coffee tables. The medium-sized rooms have ceramic floors, Tuscan-style matching coverlets and curtains, double-glazed windows, safe, minibar and satellite TV. The white-tiled bathrooms have showers (some have baths) and hairdryers. There is a spacious breakfast room/bar serving a Continental breakfast, and the staff speak English.
✚ 99 H4 ✉ Via Palestro 88, 00185 ☎ 06 445 0120 🖐 €80–€160 🕐 23 🆒 🚇 Castro Pretorio 🚌 492, or any bus to Termini

HASSLER
www.hotelhasslerroma.com
The rich and famous gather at the Hassler to be cosseted by Roberto Wirth (of the Swiss hotel dynasty) and his impeccable staff. The hotel sits at the top of the Spanish Steps, surveying St. Peter's, the Villa Medici and the Vittorio Emanuele II monument. The interior is lavish, rich with marble, frescoed walls, hand-painted tiles, fringed curtains and a glass-roofed lounge. Big spenders prefer the penthouse, though corner room 403 is also much coveted. Facilities include a restaurant, bar, hair salon, massage, babysitting, laundry, room service, tennis court and the use of bicycles free of charge.
✚ 98 E4 ✉ Piazza Trinità dei Monti 6, 00187 ☎ 06 699 340 🖐 €550–€860, excluding breakfast 🕐 95 rooms, 6 suites 🆒 🛎 🚇 Spagna

HOTEL EDEN
www.edenroma.com
Just off the Via Vittorio Veneto is the Eden, one of Rome's top hotels. Its relaxed, old-fashioned luxury makes it a popular choice with visiting celebrities and royalty. All the rooms are tastefully furnished with antiques, and have marble bathrooms, satellite TV and internet access. After dinner in the award-winning La Terrazza restaurant (▷ 93), relax in the piano bar.
✚ 98 E4 ✉ Via Ludovisi 49, 00187 ☎ 06 478 121 🖐 €880–€1,200, excluding breakfast 🕐 108 rooms, 13 suites 🆒 🚇 Barberini 🚌 63, 116 or any bus to Via Veneto

HOTEL D'ESTE
www.hoteldesterome.com
This early 19th-century hotel is in a tree-lined street, directly across from the basilica of Santa Maria Maggiore and a few minutes from Termini station. There is a charming reception hall with a cobbled floor and beamed ceiling. The bar and restaurant are up on the first floor, making the hotel unsuitable for wheelchair users. Guest rooms are simple, clean and spacious. All have a TV and bathroom with hairdryer. There is alfresco dining in summer.
✚ 99 G5 ✉ Via Carlo Alberto 46, 00185 ☎ 06 446 5607 🖐 €65–€166 🕐 37 🆒 🚇 Vittorio 🚌 70, 360

HOTEL D'INGHILTERRA
www.royaldemeure.com
The wealthy Torlonia family built this palazzo, now a sumptuous hotel, near the boutique-lined Via Condotti. Outside it has an imposing golden facade, supported by arches, while beyond the entrance a black-and-white carpet runs through the lobby, punctuated by delicate antiques and plump red sofas. The guest rooms, though less dramatic, are pleasant, with thick carpeting, carved bed frames, and carefully chosen paintings and prints. There is 24-hour room service.
✚ 98 E4 ✉ Via Bocca di Leone 14, 00187 ☎ 06 699 811 🖐 €250–€640, excluding breakfast 🕐 89 🆒 🚇 Spagna

HOTEL DE RUSSIE
www.hotelderussie.it
Near Piazza del Popolo in the heart of the city, amid all the top designer shops, this is arguably Rome's top hotel. It is a historic palazzo, where the contemporary and classic are beautifully blended. Guest rooms have high ceilings and are lovingly furnished, and the bathrooms are works of art. Amenities include spa with hydropool, sauna, Turkish baths and beauty treatments. The first-class restaurant is elegant and, when its doors are opened onto the gardens, it is the most romantic spot in Rome.

✚ 98 D3 ✉ Via del Babuino 9, 00187
☎ 06 328 881 ✋ €500–€1,000 ⓘ 122
🅢 🌁 🅠 Flaminio 🚌 117

INTERNAZIONALE
www.hotelinternazionale.com
Wisteria winds up the front of this palazzo—a faint echo perhaps of the ancient Roman gardens that once stood here. The building has evolved over the years, and served as a convent in the 16th and 17th centuries. Today, the breakfast lounge is in soothing pastel blues and purples, and this tranquil scheme continues throughout, from the cupids in the cupola to the silk wall coverings in the bedrooms. There is 24-hour room service, a bar, currency exchange, babysitting and parking, and pets are welcome.

✚ 98 E4 ✉ Via Sistina 79, 00187
☎ 06 6994 1823 ✋ €180–€350 ⓘ 42
🅢 🅠 Spagna 🚌 62

ITALIA
www.hotelitaliaroma.com
The Italia is an inexpensive, friendly, family-run hotel in a 19th-century building just off Via Nazionale, the second-largest shopping street in the city. Reception is on the first floor, and there is a small elevator. Both public and guest rooms are very clean and simple throughout, and the guest rooms have TV, minibar, air conditioning (€10 extra per day), bathroom, hairdryer and safe. All are spacious, with parquet floors, functional furniture and cream-coloured walls. The hotel has a bar and a safe at reception.

✚ 99 F5 ✉ Via Venezia 18, 00184
☎ 06 482 8355 ✋ €80–€130 ⓘ 23, plus 8 in Italia 2 annexe at Via Venezia 25
🅢 🅠 Repubblica 🚌 64

KENNEDY HOTEL
www.hotelkennedy.net
This three-star hotel is situated between Termini station and the basilica of Santa Maria Maggiore. Half of the guest rooms overlook the archaeological park of the Roman Aquarium. Rooms are spacious, with fitted wardrobes, double-glazed windows, satellite TV and small but well-equipped bathrooms. The public areas are warmly lit, and there is a small reading room with some books and guides in English. The three small breakfast rooms serve a buffet breakfast.

✚ 99 G5 ✉ Via Filippo Turati 62–64, 00185 ☎ 06 446 5373 ✋ €65–€190 ⓘ 53
🅢 🅠 Termini 🚌 40, 64, 70

LOCARNO
www.hotellocarno.com
Artists and intellectuals, including Umberto Eco (author of the novel *The Name of the Rose*), opt for this art deco refuge on a sleepy street near Piazza del Popolo. The 1925 building retains original features, including a cast-iron elevator. The interiors have been skilfully designed, using period lamps and furnishings, and each room is individually decorated. Guests have free use of the business and internet facilities, and vintage bicycles.

✚ 98 D3 ✉ Via della Penna 22, 00186
☎ 06 361 0841 ✋ €130–€360 ⓘ 68
🅢 🅠 Flaminio 🚌 117

LUCE
www.romewelcome.com/hotel-luce-.htm
This modern, light, three-star hotel is close to Termini station and the shops. All public areas have attractive inlaid marble floors and comfortable sofas. The breakfast

Below *At the Hotel de Russie contemporary and classic are seamlessly blended*

room is elegant, with upholstered spoon-back chairs and gold-braided tablecloths. Guest rooms are stylish and spacious, with draped curtains, fitted wooden furniture and good lighting. All rooms have a bathroom, TV and minibar. Parking is available.

✚ 99 G4 ✉ Via Magenta 34, 00185 ☎ 06 4470 2224 ✋ €120–€280 🛏 64 ♿ ♿ Termini 🚌 40, 64

PAVIA
www.hotelpavia.it

This small, simple three-star hotel in the Termini station area overlooks the ancient remains of Terme di Diocleziano. The interior design of the rooms is not exciting and the plywood furniture is functional. However, the rooms do have satellite/pay TV, minibar, electronic safe, internet access points and basic showers. There is a pleasant bar/lounge area open 24 hours. The hotel is based over two floors, but there is no elevator.

✚ 99 G4 ✉ Via Gaeta 83, 00185 ☎ 06 483 801 ✋ €95–€200 🛏 25 ♿ €13 extra ♿ Castro Pretorio 🚌 492, 495

PRINCIPESSA ISABELLA
www.hotelprincipessaisabella.com

The Principessa Isabella presides over the Via Vittorio Veneto and Villa Borghese, providing guests with true old-world elegance—traditional and elaborate without being fussy. Oriental carpets, gilt mirrors and mauve upholstery add to the genteel atmosphere. The Ludovici Group deserves high praise for preserving the style of this grande dame hotel. There is a bar, traditional trattoria and four suites, plus indoor parking on request.

✚ 99 F3 ✉ Via Sardegna 149, 00187 ☎ 06 484 523 ✋ €150–€400 🛏 35 ♿ ♿ Spagna

RESIDENCE BARBERINI
www.residencebarberini.com

These sleek suites are packed with modern gadgets: All have a king-sized bed, marble bathroom, TV with DVD player, personal computer, internet access, printer, webcam, fax, microwave oven and refrigerator. The penthouse includes a large roof garden with wicker loungers, dining table and pavilion. Furnishings are simple and elegant, including snowy-white quilts and wrought-iron bed frames. Breakfasts are served in the guest rooms or on the terrace. Contemporary art is exhibited in the communal areas.

✚ 98 F4 ✉ Via delle Quattro Fontane 171–172, 00184 ☎ 06 4203 3418 ✋ €250–€375, excluding breakfast 🛏 12 ♿ ♿ Barberini

SCALINATA DI SPAGNA
www.hotelscalinata.com

You need to reserve months—if not years—in advance at this boutique hotel at the top of the Spanish Steps. La Scalinata's 16 rooms, especially those with the best views, are highly coveted. The breakfast terrace, overlooking red-tiled roofs and cupolas, has wrought-iron chairs and riots of blossom. Active visitors enjoy jogging in the nearby Villa Borghese park. The less active can plug in a laptop, or use the free internet TV with email service.

✚ 98 E4 ✉ Piazza Trinità dei Monti 17, 00187 ☎ 06 6994 0896 ✋ €150–€400 🛏 16 ♿ ♿ Spagna 🚌 116

STARGATE HOSTEL AND HOTEL
www.stargatehotels.com

Near Termini station, this hostel and hotel is extremely good value. The hostel's spacious dormitory rooms, sleep four to six people and have bunk-beds, desks, chairs, wardrobe, washbasin, TV and internet access. The hostel also has its own internet lounge and kitchen. Some rooms have their own shower, and there is a communal shower on each floor. Towels and linen are provided and there's a launderette. No curfew is imposed. The hotel rooms are similar but more private, catering for one or two people. A breakfast of coffee and brioche is included in the room rate.

✚ 99 H4 ✉ Via Palestro 88, 00185 ☎ 06 445 7164 ✋ Hostel: €60–€80, hotel: €80–€120 🛏 Hostel 20, hotel 10 ♿ Castro Pretorio or Termini 🚌 492

SWEET HOME
www.hotelsweethome.it

Near Termini station, Sweet Home is a mid-range hotel with a late 19th-century feel to it. It has high ceilings and spacious rooms with simple, painted wooden tables, TV, comfortable sofas and bright design; the rooms have either a bath or a shower. The breakfast room doubles as a bar, which is open throughout the day, and there is a charming, private room with a chandelier available for meetings. There's also an internet access point. Hotel staff are friendly and helpful.

✚ 99 G5 ✉ Via Principe Amedeo 47, 00185 ☎ 06 488 0954 ✋ €150–€200 🛏 11 ♿ Termini 🚌 40, 64, 70

TRITONE
www.travelroma.com

This modern three-star hotel has a great location, just 100m (110 yards) from the Trevi Fountain, and makes an ideal base from which to explore the *centro storico* and Rome's key sights. Breakfast is served on the roof terrace, which has fabulous, panoramic views of the city. The rooms are clean and simply furnished, and all are soundproofed.

✚ 98 E4 ✉ Via del Tritone 210, 00187 ☎ 06 6992 2575 ✋ €140–€270 🛏 43 ♿ ♿ Barberini 🚌 175, 204, 492, 590

VICTORIA
www.hotelvictoriaroma.com

Efficiently run by its Swiss management, the Victoria is just inside the Aurelian Walls, at the top of Via Veneto and within striking distance of the area's restaurants. The bedrooms are large, as are the bathrooms, and all rooms have satellite TV. In the summer months, the buffet breakfast is served in the roof garden. The hotel also has a bar and restaurant, and private parking is available.

✚ 99 F3 ✉ Via Campania 41, 00187 ☎ 06 423 701 ✋ €150–€250, excluding breakfast 🛏 111 ♿ ♿ Spagna 🚌 95, 116, 116T, 119, 204

Via S Andrea
Flaminia (Belle Arti)
Via B Ammannati
Buozzi
Via G Cuboni
Via de' Tre Orologi
Via G de Notaris
Galleria Michele
Via C Linneo
Mercati
Via A Tallisser
ALDROVANDI
LUNG OBERDAN
VIALE
FLAMINIA
TIZIANO
VIA
VIA F Jacovacci
BRUNO
Via G Mangili
Aldrovandi
VIA
ULISSE
Convito Nazionale
PONTE DEL RISORGIMENTO
VIALE
di Villa Giulia
Sant' Eugenio
VIA
Museo Etrusco Villa Giulia
VIALE DELLE
Piazza Thorwaldsen
Galleria Nazionale d'Arte Moderna
VIA
Aldrovandi
Bioparco
Zoo
LUNGOTEVERE DELLE NAVI
Via G V Gravina
Belle Arti
Belle Arti
Villa Giulia E Museo Nazionale Etrusco
Piazza Thorwaldsen
BELLE
Piazza Firdusi
ARTI
Museo Canonica
Zoologico
Via C Menotti
Via G Filangieri
FLAMINIA
Piazza della Marina
Galleria Arte Moderna Piazzale Firdusi
Ministero Marina
Via di Villa Giulia
Viale di
Piazza di Siena
Villa Borghese
Via Montanelli
Via D A Azuni
Azuni (Ministero Marina)
Via M Fortuny
Villa Strohl Fern
Galoppatoio
Ponte Giacomo Matteotti
Via P S S Man li cini
Stazione Roma Flaminio
Viale Esculapio
Viale Fiorello La Guardia
Museo Carlo Bilotti
VIA
Ponte Pietro Nenni
Via degli Scialoia
Piazza Cinque Giornate
Via Cesare Beccaria
Flaminio Piazza del Popolo
Viale Washington
VIALE
Piazzale delle Canestre
Via L DI SAVOIA
Via F Carrara
Piazzale Flaminio
Giardino del Pincio
DEL
Viale delle Magnolie
Viale Goethe
Tevere
PONTE REGINA MARGHERITA
Via degli Scipioni
Santa Maria del Popolo
Monte Pincio
MURO
Viale San Paolo del Brasile
Via Maria Adelaide
Piazza del Popolo
Trinità del Monti
TORTO
Via Virginio Orsini
Piazza della Libertà
Locarno
Hotel de Russie
Via Ferdinando di Savoia
Lowenhaus
Villa Medici
Via Porta Pinciana
Antico Bottaro
Il Brillo Parlante
Casa di Goethe
Hotel Eden
Via Lombardia
LUNGOTEVERE IN AUGUSTA
Via del Vantaggio
Via Margutta
Il Margutta
La Terrazza
Ara Pacis Augustae
Gusto
Via della Frezza
Via del Babuino
Otello alla Concordia
Babington's Tea Rooms
S Isidoro
Internazionale
PONTE CAVOUR
Mausoleo di Augusto
Piazza Augusto imperatore
Al 34
Via della Croce
Hassler
SS Trinità dei Monti
Via F Crispi
Teatro Adriano
Via V Colonna
Fiaschetteria Beltramme
Piazza di Spagna
Scalinata
Palazzo di Giustizia
SS Ambrogio e Carlo al Corsa
Antico Caffè Greco di Spagna
LUNGOTEVERE MARZIO
Via Tomacelli
Le Pain Quotidien
Borgognona
Casa Howard
VIA TRIBONIALE
PONTE UMBERTO I
Palazzo Borghese
Hotel d'Inghilterra
Via Frattina
T-Bone Station
Barocco
Vitti
Palazzo Ruspoli
Via della Mercede
Residence Barberini
Fontana del Tritone
El Toulà
San Lorenzo in Lucina
Pizza Ciro
The Albert
Obika
Piazza's Silvestro V
Galleria dell'Accademia di San Luca
Palazzo Marignoli
Il Gelato di San Crispino
Palazzo della Stamperia
Il Bacaro
Palazzo di Montecitorio
Palazzo Chigi
Tritone
Fontana di Trevi
Museo Nazionale delle Paste Alimentari
Gelateria della Palma
Colonna di Marco Aurelio
Piazza Colonna
Bruschetteria Nonna Papera
Palazzo del Quirinale
Palazzo Montecitorio
Via della Dataria
Palazzo Taverna
Santa Maria della Pace
Palazzo Sciarra
Piazza del Quirinale
Sant'Agnese
Palazzo G Vecchio
Scuderie del Quirinale
Via della Consulta
Chiesa Nuova
Palazzo del Governo vecchio
Pantheon
Sant'Ignazio di Loyola
Santi Apostoli
Villa Colonna
Santa Maria sopra Minerva
Palazzo Odescalchi
Palazzo Colonna
Sant'Ivo alla Sapienza
Piazza della Minerva
Palazzo-Galleria Doria Pamphilj
Palazzo dei Santi Apostoli
Colonna Traiana
Palazzo della Cancelleria
Sant'Andrea della Valle
Teatro Argentina
Palazzo Altieri
Piazza Venezia
Mercati di Traiano
CORSO VITTORIO EMANUELE II
Museo del

98

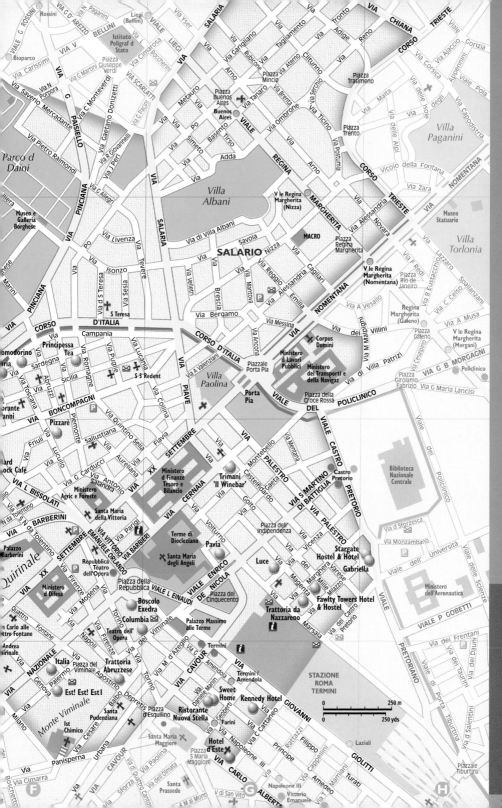

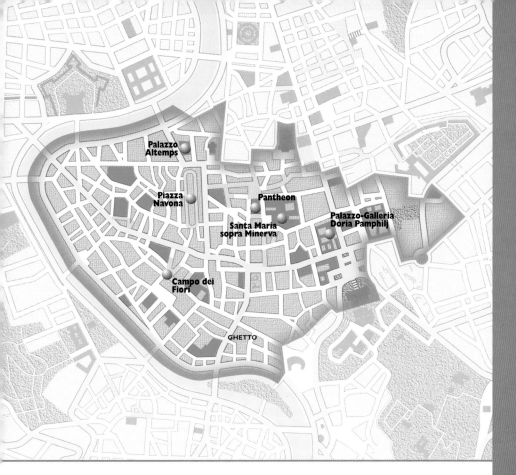

CENTRAL ROME

The heart of the present city is bounded by the sweeping curve of the River Tiber in the west, bisected by the busy Corso Vittorio Emanuele II, and flanked by Piazza Venezia in the east. After the Foro Romano and other sights of the ancient city, it is the area in which many visitors will spend most of the time, thanks to its rich mixture of churches, galleries, shops and pretty streets and piazzas.

The area is often referred to as Rome's medieval or Renaissance core, although this is only partly true, for it also contains many baroque and ancient monuments, not least the Pantheon, the best preserved of any building from the ancient world. Here, too, is Piazza Navona, Rome's most beautiful square, a mixture of medieval, Renaissance and baroque elements, built over the ruins of ancient Rome's race track.

Campo dei Fiori may be a less elegant piazza but is equally beguiling, thanks to its picturesque morning market, and, like Piazza Navona, is a key dining and nightlife district. The cobbled streets around both squares are full of bars and restaurants, but there are also plenty of vestiges of old Rome, such as the artisans' workshops in Via dei Cappellari and the surrounding area, grand residential enclaves (Via Giulia) and the traditional shops of Via dei Banchi Vecchi and Via del Governo Vecchio.

There are innumerable things to see, from major museums such as the Palazzo Altemps and Palazzo-Galleria Doria Pamphilj to key churches such as Il Gesù and Santa Maria sopra Minerva. But there are also countless smaller gems, such as San Luigi dei Francesi, which is noted for its three paintings by Caravaggio, the Palazzo Spada, with its collection of fine art and sculpture, and the former Jewish Ghetto, a delightful area to explore on foot.

S Maria d'Carm

Via CRESCENZIO

Piazza Cavour

Via V COLONNA

PONTE Cavour

PIAZZA ADRIANA

Via Alberico II

Bastioni

Via G Vitelleschi

Terenzio

Via TRIBONIANO

Palazzo di Giustizia

Via Ulpiano

LUNGOTEVERE PRATI

Via di Ripetta

Borgo Pio

Borgo Sant'Angelo

Via della Scrofa

Castel Sant'Angelo

Piazza Tribunali

Santa Maria in Traspontina

PONTE UMBERTO I

LUNGOTEVERE MARZIO

Piazza Pia

LUNGOTEVERE CASTELLO

Via Monte Brianzo

VIA DELLA CONCILIAZIONE

LUNGOTEVERE VATICANO

Sant'Angelo

Ponte Sant'Angelo

LUNGOTEVERE TOR DI NONA

Via dell' Orso

Sant' Agostino

Via G ZANARDELLI

Palazzo Altemps

Piazza Cinque Lune

Maddale

Via del B di S Spirito

Piazza S Salv in Lauro

S Salvatore

S Simeone

LUNGOT IN SASSIA

Piazza Coronari

Via dei Coronari

Via Paola

Via Panico

Palazzo Taverna

Santa Maria della Pace

San Luigi dei Francesi

PONTE VITTORIO EMANUELE II

Via Banchi Nuovi

Via M Giordano

Sant'Agnese

CORSO DEL RINASCIMENTO

PONTE PRINCIPE AMEDEO SAVOIA AOSTA

San Giovanni dei Fiorentini

Via del Governo Vecchio

Palazzo G Vecchio

Piazza Navona

Sant'Agnese in Agone

Piazza di Sant' Eustacch

Via del Banchi Vecchi

Chiesa Nuova

Via S M dell'Anima

Via Teatro Pace

Sant'Ivo alla Sapienza

Via Monterone

Palazzo Salviati

LUNGOTEVERE SANGALLO

Via Giulia

CORSO VITTORIO EMANUELE II

Piazza San Pantaleo

Via del Pellegrino

Palazzo della Cancelleria

Sant'Andrea della Valle

Ponte Mazzini

Largo Lorenzo Perosi

Via del Cappellari

del Sudario

Via degli Orti d'Alibert

S Eligio

S M d Monserato

Via Baullari

Teatro Pompeo

Te Arger

Via delle Mantellate

Campo dei Fiori

Via di San Francesco di Sales

Piazza Farnese

LUNGOTEVERE DEI TEBALDI

Palazzo Falconieri

Palazzo Farnese

Via Giubbonari

Via di San

Lungara

Tevere

Via del Riari

Palazzo Corsini

Villa Farnesina

LUNGOTEVERE DELLA FARNESINA

Palazzo Spada

Via Pettinari

Cairoli

VIA ARENULA

GHET

Via delle Zoccolette

Ministero Grazia Giustizia

Ministero G Giustizia

LU

Palazzo Torlonia

Ponte Sisto

LUNGOTEVERE DEI VALLATI

Gianicolo

Orto Botanico

250 m

250 yds

VIA GARIBALDI

Via della Scala

Santa Maria della Scala

Piazza de' Renzi

Via della Renella

PONTE GARIBALDI

LUNGOTEVERE DEI SANZIO

Piazza G G Belli

LU

Vicolo di Cedro

Via Moro

Piazza di S Maria in Trastevere

della

Belli

Passeggiata del Gianicolo

Vicolo di Cedro

S Egidio

Santa Maria in Trastevere

Lungare

Piazzale Aurelio

VIA GARIBALDI

San Pietro in Montorio

San Crisogono

Piazza Sidney Sonnino

Via di Porta San Pancrazio

SS Ambrogio e
Carlo al Corsa

Tomacelli

dell' Arancio

Borgognona

Via di S. Basilio

Santa Maria della
Concezione

VIA DI VITTORIO VENETO

V S N da Tolentino

Palazzo Ruspoli

Via Condotti

Via di Bocca di Leone

Via Belsiana

Via Frattina

Via della

Via delle Vite

Via dei Due Macelli

C le

Via Gregoriana

Sistina

Via F Crispi

Via della Purificazione

Fontana
del Tritone

Barberini
Fontana di Trevi

Piazza
Barberini

Palazzo
Barberini

Via delle Quattro Fontane

San Lorenzo
in Lucina

Via della Mercede

Piazza S
Silvestro V

Palazzo
Marignoli

Via

VIA   DEL

TRITONE

Via Poli

Galleria dell'
Accademia
di San Luca

Via Rasella

Via dei Giardini

Via di Campo

Palazzo di
Montecitorio

Palazzo
Chigi

Palazzo della
Stamperia

Museo Nazionale
delle Paste Alimentari

Giardino del
Quirinale

San Carlo
alle Quattro
Fontane

Sant'Andrea
al Quirinale

dei Prefetti

Marzio

Colonna di
Marco Aurelio

Fontana
di Trevi

Monte   Quirinale

VIA DEL QUIRINALE

Via Placenza

Piazza
Montecitorio

Piazza
Colonna

VIA

Via delle Muratte

Via dell'Umiltà

Via della Dataria

Palazzo del
Quirinale

Piazza del
Quirinale

Via della Consulta

Via Parma

Via

Via Pastini

Via del Seminario

DEL   CORSO

Palazzo
Sciarra

Via Lucchesi

Scuderie del
Quirinale

Palazzo
Consulta

Palazzo del
Quirinale

NAZIONALE

Milano

Piazza
della
onda

Pantheon

Santa Maria
sopra Minerva

Sant'Ignazio
di Loyola

P

Santi
Apostoli

Villa
Colonna

VIA XXIV MAGGIO

dei

Boschetto

Piazza della
Minerva

Via d Cestari

Palazzo
Odescalchi

Piazza
dei Santi
Apostoli

Palazzo
Colonna

del

Via Mazzarino

Serpenti

Palazzo-Galleria
Doria Pamphilj

Via del Gesù

VIA   DEL   PLEBISCITO

Largo
Magnanapoli

Via di Sant'Agata
dei Goti

CORSO VITTORIO EMANUELE II

Palazzo
Altieri

Palazzo
Venezia

San Marco

Piazza

Colonna
Traiana

Via Panisperna

Templi
Repubblicani

ntina

P

Il Gesù

Museo del
Palazzo Venezia

Venezia

Mercati
di Traiano

Via della Madonna dei Monti

Via delle Botteghe Oscure

Monumento a Vittorio
Emanuele II

Via dei Delfini

Fori
Imperiali

Via Baccina

VIA   CAVOUR

Crypta
Balbi

Via

VIA DEI FORI IMPERIALI

dei Colosseo

dei Funari

Santa Maria
in Aracoeli

Via dei Fori

Fontana delle
Tartarughe

Piazza del
Campitelli

Musei
Capitolini

Portico d'Ottavia

Piazza del
Campidoglio

Palazzo
Senatorio

Via Salaria Vecchia

Arco di
Settimio
Severo

Via Catalana

Sinagoga

CENCI

Teatro di
Marcello

Palazzo dei
Conservatori

Monte Capitolino

Via d Consolazione

Foro
Romano

Santi Cosma
e Damiano

Piazza
Monte Savello

Santa Nicola
in Carcere

Piazza della
Consolazione

Via dei Fienili

S Teodoro

Orti
Farnesiani

Arco di
Tito

Via Sacra

Arco di
Costantino

sola
erina

San Bartolomeo
all' Isola

LUNGOTEVERE DEI PIERLEONI

VIA LUIGI PETROSELLI

P

Via di San Teodoro

Palatino

L' ANGUILLARA

PONTE
PALATINO

Tempio della
Fortuna Virilis

Tempio
di Vesta

E

Piazza di
S Anastasia

Casa di Livia

Palazzo
dei Flavi

F

103

CAMPO DEI FIORI

For a slice of real Roman life, head for the Campo dei Fiori during the morning market (established here in 1869) when the stalls are in full swing and the surrounding shops busy with people. Around lunchtime, it's a good place to pause for a snack or meal, while evenings see the piazza crowded with locals and visitors making the most of the area's bars and restaurants.

The origin of the square's name is disputed. In ancient times, this area was part of a temple to Venere Vincitrice annexed to the nearby Teatro di Pompeo (Theatre of Pompey). Some scholars believe the name may derive from Flora, Pompey's lover, although the area was also later used as grazing land for cattle, hence, possibly, another source for the square's present name—the Field of Flowers. In those days, buildings stood on one side of the square only, with a spacious view over the Tiber on the other. By the 12th century the Palazzo Orsini, where the Palazzo Righetti now stands, dominated the scene, and the Campo became the heart of an exclusive residential and business district. It was also an important crossing point, as papal processions and pilgrims on their way to Rome's basilicas had to pass through Via del Pellegrino. Once it had been used for executions it lost its cachet, and became the heart of one of Rome's most vibrant working-class areas.

STATUE OF GIORDANO BRUNO

A hooded statue of the philosopher Giordano Bruno was erected in 1887 to replace a fountain, the Campo's original focal point. Bruno advocated the separation of political and religious power and, in 1600, he was condemned for heresy and burned alive by the Inquisition on this very spot, the first of a series of executions carried out here during the 17th century. Ettore Ferrari was the sculptor, and the statue soon became a meeting point for intellectuals and anti-establishment thinkers.

PALAZZO RIGHETTI AND PALAZZO DELLA CANCELLERIA

The Palazzo Righetti, at the east end of the square, was built on the site of an old palazzo, over the remains of the Theatre of Pompey. It was bought in the 18th century by the banker Righetti, from whom it takes its name. The late 15th-century Palazzo della Cancelleria is attributed to Bramante, though the interior courtyard is his sole contribution.

THE SURROUNDING STREETS

The Campo is part of the Regola district, traditionally famous for its craftsmen. Many nearby streets owe their names to the artisan workshops that once stood there: Via dei Giubbonari (jacket-makers) and Via dei Cappellari (hat-makers). These streets are still crammed with tiny shops, great trawling ground for local goods. In Via del Pellegrino look for a charming old interior courtyard—it's through a gate just round the corner of the west side of the square. Via di Monserrato, farther on, is home to the English College, where young British men train for the priesthood.

Much of the area on the left, as you walk southeast out of the square along Via dei Giubonnari, was once occupied by the vast Theatre of Pompey, built between 61BC and 55BC and restored in AD32 by Augustus and again in AD80 by Diocletian after a fire. With a diameter of 150m (480ft), it could accommodate 18,000 spectators, and extended as far east as the present-day Largo di Torre Argentina, where (in the sunken area at the centre of the square) traces of the structure can still be seen. The curve of the theatre, still followed by the medieval buildings on your right, can also be traced if you walk out of Campo dei Fiori's eastern corner, into Piazza del Biscione and then round into Piazza Paradiso and Largo dei Chiavari. Remains of the Theatre of Pompey are also visible in the cellar of the restaurant San Pancrazio on the east corner of the square—you don't have to eat there to have a look.

INFORMATION

✚ 102 D5 🚌 23, 40, 46, 62, 64, 116, 280, 870, 916; tram 8 ☕ Streetside cafés in the square 📖 Souvenir shops in the square sell guidebooks

Opposite *The daily market in Campo dei Fiori is one of the most atmospheric in the city*

CRYPTA BALBI

www.archeoroma.beniculturali.it

Part of the Museo Nazionale Romano, this museum focuses on how the city has changed over the centuries. The main display by the entrance has a rich collection of objects to illustrate social, economic and urban planning changes from ancient times to the present day.

Two other sections have displays of vases, glass items, mosaics and other items dating from between the fifth and eighth centuries.

The museum also has an interesting collection of ancient coins and archaeological finds from the Foro Romano.

✚ 103 E5 ✉ Via delle Botteghe Oscure 31, 00186 ☎ 06 678 0167; 06 3996 7700 🕐 Tue–Sun 9–7.45 ✋ Adult €7, EU citizens 18–24 €3.50, EU citizens under 18 and over 65 free. For details of the Roma Archeologica Card and Museum Card ▷ 259. Guided visit to Esedra and Portico excavations at 10, 12, 3 and 5 Sat–Sun. Must be prebooked (€3.50) 🚌 30, 40, 46, 62, 63, 64, 70, 81, 492, 628, 630, 780, 787, 916 stopping at Largo di Torre Argentina

IL GESÙ

The inside of this church, dedicated to the Holy Name of Jesus, was undecorated when it was completed in 1584. However, at the end of the 17th century, exquisite marble decorations, stuccowork and baroque frescoes, masterpieces of illusionism, were added to make the Jesuits' principal church one of the most beautiful in Rome.

The church's facade is divided in two: At the top, a triangular tympanum includes a large central window and two lateral niches; below is a line of pilasters with Corinthian capitals. The interior consists of a central nave with side chapels. The chapel on the left, dedicated to St. Ignatius Loyola, adorned with stuccowork, golden bronzes, sculptures and precious stones, is the work of the Jesuit architect Andrea Pozzo. Pietro da Cortona added the right-hand chapel, and on the altar there is a painting by Carlo Maratta. On the ceiling above the central nave is a *trompe l'oeil* fresco by Baciccia, dating from 1679. It depicts the *Triumph of the Name of Jesus*: Light descends through a fake window in the sky, figures representing the races and vocations of humankind float in clouds, while others, representing the cardinal sins, fall into darkness.

✚ 103 E5 ✉ Piazza del Gesù/Via degli Astalli 16, 00186 ☎ 06 697 001 🕐 Church: daily 7–12.30, 4–7.45. Chapel of Sant'Ignatius Loyola: Mon–Sat 4–6, Sun 10–12 ✋ Free 🚌 30, 40, 46, 62, 63, 64, 70, 81, 492, 628, 630, 780, 787, 916 stopping at Largo di Torre Argentina; tram 8

GHETTO AND SINAGOGA

The Ghetto is a picturesque place today, its narrow, bustling streets full of Jewish restaurants, pastry shops and workshops—despite its history, the area is still a meeting point for the Roman-Jewish community.

In 1555, Pope Paul IV created the Ghetto to segregate Rome's Jewish population. They were confined in unsanitary conditions within the Ghetto walls, where three gates were opened in the morning and closed at dusk. They were also limited in their rights to worship and to trade. In 1888 the gates opened for the final time; the walls and houses of the Ghetto were demolished, and Rome's Jewish population were given back the same civil rights as other residents.

The Synagogue, built in 1904, overlooks the Tiber, its great dome visible from all over the city. It houses the Jewish Museum. Behind runs Via Portico d'Ottavia, named after the ruins of the portico built in the first century BC by Augustus and his sister. Inside is the church of Sant'Angelo in Pescheria, which owes its name to the open-air fish market held nearby. This was one of the four Christian churches Jews were forced to attend every Sunday.

✚ Ghetto: 102 D6. Synagogue: 103 E6 ✉ Synagogue: Lungotevere Cenci 15 ☎ Synagogue: 06 6800 0661 🕐 Mon– Thu 9–4.30, Fri 9–1.30, Sun 9–12.30 ✋ Synagogue: €6 🚌 23, 63, 280, 630, 780; tram 8 ☞ Tours of Ghetto in English, lasting up to 1 hour, at 12.30 on Fri and Sat; €7. Meet at the Synagogue

MONUMENTO A VITTORIO EMANUELE II

There is no mistaking the colossal white monument that dominates Piazza Venezia. Dubbed the Wedding Cake, it is dedicated to Vittorio Emanuele II, the first king of a united Italy. The monument also houses the shrine of Italy's Unknown Soldier, interred here in 1921. The monument, built between 1885 and 1911, was controversial from the outset, not least because of its impact on its surroundings, large areas of which were sacrificed or remodelled to make way for it. It's worth a visit for the fine views of the Fori Imperiali from its terraces.

✚ 103 E5 ✉ Piazza Venezia, 00184 ☎ 06 699 1718 🕐 Apr–Sep daily 9.30–5.30; Oct–Mar 9.30–4.30 ✋ Free 🚇 Colosseo 🚌 44, 46, 84 and all other services to Piazza Venezia

PALAZZO ALTEMPS

▷ 108–109.

PALAZZO–GALLERIA DORIA PAMPHILJ

Not far from trafffic-filled Piazza Venezia stands one of the largest palaces in Rome, Palazzo Doria Pamphilj, whose art collection is among the city's most prestigious. Owned and inhabited by the same family since the 17th century, the palace has remained untouched through the centuries; as you wander around the magnificent rooms, it is like stepping back in time.

The vast palace, with its five courtyards, four colossal staircases and over 1,000 rooms, is today in the hands of two half-British siblings, the adopted descendants of a venerable papal dynasty. This was created when two families were united by marriage: the Doria, an important Genoese merchant dynasty, and the Pamphili (or Pamphilj), pillars of the Roman aristocracy.

INSIDE THE PALACE

From the entrance, climb the monumental stairway to the *piano nobile*, and pick up one of the excellent multilingual audioguides (included in the ticket price). This will guide you around the palace, picking out highlights along the way; you should allow about 90 minutes for your visit. Five superbly decorated saloons, the state apartments, each more sumptuous than the last, open out one from the other. The ballroom is indubitably the finest room, with white and gold stucco decoration, chandeliers, mirrors and walls hung with figured silk. From here, you reach the private chapel, designed by Carlo Fontana in 1690, and the entrance to the picture galleries. These run round the sides of the largest of the inner courtyards and perfectly reflect 18th-century taste, with Italian and Flemish works hung beside and above and below one another, the arrangement preferred by Prince Andrea Doria IV in 1760.

THE GALLERIES

The collection's most famous work is Velázquez's *Portrait of Innocent X* (1650). Innocent, a pope of notoriously weak character, is said to have remarked of the likeness that it was 'too true, too true'. Bernini's bust of Innocent, which stands beside Velázquez's painting, makes an interesting comparison. Most of the great names in Italian art are represented here: Look in particular for Caravaggio's *Rest on the Flight into Egypt* and his very beautiful *Magdalen*, Raphael's *Double Portrait* and Titian's alluring *Salome with the Head of John the Baptist*. Other highlights include Breughel's *Terrestial Paradise*, Filippo Lippi's *Annunciation* and Parmigianino's *Nativity*.

INFORMATION

www.dopart.it
✚ 103 E5 ✉ Piazza del Collegio Romano 2 ☎ 06 679 7323. Advance tickets: 06 3996 7700 🕐 Daily 10–5 ✋ Adult €10.50, child (under 18) €7.50, adult over 65 €7.50 🚇 Barberini, Colosseo 🚌 64, 95, 175, 492, 62, 630 📖 Free guide, *Breve Guida della Galleria Doria Pamphilj*, available in several languages ☕ Tea room

TIPS

» Use the audioguide, which is included in the price and helps you make sense of what you're seeing.
» The paintings are not well lit so it is better to visit during daylight hours.

Above *The opulent interior of the Palazzo-Galleria Doria Pamphilj*
Opposite *The Monumento a Vittorio Emanuele II in Piazza Venezia*

INFORMATION

www.archeoroma.beniculturali.it
www.pierreci.it (for online reservations)
✚ 102 D4 ✉ Piazza Sant'Apollinare
46, 00186 ☎ 06 687 2719. Advance
tickets: 06 3996 7700 🕐 Tue–Sun 9–7
(exit 7.45) 👍 Adult €7, EU citizens
18–25 €3.50, EU citizens under 18 and
over 65 free. For details of the Roma
Archeologica Card and Museum Card,
▷ 259. 🚌 70, 81, 87, 116, 186, 492, 628,
916 🎧 Audiotours: English, Italian, €5
📖 Available in museum shop: brief guide
€10, full catalogue €49 🏛 Sells guides
and souvenirs

Above *Some of the collection is exhibited in the loggia on the upper floor, a mid-16th century addition to the palazzo*

INTRODUCTION

The superbly restored 15th-century Palazzo Altemps forms part of the Museo Nazionale Romano, along with the Palazzo Massimo alle Terme, Crypta Balbi and Terme di Diocleziano, and is as beautiful as its exhibits, which include some of the city's finest Roman sculpture.

Originally the site of a Roman warehouse, the area of the future palazzo became part of a fortification dividing two rival Roman families, the Orsini and the Colonna. The present building dates from 1477, when Girolamo Riario, a nephew of Pope Sixtus IV, commissioned the palace. It was extended by members of the Altemps family in 1568; they added the courtyard, designed by Martino Longhi the Elder, with its portico and loggias. Between 1621 and 1623, Cardinal Ludovico Ludovisi assembled his 500-piece collection, still the core of today's museum. Later owner-collectors included Cardinal Marco Sittico Altemps, who bought the palace and made it a suitable setting for his magnificent collection of books and antique sculptures. The Italian state acquired the Palazzo Altemps in 1982, and restored the building to reflect 16th- and 17th-century taste and display methods.

The museum is set out over three floors around a courtyard, with statuary exhibited in arcades, loggias, courtyards and the beautifully frescoed rooms. The number of exhibits is not overwhelming, but the standard is high. Don't try to see everything, but concentrate on what appeals. The exhibits are stunningly lit, and it's well worth trying to time a visit while dusk falls.

WHAT TO SEE

COURTYARD, GROUND-FLOOR ARCADES AND LOGGIA

The courtyard is probably the most handsome feature of the building. A fountain made from seashells, pumice stones and vitreous paste stands to one side; look for the Altemps family coat of arms here showing lightning striking a bridge. Around the courtyard, the arcades are the perfect setting for larger-than-life-size statues, while the open space is overlooked by a loggia, its ceiling decorated with cherubs. The room behind here has *trompe l'oeil* landscapes and views covering the walls and columns, while nearby is the Sideboard Room, the scene in 1477 of Girolamo Riario's marriage to Caterina Sforza, a member of the powerful Milanese dynastic family.

THE LUDOVISI THRONE

One of the most beautiful of all surviving Greek sculptures in Rome, the Ludovisi Throne was thought for years to have been part of a fifth-century BC altar. More probably it was the throne for a statue of the goddess Aphrodite of Eryx, whose ancient cult is associated with Erice in Sicily. She was the patron goddess of mariners and love, revered throughout the Mediterranean. The throne portrays the birth of the goddess from the sea foam; she rises between two nymphs, her draperies clinging to her body and drops of water falling from her hair, supremely delicate, the embodiment of all that was finest in the Greek world. Find it in the Tales of Moses Room on the upper floor.

THE FIREPLACE SALON

The Roman copy of the Greek *Gaul and His Wife Committing Suicide* has been admired for centuries for its realism and pathos; it was probably commissioned by Julius Caesar as a memento of his time in Gaul. If you've seen the *Dying Gaul* in the Musei Capitolini (▷ 159), it's easy to see that these two pieces were part of a group, erected in 197–159BC to celebrate a Greek victory. The room's highlight, though, is the action-packed relief on the side of the Ludovisi Sarcophagus. Carved from a single block of marble, it's full of life and movement, and shows Roman soldiery giving a thorough beating to some hapless barbarians.

THE CHURCH OF SANT'ANICETO

Leading off the Fireplace Salon is this highly decorated church, which was commissioned in 1603 by Giovanni Angelo Altemps to house the relics of St. Aniceto. Altemps invented a story of Aniceto's martyrdom by beheading, which mirrors his own father's death and is shown in painted cycles around the church. Don't miss the *confessio*, behind the altar, which has a wonderful ceiling decorated with mother of pearl.

GALLERY GUIDE

Ground floor: Roman copies of ancient Greek statues; remains of ancient Roman buildings (Tower Room); portraits from the Ludovisi collection (Portrait Room); Teatro Goldini (16th-century private theatre).
Upper floors: Frescoed rooms (particularly the Painted Views Room and the Painted Loggia); Roman copies of ancient Greek statues, including the Ludovisi Throne (Tales of Moses Room), the Ludovisi Sarcophagus and *Gaul and His Wife Committing Suicide* (both in the Fireplace Salon) and *Aphrodite* bathing (Duchess' Room); Church of Sant'Aniceto; Octagonal Chapel.

Below left Gaul and his Wife Committing Suicide, *a Roman copy of a Greek sculpture*
Below *A bust of Aphrodite*

REGIONS • CENTRAL ROME • SIGHTS

PALAZZO SPADA

www.galleriaborghese.it

Cardinal Spada's private collection of 17th-century paintings are displayed in the palace he acquired in 1632. The gallery consists of four rooms, all frescoed and decorated with statues and friezes.

The collection includes many fine works of art; to get the best from your visit, use one of the information leaflets available in several languages. Look out, in particular, for Guercino Didone's painting of *Death* in room 3, with its beautiful background, and the canvases by Artemisia Gentileschi and her father Orazio, in room 4. Also in room 4 is the octagonal painting of *The Halt at the Inn* by the Flemish painter Pieter van Laer (also known as 'Il Bamboccio'), one of Cardinal Spada's best-loved artists.

The palace's courtyard is most interesting for the Borromini perspective, a corridor only 8m (26ft) long, but appearing about four times longer. The columns are not parallel, but converge towards a focal point, and the floor slopes gently upwards. The statue at the end of the corridor is smaller than it appears.

✚ 102 D5 ✉ Piazza Capo di Ferro 13/ Vicolo del Polverone, 00186 ☎ Information and advance tickets: 06 683 2409 ⏱ Tue– Sun 8.30–7.30; Borromini perspective: 9.30–6.30 every hour ♿ Adult €5, EU citizens 18–25 €2.50, EU citizens under 18 and over 65 free 🚌 63, 116, 630, 780; tram 8 🍴 ▯ 🛍

Above *A 15th-century painting of the Nativity, part of Palazzo Venezia's permanent collection*
Above left *The Palazzo Spada houses a fine collection of 17th-century paintings*

PALAZZO VENEZIA

www.galleriaborghese.it

The imposing palace dominating Piazza Venezia (▷ 115) was one of the first major civil buildings to be erected in Rome during the Renaissance. Today, it houses the Museo del Palazzo Venezia, with collections of paintings and *objets d'art*. The palace also hosts excellent temporary art exhibitions, which are well worth seeing.

The Venetian Pietro Barbo started building the palace in 1455 when he became a cardinal, and it was enlarged when he was elected Pope Paul II in 1464. The palace acquired its present name in 1564, when Pope Pius IV gave it to the Republic of Venice as a diplomatic residence. The popes continued to live in a wing of the palace until the 16th century. In the 19th century Napoleon made it the seat of the French administration, and between 1930 and 1944 Mussolini established his government here and used the first floor of the palace for his office.

Exhibits in the permanent museum include ivory, silver and gold items, 16th- and 17th-century bronze statues, religious works of art, Renaissance models in plaster and terracotta, oriental pottery and 15th-century tapestries.

✚ 103 E5 ✉ Via del Plebiscito 118, 00184 ☎ 06 6999 4388; 06 678 0131 ⏱ Tue–Sun 8.30–7 ♿ Adult €4, EU citizens 18–25 €2, EU citizens under 18 and over 65 free 🚇 Colosseo 🚌 44, 46, 84, 715, 716, 780, 781, 810, 916 🛍

PANTHEON

▷ 112–114.

PIAZZA FARNESE

Close to Piazza Campo dei Fiori, at the historical heart of the Regola quarter, Piazza Farnese is akin to an elegant open-air drawing room, furnished by the majestic Renaissance Palazzo Farnese (now the French Embassy) and twin fountains to each side. The lily, emblem of the Farnese family and symbol of France, is the dominant theme in the square, visible on the palace facade and on the fountains. The Palazzo Farnese is the highlight of the square but can only be visited by appointment or with a private tour. However, it is pleasant to admire the splendid exterior from one of the square's outdoor cafés.

✚ 102 D5 🚌 23, 40, 46, 62, 64, 116, 280, 916; tram 8

PIAZZA NAVONA

Rome's most dazzling piazza was laid out in the mid-17th century on the ruins of Domitian's stadium (AD86), hence its elliptical shape. The stadium was originally called the Circus Agonalis (*Agones* means 'games' in ancient Greek), but in the Middle Ages it became known as Campus Agonis, which in turn was corrupted by Roman dialect to become *n'agnona* and eventually Navona. The arena was used for festivals and sporting events until the late 15th century, when it was paved over and transformed into a marketplace and public square.

You're likely to be drawn time and again to the piazza, so plan several visits to appreciate the square at different times of day. You could spend your first visit sightseeing, but be sure to return to relax, sit at a café table (but beware that prices are high), take in the street performers and local worthies, or eat one of Rome's best ice creams: the wicked chocolate *tartufo* at Tre Scalini.

THE PIAZZA

Harmonious, regularly shaped Piazza Navona is one of the most remarkable examples of town planning in Rome. Notable buildings include the Palazzo Braschi, renovated by Antonio da Sangallo in 1793 and now hosting exhibitions, and the elegant 17th-century Palazzo Pamphilj, the largest building in the piazza, which is now home to the Brazilian Embassy.

FONTANA DEI FIUMI

You'll be drawn at once to Bernini's famous Fountain of the Four Rivers, (1651), which gained him the admiration and protection of Pope Innocent X. The fountain shows the main rivers of the four then known continents: the Danube in Europe, the Ganges in Asia, the Nile in Africa and the Rio de la Plata in the New World. An obelisk (from the Circus of Maxentius) rears boldly into the air surrounded by animals. Legend has it that the fountain symbolizes the rivalry between Bernini and Borromini. Innocent X asked Borromini to do the work, but Bernini obtained the commission by flattering the Pope's sister. According to popular belief, Borromini built the church of Sant'Agnese in Agone in front of Bernini's fountain out of revenge, and the statue of the Nile seems to cover its face to shield its eyes from Borromini's work. Sadly, this is purely hearsay, since the fountain pre-dates the church—the Nile's face is covered because its source was as yet unknown.

SANT'AGNESE IN AGONE

The church of Sant'Agnese in Agone stands where, according to tradition, 12-year-old Agnes was martyred by the Emperor Diocletian. Exposed naked, the saint was miraculously covered by the prodigious growth of her own hair. Pope Innocent X commissioned the church in 1652 and Borromini took control of the project, radically changing the design of the facade and building the twin bell towers.

THE FONTANA DEL MORO AND THE FONTANA DEL NETTUNO

The Fontana del Moro at the southern end of the piazza was commissioned by Pope Gregory XIII and designed by Giacomo della Porta in 1576, with sculptures of tritons, dragons and dolphins. Bernini altered the fountain in the mid-17th century, adding the central figure of the Moor, apparently wrestling with a dolphin. At the northern end of the piazza, the 19th-century Fontana del Nettuno shows Neptune flanked by nymphs as he battles with a sea monster.

DOMITIAN'S STADIUM

To see the remains of Domitian's stadium, you can visit the building at Piazza di Tor Sanguigna, off the northern end of the square. A maximum of five people are allowed in at any one time, but it is well worth a visit.

INFORMATION

✚ 102 D5 ☎ Church of Sant'Agnese in Agone: 06 6819 2134. Domitian's stadium: 06 0608 for guided tours ⏱ Church of Sant'Agnese in Agone: Mon–Sat 9.30–12.30, 3.30–7, Sun 10–1, 4–7. Domitian's stadium: Mon–Fri 9–1, 2–5; open only by prior arrangement ✋ Church: free. Domitian's stadium: €7 🚌 23, 30, 62, 64, 70, 81, 87, 116, 280, 492, 628, 810, 916

Below *The 19th-century Fontana del Nettuno, one of the piazza's trio of fountains*

REGIONS CENTRAL ROME • SIGHTS

111

INTRODUCTION

The Pantheon is the best-preserved Roman monument in the world, still as impressive today as it must have been nearly 2,000 years ago. The original temple here, in the style of a traditional pagan Greek temple, was built in 27BC by Augustus' general and son-in-law, Marcus Agrippa, whose name can still clearly be seen on the inscription on the facade: 'M Agrippa L.F. Cos Tertium fecit' ('Marcus Agrippa, son of Lucius, built this during his third consulate'). Destroyed by a great fire in AD80, the temple was rebuilt by Emperor Hadrian in the early second century, but retained the original inscription.

In the sixth century, the Byzantine Emperor Phocas gave the Pantheon to Pope Boniface IV, who transformed it into a Christian church (thus helping preserve it), dedicating it to St. Mary of the Martyrs. To consecrate the church, the Pope is said to have brought 28 cartloads of bones of martyrs from the Roman catacombs and buried them beneath the altar.

From Piazza della Rotonda, a single door in the portico leads into the immense interior, distinguished by, among other things, the oculus, or hole in the dome, deliberately requested by Hadrian to allow worshippers a direct meditation on the heavens. If possible, visit during a downpour for the memorable sight of rain tumbling through the opening.

WHAT TO SEE

THE BUILDING

The portico is 14m (46ft) high and consists of 16 Egyptian granite columns with Corinthian capitals. The church is paved with marble and granite, and at one time the ceiling was entirely covered in bronze. When Pope Urban VIII restored the roof in the 17th century, the precious material was removed and used for the altar of St. Peter's and other works. The bronze doors are probably original. Around the interior are seven niches where statues of divinities once stood, with the statue of Jove Ultor, the Avenger, at the middle.

INFORMATION

✚ 103 D5 ✉ Piazza della Rotonda, 00186 ☎ 06 6830 0230 🕐 Mon–Sat 8.30–7.30, Sun 9–6, public hols 9–1. Closed to visitors during Mass on Sat at 5pm, Sun at 10.30am 🖐 Free 🚌 116 to Via della Palombella; 30, 40, 46, 62, 63, 64, 70, 81, 492, 628, 630, 780, 787, 916 or tram 8 to Largo di Torre Argentina ❓ There is an information/security point inside the building with basic information 📖 Guidebooks to the Pantheon in several languages are available in souvenir shops on Piazza della Rotonda

Above *The Pantheon faces onto Piazza della Rotonda*
Opposite *The central oculus in the dome is the building's only natural source of light*

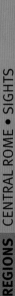

» The Pantheon is often very crowded, especially at the weekend. To make the most of a visit, go on a weekday or early in the morning.

» Relax in one of Piazza della Rotonda's cafés to enjoy the exterior view of the Pantheon and the atmosphere of the lively piazza.

Below *The Pantheon serves as a mausoleum for the members of Italy's short-lived monarchy, as well as other illustrious figures, including Raphael*

THE DOME

The dome, spanning 43.3m (142ft), is the largest ever built before the introduction of reinforced concrete in the 20th century; its diameter is greater than that of the dome of St. Peter's. As seen from outside, it is actually a cheat—a thick skin of brickwork over the smaller structure of the actual cupola inside. This consists of concrete, cast over a temporary framework, the material being thinner and lighter at the base of the dome than at its apex. The cupola represents the sky, while the oculus, the great central opening— the only source of natural light for the building—stands for the sun.

THE TOMBS

Today, the Pantheon acts as the mausoleum of the royalty of Italy, accommodating the tombs of Vittorio Emanuele II, Umberto I and Queen Margherita of Savoy, and of a few notable Italians. In the first chapel on the right, next to the tomb of Vittorio Emanuele II, is a fresco of the Annunciation by Melozzo da Forlì. The third chapel contains the funerary monument by the Norwegian sculptor Thorvaldsen of Cardinal Consalvi (d.1824), and the third niche on the left holds the remains of Raphael (d.1520). Also in the chapel are a sculpture of the Madonna by Raphael's pupil Lorenzetto and an epitaph to Maria Bibbiena, Raphael's betrothed, who died three months before the artist. The tombs of King Umberto I and Queen Margherita of Savoy are beyond, followed by the tomb of the painter and architect Baldassare Peruzzi (1481–1536).

PIAZZA DELLA ROTONDA

The Pantheon faces Piazza della Rotonda, which resembles in shape the arcade thought to have surrounded the ancient Roman temple. The central fountain was designed by Giacomo della Porta in 1575. Pope Clement XI erected a 13th-century BC Egyptian obelisk dedicated to Rameses II at the centre of the basin in 1711. The granite monolith, 6.43m (21ft) tall, stood in the temple dedicated to Isis and Serapis in the nearby area of Campo Marzio before it was moved here.

PIAZZA VENEZIA

This busy traffic junction owes its name to the Palazzo Venezia (▷ 110). Next to it, in fact incorporated in the palace complex, is the church of San Marco (▷ 116). With origins in the fourth century, this venerable basilica has been much altered over the centuries. It is worth a visit for a wonderful ninth-century mosaic in the apse. Between the palace and the church, look for *Madama Lucrezia*, one of the six 'talking statues'.

Dominating the square, however, is the theatrical Monumento a Vittorio Emanuele II (▷ 106), built between 1885 and 1911.
➕ 103 E5 🅜 Colosseo 🚌 44, 46, 84, 715, 780, 781, 810, 916

SANT'AGOSTINO

One of Rome's first Renaissance churches, Sant'Agostino dates from between 1479 and 1483. Although now tucked away, in its day it was at the heart of Roman life, and many great artists, including Raphael and Michelangelo, came here to pray.

Inside, the church retains its original Latin-cross plan, but much of the interior was extravagantly remodelled in the 17th century, and again in the 19th century. Fortunately, the church's artistic masterpieces, including works by Raphael, Caravaggio and other renowned artists, survived the various changes.

To the left of the central portal, near the main door, is the *Madonna del Parto (Madonna of Childbirth)*, a statue by Jacopo Sansovino dating from 1521. The statue is much venerated by pregnant women and childless couples and many votive gifts are still left at its foot.

A fresco of the Prophet Isaiah (1512) by Raphael adorns the third pillar of the nave on the left. It was clearly inspired by Michelangelo's frescoes in the Sistine Chapel, and Michelangelo is known to have been an admirer of the painting. When the Vatican official who commissioned the work complained of the cost, Michelangelo, not one

Above *The extravagant Monumento a Vittorio Emanuele II, built between 1885 and 1911 in honour of the first king of a united Italy, dominates Piazza Venezia*

who readily admitted his rival's genius, told him: 'The knee alone is worth what you paid'.

Below the fresco is a sculpture of *St. Anne and the Virgin Mary with the Christ Child* by Andrea Sansovino. The first chapel on the left contains Caravaggio's magnificent *Madonna di Loreto*.
➕ 102 D4 ✉ Piazza di Sant'Agostino 80, 00186 ☎ 06 6880 1962 🕐 Daily 7.30–12.30, 4–6.30 🖐 Free 🚌 116 to Via Zanardelli; 30, 70, 81, 87, 130, 186, 492, 628 to Corso del Rinascimento

SANT'IGNAZIO DI LOYOLA

St. Ignatius of Loyola, founder of the Jesuit order and of the nearby Roman College, is the dedicatee of this lavishly decorated church, designed by the Jesuit architect Orazio Grassi. The church was completed in 1685 without a cupola, but another Jesuit, the architect and painter Andrea Pozzo, remedied this by painting a superb *trompe l'oeil* dome above the crossing, imitating the lighting and depth of a cupola. Pozzo's work dominates the interior. The corners of the crossing glorify the Jesuits' missionary activities, with paintings showing the Glory of St. Ignatius in each of the four known continents. In the middle of the nave Pozzo used the same technique to give a three-dimensional effect to the figures in the fresco of St. Ignatius bathed in divine light. Stand on the disc in the centre of the nave and then move towards the transept to get the best view.
➕ 103 E5 ✉ Piazza di Sant'Ignazio 8, 00186 ☎ 06 679 4406 🕐 Daily 7.30–12.20, 3–7.20. Closed to visitors during Sun morning Mass 🖐 Free 🚌 116 to Via del Seminario; 30, 40, 46, 62, 63, 64, 70, 81, 492, 628, 630, 780, 787, 916 to Largo di Torre Argentina

SANT'IVO ALLA SAPIENZA

This domed church is one of Francesco Borromini's masterpieces. Built in the grounds of the Palazzo alla Sapienza (Palace of Wisdom), it is worth visiting for its extraordinary spiral dome surmounted by a crown of flames. It is dedicated to St. Ives, patron saint of lawyers, who gave his services free to the poor.

The facade is baroque, and has two rows of arches running along the side walls. The hexagonal plan suggests a honeycomb, an allusion to the Barberini bee emblem (Barberini Pope Urban VIII gave Borromini the commission).

The culmination is the extravagant dome with its spiral crown, possibly inspired by the architect's collection of shells.

✠ 102 D5 ✉ Corso del Rinascimento 40, 00186 ☎ 06 361 2562 🕐 Sun 9–12 ✋ Free 🚍 23, 30, 40, 46, 62, 64, 70, 81, 87, 116, 280, 492, 628, 916; tram 8 to Largo di Torre Argentina

SAN LUIGI DEI FRANCESI

San Luigi dei Francesi, the national church of the French in Rome, is essential viewing for lovers of Caravaggio's work—the church contains no less than three canvases by him.

The church was begun in 1518 by Cardinal Giulio de' Medici, the future Pope Clement VII, and completed in 1589 by Domenico Fontana, with money from France provided by Henri II, Henri III and Catherine de' Médici. On the facade, by Giacomo della Porta, is the salamander emblem of François I. The French theme continues with statues of Charlemagne and St. Louis in the lower part of the facade, and St. Clotilde and St. Joan of Valois in the upper part.

The church received much embellishment in the baroque period, with marble, paintings, gilding and stucco. There are frescoes by Domenichino in the chapel of St. Cecilia, but the church's principal draw—the Caravaggio paintings—are in St. Matthew's chapel. They are dramatic depictions of three episodes from the saint's life: *St. Matthew and the Angel*, *The Calling of St. Matthew* and *The Martyrdom of St. Matthew*.

✠ 102 D5 ✉ Piazza San Luigi dei Francesi 5, 00186 ☎ 06 688 271 🕐 Fri–Wed 10–12.30, 4–7, Thu 10–12.30 ✋ Free 🚍 23, 30, 40, 46, 62, 64, 70, 81, 87, 116, 280, 492, 628, 916; tram 8 to Largo di Torre Argentina

SAN MARCO

San Marco is well worth visiting for its ninth-century mosaic. It was founded by Pope Mark in AD336, and is dedicated to St. Mark the Evangelist, who is believed to have written his gospel in Rome.

Pope Gregory IV rebuilt the church in the ninth century, and the crypt, which contains the relics of the Persian saints Abdon and Senna, dates from the same period. Inside the porch, look for the 16th-century funerary plaque of Vanozza Catanei, who was the mistress of Pope Alexander VI and mother of Cesare and Lucrezia Borgia. The elegant Renaissance facade is attributed to Leon Battista Alberti, who reused materials from the Colosseo and the Theatre of Marcellus.

The interior of the church is a mixture of styles. In the 15th century, a coffered ceiling showing the coat of arms of Pope Paul II was added, and there were baroque additions in the 18th century. The real gem is the ninth-century mosaic in the apse, which shows Christ, his hand raised in blessing, surrounded by saints. Pope Mark (or St. Gregory) holds a model of the church.

✠ 103 E5 ✉ Piazza di San Marco 48, 00186 ☎ 06 679 5205 🕐 Tue–Sat 7.30–12.30, 4–7, Sun 7.30–12.30, 4–7.30, Mon 4–7 ✋ Free 🚇 Colosseo 🚍 44, 46, 84, 715, 716, 780, 781, 810, 916 to Piazza Venezia

Below right The spiral dome of Sant'Ivo alla Sapienza, a masterpiece by Borromini
Below San Marco's ninth-century apse mosaic depicting Jesus surrounded by the saints

SANTA MARIA SOPRA MINERVA

Behind its Renaissance facade, Santa Maria sopra Minerva is a rarity in being Rome's only Gothic church (although much restored in the 19th century). Some of the most prominent Italian families called upon the finest artists of their time to embellish their chapels, so there is plenty of interest inside.

THE TEMPLE OF MINERVA

The first church was built in the eighth or ninth century on top of *(sopra)* a temple of the pagan goddess Minerva. In 1280, two Dominican friars, Sisto and Ristoro, began reconstructing the church in Gothic style, apparently on the model of Santa Maria Novella in Florence, of which they were also the architects. In the 16th and 17th centuries, the interior was redecorated in baroque style, and in the 1840s, restorers indulged their taste for the Gothic style.

THE CHURCH'S INTERIOR

The interior, divided into a nave and two aisles, has chapels on either side. In the right transept is the splendid Cappella Carafa, built and decorated by order of Cardinal Carafa in honour of the philosopher-saint Thomas Aquinas (1224–74). Filippino Lippi frescoed the walls of this chapel in the 1480s with scenes from the life of St. Thomas Aquinas and a beautiful *Assumption of the Virgin*. The tomb of Pope Paul IV (d.1559) is also here.

Near the high altar in the choir is a statue of the *Risen Christ with the Cross* by Michelangelo. The remains of St. Catherine of Siena, one of the patron saints of Italy, lie under the altar. In the apse are the tombs of the Medici popes Leo X and Clement VII, the work of Antonio Sangallo the Younger.

BERNINI'S ELEPHANT

Outside, in Piazza della Minerva, stands one of Rome's best-loved oddities: a sixth-century BC Egyptian obelisk, supported on the back of a marble elephant. The work was designed by Bernini and sculpted by his pupil Ercole Ferrata in 1667. The inscription on the statue's base, by Pope Alexander VII, reads: 'A strong mind is necessary to support solid wisdom'—meaning that the obelisk represents the wisdom that grows from, and is supported by, the strong mind of the elephant.

INFORMATION

www.basilicaminerva.it

✚ 103 E5 ✉ Piazza della Minerva 42, 00186 ☎ 06 679 3926 🕐 Mon–Sat 7.10–7, Sun 8–12, 2–7. Closed to visitors during Mass ✋ Free 🚌 116 to Via della Palombella; 30, 40, 46, 62, 63, 64, 70, 81, 492, 628, 630, 780, 787, 916 or tram 8 to Largo di Torre Argentina 📖 Guide published by the Dominican friars in English, French, German, Spanish, Italian €5 📖 Religious books on church history and on the basilica's artworks sold by the Dominican friars. Ask at sacristy for information

TIPS

» Use the lighting system (€1) to get a better look at the chapel frescoes, as the church is very dark.

» Look for the plaques and inscriptions on the central portal. They show the flood levels reached by the Tiber before the river embankments were built up in the 19th century.

Above *Soaring Gothic arches and gilding characterize the interior of the church*

AROUND PIAZZA NAVONA

Leading from Piazza Navona to Piazza di Spagna and back, via the Fontana di Trevi, this walk takes in some of Rome's best-known sights, including the Spanish Steps and Trevi Fountain.

THE WALK
Distance: 2.5km (1.5 miles)
Allow: 3 hours
Start at: Piazza Navona
End at: Piazza Navona

HOW TO GET THERE
Take a bus to Piazza Navona:
Nos. 23, 46, 64, 87, 119 and others
all pass nearby.

★ Leave Piazza Navona from the
northern end (near the Fontana del
Nettuno). From Via Agonale, turn
right onto Piazza Sant'Agostino.
On your left is the church of
Sant'Agostino (▷ 115).

❶ Sant'Agostino is known for its
works of art, including Caravaggio's
Madonna di Loreto (or *Madonna of
the Pilgrims*, 1605) in the first chapel
off the left aisle. The painting's
realism caused a scandal when it
was first unveiled—the Virgin was
depicted with dirty feet and some
pilgrims shown as old and sick.

Cross the piazza and bear left
on Via della Scrofa, which becomes
Via di Ripettai. Turn right onto Via
Tomacelli and then bear left onto
Piazza Augusto Imperatore. Cross
the piazza, then turn right onto
Via dei Pontefici. At the end of the
street is the Accademia Nazionale
di Santa Cecilia (▷ 87).

❷ L'Accademia Nazionale di
Santa Cecilia is the national school
of music, founded in 1585. Its
orchestra has performed more than
14,000 concerts.

Turn right onto Via del Corso, a busy
street lined with shops. A short way
along the street, turn left onto Via
della Croce, renowned for its food
shops and cafés; at No. 76 is Antica
Enoteca, an old wine bar. Follow
the road until it opens out into lively
Piazza di Spagna (▷ 74–75).

❸ One of Rome's focal piazzas,
Piazza di Spagna is the site of the

city's most beautiful stairway, the
Scalinata della Trinità dei Monti
(Spanish Steps), and the French
church Trinità dei Monti.

Turn right to reach the bottom of
the Spanish Steps. With your back
to the steps, cross the piazza onto
Via Condotti, one of Rome's most
exclusive shopping streets. Bear left
onto Via Belsiana just before you
reach Via del Corso again. Continue
as far as Piazza San Silvestro,
crossing Via Frattina and Via della
Vite, and go diagonally across the
square to turn down a little street
called Via del Pozzetto. Take the first
right, Via Poli, which crosses Via del
Tritone and takes you to Piazza di
Trevi and the theatrical Fontana di
Trevi (▷ 62).

❹ Nicola Salvi's baroque
masterpiece is Rome's most
spectacular and popular fountain,
immortalized in Fellini's film,
La Dolce Vita. Opposite the Trevi

Opposite Fontana del Nettuno, at the northern end of Piazza Navona

Fountain is the church of Santi Vincenzo e Anastasio, notable for its grisly relics: Between 1590 and 1903, the hearts and lungs of 22 popes, preserved in urns, were interred in the crypt.

Facing the Trevi Fountain, take the traffic-free street to the left, Via delle Muratte, which leads back to Via del Corso. Turn right onto the Corso, towards Piazza Colonna, named after Marcus Aurelius' column, which stands in the middle of the square. Erected between AD180 and AD193, the monument illustrates victorious episodes in the Emperor's war campaigns. With your back to the Corso, take Via dei Bergamaschi, the narrow street in the far left-hand corner of the piazza, which leads to Piazza di Pietra.

5 On the right-hand side of the Piazza di Pietra, you can see the last remaining columns of Hadrian's temple, now incorporated into the 17th-century Borsa, the stock exchange. These imposing 15m (50ft) columns formed part of a temple built and dedicated to the Emperor Hadrian in AD145 by his successor Antoninus Pius.

Continue along Via de' Burro to reach the rococo Piazza di Sant'Ignazio, with its beautiful 17th-century church.

6 Step inside Sant'Ignazio di Loyola (▷ 115) to admire the magnificent *trompe l'oeil* dome painted by the Jesuit architect and artist Andrea Pozzo.

Walk down Via di Sant'Ignazio—the Jesuit Collegio Romano is on your left—until you emerge onto Piazza del Collegio Romano. Turn right onto Via Piè di Marmo, which leads to Piazza della Minerva and the church of Santa Maria sopra Minerva (▷ 117).

7 Bernini's delightful statue of an elephant stands outside the church. On the right-hand side of its facade are several plaques showing the water levels when the Tiber flooded between 1598 and 1870.

With the church on your right, continue down Via della Minerva to Piazza della Rotonda and the Pantheon (▷ 112–114).

8 The best-preserved of Rome's ancient monuments, the Pantheon is a magnificent feat of Roman engineering.

Facing the Pantheon, take Via della Rotonda, the road that runs up the right-hand side of the building, then take the first right, Via della Palombella, which leads onto Piazza di Sant'Eustachio. Here you will find Sant'Eustachio il Caffè where, some say, they serve the best coffee in Rome (▷ 131). Leave the square on the opposite side, down Via dei Staderari. This takes you along the side of the church of Sant'Ivo alla Sapienza (entrance on Corso del Rinascimento; ▷ 116).

9 Sant'Ivo alla Sapienza, a masterpiece by Francesco Borromini, is crowned by a spectacular spiral dome.

Via dei Sediari, opposite the church's entrance, will take you back to Piazza Navona.

WHEN TO GO
Any time is fine, but remember that many churches are closed in the afternoon and during Mass.

WHERE TO EAT
ANTICA ENOTECA
Order wine by the bottle or by the glass in this traditional wine bar. There is a restaurant at the rear. ✉ Via della Croce 76b, 00187 ☎ 06 679 0896 🕐 Daily 11am–1am; restaurant daily 12.30–12

PLACE TO VISIT
SANTI VINCENZO E ANASTASIO
✉ Vicolo dei Modelli 73, 00187 ☎ 06 678 3098 🕐 Daily 7.30–12, 4–7 🎫 Free

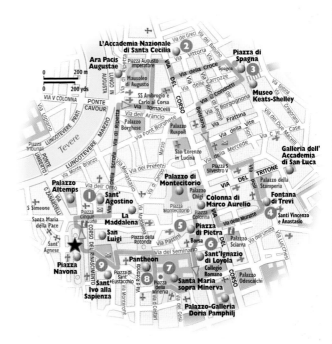

SHOPPING

AI MONASTERI
www.monasteri.it
This late 19th-century pharmacy has a fascinating array of edible goods (chocolate, honeys and jams) and cosmetics made in monasteries throughout Italy to traditional recipes. For ladies of a certain age, there's *olio alla trigonella* (fenugreek oil) to firm up the bust and smooth neck wrinkles.
✚ 134 D5 ✉ Corso del Rinascimento 72, 00186 ☎ 06 6880 2783 🕒 Fri–Wed 9–1, 4.30–7.30, Thu 9–1. Closed 1 week in Sep 🚌 40, 64, 116, 492, 571, or any bus that goes along Corso Vittorio Emanuele II, or 30, 70, 81, 87, 186, 628 to Corso del Rinascimento

AL SOGNO
www.alsogno.com
This shop will enthral adults and children alike. It's packed with beautifully made toy animals, from miniature to life size, exquisite Italian handmade dolls and wooden Pinocchios, Venetian masks and handcrafted chess sets.
✚ 134 D5 ✉ Piazza Navona 53, 00186 ☎ 06 686 4198 🕒 Daily 10–8 🚌 64, 87, 116, 492

ANTICA LIBRERIA CROCE
www.libreriacroce.it
This primarily Italian bookshop, with some titles in English, specializes in books on all aspects of classical and contemporary art and photography. It has an extensive selection over two floors, and from time to time art exhibitions are held here.
✚ 134 D5 ✉ Corso Vittorio Emanuele II 156, 00186 ☎ 06 6880 2269 🕒 Mon–Fri 9.30–8, Sat–Sun 10–8 🚌 40, 62, 64, 116

AUREA AETAS VALLICELLA
Under the arch in a side street off Corso Vittorio Emanuele II are two linked shops, the workshops of three master goldsmiths. Pieces are designed to your own specifications, or you can choose an existing design from the catalogue. Items are usually good value for money, with prices starting at around €80. Orders can be made by email, and worldwide shipping is possible. Staff speak English. Note that credit cards are not accepted in the shop.
✚ 134 D5 ✉ Arco della Chiesa Nuova 8, 00186 ☎ 06 686 1840 🕒 Mon–Sat 9–4 🚌 40, 62, 64

BARTOLUCCI
www.bartolucci.com
Not far from the Pantheon is this master craftsman's workshop. All the wooden articles, including marionettes, toy horses, children's furniture and animal-shaped clocks with moving eyes, are handmade, the result of the most skilled and patient work. Prices start at just a few euros.
✚ 135 E5 ✉ Via dei Pastini 98, 00186 ☎ 06 6919 0894 🕒 Daily 9.30am–10.30pm 🚌 116

CAMPO DEI FIORI
This 'field of flowers' (▷ 105) hosts Rome's liveliest produce market. Traders hawk displays of vegetables, seafood, meat, household goods and flowers. Order small items by the *etto* (100g/4oz). An art fair is held on Sundays. Credit cards are not accepted.
✚ 134 D5 ✉ Campo dei Fiori, 00186 🕒 Mon–Sat am 🚌 46, 62, 64, 87, 116, 492

CAPPELLERIA TRONCARELLI
www.troncarelli.it
This family-run hat shop close to Piazza Navona, catering

predominantly to men, is a pleasant throwback to a bygone age. Every conceivable hat is here, from panamas and Florentine straw hats to trilbies and flat caps, all handcrafted and to suit every occasion. Prices range from €50 to €180.

➕ 134 D5 ✉ Via della Cuccagna 15, 00186 ☎ 06 687 9320 🕓 Tue–Sat 10–1.30, 3–7.30, Mon 3–7.30 🚌 46, 62, 64, 70, 87, 116, 492

CENTRO RAKU

www.raku.it

Here, in one of the most beautiful areas of Rome, near the Pantheon, are hundreds of handmade raku clocks (from €25 to €100). The raku ceramic technique of glazed earthenware originated in 16th-century Japan, where it is mainly reserved for the tea ceremony. Raku means 'to celebrate the day', or 'to live in harmony'.

➕ 135 E5 ✉ Via dei Pastini 20, 00186 ☎ 06 678 7682 🕓 Daily 10.30–8.30 🚌 116

LA CITTÀ DEL SOLE

www.cittadelsole.com

This toy store, between Piazza Navona and the Pantheon, is crammed with educational toys, puzzles, games and books. It is divided into sections for children aged 0–14, with a focus on creative playing and learning. All the best toys are in safe plastics and wood.

➕ 134 D5 ✉ Via della Scrofa 65, 00186 ☎ 06 6880 3805 🕓 Tue–Sat 10–7.30, Sun 11–7.30, Mon 3.30–7.30 🚌 116

COMICS BAZAR

This veritable Aladdin's cave specializes in early 20th-century Viennese Thonet lamps, and furniture dating from the 1800s to the 1920s. One of two entrances is just beyond Via Sforza Cesarini, on your left going towards Campo dei Fiori, while the other is a little farther down.

➕ 134 C5 ✉ Via dei Banchi Vecchi 127–128, 00186 ☎ 06 6880 2923 🕓 Tue–Sat 9.30–7.30, Mon 2.30–7.30 🚌 46, 62, 64, 116, 492, 571, or any bus to Corso Vittorio Emanuele II

D CUBE

www.dcubedesign.it

D Cube is packed with design objects from around the world, each labelled with its country of provenance. The range includes everything from tableware, kitchenware, candles and bags to quirkier items such as ecological radios, either clockwork or powered by solar energy. What's on offer is very original, with something for every budget.

➕ 134 D5 ✉ Via della Pace 38, 00186 ☎ 06 686 1218 🕓 Daily 11–9 🚌 40, 64, 116, 492, 571, or any bus to Corso Vittorio Emanuele II

DITTA POGGI

www.poggi1825.it

Whether the marvellous paintings in Rome's galleries and churches have inspired you to take up a paintbrush, or if you're simply an artist with an eye for a beautiful shop, then visit Ditta Poggi, a glorious old-fashioned store on a corner just east of Santa Maria sopra Minerva selling paints, papers, card, pens and a wealth of other artists' materials. It has been in business since 1825.

➕ 135 E5 ✉ Via del Gesù 74–75, 00186 ☎ 06 679 3674 🕓 Mon–Sat 9–1, 4–7.30. Closed for a period in Aug Ⓜ Colosseo 🚌 116 or 40, 46, 64 and other services to Largo di Torre Argentina

FABINDIA

www.fabindia.it

Facing the Ponte Sant'Angelo is this delightful emporium selling Indian fabrics, scarves and garments, all hand-woven and made in Indian villages. The company is devoted to developing fair and equitable relationships with the producers. The style is both traditional and more contemporary. The store also stocks bags, pillows and photograph albums, made with, or covered in, Indian cottons and silks.

➕ 134 C5 ✉ Via del Banco di Santo Spirito 40, 00186 ☎ 06 6889 1230 🕓 Mon–Sat 10–1.30, 3–7.30 🚌 40, 64, 116, 492, 571, or any bus to Corso Vittorio Emanuele II

Below Whatever you collect, the city's wide range of stores is unlikely to disappoint

FELTRINELLI LIBRI E MUSICA
www.lafeltrinelli.it
This attractively designed music store is in a building that once housed the Verdi archives. It has the largest classical DVD/CD collection in Rome, plus an extensive selection of Italian music, sheet music and musical instruments. Other outlets are at Termini, Viale Guilio Cesare, Galleria Colonna and Via del Corso.
✚ 135 D5 ✉ Largo di Torre Argentina 11, 00186 ☎ 06 6866 3001 ✪ Mon–Fri 9–9, Sat 9am–10pm, Sun 10–9 🚌 40, 62, 64, 117 to Piazza Venezia

IL FORNO DI CAMPO DE' FIORI
This tiny bakery has been on the Campo dei Fiori since 1850 and is always packed. There is no discernible order in which people are served, but hang in there—all is forgiven with one bite of their *pizza bianca*, fresh from the oven, with a hint of rosemary, olive oil and sea salt, served as bread. Home-made biscuits and cakes are also on offer. Credit cards are not accepted.
✚ 134 D5 ✉ Campo dei Fiori 22/22a, 00186 ☎ 06 6880 6662 ✪ Jul–Aug Mon–Fri 7.30–2.30, 4.45–8, Sat 7.30–2.30; Sep–Jun Mon–Sat 7.30–2.30, 4.45–8 🚌 46, 64, 116

MAGA MORGANA
Two shops on Via del Governo Vecchio sell clothes by designer Luciana Iannace. The shop at No. 27 has mostly hand-knitted jumpers, skirts and dresses. At No. 98 (on the other side of the road), delve into designs for the evening or for special occasions, even weddings. Prices are high, but you can still pick up a bargain.
✚ 134 D5 ✉ Via del Governo Vecchio 27 and 98, 00186 ☎ 06 687 9995 ✪ Tue–Sat 10–8, Mon 4–7. Occasional Sun opening 🚌 40, 64, 116, 492, 571, or any bus to Corso Vittorio Emanuele II

MARIA GRAZIA LUFFARELLI
www.mgluffarelli.com
Prices for Luffarelli's bright watercolour landscapes of hills, sea and sun range from very low to moderate for original works.

Also on sale is a beautiful range of Rome watercolour reproductions in postcard format, as well as prints of Luffarelli's work mounted on brightly painted tables.
✚ 134 C5 ✉ Via dei Banchi Vecchi 29, 00186 ☎ 06 683 2494 ✪ Mon–Fri 11–8, Sat 10–8 🚌 40, 64, 116, 492, 571, or any bus to Corso Vittorio Emanuele II

MONDELLO OTTICA
www.mondelloottica.it
Eyewear with a difference: This minimalist boutique has regular installations by local artists. Prices may be higher than average, but the glasses are superlative in quality and sheer chic. All have that little extra something special that makes the price worth paying. The owners provide friendly service.
✚ 134 D5 ✉ Via del Pellegrino 97–98, 00186 ☎ 06 686 1955 ✪ Tue–Sat 10–1, 4–7.30 🚌 46, 62, 64, 116, 492, 571, or any bus to Corso Vittorio Emanuele II

NATOLLI
Natolli is on a street parallel with Piazza Navona and sells exquisitely crafted Murano glass, with items ranging from chandeliers to mirrors, glasses and even sculptures. All items are sold with a certificate of authenticity and signed in limited editions. Up the road, at No. 43, is another shop selling smaller items. Shipping is possible worldwide.
✚ 134 D5 ✉ Corso del Rinascimento 55, 00186 ☎ 06 6830 1170 ✪ No. 55: daily 10–1, 2–7.30. No. 43: Mon–Sat 10–8, Sun 10–7 🚌 64, 87, 116, 492

OFFICINA PROFUMO—FARMACEUTICA DI SANTA MARIA NOVELLA
www.smnovella.com
This elegant branch of the pharmacy in Florence's Via della Scala, founded in 1612, sells creams, soaps and perfumes from original recipes by Dominican friars. Some of the recipes go back to medieval times. Their signature and extremely fragrant pot-pourri is made with herbs from the Florentine hills.
✚ 134 D5 ✉ Corso del Rinascimento 47, 00186 ☎ 06 687 9608 ✪ Mon–Sat

10–1.30, 2–7.30 🚌 40, 64, 116, 492, 571 to Corso Vittorio Emanuele II, or 30, 70, 81, 87, 186, 628 to Corso del Rinascimento

PIAZZA DELLE COPPELLE
This tiny but very scenic food market wedged in among the cars and tourists just north of the Pantheon makes a welcome respite from a tiring morning's sightseeing. There are fresh flowers as well as food to tempt you. Credit cards are not accepted.
✚ 134 D5 ✉ Piazza delle Coppelle ✪ Mon–Sat 7–1 🚌 23, 30, 75, 280, 716 or buses to Via Marmorata; tram 3

RACHELE
Tucked down a side alley close to Campo dei Fiori, this delightful shop sells kids' clothes, from classic and retro to the latest fashions. All are handmade by the Swedish owner in high-quality cottons and wools. Stock items are for children up to age 6; special orders up to age 12. There is a good line of amusing accessories, including a range of hats inspired by animals and fruits.
✚ 134 D5 ✉ Vicolo del Bollo 6–7, 00186 ☎ 06 686 4975 ✪ Sep–Jul Tue–Sat 10.30–2, 3.30–7.30 🚌 46, 62, 64, 116, 492, 571, or any bus to Corso Vittorio Emanuele II

SPAZIO SETTE
Housed in a 17th-century cardinal's palace, this is one of the few stores in Rome that will make even the most hardened shopper salivate over must-have furnishings for the kitchen, living room and bathroom. The range includes vases, lamps and various other ornaments from the biggest names in Italian and international design.
✚ 134 D5 ✉ Via dei Barbieri 7, 00186 ☎ 06 686 9708 ✪ Tue–Sat 9.30–1, 3.30–7.30, Mon 3.30–7.30 🚌 30, 40, 46, 62, 64, 81, 87, 186, 492, 628, 916; tram 8 to terminus

LE TRE GHINEE
www.letreghinee.com
A mother and daughter team design jewellery and *objets d'art* using Tiffany glass and pottery techniques. The mother deals in

glass and the daughter is a pottery wizard. Items range from expensive vases to very reasonable cups and goblets. Pottery Nativity scenes are on sale at Christmas. Evening classes are offered.

🚩 134 D5 ✉ Via del Pellegrino 90, 00186 ☎ 06 687 2739 🕐 Tue, Thu–Sat 10–8, Mon 11–8, Wed 10–7 🚌 46, 62, 64, 116, 492, 571, or any bus to Corso Vittorio Emanuele II

TREPPIEDI

Two minutes from Piazza Navona, this quaintly old-fashioned shop has been famous for years in Rome for its women's lingerie and made-to-measure swimwear. Prices are high but so is the quality. Large sizes are kept in stock.

🚩 134 D5 ✉ Via del Teatro Valle 55d, 00186 ☎ 06 6880 6268 🕐 Tue–Sat 9.30–1, 4–7.30. Closed Sat 4–7.30 summer; Mon 9.30–1 winter 🚌 40, 62, 64, 116

VOLPETTI

www.volpetti.com

Prices at this delicatessen (related to the more famous branch in Testaccio) may be high, but quality is higher. Delicacies include truffles, cheese, home-made salamis and pâtés, and a good selection of wine. Try their delicious sliced *porchetta* (roast suckling pig).

🚩 134 D4 ✉ Via della Scrofa 21/32, 00186 ☎ 06 6880 6335 🕐 Mon–Sat 9–8.30 🚌 62, 64, 87, 116, 492 to Piazza Navona

YAKY

www.yaky.it

Real collectors' items can be found in this treasure trove of beautifully handmade Chinese furniture and household items of the finest quality. Dark polished wooden objects contrast with bright, shimmering silks and polished lamps, creating a rich interior. Willing, friendly staff are there to help you make your choice and arrange shipping worldwide.

🚩 135 D6 ✉ Via S. Maria del Pianto 55, 00186 ☎ 06 6880 7724 🕐 Sun–Fri 10–2, 3.30–7.30, Sat 10–7.30 🚇 Spagna 🚌 63, 271, 630

Above *Cheeses are among the delicacies sold at the renowned delicatessen Volpetti*

ENTERTAINMENT AND NIGHTLIFE

ANIMA

Anima lies close to the heart of the nightlife district, west of Piazza Navona, and is a small but humming spot distinguished by its gloriously over-the-top baroque decor. Drinks prices are reasonable for central Rome, and the eclectic music policy keeps the many customers—visitors and locals alike—glued to the dance floor.

🚩 134 D5 ✉ Via Santa Maria dell'Anima 57, 00186 ☎ 347 850 9256 🕐 Daily 6pm–3 or 4am 👋 Free 🚌 46, 62, 64 and other services to Corso Vittorio Emanuele II

ANTICA BIRRERIA

www.anticabirreriaperoni.com

German beer is served in large steins at this art nouveau beer hall close to Piazza Venezia. It's an inexpensive place, brimming with alcohol-fuelled cheer.

🚩 135 E5 ✉ Via di San Marcello 19, 00187 ☎ 06 679 5310 🕐 Mon–Sat 12–12 👋 Free 🚌 40, 46, 62, 64, 916

ASSOCIAZIONE MUSICALE ROMANA ALL'ORTO BOTANICO

Rome's botanical gardens provide a much-loved venue for music events, mainly hosted by the Roman Music Association. Concerts range from Gershwin to Classical, and there is even a harpsichord festival.

🚩 134 C5 ✉ Via dei Banchi Vecchi 61, 00186. Botanical gardens: Largo Cristina di Svezia 23b, 00186 ☎ 06 686 8441 🕐 Box office open 1 hour before concert, no advance tickets. Season: Mar–Sep 👋 €10–€25 🚌 H, 630, 780

BARTARUGA

www.bartaruga.com

This retro kitsch venue has it all: a grand piano, Murano crystal, comfortable sofas and subdued lighting. In summer, it spills out onto Piazza Mattei, one of the most beautiful little piazzas in Rome. It also hosts occasional live music and cabaret nights. Credit cards are not accepted.

🚩 135 D5 ✉ Piazza Mattei 7, 00186 ☎ 06 689 2299 🕐 Mon–Sat 6pm–3am 👋 Free 🚇 Largo di Torre Argentina

BLOOM

Enjoy sushi upstairs and cool sounds in a futuristic setting downstairs. Bloom is the trendiest of the Roman *fashionista* hang-outs, so you may well have trouble getting in—but it's worth a go.

🚩 134 D5 ✉ Via del Teatro Pace 29–30, 00186 ☎ 06 6880 2029 🕐 Sep–Jun Mon–Tue, Thu–Sat 7pm–3am 👋 Free 🚌 30, 40, 46, 62, 64, 87, 116, 916

IL CENTRALE

www.centraleristotheatre.it

Il Centrale is a *ristotheatre*, taking its name from the fact that it is in a former theatre from the 1920s. It has a bar with a DJ, a lounge area and a restaurant where you can eat while watching a live cabaret or music show. *Aperitivo* time is 7–10pm, and for €18 you can have a drink and all you can eat from a buffet of pasta salads.

✚ 135 E5 ✉ Via Celsa 6, 00186 ☎ 06 678 0501 🕐 Mon–Fri, Sun 7pm–midnight, Sat 7pm–2am 🍽 From €8 🚍 30, 40, 46, 64 or any bus to Piazza Venezia or Largo di Torre Argentina

ESCOPAZZO

www.escopazzo.it

This wine and cocktail bar, very near Piazza Venezia, is an intimate place perfect for a romantic soirée. The music is live most days, the atmosphere relaxed and relaxing. Credit cards are not accepted.

✚ 135 E5 ✉ Via d'Aracoeli 41, 00186 ☎ 389 683 5618 🕐 Tue–Sun 9pm–5am 🍽 Free 🚍 40, 64, 170, 175 to Piazza Venezia

HABANA CAFÉ

www.habanaroma.it

There is a real buzz at this small, chaotic cocktail bar with live music. And some potentially mind-blowing combinations—their mojito has to be tried to be believed. This is the place to be if you like to be in the thick of it. Snacks are served.

✚ 135 E5 ✉ Via dei Pastini 120, 00186 ☎ 06 678 1983 🕐 Tue–Sun 9.30pm–3am 🚍 62, 64, 70, 81, 571; tram 8

JONATHAN'S ANGELS

This popular haunt is a must for both casual visitors and hardened night-owls. The music is cheesy (bad Italian or French retro), which matches the quirky decoration. Credit cards are not accepted.

✚ 134 D5 ✉ Via della Fossa 16, 00186 ☎ 06 689 3426 🕐 Daily 8pm–2.30am 🍽 Free 🚍 46, 62, 64, 492 to Corso Vittorio Emanuele II (ask for Campo dei Fiori); 116 to Campo dei Fiori

Above *Unwind with the gentle sounds of chamber music at the Oratorio il Gonfalone*

MAD JACK'S

This Irish pub will suit those looking for a festive place in which to pass the night hours. The music is loud and drinks are flowing.

✚ 134 D5 ✉ Via Arenula 20, 00186 ☎ 06 6880 8223 🕐 Daily 10am–2am 🍽 Free 🚍 40, 64 to Largo di Torre Argentina; tram 8

LA MAISON

www.lamaisonroma.it

Mingle with TV and film stars at this fashionable venue. The interior is opulent and the music is varied.

✚ 134 D5 ✉ Vicolo dei Granari 4, 00186 ☎ 06 683 3312 🕐 Oct–May Wed–Sat 11pm–4am 🍽 €10–€15 🚍 40, 46, 62, 64 to Corso Vittorio Emanuele II, or 30, 70, 81, 204, 628 to Corso del Rinascimento

ORATORIO IL GONFALONE

Specializing in chamber music, Il Gonfalone hosts excellent groups from around the world. Events are held in the 16th-century Oratorio del Gonfalone, complete with frescoes and a gilded ceiling.

✚ 134 C5 ✉ Via del Gonfalone 32a, 00186. Box office: Vicolo della Scimmia 1b, 00186 ☎ 06 687 5952 🕐 Oct–May Mon– Fri 9.30–4 🍽 From €10 🚍 116, or 46, 62, 64, 87, 492 to Campo dei Fiori, then walk

RIALTO SANTAMBROGIO

www.rialto.roma.it

This *centro sociale*, or semi-formal squat, in the Ghetto district organizes inexpensive concerts, art exhibitions, cutting-edge DJs and other cultural events. Some *centri sociali* disappear quickly, so check the latest listings before hunting out this venue.

✚ 135 E6 ✉ Via Sant'Ambrogio 4, 00186 ☎ 06 6813 3640 🕐 Sep–Jul hours and days vary 🍽 Free or up to €5 🚍 All services to Piazza Venezia then a short walk; 8, 40, 64, 70 to Lungotevere dei Cenci

SALOTTO 42

www.salotto42.it

Salotto 42, two minutes' walk east of the Pantheon, is often a quieter choice than its competitors in and around Piazza Navona. It has a contemporary interior, friendly staff and innovative cocktails.

✚ 135 E5 ✉ Piazza di Pietra 42, 00186 ☎ 06 678 5804 🕐 Tue–Sat 10am–2am,

Sun 10am–midnight  Spagna 52, 53, 61, 85, 117 and all services to Via del Corso

SANTA MARIA DELLA PACE
Piano recitals and ensembles take place in the church in summer. Stop at the adjacent Bar della Pace for a post-concert espresso.
134 D5 Box office: Chiostro del Bramante, Vicolo della Pace 2 06 780 7695 Aug €11–€15 46, 62, 64, 87, 116, 492 to Piazza Navona

LA TAVERNA DEL CAMPO
This tavern is always full and has reasonably priced food and loud music, with tables on the piazza.
134 D5 Campo dei Fiori 16, 00186 06 687 4402 Tue–Sun 7.30am–2am Free 46, 62, 64, 87, 116, 492

TEATRO ELISEO
www.teatroeliseo.it
Large, modern and popular, the Eliseo puts on plays by major and established Italian and international playwrights. The smaller Piccolo Eliseo next door pays more attention to contemporary and fringe theatre.
135 F5 Via Nazionale 183, 00184 06 488 2114; 06 488 721 Theatre: Sep–May. Box office: Mon–Sat 9.30–2.30, 3.30–7. Closed Aug, and Sat in Jun–Jul €15–€45 40, 64, 70, 71, 170

TEATRO DI ROMA–ARGENTINA
www.teatrodiroma.net
This is one of Rome's most historic theatres and a leading venue for beautifully staged productions.

A performance here is a night out and the audience dresses up accordingly.
135 D5 Largo di Torre Argentina 52, 00186 06 684 0001 Box office: Mon–Sat 10–2, 3–7 €15–€35 64, 87, 492 to Largo di Torre Argentina; tram 8

TEATRO ROSSINI
www.palazzosantachiara.it
Performances at Teatro Rossini are dedicated to comedy, local dialect and the characters of popular and traditional Roman theatre.
135 E5 Piazza Santa Chiara 14, 00186 06 687 5579 Box office: daily 10–8 €15–€18 64, 87, 492 to Largo di Torre Argentina; tram 8

TEATRO VALLE
www.teatrovalle.it
This is a charming little theatre with excellent dramatic performances, including the classics, all produced with great attention to detail, which also makes it popular with students.
134 D5 Via del Teatro Valle 21a, 00186 06 6880 3794 Tue–Sat 10–7 €16–€30 Barberini 64, 87, 492 to Largo di Torre Argentina, or any bus to Corso Vittorio Emanuele II; tram 8

TRINITY COLLEGE
www.trinity-rome.com
This Gothic-looking building houses one of Rome's most reliable Irish pubs, in the affluent area between the Pantheon and Via del Corso.
135 E5 Via del Collegio Romano 6, 00186 06 678 6472 Daily noon–3am Free 62, 63, 81, 85, 95, 117, 119, 175

IL VINAIETTO DI MARIO E GIANCARLO
Just off the crowded and expensive Campo dei Fiori, Il Vinaietto has somewhat flexible opening hours, but some of the best prices for a good glass of wine in the city. Credit cards are not accepted.
134 D5 Via Monte della Farina 38, 00186 06 6880 6989 Mon–Sat 10–2, 5–9.30 Free 40, 46, 62, 64, 492, 630; tram 8

SPORTS AND ACTIVITIES
CLIMBING THE MONUMENTO A VITTORIO EMANUELE II
Mussolini built the much-ridiculed monument to Vittorio Emanuele II (▷ 106), the vast marble edifice dominating the area around Piazza Venezia. It is well worth climbing to the top of the monument for the superb views of the Fori Imperiali.
135 E5 Piazza Venezia, 00187 06 699 1718 Daily 9–4.30 Free Colosseo 44, 46, 84, 715, 716, 780, 781, 810, 916

FOR CHILDREN
TIME ELEVATOR
www.timeelevator.it
Older children will love—and learn from—this hour-long, three-screen show that uses state-of-the-art sound and graphics to recreate Rome's history and the heyday of its most ancient famous monuments.
135 E5 Via dei Santi Apostoli 20, 00187 06 6992 1823 Daily 10.30–7.30 Adult €21, child €15 Barberini, Colosseo 40, 60, 64, 170, 175

PRICES AND SYMBOLS

The restaurants are listed alphabetically (excluding La, Il, Le and I). The prices given are the average for a two-course lunch (L) and a three-course dinner (D) for one person, without drinks. The wine price is for the least expensive bottle. All the restaurants listed accept credit cards unless otherwise stated.

For a key to the symbols, ▷ 2.

AL BRIC

www.albric.it

This is a very stylish *osteria* and wine bar overlooking Via del Pellegrino, near Campo dei Fiori. The wine list is huge, featuring more than a thousand labels. The menu has a wide selection of creative dishes, which are matched perfectly with wine suggestions. Try the tasty spaghetti with anchovies and pecorino cheese or pears with Gorgonzola cheese and the delicious home-made bread. Among the desserts, don't miss the strudel with cinnamon ice cream.

✚ 134 D5 ✉ Via del Pellegrino 51–52, 00186 ☎ 06 687 9533 ◷ Jun–Sep Tue–Sat 7.30pm–11.30pm, Sun 12.30–2.30; Oct–May daily 7.30pm–11.30pm ✋ D €60, Wine €18 🚌 64, 87, 492 to Largo di Torre Argentina; tram 8

ANTICO CAFFÈ DELLA PACE

www.caffedellapace.it

Caffè della Pace is a real Roman institution, an art nouveau café just off Piazza Navona, with marble interior and wrought-iron tables under an ivy cascade outside. Attracting a showbiz crowd, it is possibly the last stronghold of *la dolce vita*. Good for light meals or an *aperitivo*. Credit cards are not accepted.

✚ 134 D5 ✉ Via della Pace 3/7, 00186 ☎ 06 686 1216 ◷ Tue–Sun 8.30am–3am, Mon 5pm–3am ✋ Cocktails from €12, sandwiches from €9 🚌 46, 62, 64, 87 and other services to Largo di Torre Argentina or Corso del Rinascimento

ANTONIO AL PANTHEON

The food is quintessentially Roman and the clientele local at this family-run restaurant in a pedestrian street near the Pantheon. Try the fresh fettuccine with creamy walnut sauce and, for a main course, the calves' liver cooked in chilli, olive oil and wine. The portions are very generous and the service is a joy.

✚ 135 E5 ✉ Via dei Pastini 12, 00186 ☎ 06 679 0798 ◷ Mon–Sat 12–3, 7–11. Closed 3 weeks in Aug ✋ L €18, D €30, Wine €16 🚌 40, 62, 64, or any bus to Piazza Navona and Corso Vittorio Emanuele II

L'ARCHETTO

L'Archetto serves pizza and grilled meat, but, most of all, spaghetti— there are more than 100 different kinds to choose from and portions are always generous. Dishes range from traditional recipes such as carbonara and *spaghetti alle vongole* (with clams) to more creative incarnations: The lemon spaghetti is especially good. There are a few tables outside.

✚ 135 E5 ✉ Via dell'Archetto 26, 00186 ☎ 06 678 9064 ◷ Daily 12–3, 7–1 ✋ L €12, D €22, Wine €8 Ⓜ Barberini 🚌 117, 119, or any bus to Piazza Venezia or Via del Corso

BAIRES

www.baires.it

The bright walls and floors, and the sounds of tango create a South American atmosphere in which to enjoy Argentinian grilled meat served with various sauces. Starters include marinated chicken (*pollo all'escabeche*), and there's a wide choice of salads and soups. The wine list focuses on Argentina; the house red and white are organic.

✚ 134 D5 ✉ Corso del Rinascimento 1, 00186 ☎ 06 686 1293 ◷ Daily 12–3.30, 7.30–12 ✋ L €18, D €30, Wine €12 Ⓜ Colosseo 🚌 87, 116, 492

Opposite Head to one of the city's many pizzerie to enjoy an inexpensive, informal evening out

BRUSCHETTERIA DEGLI ANGELI

Just behind Campo dei Fiori, this eatery offers an alternative to pizza. Huge *bruschette* (toasted breads) are served with more than 50 different toppings, from tomatoes and rocket (arugula) salad to Asiago cheese and *speck* (bacon), plus pasta and meat dishes and huge salads. The international beer list is ample. There are tables available outside during the summer. Paper tablecloths and wooden furniture contribute to the rustic image.
☩ 134 D6 ✉ Piazza B. Cairoli 2a, 00186 ☎ 06 6880 5789 ◷ Sep–Jun Mon–Sat 12–3, 7–1, Sun 7pm–1am; Jul–Aug daily 7pm–1am ✋ *Bruschette* from €10, Beer from €6 🚌 64, 87, 492 to Largo di Torre Argentina; tram 8

IL CAPRICCIO

Pizza a taglio (pizza by the slice) to go is a Roman institution. This establishment is just along from Piazza Navona. You decide how much they should slice off the large rectangular tray-baked pizzas and then pay by weight—no slice is too small. Other tasty morsels are the olives *ascolane* (large green olives, stuffed with meat and herbs and deep fried) or *supplì* (deep-fried tomato risotto and cheese balls). Credit cards are not accepted.
☩ 134 D5 ✉ Via della Pace 27a, 00186 ☎ 06 6880 4458 ◷ Daily 10am–2am or later. Closed 2 weeks in Feb, end Aug ✋ Pizza slice approx. €2 per 100g (4oz), Beer €4 🚌 46, 62, 64, 87, 116, 492 to Piazza Navona

CASA BLEVE

www.casableve.it
The impressive main room of this *enoteca* (wine bar) between Largo di Torre Argentina and the Pantheon is a large, high-ceilinged salon of pillars and colonnades. In these airy, pleasing and unpretentious surroundings you sit down at robust wooden tables to enjoy a wide selection of wines and a buffet choice of cheeses, salamis, salads, and smoked and cured meats and fish. The same owners run a smaller wine bar in the Ghetto at Via Santa Maria del Pianto 9–11, open Monday to Saturday 8am to 8pm.
☩ 135 D5 ✉ Via del Teatro Valle 48–49, 00186 ☎ 06 686 5970 ◷ Tue–Sat 12.30–3, 7–10 ✋ Light meal €12, Wine (by the glass) €6 🚌 30, 40, 46, 62, 63, 64 and other services to Largo di Torre Argentina

CICCIA BOMBA

Just round the corner from Piazza Navona, this tiny, cosy place serves excellent pizzas and has its wood-burning oven in full view. Try some of the *antipasti* with grilled and marinaded vegetables, accompanied by freshly baked focaccia. The restaurant is air conditioned in summer.
☩ 134 D5 ✉ Via del Governo Vecchio 76, 00186 ☎ 06 6880 2108 ◷ Jun–Sep daily 12.30–3, 7.30–11.30; Oct–May Thu–Tue 12.30–3, 7.30–11.30; no pizza Mon lunchtime ✋ L/D €25, Wine €10 🚌 62, 64, 81, 571

IL CONVIVIO

www.ilconviviotroiani.com
The interior of this restaurant, down a narrow cobbled street behind Palazzo Altemps in the heart of Rome, is high-tech and gloriously spacious. Service is excellent. The *degustazione* (tasting) menu includes a bit of everything, while the creative regional menu changes frequently. If available, try the courgette (zucchini) flowers filled with porcini mushrooms and goat's cheese, or the rabbit stuffed with olives and sausage with a fennel sauce. The excellent wine list has more than 2,000 different bottles.
☩ 134 D4 ✉ Vicolo dei Soldati 31, 00186 ☎ 06 686 9432 ◷ Mon–Sat 8pm–11pm ✋ D €75, Wine €24 🚌 46, 62, 64, 87, 116, 492 to Piazza Navona

CORALLO

This restaurant/pizzeria is divided into different rooms, all with a maritime theme and a quiet atmosphere. Very thin pizza baked in a wood oven is the house special, and the focaccia is very popular. The beef fillet is also delicious and perfectly cooked, and there's fresh fish on Tuesday and Friday. Reservations are advised. There are tables outside in summer.
☩ 134 D5 ✉ Via del Corallo 10, 00186 ☎ 06 6830 7703 ◷ Tue–Sun 12–3, 7.30–1, Mon 7.30pm–1am ✋ L €20, D €25, Wine €8 🚌 64, 87, 492 to Largo di Torre Argentina; tram 8

CUL DE SAC

Very close to Piazza Navona, Cul de Sac was originally just a wine bar, but it has gradually built a reputation for its food as well. It's well known for its pâtés—such as the sweet-and-sour wild boar pâté—served with toasted bread (€8). The interior is reminiscent of a 1950s train, furnished in beautiful solid white wood. Thirty-five wines are available by the glass and over 1,400 are in stock.
☩ 134 D5 ✉ Piazza Pasquino 73, 00186 ☎ 06 6880 1094 ◷ Daily 12–4, 6–12.30 ✋ L €21, D €35, Wine €15 🚌 46, 62, 64, 87, 116, 492 to Piazza Navona

DA BAFFETTO

Come early or be prepared to wait, joining the exuberant mob outside one of Rome's best pizzerias. Sixties radicals headed here; now the whole world seemingly vies for a seat. Don't miss the *bruschetta al pomodoro* (toasted bread topped with tomato, basil and olive oil). Be prepared for more genial jostling at the outdoor tables, and long waits for the superb pizzas. Credit cards are not accepted.
☩ 134 D5 ✉ Via del Governo Vecchio 114, 00186 ☎ 06 686 1617 ◷ Daily 6.30pm–1am ✋ D €30, Wine €10 🚌 46, 62, 64, 87, 116, 492 to Campo dei Fiori

DA BENITO

This friendly, family-run spot in a quiet, cobblestone side street near Largo di Torre Argentina serves hot and cold food cafeteria-style; just choose and point, then take it to your table. When you've finished, simply tell the cashier what you had. There are always a couple of fresh specials of the day, including home-made pasta. A plateful of assorted mixed vegetables with olive oil dribbled over, together with *polpette* (meatballs), makes a perfect quick lunch. Credit cards are not accepted.

✚ 135 D5 ✉ Via dei Falegnami 14, 00186 ☎ 06 686 1508 🕐 Mon–Sat 7.30–7.30 ✋ L €10, D €30, Wine €12 🚇 Cavour 🚌 64, 87, 492 to Largo di Torre Argentina; tram 8

DA FRANCESCO

Set on a jewel of a square just a few minutes from Piazza Navona, this trattoria is very popular with locals (expect to wait if you come after 8pm). With paper tablecloths and no frills, the best tables are outside. Try their fantastic focaccia with Parma ham, which is served alongside the vegetable and fish buffet. Shellfish pastas are good (Tuesday and Friday), as is the porcini mushroom pasta. Pizzas are available evenings only (from €9). The draught beer and house wine are good. Credit cards are not accepted.

✚ 134 D5 ✉ Piazza del Fico 29, 00186 ☎ 06 686 4009 🕐 Wed–Mon 12–3, 7–1, Tue 7–1 ✋ L €30, D €60, Wine €7 🚌 46, 62, 64, 87, 116, 492 to Piazza Navona

DA SETTIMIO

Wrought-iron flourishes and piles of fruit greet you at this vivid gem of a restaurant by the Pantheon. Graffiti covers the walls, old beams and terracotta tiles. The fare is simple but spot on, including the best *penne all'arrabiata* (pasta with fiery chilli, tomato and garlic sauce) in town, and superb truffles and game dishes. Reserve a table for dinner, as both tiny rooms quickly overflow with cheerful customers.

✚ 135 D5 ✉ Via delle Colonnele 14, 00186 ☎ 06 678 9651 🕐 Sep–Jul Tue–Sat 12.30–3, 7.30–11.30 ✋ L €20, D €30, Wine €11 🚌 116, or any bus to Largo di Torre Argentina, such as 64, 87, 492

DAI TRE AMICI

In a 16th-century building behind the Pantheon, this unpretentious trattoria with simple wooden tables

epitomizes the Roman spirit of dining—lots of noise and organized chaos. Waiters weave their way through the packed tables with dishes such as *farfalle alla calabrese* (pasta with garlic, butter and cheese) followed by wafer-thin beef with porcini mushrooms. The *antipasto* buffet is extensive and great for vegetarians. Fresh fish Tuesday and Friday. Either make a reservation or go before 8pm.

✚ 135 D5 ✉ Via della Rotonda 7, 00186 ☎ 06 687 5239 🕐 Daily 12–3, 7–midnight ✋ L €20, D €30, Wine €12 🚌 116, or any bus to Largo di Torre Argentina, such as 64, 87, 492

DER PALLARO

Enjoy traditional Roman cooking at this timeless trattoria right behind Campo dei Fiori. There's no need to choose from a menu, as the waiter will bring you everything that's on that day, from starter to dessert, for the price of €25, including house wine. The cooking is simple but good, and the portions generous. It's an excellent choice if you are looking for a late dinner. In summer you can eat outside in the square. Credit cards are not accepted.

✚ 134 D5 ✉ Largo der Pallaro 15, 00186 ☎ 06 6880 1488 🕐 Jun–Sep daily 12–3, 7.30–1; Oct–May Tue–Sun 12–3, 7.30–1. Closed 2 weeks in Aug ✋ L €20, D €25 (includes house wine) 🚌 64, 87, 492 to Largo di Torre Argentina; tram 8

DITIRAMBO

www.ristoranteditirambo.it
One block south of Corso Vittorio Emanuele II, this downtown trattoria even satisfies the difficult-to-please *bel mondo* of Rome. The kitchen uses organic ingredients, and produces home-made bread, pasta (including its showcase dish with zucchini flowers) and desserts. Furnishings lean towards country chic. The wine list is legendary. Reservations are essential.

✚ 134 D5 ✉ Piazza della Cancelleria 75, 00186 ☎ 06 687 1626 🕐 Sep–Jul Tue–Sun 1–3, 7.30–11.30, Mon 8pm–11.30pm ✋ L €20, D €42, Wine €12 🚌 46, 62, 64, 87, 116, 492 to Campo dei Fiori

L'EAU VIVE

www.restaurant-leauvive.net
An international order of nuns runs this restaurant, in a Renaissance building with frescoed vaulted ceilings. Cuisine is international, mainly French, and includes soups, main courses and desserts. Classical music plays in the background. The wine list is excellent. The restaurant helps the nuns raise funds for missions to developing countries. You can join the sisters for evening prayers at 10pm.

✚ 134 D5 ✉ Via Monterone 85, 00186 ☎ 06 6880 2101; 06 6880 1095 🕐 Sep–Jul Mon–Sat 12.30–2.30, 7.30–10 ✋ L €25, D €40, Wine €12 🚌 64, 87, 492 to Largo di Torre Argentina; tram 8

EDOARDO II

www.edoardosecondo.com
One of Rome's most popular gay bars, very close to the Jewish quarter and Piazza Venezia, has been transformed into a sophisticated gay restaurant as well. Candles and soft lighting complement pale stucco walls decorated with modern paintings and photographs. The cuisine is mainly Mediterranean—meat and fish, plus delicious vegetable pies and an array of cakes and pastries. There are also more than 100 wines.

✚ 135 E5 ✉ Vicolo Margana 14, 00187 ☎ 06 6994 2419 🕐 Wed–Mon 8pm–midnight. Closed 1 week in Aug ✋ D €35, Wine €12 🚌 40, 64, 87, 628 to Piazza Venezia

ETABLI

www.etabli.it
Etabli is in the dining and nightlife area known as the 'Triangolo della Pace', the triangle of streets around Via della Pace. There are many bars and restaurants in this area, including Antico Caffè della Pace (▷ 126), but it is less trendy than it was and some establishments are unashamedly aimed at visitors. Etabli, however, draws chic young Romans with its pared-down elegance, amiable staff, welcoming ambience and deep leather armchairs. You can eat light lunches

in a room off to the side, or there's a more formal but rather over-priced restaurant upstairs. Most people, however, come here for a morning coffee and brioche or evening drink.
🚹 134 D5 ✉ Vicolo delle Vacche 9, 00186 ☎ 06 9761 6694 🕓 Tue–Sun 12–3, 7–12. Wine bar: 6pm–2am 🍴 Coffee €1.20, light lunch €20 🚌 30, 70, 80, 81 and other services to Corso del Rinascimento

EVANGELISTA
www.ristorantevangelista.com
In this genteel restaurant near the Tiber, ideal for long, intimate meals, the stars of the rich menu are its artichoke dishes. Try them *alla giudia* (Roman-Jewish style, fried whole in batter) or *al mattone* (crushed between two bricks, then baked). Also recommended is the pasta with aubergines (eggplant), almonds and ricotta. The interior design is elegant and the service gracious.
🚹 134 D6 ✉ Via delle Zoccolette 11a, 00186 ☎ 06 687 5810 🕓 Sep–Jul Mon–Sat 7.30pm–11.30pm 🍴 D €75, Wine €26 🚌 H, 23, 280, 780 to Lungotevere Ponte Sisto; tram 8

GIGGETTO AL PORTICO D'OTTAVIA
www.giggettoalportico.it
For more than 80 years, this family-run restaurant in the heart of the Ghetto has specialized in traditional Roman-Jewish cuisine. Without a doubt the *pièce de résistance* is the *carciofi alla giudia* (Jewish artichoke). You should also try the unusual salad featuring wild chicory shoots with an anchovy dressing—all prepared to perfection. There's a wine cellar with more than 500 labels, and some exceptional desserts, too.
🚹 135 E6 ✉ Via Portico d'Ottavia 21a, 00186 ☎ 06 686 1105 🕓 Tue–Sun 12.30–3, 7.30–11 🍴 L €30, D €50, Wine €12 🚌 62, 64, 87, 492, 628 to Largo di Torre Argentina

GIOLITTI
www.giolitti.it
This family-run *gelateria* has been tempting Romans with its delicious

ice creams since 1900. Ever popular with Roman families, the Liberty-style (art nouveau) room, with olive-green ceilings and marble floors, is the perfect setting in which to linger over an ice cream (there are more than 60 varieties), or a home-made pastry and a drink. For pure indulgence, ask for *panna* (whipped cream) on top of your ice cream. There is also a takeaway counter.
🚹 135 E4 ✉ Via degli Uffici del Vicario 40, 00186 ☎ 06 699 1243 🕓 Daily 7am–2am 🍴 Ice creams €4.80–€9 (to take away €1.80–€3) 🚌 52, 53, 61, 71, 80, 85, 160, 850

IL GOCCETTO
This wine bar is in a medieval bishop's house between Corso Vittorio Emanuele II and the Tiber. Frescoes on the walls combine with bottles and glasses stored on the shelves and in open cupboards to create a relaxed atmosphere. Not only is there a vast wine list (800 different labels), but there's also an extensive cheese list and other regional delicacies, including various kinds of salami and ham.
🚹 134 C5 ✉ Via dei Banchi Vecchi 14, 00186 ☎ 06 686 4268 🕓 Tue–Sat 11.30–2, 7–11, Mon 7–11 🍴 Selection of salami/cheese from €10, desserts from €5, Wine €4 (by the glass) 🚌 64, 87, 492 to Largo di Torre Argentina; tram 8

GROTTE DEL TEATRO DI POMPEO
www.grotteteatropompeo.it
The back rooms of this restaurant, which is just behind the spot where Julius Caesar was assassinated, are carved out of the first stone theatre in Roman history. Some of the best fish dishes around are served here: Spaghetti with seafood, oven-baked turbot or grilled scampi are all excellent. There's also a good wine list. In summer, sit outside and try the Prosecco Mionetto (€14), a sparkling wine perfect with fish.
🚹 134 D5 ✉ Via del Biscione 73, 00186 ☎ 06 6880 3686 🕓 Sep–Jul Tue–Sun 12–3, 7–11 🍴 L €22, D €35, Wine €10 🚌 64, 87, 492 to Largo di Torre Argentina; tram 8

INSALATA RICCA
This Italian chain concentrates on salads and *bruschette* (toasted bread with toppings) to marvellous effect. Start with artichoke pâté or sesame goat's cheese on seared bread. Then tuck into a massive salad, such as mozzarella and tomato or greens drizzled with honey and topped with walnuts and Parmesan. The interior incorporates exposed brick and sponge-painted walls, but most prefer the crowded outdoor tables. The bilingual staff make visitors welcome.
🚹 134 D5 ✉ Largo de' Chiavari 85, 00186 ☎ 06 6880 3656 🕓 Daily 12–12 🍴 L €10, D €12, Wine €4 🚌 46, 62, 64, 87, 116, 492 to Campo dei Fiori

MACCHERONI
This is a funky place, which is popular more for its lively atmosphere and young staff than its food. The pasta dishes are very good, but the rest is average.
🚹 134 D5 ✉ Piazza delle Coppelle 44, 00186 ☎ 06 6830 7895 🕓 Daily 1–3, 7.30–12 🍴 L/D €15, Wine €7 🚌 23, 30, 75, 280, 716 or any bus to Via Marmorata; tram 3

NAVONA NOTTE
This pizzeria/restaurant near Piazza Navona is one of the few in the *centro storico* that offers a set-price tourist menu. For around €8.50, you can enjoy mussels with focaccia, followed by either spaghetti or a pizza and a glass of wine. The typical Roman thin-crust pizzas are made in a traditional wood-burning oven. Expect good, honest fare and simple style. If you can, get a seat outside and enjoy the bustle of central Rome.
🚹 134 D5 ✉ Via del Teatro Pace 44, 00186 ☎ 06 686 9287 🕓 Daily 5.30–10.30pm, Sun also 12.30–2.30 🍴 D €20, Wine €6 🚌 62, 64, 87, 116, 492

OSTERIA DELL'ANIMA
The seascape frescoes give this refined restaurant behind Piazza Navona a refreshingly different look. The chef invests great thought in the seasonal cuisine and its

presentation. Prices are surprisingly reasonable. Try the ravioli filled with scampi and artichokes in a tomato and cream sauce, or thinly sliced beef with *caciotta* (ewe's milk cheese), tomatoes and salad leaves. All the bread is home-made. More than 150 wines, many from Tuscany, are served.

✚ 134 D5 ✉ Via Santa Maria dell'Anima 8, 00186 ☎ 06 686 4021 ⏰ Daily 12–12 ✋ L €15, D €30, Wine €13 🚌 40, 62, 64, or any other bus to Piazza Navona or Corso Vittorio Emanuele II

OSTERIA 'AR GALLETTO'
This family-run trattoria, with tables spilling outside into the corner of Piazza Farnese, has one of the most soothing views in Rome. It offers a fine array of largely vegetarian *antipasti*, excellent home-made ravioli and pasta, grilled lamb or beef, and classic *dolci*. It gets very busy, and is not a place to come if you are in a hurry.

✚ 134 D5 ✉ Vicolo del Gallo 1, Piazza Farnese 102, 00186 ☎ 06 686 1714 ⏰ Mon–Sat 12.30–3, 7.30–11 ✋ L €25, D €40, Wine €12 🚌 117

IL PAGLIACCIO
www.ristoranteilpagliaccio.it
Elegant Il Pagliaccio has been awarded two Michelin stars thanks to the daring cooking of chef Anthony Genovese, whose first-hand experience of kitchens in Japan, Thailand and Malaysia adds a Far Eastern tinge to his otherwise mainly Italian dishes. You might be offered veal gently marinated with lemon grass, grilled scallops with teriyaki-marinated beef, or baked red mullet with red onions and wild asparagus. Leave room for the sublime desserts. The two dining rooms are soberly but elegantly decorated, and help make this an excellent choice for an expensive gastronomic treat.

✚ 134 C5 ✉ Via dei Banchi Vecchi 129, 00186 ☎ 06 6880 9595 ⏰ Mon–Tue 7.30–10, Wed–Sat 1–2.30, 7.30–10. Closed for periods in Jan and Aug ✋ L €100, D €150, Wine €40 🚌 64, 87, 492 and other services to Largo di Torre Argentina

PANE VINO E SAN DANIELE
In a charming piazza, this wine bar serves wine by the glass—including good full-bodied reds from the Fantinel vineyards—and dishes from Friuli. It offers generous platters of *prosciutto*, salami and cheese, and salads and soups; try the polenta with mushrooms, or wild boar followed by a slice of home-made ricotta cake or fruit salad.

✚ 135 D5 ✉ Piazza Mattei 16, 00186 ☎ 06 687 7147 ⏰ Mon–Sat 11–2, 7.30–10.30 ✋ L/D €20, Wine €15 🚌 60, 64, 70, 170, 571 (Largo di Torre Argentina)

IL PICCOLO
In this lovely wine bar near the beginning of Via del Governo Vecchio bottles of wine are stored up to the ceiling. There are a few tables outside, plus just a couple inside that add to the intimate atmosphere. The ample wine list includes white *fragolino* (a sweet wine with a strawberry aroma) and blackberry and raspberry sangria. There's a selection of different cheeses and meats: Try the *bresaola* (dried fillet of beef) or sun-dried tomatoes from Calabria. Credit cards are not accepted.

✚ 134 D5 ✉ Via del Governo Vecchio 74, 00186 ☎ 06 6880 1746 ⏰ Daily 10.30am–2am ✋ L €14 (selection of salami/cheeses from €7), Wine €3 (by the glass) 🚌 87, 492 to Largo di Torre Argentina; tram 8

PIERLUIGI
www.pierluigi.it
Prices at this excellent fish restaurant are reasonable considering its setting and quality. It's on a gem of a piazza, with plenty of tables outside. Inside, cool terracotta floors, brick arches and medieval beams are beautifully spotlit. Scampi risotto is a good choice, as is the *carpaccio* of tuna or swordfish. Fresh fish of the day is displayed in a glass cabinet. Ask to see the wine cellar. Service is good.

✚ 134 D5 ✉ Piazza dei Ricci 144, 00186 ☎ 06 686 1302 ⏰ Tue–Sun 12.30–3, 7.30–midnight ✋ L €30, D €40, Wine €14 🚌 46, 62, 64, 87, 116, 492 to Campo dei Fiori

PIZZERIA LA MONTECARLO
Expect simple, unfussy food and service at this typical Roman pizzeria near Piazza Navona. The walls are covered with photographs of more (or less) famous diners. Pizzas are baked in wood-fired ovens. The house special is the *pizza montecarlo:* tomato, mozzarella, mushrooms, artichokes, sausage, eggs, peppers, onion and olives. Arrive before 8.30pm or be prepared to wait. Credit cards are not accepted.

✚ 134 D5 ✉ Vicolo Savelli 11A–12–13, 00186 ☎ 06 686 1877 ⏰ Tue–Sun 12–3.30, 6.30–1. Closed 2 weeks in Aug ✋ Pizza €6, L €6, D €18, Wine €11 🚌 40, 62, 64, or any other bus to Piazza Navona or Corso Vittorio Emanuele II

QUINZI E GABRIELI
www.quinziegabrieli.it
This well-established, if pricey, fish restaurant, in a splendid 15th-century palazzo not far from Piazza Navona, has three dining rooms, wonderfully decorated with murals of exotic beaches, stone columns and a wooden canopy. Service is efficient, with Italian flair. A house special is the raw fish platter, with bass, crayfish, tuna and squid. Try the spaghetti with lobster, which is the best in Rome.

✚ 135 D5 ✉ Via delle Coppelle 5, 00186 ☎ 06 687 9389 ⏰ Tue–Sat 12.30–2.30, 7.45–11 ✋ L €100, D €100, Wine €25 🚌 116, 492

RENATO E LUISA
www.renatoeluisa.it
For traditional Roman cuisine with a touch of creativity, head to this tiny restaurant (only 10–15 tables) behind Largo di Torre Argentina. Starters include mozzarella cheese with pesto or truffles, grilled or au gratin vegetables and focaccia. Among the pastas, the special is fettuccine with cherry tomatoes and ricotta cheese. The house wine is good.

✚ 134 D5 ✉ Via dei Barbieri 25, 00186 ☎ 06 686 9660 ⏰ Tue–Sun 8.30pm–12 ✋ D €40, Wine €12 🚌 64, 492 to Largo di Torre Argentina; tram 8

SANT'EUSTACHIO IL CAFFÈ

www.santeustachioilcaffe.it

The scent of Arabian coffee hangs in the air here, in a square with a view of the church of Sant'Eustachio and the Senate buildings. Connoisseurs come to this café, which has been here since 1938 (the mosaic floor dates from the 1930s), to try what is generally regarded as the best coffee there is. The blends are roasted in wood-fired ovens on site—hence the glorious aroma. Credit cards are not accepted.

✚ 134 D5 ✉ Piazza di Sant'Eustachio 82, 00186 ☎ 06 6880 2048 🕐 Daily 8.30am–1am ✋ Coffee from €1.20 🚌 40, 62, 64, 85, 87, 117, 492 to Corso del Rinascimento

TAPA LOCA

Between Piazza Navona and the beautiful Piazza della Pace is a real rarity: a Spanish restaurant in Rome. The comfortable, large dining area, with chunky tables and chairs, lies within a 16th-century palazzo. Four different paellas, including vegetarian, are on offer, plus a wide variety of meat, fish and vegetarian tapas. There is also a good selection of Torres wines.

✚ 134 D5 ✉ Via di Tor Millina 4–5, 00186 ☎ 06 683 2266 🕐 Daily 6.30pm–2am ✋ D €25, Wine €11.50 🚌 46, 64, 87, 116, 492 to Piazza Navona

LA TAVERNA DEL GHETTO

www.latavernadelghetto.com

This kosher restaurant is just along the street from the Portico d'Ottavia in the heart of the Ghetto district. The dining area, within a 14th-century building, is an attractive brick-pointed room with an arched Gothic ceiling. The kosher kitchen serves Roman-Jewish dishes. Chicory and anchovy pie and baked salted cod with pine nuts, raisins and cherry tomatoes are two typical dishes. There's a good wine list, including Israeli selections.

✚ 135 E6 ✉ Via Portico d'Ottavia 8, 00186 ☎ 06 6880 9771 🕐 Sun–Thu 12–3, 7–11, Fri 12–3, Sat 7–11 ✋ L €28, D €45, Wine €21 🚌 62, 64, 87, 628, or any other bus to Largo di Torre Argentina

TAVERNA PARIONE

www.tavernaparione.com

There has been a restaurant in this 15th-century palazzo, near Piazza Navona, for over 60 years. It is a spacious, simple place where you can enjoy wholesome Roman food, including pizzas, accompanied by wine from its own cellar. It is popular with local celebrities—look for their pictures on the photo board. There are tables outside in warm weather.

✚ 134 D5 ✉ Via dei Parione 38–39 ☎ 06 686 9545 🕐 Daily 12–3, 7–12 ✋ L €15, D €30, Wine €15 🚇 Spagna 🚌 46, 64

TAZZA D'ORO

www.torrefazionetazzadoro.com

This bustling bar/coffee shop near the Pantheon sparks major arguments: Does it serve the city's best coffee or is it merely a contender? The standard blend is creamy and fragrant, but the Jamaican Blue Mountain provides the smoothest buzz. Seasonal choices include *granita di caffè* (coffee sorbet) and the indulgent *cioccolata calda con panna* (hot chocolate with whipped cream). A bag of beans or a bottle of Aroma di Roma coffee liqueur from the gift shop makes an ideal gift to take home. Bar service only, no seating.

✚ 135 E5 ✉ Via degli Orfani 84, 00186 ☎ 06 678 9792 🕐 Mon–Sat 7am–8pm ✋ Coffee from €0.90, *granita* €1.30 🚌 40, 62, 64, or any bus to Piazza Navona or Corso Vittorio Emanuele II

TRE SCALINI

You cannot visit Piazza Navona without sampling Tre Scalini's chocolate *tartufo* ice cream—reputed to be the finest in the city. There are tables outside, but these come at a premium. For a less expensive alternative, take your ice cream away to enjoy in the piazza in the shade of Bernini's fountain?

✚ 134 D5 ✉ Piazza Navona 28–32, 00100 ☎ 06 6880 1996 🕐 Sun–Fri 10am–midnight, Sat 10am–3am ✋ €2.50 (small ice cream to take away) 🚌 63, 492 or any bus to Largo Argentina

VECCHIA ROMA

Despite its popularity, Vecchia Roma has remained unspoiled. In summer, enjoy salads in the pretty piazza, and in winter move to the 18th-century interior for more substantial meals, based around polenta. Reservations are recommended.

✚ 135 E6 ✉ Piazza del Campitelli 16, 00186 ☎ 06 686 4604 🕐 Mon–Tue, Thu–Sun 1–3, 8–11. Closed 3 weeks in Aug ✋ L €22, D €35, Wine €8 🚌 44, 46, 56, 60, 75, 85, 87, 95

VINERIA REGGIO

If you are looking for somewhere to have a light lunch and a glass of wine after a visit to the Campo dei Fiori market, this wine bar on the market square is an ideal place to go. It is set in an original 16th-century building, with exposed beams, terracotta floors and a marble bar. The wine selection is vast, with fine choices from all over Italy. In the evening, the atmosphere is vibrant, with people spilling out onto the piazza. Prices for wines per glass start at €2.50 and go up to €10.50.

✚ 134 D5 ✉ Piazza Campo dei Fiori 15, 00186 ☎ 06 6880 3268 🕐 Mon–Sat 9am–2am, Sun 4pm–2am. Closed 2 weeks in Aug ✋ L €11, Wine €4 🚌 46, 62, 64, 87, 116, 492 to Campo dei Fiori

WINE TIME

www.winetime.it

This wine bar offers panoramic views of Castel Sant'Angelo, and an ample wine list of about 300 labels, mainly Italian in origin. Glossy wood tables, open cupboards displaying bottles and glasses, and a 10m (33ft) wooden counter running through the main room create a stylish yet welcoming environment. All dishes are coupled with a suitable wine, from creative starters (roasted Piedmont cheese, smoked ham with vegetables) to the salads and tasty meat dishes. Reservations are advised.

✚ 134 C5 ✉ Piazza Pasquale Paoli 15, 00186 ☎ 06 687 5706 🕐 Mon–Sat noon–2am ✋ L €25, D €35, Wine €15 🚌 40, 64 to Corso Vittorio Emanuele II

PRICES AND SYMBOLS

Prices are the lowest and highest for a double room for one night. Breakfast is included unless noted otherwise. All the hotels listed accept credit cards unless otherwise stated. Note that rates vary widely throughout the year.

For a key to the symbols, ▷ 2.

ABRUZZI

www.hotelabruzzi.it

Although its prices have increased, this hotel is still a steal, considering its dramatic view of the Pantheon. Most rooms have private bathrooms, and all have double glazing and air conditioning.
✚ 135 D5 ✉ Piazza della Rotonda 69, 00186 ☎ 06 9784 1351 ✋ €120–€220 ⓘ 25 ⑤ 🚌 116

ALBERGO CESARI

www.albergocesari.it

Its quiet but central position ensures that this friendly hotel has a loyal client base, so early reservations are recommended. Built in 1787, close to the Pantheon, the building includes 11 pillars from the second-century AD Temple of Hadrian. Its large rooms all have satellite TV.
✚ 135 E5 ✉ Via di Pietra 89a, 00186 ☎ 06 674 9701 ✋ €130–€280 ⓘ 47 ⑤ 🚌 60, 62, 85, 117, 119, 160 to Via del Corso

ALBERGO DEL SENATO

www.albergodelsenato.it

An elegant Renaissance palace houses this hotel with spectacular views of the Pantheon. The roof terrace makes an ideal setting for relaxing and enjoying being in the heart of old Rome. Rooms are very comfortable and the service is efficient and welcoming.
✚ 135 D5 ✉ Piazza della Rotonda 73, 00186 ☎ 06 678 4343 ✋ €165–€415 ⓘ 56 ⑤

ALBERGO DEL SOLE AL BISCIONE

www.solealbiscione.it

Rooms at this competitively priced hotel just off Campo dei Fiori are clean, if on the small side. All have a TV and bathroom with shower. Staff are friendly and there is a gem of a roof terrace. There is no access for wheelchair users. Paid parking. Credit cards are not accepted.
✚ 134 D5 ✉ Via del Biscione 76, 00186 ☎ 06 6880 6873 ✋ €125–€145, excluding breakfast ⓘ 59 ⑤ 20 rooms 🚌 40, 62, 64, 87, 116, 492

ALBERGO DE SOLE AL PANTHEON

www.hotelsolealpantheon.com

This chic hotel, dating from 1467, claims to be the oldest in Rome. In the same square as the Pantheon, it has stunning views from the windows at the front of the building. Some rooms have painted ceilings or tiled floors, and more than half have a jacuzzi; all have satellite TV. In warm weather, breakfast is served in the courtyard.
✚ 135 D5 ✉ Piazza della Rotonda 63, 00186 ☎ 06 678 0441 ✋ €225–€338 ⓘ 33 ⑤ Ⓜ Spagna 🚌 119 to Piazza della Rotonda, 70, 81, 87 to Corso del Rinascimento, or any bus to Largo di Torre Argentina

Above *Gilded opulence and lavish design, characteristic of many of the city's top hotels*

COLONNA PALACE
www.itihotels.it
Overlooking the Parliament buildings in the hub of 16th-century Rome, the Colonna makes a superb base for discovering the city. Rooms are spacious, with bathroom, TV and minibar. The breakfast room overlooks the presidential palace and there is also a roof terrace bar and a solarium.

✚ 135 E4 ⊠ Piazza di Montecitorio 12, 00186 ☎ 06 675191 ✋ €300–€370 ⓘ 104 ⑤ 🚌 46, 62, 116

GENIO
www.leonardihotels.com
With good-sized, high-ceilinged rooms, marble bathrooms and antique furniture, this hotel, just seconds away from Piazza Navona, has a nice old-world touch about it. The bar and roof terrace have fine views of nearby St. Peter's and Castel Sant'Angelo. A free airport shuttle service is available, as is private parking.

✚ 134 D5 ⊠ Via G. Zanardelli 28, 00186 ☎ 06 683 3781 ✋ €90–€450 ⓘ 60 ⑤ 🚌 70, 81, 87, 116, 492

GRAND HOTEL DE LA MINERVE
www.grandhoteldelaminerve.it
This historic 17th-century hotel is close to the Pantheon. The classically furnished lobby has Roman statues, palm trees, marble flooring and an art nouveau glass cupola. Guest rooms are elegantly furnished and some have exposed beams or frescoed ceilings. All have marble bathrooms, satellite/pay TV, coffee-maker, trouser press, safe and internet access. Amenities include a restaurant, bar, roof garden, sauna and fitness facilities. The staff are always ready to help.

✚ 135 E5 ⊠ Piazza della Minerva 69, 00186 ☎ 06 695 201 ✋ €280–€480 ⓘ 135 ⑤ 🍷 🚌 116, or any bus to Via del Corso

HOTEL GIARDINO
www.hotel-giardino-roma.com
The English owner Katie offers her guests a warm welcome. Her rooms are decorated in soft pastels and comfortably furnished. Ask for a room on the road side for views up to the Palazzo del Quirinale—double glazing shuts out the traffic noise.

✚ 135 E5 ⊠ Via XXIV Maggio 51, 00187 ☎ 06 679 4584 ✋ €90–€150 ⓘ 11 ⑤ Ⓜ Cavour, Barberini 🚌 H, 40, 60, 64, 70, 117, 170

HOTEL NAVONA
www.hotelnavona.com
There's a friendly atmosphere in this popular hotel in a quiet side street close to Piazza Navona and the Pantheon. Some parts of the building date from the first century AD, and were built over the Baths of Agrippa; Keats and Shelley once stayed on the top floor. The rooms are basic and simple, most have bathrooms, and air conditioning is available at a €15 supplement. Credit cards are not accepted.

✚ 134 D5 ⊠ Via dei Sediari 8, 00186 ☎ 06 6830 1252 ✋ €110–€160 ⓘ 21 ⑤ 🚌 30, 70, 86, 87, 116

NAZIONALE A MONTECITORIO
www.nazionaleroma.it
Next to the Parliament buildings, and close to the Trevi Fountain and Piazza di Spagna, this charming hotel has an old-world feel. The medium-sized rooms have high ceilings and period furniture; all have a bathroom, satellite/pay TV, minibar and safe. Continental cuisine is served in the old-fashioned bar and restaurant.

✚ 135 E5 ⊠ Piazza Montecitorio 131, 00186 ☎ 06 695 001 ✋ €205–€500 ⓘ 80 ⑤ 🚌 46, 62, 116

PONTE SISTO
www.hotelpontesisto.it
This grand hotel is in Rome's famed jewellers' row, just along from the Tiber and the bridge from which it takes its name. The interior is truly splendid: marble floors, glass foyers and ample reception space, with a fine courtyard creating an oasis for its guests. The guest rooms are tastefully furnished with cherrywood suites and all-marble bathrooms; satellite TV with the option of internet access is also available.

The roof terrace has a breathtaking 360-degree view of baroque Rome.

✚ 134 D6 ⊠ Via Pettinari 64, 00186 ☎ 06 686 3100 ✋ €200–€360 ⓘ 103 ⑤ 🚌 116, 280

PORTOGHESI
www.hotelportoghesiroma.it
This gem of a hotel is tucked into the labyrinth of the Tor di Nona area, north of Piazza Navona, well away from the main tourist trail. It's easy to miss the unassuming entrance, flanked by potted evergreens: Keep an eye out for the row of dainty flags. Highlights include the breakfast solarium and roof terrace.

✚ 134 D4 ⊠ Via dei Portoghesi 1, 00186 ☎ 06 686 4231 ✋ €170–€190 ⓘ 27 ⑤ Ⓜ Spagna 🚌 116, 280

RAPHAEL
www.raphaelhotel.com
The ivy-covered facade of this hotel, just steps away from Piazza Navona, always looks a dream. There is a period feel to the antique-filled lobby, and the beautifully furnished guest rooms are littered with *objets d'art*. Facilities in the rooms include satellite TV, safe and minibar. There is an internationally acclaimed restaurant and the roof terrace has unparalleled views of the city. There are also fitness facilities.

✚ 134 D5 ⊠ Largo Febo 2, 00186 ☎ 06 682 831 ✋ €250–€380, excluding breakfast ⓘ 50 ⑤ 🍷 🚌 40, 62, 64, 87, 116, 492, 628 to Piazza Navona

TEATRO DI POMPEO
www.hotelteatrodipompeo.it
The Theatre of Pompey—site of Caesar's assassination—was absorbed into the medieval palazzo that now houses this boutique hotel. It is just steps away from the Campo dei Fiori, but insulated from its noise. All rooms are double or twin, with private bath and simple interiors. Avoid the less pleasant annexe. Amenities include room service, babysitting and laundry.

✚ 134 D5 ⊠ Largo del Pallaro 8, 00186 ☎ 06 6830 0170 ✋ €146–€210 ⓘ 13 ⑤ 🚌 46, 62, 64, 87, 116, 492 to Campo dei Fiori

REGIONS • CENTRAL ROME • EATING AND STAYING MAP

Streets and places (labels):

S Maria d Carm
Via G Vitelleschi
Bastioni
Via Alberico II
Via Terenzio
PIAZZA ADRIANA
VIA CRESCENZIO
PIAZZA CAVOUR
VIA V COLONNA
PONTE CAVOUR
VIA TRIBONIANO
Palazzo di Giustizia
VIA ULPIANO
LUNGOTEVERE PRATI
LUNGOTEVERE MARZIO
Via di Ripetta
Borgo Pio
Via
Via
Borgo Sant'Angelo
Santa Maria in Traspontina
Castel Sant'Angelo
Piazza Pia
Piazza Tribunali
P
VIA DELLA CONCILIAZIONE
VIA DELLA CONCILIAZIONE VATICANO
Ponte Sant'Angelo
LUNGOTEVERE CASTELLO
PONTE UMBERTO I
Via Monte Brianzo
Via G Zanardelli
VIA della Scrofa
Via dell' Orso
Portoghesi
Il Convivio
Sant' Agostino
La Madd
Maccher
LUNGOT IN SASSIA
PONTE VITTORIO EMANUELE II
Wine Time
Via Paola
Via dei B d S Spirito
LUNGOTEVERE TOR DI NONA
Piazza S Salv in Lauro
S Simeone
S Salvatore
Palazzo Altemps
Genio
Piazza Cinque Lune
Tre Scalini
PONTE PRINCIPE AMEDEO SAVOIA AOSTA
San Giovanni dei Fiorentini
Via Banchi Nuovi
Via Panico
Via M Giordano
Piazza Coronari
Via dei Coronari
Palazzo Taverna
Etabli
Da Francesco
Antico Caffè della Pace
Santa Maria della Pace
Raphael
Osteria dell'Anima
Piazza Navona
San Luigi dei Francesi
Sant' Eustach
Il Caff
Corallo
Il Capriccio
Palazzo G Vecchio
Tapa Loca
Sant'Agnese in Agone
Sant'Ivo alla Sapienza
Chiesa Nuova
Il Piccolo
Via del Governo Vecchio
CORSO VITTORIO EMANUELE II
Taverna Parione
Navona Notte
Ciccia Bomba
CORSO DEL RINASCIMENTO
Il Goccetto
Via dei Banchi Vecchi
Da Baffetto
Pizzeria la Montecarlo
Cul de Sac
Hotel Navona
Via
Via
Via Giulia
Il Pagliaccio
Pierluigi
Via del Pellegrino
Piazza San Pantaleo
Baires
Via del Cappellari
Palazzo della Cancelleria
Ditirambo
Insalata Ricca
Sant'Andrea della Valle
Via del Suda
Largo Lorenzo Perosi
S M d Monserato
Al Bric
Via Baullari
Grotte del Teatro di Pompeo
Arge
Renato e Luisa
S Eligio
Osteria 'Ar Galletto'
Albergo del Sole al Biscione
Vineria Reggio
Campo dei Fiori
Teatro Pompeo
Teatro di Pompeo
Der Pallaro
P
LUNGOTEVERE SANGALLO
LUNGOTEVERE GIANICOLENSE
Palazzo Salviati
Ponte Mazzini
LUNGOTEVERE DEI TEBALDI
Palazzo Falconieri
Palazzo Farnese
Piazza Farnese
Via Giubbonari
Bruschetteria degli Angeli
Da B
Cairoli
Palazzo Corsini
Palazzo Torlonia
Villa Farnesina
Via dei Orti d'Alibert
Via delle Mantellate
Via di San Francesco di Sales
della
Lungara
Via dei Riari
Palazzo Spada
Via Pettinari
VIA ARENULA
VIA GHET
Ministero G Giustizia
Tevere
LUNGOTEVERE DELLA FARNESINA
Ponte Sisto
Ponte Sisto
Via delle Zoccolette
Ministero Grazia Giustizia
Evangelista
LU
Orto Botanico
Gianicolo
Passeggiata del Gianicolo
Piazzale Aurelio
VIA GARIBALDI
VIA GARIBALDI
San Pietro in Montorio
S Egidio
Vicolo del Cedro
Santa Maria della Scala
Via della Scala
Vicolo del Cinque
Piazza de' Renzi
Via del Moro
Piazza di S Maria in Trastevere
Santa Maria in Trastevere
PONTE GARIBALDI
PONTE SISTO
LUNGOTEVERE DEI VALLATI
LUNGOTEVERE DEI SANZIO
Piazza G-G Belli
Piazza Renella
San Crisogono
Piazza Sidney Sonnino
Belli
Lungaret
LU
della
Via
Palazzo Spada

Scale:
0 — 250 m
0 — 250 yds

4
5
6

C
D

SS Ambrogio e Carlo al Corso
Tomacelli
dell' Arancio
Borghese
VIA DEL CORSO
Palazzo Ruspoli
VIA Condotti
VIA Bocca di Leone
VIA Belsiana
VIA Borgognona
VIA Frattina
VIA della Vite
Fiori
VIA delle
C le Due Case
VIA dei Due Macelli
VIA Gregoriana
Sistina
Via della Purificazione
VIA VITTORIO VENETO
Santa Maria della Concezione
Via di S Basilio
VIA S N da Tolentino
Fontana del Tritone
Barberini Fontana di Trevi
Piazza Barberini
Palazzo Barberini

San Lorenzo in Lucina
Marzio
dei Prefetti
Via di Campo
Palazzo Marignoli
Piazza S Silvestro V
Via della Mercede
VIA Poli
VIA DEL TRITONE
Galleria dell' Accademia di San Luca
Palazzo della Stamperia
Via delle Scuderie
Museo Nazionale delle Paste Alimentari
Via Rasella
Via dei Giardini
Giardino del Quirinale
San Carlo alle Quattro Fontane
Sant'Andrea al Quirinale

Palazzo di Montecitorio
Palazzo Chigi
Giolitti
Piazza Montecitorio
Colonna Palace
Colonna di Marco Aurelio
VIA DEL CORSO
Fontana di Trevi
Palazzo del Quirinale
Monte Quirinale
VIA DEL QUIRINALE
Via Placenza
Magdalena
rizi e Gabrieli
Nazionale a Montecitorio
Tazza d'Oro
Piazza Colonna
Via delle Muratte
Via della Dataria
Piazza del Quirinale
VIA della Consulta
Via della Parma
NAZIONALE
Milano
Da Settimio
Via Pastini
Antonio al Pantheon
Albergo Cesari
Via dell'Umiltà
Palazzo Sciarra
L'Archetto
Lucchesi
Scuderie del Quirinale
Palazzo Consulta
zza
onda
Abruzzi
Albergo del Senato, Albergo de Sole al Pantheon
Seminario
Sant'Ignazio di Loyola
Pantheon
Dai Tre Amici
Piazza della Minerva
Santa Maria sopra Minerva
Palazzo Odescalchi
P
Santi Apostoli
Villa Colonna
VIA XXIV MAGGIO
Hotel Giardino
asa Bleve
Grand Hotel de la Minerve
Palazzo-Galleria Doria Pamphilj
Piazza dei Santi Apostoli
Palazzo Colonna
Via Mazzatino
VIA d Cestari
Via del Gesù
Palazzo Altieri
VIA DEL PLEBISCITO
San Marco
Largo Magnanapoli
CORSO VITTORIO EMANUELE II
Templi Repubblicani
gentina
Il Gesù
Palazzo Venezia
Museo del Palazzo Venezia
Piazza Venezia
Colonna Traiana
Mercati di Traianei
Via Panisperna
Via di Sant'Agata dei Goti
Via del Boschetto
Via delle Botteghe Oscure
Crypta Balbi
Delfini
Edoardo II Vecchia Roma
Via dei
Monumento a Vittorio Emanuele II
Fori Imperiali
Via Baccina
VIA CAVOUR
Pane Vino e San Daniele
Via dei Funari
Fontana delle Tartarughe
La Taverna del Ghetto
Piazza del Campitelli
Santa Maria in Aracoeli
Musei Capitolini
VIA DEI FORI IMPERIALI
Via della Madonna dei Monti
Giggetto al Portico d'Ottavia
Via Catalana
Portico d'Ottavia
Sinagoga
I CENCI
Teatro di Marcello
VIA DEL TEATRO DI MARCELLO
Monte Capitolino
Piazza del Campidoglio
Palazzo Senatoriale
Via Salaria Vecchia
Arco di Settimio Severo
Santi Cosma e Damiano
Via del Colosseo
sola
erina
Piazza Monte Savello
Santa Nicola in Carcere
Palazzo dei Conservatori
Piazza della Consolazione
Via d Consolazione
Foro Romano
Arco di Tito
San Bartolomeo all' Isola
LUNGOTEVERE DEI PIERLEONI
VIA LUIGI PETROSELLI
P
Via dei Fienili
S Teodoro
Orti Farnesiani
Arco di Costantino
Via sacra
LL' ANGUILLARA
PONTE PALATINO
Tempio della Fortuna Virilis
Tempio di Vesta
E P
Piazza di S Anastasia
Via di Casa d'Iseo
Via Teodoro
Palatino
Casa di Livia
Palazzo dei Flavi
F

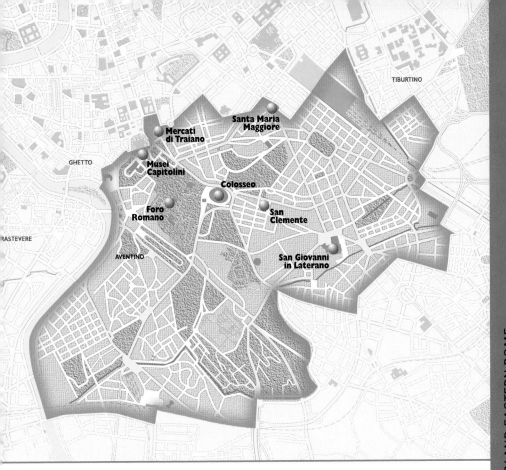

TIBURTINO

Santa Maria
Maggiore

Mercati
di Traiano

GHETTO

Musei
Capitolini

Colosseo

Foro
Romano

San
Clemente

RASTEVERE

AVENTINO

San Giovanni
in Laterano

THE ANCIENT CITY AND EASTERN ROME

While the monuments of ancient Rome are scattered far and wide, much of the heart of the city of Caesar, Nero and Hadrian is still confined—albeit in ruins—to the area on and around the Foro Romano (Roman Forum), the social, political and economic hub of the Roman Empire.

This only partially excavated area, largely free of modern buildings, embraces four of the original seven hills of Rome, stretching west to east from the Capitoline Hill (now largely dominated by the vast white monument to Vittorio Emanuele II), through the Palatine Hill, in whose shadow lie the Roman Forum and later Fori Imperiali (Imperial Fora), through to the Colosseum, built close to the Caelian and Esquiline hills.

The Roman and Imperial fora are easily seen, accessed from Via dei Fori Imperiali, the vast road that Mussolini drove through the area in the 1930s. So, too, are the Colosseum and Palatino, both close to the Roman Forum and entered with the same ticket. Fewer people visit the area's more outlying Roman sites—the Circo Massimo and Terme di Caracalla—but make a point of seeing the pretty Colle Oppio park and Parco di Traiano, both for their ruins and the views they offer of the Colosseum.

There is far more in this eastern and southern part of the city than simply Roman monuments. Santa Maria Maggiore and San Giovanni in Laterano are Rome's most important churches after St. Peter's, while San Clemente and Santa Maria in Cosmedin have the city's most beautiful medieval interiors. Then there are smaller gems, such as tiny Santa Prassede and San Pietro in Vincoli, with its Michelangelo sculpture. On the area's southern fringes, beyond the leafy streets of the Aventine Hill, are Testaccio and Ostiense, too far, perhaps, for most casual visitors, but a key area if you want to explore Rome's cutting-edge nightlife.

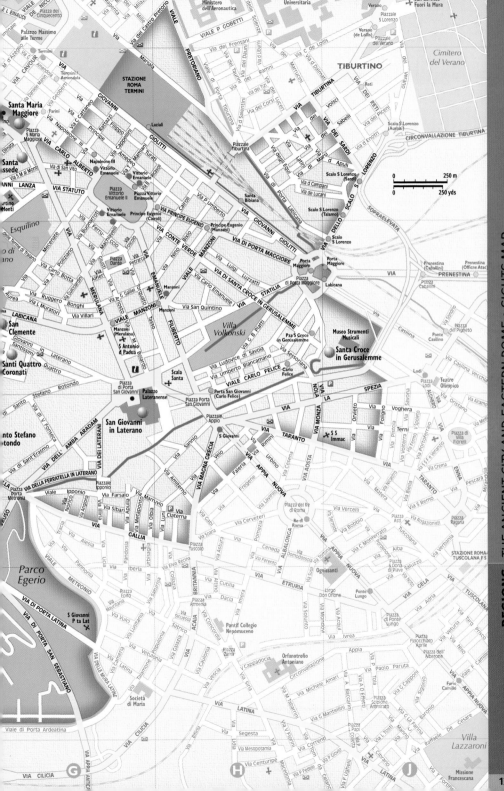

AVENTINO

The Aventine is one of the most beautiful quarters of Rome. Here, the traffic and chaos of the city are left far behind, replaced by peaceful churches, charming cloisters, beautiful gardens and panoramic views over the Trastevere and St. Peter's.

This is the most southerly of Rome's seven hills. Trajan lived here before he became emperor, and his friend Licinius Sura built his private baths here. It became such an affluent area that the Visigoths destroyed it when they sacked Rome in AD410.

From the Circo Massimo (▷ 145) at the foot of the hill there is a delightful walk up to the churches of Santa Sabina (▷ 170) and Sant'Alessio.

One of the finest views of Rome can be had from the Giardino degli Aranci (Garden of Orange Trees), which extends over the site of the Savelli family's stronghold in the Middle Ages. The orange trees were planted here in 1932 to commemorate the first orange tree planted in Italy, brought from Spain by St. Dominic early in the 13th century. Legend has it that the tree can still be seen in the cloister of the Dominican monastery of Santa Sabina.

One of Rome's most popular 'secret' views of St. Peter's can be seen through the keyhole in the main entrance to the Priory of the Knights of Malta.

✚ 138 E7 ✉ Circo Massimo 🚋 3, 44, 60, 73 to Viale Aventino, 75, 81, 95, 118, 160, 175, 204, 231, 628, 715

Clockwise from opposite *Monumento a Vittorio Emanuele II seen from the Aventine Hill; the view of St. Peter's from the Priory of the Knights of Malta; mosaics from Santa Sabina*

ARCO DI COSTANTINO

One of Rome's best-preserved Imperial monuments, the Arch of Constantine stands proudly on the ancient triumphal way where victorious armies once marched.

The Senate and people of Rome built the arch in AD315 to commemorate the victory of Constantine the Great over Maxentius, the last pagan emperor of Rome, in the battle of Ponte Milvio (AD312), after which Constantine granted freedom of worship to the Christians.

The highly decorated structure stands nearly 25m (80ft) high and consists of a large arch flanked by two smaller ones. It carries an inscription, repeated on both sides, celebrating Constantine's coming to power. Many of the arch's sculptures were actually taken from other monuments and reused: The bas-reliefs between the statues originally showed episodes in Marcus Aurelius' life, but his features were remodelled to resemble those of Constantine.

✚ 138 F6 ✉ Piazza del Colosseo, 00184 ✋ Free 🚇 Colosseo 🚋 60, 75, 81, 85, 117, 175, 204, 673, 810, 850

INTRODUCTION

The Colosseo, the Roman Empire's biggest amphitheatre, lies at the west end of the Foro Romano, all but encircled by the Caelian, Palatine and Esquiline hills. To get a sense of the building's scale and size, approach it along Via dei Fori Imperiali, or view it from the Colle Oppio park or the terrace above the Colosseo metro station.

The Colosseo was known as the Flavian Amphitheatre until the eighth century, as it was built by the three emperors from the Flavian family. Construction started under Vespasian in AD72, and the inaugural games, held in a partially completed building, took place during the reign of his son Titus in AD80. The Colosseo was completed by Titus' brother Domitian.

This was the first permanent amphitheatre to be built in Rome and one of the first buildings to combine a grandiose design with immense practicality. Games and fights were held here right up until the end of the Empire, with the last recorded exhibition of wild beasts in the sixth century. During the Middle Ages, the amphitheatre was used as a fortress, and from the 15th century as a quarry, providing the stone for some of Rome's finest churches and palaces. By the late 1700s the crumbling structure was a romantic and overgrown ruin, dedicated since 1750 to the Christian martyrs who had been killed in its arena. Serious conservation started in the 19th century and continues still.

Walk round the outside before you enter to take in the exterior architectural details. The Colosseum's interior has been severely damaged over the years, so joining the guided tour, or using an audioguide, is almost essential for understanding what you are seeing.

WHAT TO SEE
THE EXTERIOR

Only a small part of the Colosseo survives after centuries of pillaging for building stone. What's left is still impressive, and gives a good idea of the original external architecture, although the marble facings, painted stucco and statues have all gone. The Colosseo covers about 2.5ha (6 acres). It was built on marshy ground, which had to be drained, and beneath its visible arches are others sunk in the earth on cores of concrete. The external arches, and arcades behind them, are built of travertine stone. Behind the travertine facing there is a tufa infill, while the upper storeys of the arcades behind the facade are built of brick-faced concrete.

Externally, the Colosseo measures 188m by 156m (615ft by 510ft) and rises to 48.5m (158ft), with a facade of three tiers of arches and an attic level. The tiers are faced with three-quarter columns in the Classical architectural orders: Doric on the first floor, Ionic on the second and Corinthian on the third, each more elaborate than the one below. The attic has small square window openings and blank walls between Corinthian pilasters, where bronze shields once hung. At the top were 240 brackets and sockets that anchored the huge *velarium*, a shade and bad-weather canopy that could be pulled right over the interior. The holes all over the walls once housed the metal clamps that held the massive stone blocks together; these, along with huge amounts of stone, were pillaged for building in the Middle Ages and in Renaissance times.

THE ARCADES AND SEATING

Behind the facade, on the outside edge of the building, superb arcades run the whole way round the Colosseo on each floor, linking the stairways that connect the different levels. Farther in, 80 walls radiate out from the central arena and support vaults for the access passageways and the tiers of seats.

INFORMATION

www.archeorm.arti.beniculturali.it
www.pierreci.it

✚ 138 F6 ✉ Piazza del Colosseo, 00184 ☎ 06 0608. Advance tickets: 06 3996 7700 🕐 Last Sun in Mar to Aug daily 8.30–7.15; Sep 8.30–7; Oct 8.30–6.30; Nov to mid-Feb 8.30–4.30; mid-Feb to mid-Mar 8.30–5; mid-Mar to last Sat in Mar 8.30–5.30. Last entrance 1 hour before closing 🖐 Adult €12, plus €3 for special exhibitions, EU citizens 18–24 €7.50, EU citizens under 18 and over 65 free. Ticket valid for two days and includes access to the Foro Romano (▷ 146–151) and Palatino (▷ 160). Tickets can be booked in advance online at www.pierreci.it/it/acquista-il-biglietto/biglietto-on-line.aspx or by phone on 06 0608. Alternatively, buy tickets at the visitor centre at Via Parigi 5. If you intend visiting many of the city's ancient sites, it may be worth buying the Roma Archeologica Card (▷ 259). Guided visits €4. 🚇 Colosseo (line B) 🚌 60, 75, 85, 87, 175, 810, 850 🚶 English-language tours available; hours vary. Audioguides available in Italian, English, French, German, Spanish and Japanese: €5 📖 Official guidebook in English published by Sovrintendenza dei Beni Culturali; unofficial guidebooks in English available at stands all over Rome 🏪 Two well-stocked souvenir and book shops selling guidebooks, postcards and souvenirs

Opposite The Colosseum, which was designed to hold more than 50,000 people, is the largest surviving ancient Roman structure in the world

TIPS

» The Colosseo's ticket office can be very busy—buy your ticket online or at the Palatine to avoid waiting.

» It's hard to work out what's what, so take the guided tour to get the most out of your visit.

» Viewing the outside of the Colosseo after dark, when it is floodlit, adds an extra dimension.

WHAT'S IN A NAME?

The name Colosseum first appeared in the writings of the English monk the Venerable Bede in the eighth century. Despite the fact that Bede had never been to Rome, it was soon accepted that he derived the name either from the size of the structure, or because of the huge statue of Nero that once stood nearby. Another theory is that it may once have been called *amphitheatrum ad Colle Isaeum*—'the amphitheatre near the Iseum Hill'. Constant use would have led to the dropping of *amphitheatrum*, and as initial vowels elide in Latin the resultant word would have been very close to Colosseum. Whatever the derivation, English travellers may then have taken the name back from Rome to Bede.

Off the arcades, about 80 entrances—called *vomitoriae*—led into the arena itself, allowing vast numbers of people to pass rapidly through.

Inside, there were tiers of marble benches, some of which can still be seen, where more than 50,000 people could be seated. In the later days of the Empire, cushions were provided, probably much appreciated since the games usually lasted throughout the day. Seating was arranged by rank, with the least important members of the crowd—including women—assigned places nearest the top. Closest to the arena was a special box for the emperor, his family and the Vestal Virgins. Senators were also allotted ringside seats, and the rest of the tickets were distributed through the heads of families, with better-born citizens getting the better seats.

The tickets themselves were wooden plaques, carved with the relevant entrance, aisle, row and seat number. Spectators found the right entrance by looking for the numbers over the exterior arches, and you can still see traces of these. The system was supremely efficient, capable of moving up to 70,000 people in or out in a matter of minutes. The design has never been bettered; in essence, the Colosseo is the prototype for every modern sports stadium.

THE ARENA

Right in the middle of the Colosseo is a jumble of ruins, all that's left of the labyrinthine passages beneath the arena itself. In Roman times, this area was covered by wooden flooring, topped with a waterproof layer of canvas and overlaid with sand—the word arena comes from the Latin word for sand. The four principal entrances were mainly used by the gladiators and corpse removers, but far more dramatic entrances were made through the floor itself, and you can see outlines of the stone rims of trapdoors among the ruins.

During the Colosseo's history, tens of thousands of animals were slaughtered here, sent to Rome from all over the Empire by specialist animal collectors. Such vast numbers were needed that elephants disappeared from North Africa, hippos from Numidia and lions from Mesopotamia as the Roman appetite for ever-more extravagant spectacles grew. Once in Rome, the animals were transported in cages to the Colosseo, then harried through underground passages onto elevators that rose up to arena level through the trapdoors. With this in mind, the maze of ruins begins to make sense.

Not all the channels were used for men and beasts. Some were water conduits, and the arena was regularly flooded for entertainments known as *naumachia*, when criminals fought to the death in re-enactments of naval battles in scaled-down galleys. Gladiatorial games began in the morning with an elaborate procession led by the games' sponsor, the prelude to a morning of staged hunts with wild animals pitted against each other or pursued by *bestiarii*, gladiators specializing in animal slaughter. The lunch break was accompanied by executions of the worst criminals, a taster for the climax of the day—the individual gladiatorial combats.

Below *A complex network of passageways lay beneath the floor of the arena*

CIRCO MASSIMO

Even if there is no longer much to see, the Circo Massimo has kept its magical atmosphere and the feeling of past glories. Wandering around the huge elliptical track, now a peaceful garden (if you can ignore the noise of the traffic beyond its boundaries), it is not difficult to imagine the cheers of 300,000 spectators watching the chariot races organized for the emperors of Imperial Rome.

Nestling in a hollow between the Aventine and Palatine hills, the Great Circus was more than 600m (1,970ft) long and 140m (460ft) wide, and was probably built as early as 326BC. Mainly used for two- and four-horse chariot races, it remained in use until AD549.

Emperor Augustus erected the obelisk of the Pharaoh Rameses II (now in Piazza del Popolo) on the *spina*, the dividing wall running down the middle of the track; Constantine also put up an obelisk, later moved to Piazza di San Giovanni in Laterano. The ruins of Porta Capena were part of the circus during Trajan's period. In 1145 the circus was granted to the Frangipani family—the tower at the end towards the FAO building is what remains of their fortress. Excavation and restoration works started in the 1930s.

✠ 138 E7 ✉ Viale Aventino, 00184 🚇 Circo Massimo 🚌 81, 160, 204, 628, 715

COLONNA TRAIANA

Trajan's Column is one of the oldest and most intact ancient monuments in present-day Rome. It is an exquisite work of art, with more than 100 bas-relief scenes of the Dacian wars (waged in the region of present-day Romania) conducted by Emperor Trajan during the second century AD. More than 2,500 figures decorate 25 great blocks of marble, each one about 3.5m (11ft) wide. These magnificent carvings were probably originally painted in brilliant hues. The column stands in Trajan's Forum, part of the Fori

Above *The ruins of the Foro di Augusto (Forum of Augustus), one of the five Fori Imperiali*

Imperiali (▷ below), where you can also see the Mercati di Traiano—Trajan's Market (▷ 152–153).

From the base of the column, which is decorated with war trophies, there is a spiral staircase leading up. A statue of St. Peter on top, by Tommaso della Porta, replaces the original statue of Trajan, which looked out over the Forum until 1587. The inside of the column can only be visited as part of an organized tour.

The marble blocks vary in diameter from the base to the top of the column. So that the 40m (130ft) column appears straight, the diameter increases gradually from about two-thirds of the way up. Look also for the windows cut in the decorative panels: Barely noticeable from the outside, they allow light to enter the staircase area.

✠ 138 E5 ✉ Via dei Fori Imperiali, 00184 🚇 Colosseo 🚌 60, 84, 85, 87, 117, 175, 810, 850

COLOSSEO

▷ 142–144.

FORI IMPERIALI

www.capitolium.org

By the first century BC the Foro Romano (▷ 146–151) had become too small to serve the needs of the growing city, and in 54BC Julius Ceasar built an additional administrative centre, the first of the five Fori Imperiali, or Imperial Fora. Successive emperors Augustus, Vespasian, Domitian and Trajan built their own fora, ostensibly to

commemorate military victories or periods of peace, but in reality, like Ceasar, as an expression of their own power.

The Fori Imperiali lie on either side of the Via dei Fori Imperiali between the Piazza Venezia and the Colosseum, sprawling across 22,000sq m (236,800sq ft). Excavations, ongoing since the 1990s, have uncovered over half of the site. While these continue, there is no public access to the fora. However, much of the jumble of archeological remains is visible from the Via dei Fori Imperiali. Head to the Centro Esposito-Informativo, where models and audiovisual displays will help you to understand more fully what you see.

From Piazza Venezia, the first forum, lying below the Mercati di Traiano (▷ 152), is that of Trajan, the last and most opulent to be built. Behind the forum stands the superb Trajan's Column (Colonna Traiana, ▷ opposite). Across the road is the earliest, Caesar's Forum. On the same side as Trajan's Forum is that of Augustus, inaugurated in 2BC. In AD75 Vespasian built a forum close to the Foro Romano, while in AD97 the Forum of Nerva was completed, sited underneath the present Via dei Fori Imperiali.

✠ 138 E5, E6, F6 ✉ Via dei Fori Imperiali, 00184. Centro Esposito-Informativo: Via dei Fori Imperiali ☎ Centro Esposito-Informativo: 06 679 7702 🕐 Centro Esposito-Informativo: daily 9.30–6.30 ♿ Free 🚇 Colosseo 🚌 60, 84, 85, 117, 810

INTRODUCTION

The ruins of the Roman Forum, once the centre of Republican and Imperial Rome, still lie at the heart of the city, shadowed by the Monumento a Vittorio Emanuele II in Piazza Venezia (▷ 106) and the Capitoline and Palatine hills.

The site is among the oldest in Rome, close to the area where the city's earliest inhabitants, seeking refuge from the marshy banks of the Tiber, first built pastoral settlements on the high ground of the Palatine Hill. New excavations reveal ever-older artefacts, but there were tribes in the area at least 1,000 years before the birth of Christ. The origins of the Forum itself lie in the eighth century BC, perhaps earlier, when villagers began to drain the land below the Palatine and construct religious and civic buildings.

Over the centuries the Forum and its associated buildings became the heart of the expanding city of Rome, graced with ever more magnificent basilicas, temples and commercial premises. It was home to the Vestal Virgins, the venue for religious ceremonies, military triumphs, sacrifices and important funerals, and the site of the law courts and banking, trading and commercial activities. It was also the city's main meeting place, fulfilling much the same purpose in Roman life as a piazza does in 21st-century Italian towns.

By the second century BC, however, the forum was too constricted for Rome's ever-expanding public needs, and in 54BC Julius Caesar built the first of a series of new administrative centres close by, the Fori Imperiali (▷ 145). With Rome's decline, the original Forum area steadily declined, its buildings either transformed into Christian churches, or abandoned. After AD800 the Forum became little more than a convenient stone quarry for medieval and Renaissance builders. Excavation started in the 19th century and has continued ever since.

The best of several entrances to the Forum is the one midway down Via dei Fori Imperiali, which leads you straight on to the Via Sacra, running through the heart of the complex. This thoroughfare is bounded to the right by the Arco di Settimio Severo, and to the left by the Arco di Tito, with most of the interesting remains lying between these two triumphal arches.

INFORMATION

www.capitolium.org

✚ 138 E6 ✉ Via dei Fori Imperiali, Via di San Teodoro, Via di San Gregorio, Piazza Santa Maria 53, Largo Romolo e Remo 5–6, 00184 ☎ 06 3996 7700 🕐 Last Sun in Mar to Aug daily 8.30–7.15; Sep 8.30–7; Oct 8.30–6.30; Nov to mid-Feb 8.30–4.30; mid-Feb to mid-Mar 8.30–5; mid-Mar to last Sat in Mar 8.30–5.30

✋ Adult €12, EU citizens 18–24 €7.50, EU citizens under 18 and over 65 free. Ticket is valid for two days and includes entry to the Colosseum (▷ 143–144) and Palatino (▷ 160). Tickets can be booked in advance online at www.pierreci.it/it/acquista-il-biglietto/biglietto-on-line.aspx or by phone on 06 0608. If you intend visiting many of the city's ancient sites, it may be worth buying the Roma Archeologica Card (▷ 259) 🚇 Colosseo 🚌 75, 85, 87, 117, 175, 186, 810, 850

🚩 Tours in English available 1–2pm daily, €5. Audioguides in Italian and English, €5. Ticket office at Arco di Tito (tel 06 3996 7700)

Above *The view from the Palatine Hill*
Opposite *The Monumento a Vittorio Emanuele II, overlooking the ruins of the Roman Forum*

TIPS

» Making sense of the Forum is quite a challenge—use an audioguide to get more out of your visit.

» Take something to drink with you. There are no cafés or bars in the Forum area.

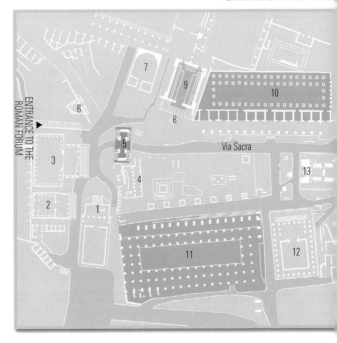

ENTRANCE TO THE ROMAN FORUM

Via Sacra

When exploring the Forum, it is vital to remember that monuments were built, rebuilt, plundered, demolished and incorporated into later buildings for at least 1,000 years, so the ruins can appear haphazard. Take time to get your bearings, however, and refer to the plan of the area, and you can begin to make sense of Rome's ancient heart of empire.

WHAT TO SEE

TEMPLE AND HOUSE OF THE VESTAL VIRGINS

Overlooking the Via Sacra rise the ruins of a circular white temple. This is the Temple of Vesta, goddess of the hearth, where the Vestal Virgins tended an ever-burning fire symbolizing the perpetuity of the Roman state. A Temple of Vesta stood here from the earliest times; the existing ruin and its columns are composed of fragments of the version dating from AD191, built by Septimius Severus after a fire. It was reconstructed in the 1930s.

The cult of Vesta was one of the cornerstones of Roman belief. In primitive times, fire was of such importance it attained an almost sacred significance. Difficult to kindle, it was vital that it should not go out, so the custom evolved of keeping the communal fire in a separate hut. Young girls, with few other responsibilities, were the appointed guardians; thus over time a practice that originated in good sense became imbued with religious symbolism. The temple itself was always circular, in imitation of the round huts of ancient Rome, and everything connected with Vesta and her worship was charged with archaic significance. The fire had to be kept burning at all costs, a difficult task when the winds blew and rain poured through the vent in the roof.

There were six Vestal Virgins, working in turns to tend the fire. They were recruited at an early age from impeccable families and appointed for 30 years by the emperor. The first 10 years were spent learning their duties, the second practising them and the last passing on their knowledge. At the end of their service, Vestals were released from their vows and were free to marry, though

Below *A detail from the third-century AD Arco di Settimio Severo*

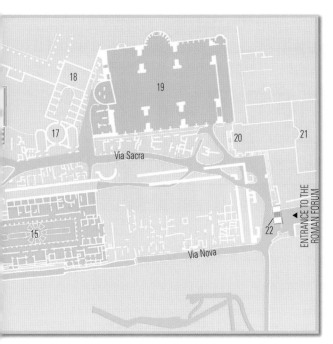

few did. In return for their service, they had immense privileges (in a society where women had few rights) — wealth, land ownership, the right to pardon criminals, and access to the emperor. If they broke their vows of chastity, however, the penalties were harsh — some were buried alive. The order survived into the Christian era, being finally disbanded in AD394.

Vestal Virgins lived in the Atrium Vestae, the sprawling site next to the temple. This was built, as were all patrician houses, around an elongated court, whose ruins survive. It was constructed in the second century AD, to replace an earlier building, and must have been immensely grand. Today, the central courtyard with its three pools, lined with statues of the Virgins in their long white robes, is the most striking thing to be seen. Behind lie the tumbled ruins of the Vestals' once-magnificent palace.

THE CURIA

Set back from the Forum proper is a wonderfully complete, austere, red building. This is the Curia, home to the Senate, the most important civil body during the days of the Republic. According to Roman legend, Romulus, father of Rome, summoned a hundred family heads to meet regularly for consultation. These so-called *patres* (fathers) were the first senators; their role evolved into that of decision-makers on Rome's policies at home and abroad. During the Republic, the Curia was politically the most important place in the Roman world, where famous orators and statesmen spoke, major legal affairs were disputed, and policies shaped. But as the role of the single ruler evolved, its influence waned, and by the second century AD the Senate had no control over affairs, although it continued as an institution right up to the fall of Rome.

The Curia was rebuilt several times over the centuries, and the present building was reconstructed after a fire during the reign of Diocletian (AD285–305). In AD630 it was incorporated into the church of Sant'Adriano, and emerged virtually intact when the church was demolished in 1937. It is by no means

Below *The sombre Arco di Tito dates from AD81*

THE TOGA

All over the Empire, free-born Romans wore the toga. It was a sign of citizenship and the privileges that went with it; it proclaimed that the wearer was protected by Roman law and could not be mistreated, flogged or crucified. The emperors issued edicts about the toga, decreeing that citizens entering the Forum or attending the games had to wear it. It was an elegant but cumbersome garment, with folds that took time to arrange; it had to be re-pleated after every wearing, and it needed constant washing. Citizens disliked putting on the toga, and avoided doing so if possible — it was difficult to do more than stroll about slowly while wearing it.

There were several types of toga: the plain white one worn by ordinary citizens; a garment with a red hem for certain priests; and the *toga praetexta*, edged with purple and worn by the 600 senators. Grandest of all was the *toga picta*, woven of purple cloth, worn by the emperor on state occasions.

grand or huge, being built to hold about 300 senators. The height of the Curia is half the sum of its length and breadth, a ratio prescribed by the great first-century BC architect Vitruvius as providing ideal acoustics. Inside, three shallow tiers of marble seats face each other across the central space, with a low dais for the presiding magistrate at the far end, and a statue of a senator in the middle. Grey marble originally covered the walls — you can see some surviving sections facing each side of the platform. The floor is a most beautiful example of a technique called *opus sectile*, in which large pieces of stone in different hues are fitted together in figured patterns. Only the doors are replacements; the originals were removed in the 17th century, by Pope Alexander VII, to the basilica of San Giovanni in Laterano.

The senate house was a consecrated building with the status of a temple; the first act of each senator on entering was to throw incense grains onto the brazier next to the goddess of victory, whose statue stood on an altar at one end. Speakers addressed the Senate from their seats, and voted by division, with those in agreement moving to one side and those against to the other.

The area outside the Curia is the Comitium. Here, during the early Republic, stood the Rostra, from which orators addressed the people. Its name comes from the *rostra* — the prows or beaks — of ships captured at the Battle of Anzio in 338BC, which once decorated it. The fenced-off, flat, black marble slab is the Lapis Niger, which the Romans believed marked the burial place of Romulus. A stele dating from the sixth century BC was found here; the inscription engraved on it is believed to be the earliest written form of Latin.

ARCO DI SETTIMIO SEVERO

Next to the Curia, on the triumphal route that led to the Capitoline Hill, stands the Arch of Septimius Severus. It was built, in AD203, on the orders of the Senate, to commemorate the 10th anniversary of the Emperor Septimius Severus' defeat of the Parthians (in what is now Iran), and to glorify his sons, Caracalla and Geta. Being the first major architectural addition to the Forum area for 80 years, it was suitably grandiose. The central arch is flanked by two lower ones, and faced with four splendid Corinthian columns, surrounded by reliefs with reclining gods and scenes from Severus' career. Originally, it was topped with a statue of Severus and his two sons riding in a chariot drawn by six horses. This has gone, but the inscriptions along the entablature are still clear. In AD212, after he became emperor, Caracalla murdered his brother Geta, co-emperor with him, and removed his name. Look at the fourth line of the inscription and you can see the missing words *'et Gatae nobilissimo cesari'* outlined by the holes left by the clamps that once held the letters.

Above Although little of the site remains intact, the Forum is one of the most captivating places in the city

ARCO DI TITO

At the opposite end of the Forum from Severus' Arch, the Arch of Titus was erected in AD81 in homage to Flavian Emperor Titus and his capture of Jerusalem 11 years earlier. This restrained and sober monument, heavily restored, is today most significant for its unique representations, on the inner jambs of the arch, of the sacred furnishings of the great Jewish temple in Jerusalem. On the south side is the triumphant procession entering Rome with the trophies from the temple—the silver trumpets, the sacred altar and the seven-branched candlestick. On the opposite jamb is Titus, crowned with laurel by Nike (goddess of victory), standing in his horse-drawn chariot, surrounded by senators and plebs. For centuries the arch has been a symbol of shame to Jews, and even today, many refuse to pass through it.

VIA SACRA

The Via Sacra runs right through the core of the Forum, from the Palatine Hill to the Capitoline. It was the most famous street in ancient Rome, its name deriving from the sanctuaries that lined it and the victorious processions of generals and emperors that walked along it. Scholars and archaeologists have argued for years over the precise function of some of the buildings along the Via Sacra, but many are well known, as they were among the most important in the city. Just by the main entrance to the Forum site are the steps of the Regia, the house of kings, probably dating from the seventh century BC. Opposite is the best-preserved temple in the Forum, that of Antoninus and Faustina, which owes its survival to its conversion into a Christian church in the seventh century. Farther along, the huge area of broken columns was once the Basilica Aemilia, built in the second century BC to house the law courts. The Via Sacra curves left from here, with the Forum proper to the right. To the left are the long steps of the ruins of the Basilica Giulia, built by Julius Caesar in the 50s BC on his return from the Gallic Wars. The romantic theory that the ruts in the stones were made by Roman chariots is unlikely to be correct, as none were allowed along the Via Sacra; they were probably gouged out by the carts of medieval builders using the Forum as a quarry.

BASILICAS

The Romans invented the architectural form of the basilica, a great hall where the central, higher space, lit by clerestory windows, was divided from the side aisles by rows of columns. Basilicas, with their exterior porticoes and colonnades, were practical buildings where crowds could gather in comfort, and they were used as meeting places for business and as law courts. They were cool and airy during stifling summer months, making it no surprise that the early Christian Church adopted the design—and the name.

Left *The three remaining columns from the Temple of Castor and Pollux*
Below *The Palatine Hill rises above the Forum*

INFORMATION

www.mercatiditraiano.it

🔲 138 E5 ✉ Via IV Novembre 94, 00184 ☎ 06 0608 🕐 Tue–Sun 9–7 ✋ Adult €11, EU citizens 18–25 and over 65 €9, child (under 6) free 🚇 Colosseo 🚌 60, 84, 85, 87, 117, 810, 850

MERCATI DI TRAIANO

Like his predecessors, the Emperor Trajan was responsible for the construction of a forum in the heart of ancient Rome. Today, his is remarkable not just for its size, but for its contents, their state of preservation and the superb restoration that has been done on them. Built between AD100 and 110, Trajan's Forum included the Colonna Traiana (▷ 145), the forum itself—one of the five Fori Imperiali (▷ 145)—and the extraordinary *mercati* (markets). These are built on six different levels against the Quirinal Hill, and are often dubbed the world's first purpose-built shopping mall. Today, they are home to the Museo dei Fori Imperiali which incorporates the main market structures, stretches of ancient streets and some of the surrounding medieval buildings. The exhibits within the rooms of the complex are devoted to beautifully illuminated statuary and archaeological finds, displayed in a succession of chambers devoted to each of the Fori Imperiali.

INSIDE THE MARKETS

The *mercati* served as an administrative hub for the Imperial authorities, where supplies were brought in, divided and redistributed. The main entrance from Via IV Novembre leads you into the Grande Aula (Great Hall), a huge space, once probably used for the distribution of corn. Today, beautifully lit and restored, it's often used for temporary exhibitions. There's access from the hall to the Great Hemicycle (AD107), open-air terraces on which six tiers of arcaded shops and apartments are set. From here there's an excellent bird's-eye view over the neighbouring fora. At the east end of the Aula, steps lead down to Via Biberatica, an ancient street running round the upper floor of the complex. Complete with its original paving, it's flanked by well-preserved shops, probably *tabernae* (bars), which may have given the street its name—*bibere* means 'to drink' in Latin.

THE SHOPS

More stairs lead down through the different floors, where you can take in the covered shopping arcade and the stores on the ground floor; in all, there are around 150 shops of different types. Those on the ground floor were quite shallow; one has been reconstructed to show the external travertine door frames, which gave the shopkeepers extra space for their goods.

Above *The Great Hemicycle, a spectacular first-century AD structure*
Opposite *The Torre delle Milizie, a medieval addition, rises above the original Roman marketplace*

INFORMATION

www.museicapitolini.org

➕ 138 E6 ✉ Piazza del Campidoglio 1, 00186 ☎ Advance tickets and information: 06 0608 🕐 Tue–Sun 9–8, 24 and 31 Dec 9–2 💷 Adult €12, EU citizens 6–25 and over 65 €9.50, child (under 6) €2. During temporary exhibitions, the ticket price may be higher and will include entrance to both the exhibition and the museum 🚇 Colosseo 🚌 40, 60, 64, 86, 88, 492, 590, 715, 716 🎧 Audioguide available in English; €5 📖 Short and full guidebooks available in the museum shops 🍴 Caffè Caffarelli, with all-day service, ice cream and bar. Rooftop terrace with stunning views. Open outside museum hours in summer 🎁 Libreria Capitolina (2 outlets). Excellent range of guidebooks, postcards, souvenirs and museum merchandise. The shops also sell a large range of other art books and multimedia works

INTRODUCTION

The Musei Capitolini, or Capitoline Museums, house much of Rome's civic art collections, and occupy two of the three palaces around Michelangelo's beautiful Piazza del Campidoglio (▷ 160). They date from the 15th century, when civic power in Rome was centred on the Capitoline, where the Palazzo Senatorio and Palazzo dei Conservatori were used for meetings of the magistrates who, together with the senators, governed the city.

In 1471 Pope Sixtus IV presented the Roman bronzes and statues that formed the nucleus of the museum to the city, creating the world's first public museum. The buildings and piazza were restored and enlarged to Michelangelo's plans in the mid-16th century, and in 1654 Girolamo and Carlo Rainaldi designed the Palazzo Nuovo to complete an architectural ensemble incorporating Roman, medieval and Renaissance elements.

The piazza and its array of buildings is approached up a graceful ramp, known as the Cordonata, just off Piazza Venezia, with the church of Santa Maria d'Aracoeli to the left. At the heart of the piazza, laid out for the triumphal entry of Emperor Charles V in 1536, is a copy of the great second-century equestrian statue of Marcus Aurelius. The main entrance to the Musei Capitolini is via the Palazzo dei Conservatori, where you'll find the ticket offices and cloakrooms. You can reach the collections in the Palazzo Nuovo either by crossing the piazza or using the underground gallery that runs beneath the Palazzo Senatorio; this gives access to the Tabularium, once the ancient Capitoline archive building.

Some 400 of the museum's sculptures are now housed at the Centrale Montemartini, a converted power station south of the city.

WHAT TO SEE
PALAZZO DEI CONSERVATORI

Your visit starts in the *cortile* (central courtyard), lined with reliefs and inscriptions, and containing the surviving fragments of a colossal statue of Constantine the Great dating from AD313, which was discovered in the Forum in 1486. Only the nude parts of the body would have been in marble, with the draperies in gilded bronze covering a supporting frame.

From this central courtyard a superb stairway leads to the upper floor where the bulk of the palazzo's collections are housed. The route takes you first through a series of frescoed halls, the Appartamenti dei Conservatori. Their grand decorative schemes are linked to their original function as rooms for official civic business, and the wall paintings and tapestries form a superb backdrop for the stunning works in the collection. Don't miss the Hall of the Horatii and Curiatii, where giant murals depicting the early days of Rome surround Bernini's statue of Urban VIII, sculpted between 1635 and 1640.

Further on, in the Sala dei Trionfi, is one of the museum's best-loved sculptures. The small bronze *Spinario* was one of the first gifts to the museum by its founder Pope Sixtus IV in 1471, and shows a seated boy pulling a thorn from his foot. The pose is unique among ancient statues and it was popular in the Renaissance, inspiring many similar works.

Next door, in the Sala della Lupa, is the *Capitoline She-Wolf*, the very symbol of Rome. Also part of Sixtus IV's gift, it originally stood on the facade of the palazzo—minus the figures of Romulus and Remus. These were added in 1509 by the Florentine sculptor Antonio del Pollaiuolo, and the group was brought inside during Michelangelo's refurbishment of the palace in the mid-16th century. The statue is Etruscan, dating from the fifth century BC, and is a wonderfully intelligent portrayal of an animal once common in Italy. Beyond the Sala della Lupa, in the Sala delle Oche, Bernini's dramatic head of Medusa (1644–48) showcases the contrast between the austere Classical style and high baroque.

TIPS
» It's worth taking a guided tour (groups only) or audioguide as the collection is huge and confusing.
» Allow plenty of time and be prepared to concentrate—this is not the easiest museum to love and is not for the faint-hearted.
» The piazza and the interiors look their best after dark, so try to go late in the day.
» Some works have been moved to the Montemartini power house on the Via Ostiense, but the best remain here.
» From the terrace of the second-floor café and restaurant there are magnificent views over the city—you can access this without paying the museum entrance fee.

Clockwise from opposite *Fragments from a colossal statue of Constantine the Great line the courtyard of the Palazzo dei Conservatori; the Capitoline Venus in the Palazzo Nuovo; the bronze* Spinario, *in the Palazzo dei Conservatori, depicts a boy picking a thorn (spina) from his foot*

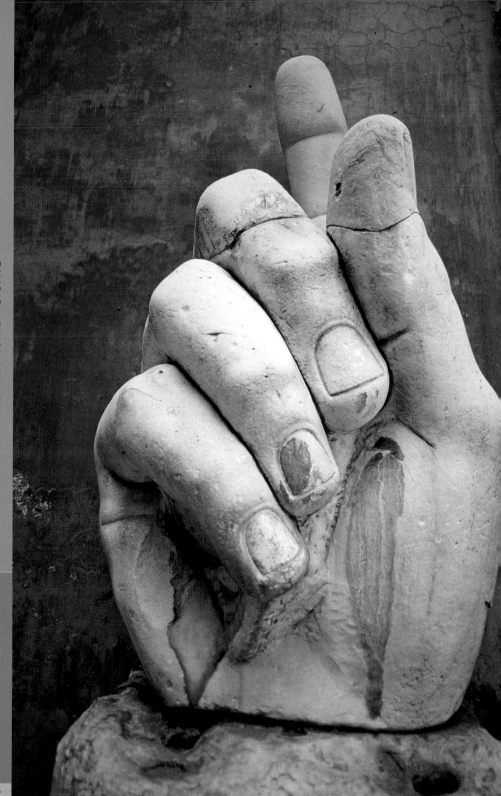

The Appartamenti lead into the Museo del Palazzo dei Conservatori proper, where a series of rooms is home to Classical statuary, busts and urns, many of them of superlative quality. The Galleria degli Horti leads into the museum's most stunning space, the Esedra, a contemporary glass and stone hall built specifically to house the magnificent gilded bronze equestrian statue of Emperor Marcus Aurelius. The statue was once the focal point of the Piazza del Campidoglio outside, residing there on a plinth designed by Michelangelo. Threatened by modern pollution, the original has been replaced by a replica.

This wonderful piece, once part of a triumphal monument, depicts Marcus Aurelius (AD161–180), astride his horse, as a majestic lawgiver. Following the fall of Rome, the statue, with its outstretched hand, was believed to be that of Constantine, the first Christian emperor, and thus survived the Dark Ages, when thousands of similar works were destroyed. It stood untouched outside the basilica of San Giovanni in Laterano until it was brought to the Piazza del Campidoglio. It is the only such statue to survive from this period, and throughout the Middle Ages was repeatedly referred to by artists and writers. The Esedra also houses a superb gilded bronze Hercules, dating from the second century BC, and the head and foot of a fourth-century AD bronze colossus of the Emperor Constantine.

The glassed-in gallery overlooking the Esedra is devoted to finds from the ruins of the ancient Temple of Jove Capitoline, which was unearthed during its construction in 2000. Segments of the temple's walls survive and there are interesting displays throwing light on the archaeological dig and its discoveries.

THE PINACOTECA

The second floor of the Palazzo dei Conservatori houses the Pinacoteca, the Capitoline picture gallery, founded in the 18th century by Pope Benedict XIV. There are far finer collections in Rome, but the gallery does contain a good cross-section of Italian painting between the 14th and 17th centuries, as well as some interesting foreign works. The gentle piety of Titian's *The Baptism of Christ* (c.1512) and Tintoretto's *Penitent Magdalene* (c.1531) contrast admirably with the sensual energy of Veronese's *The Rape of Europa* in room III. There is a fine *Madonna* in room V by Correggio, but some of the best works are in the Hall of St. Petronilla, named after *The Burial of St. Petronilla* (c.1623), an altarpiece by Guercino (Giovanni Francesco Barbieri). Here, there are two splendid works by Caravaggio, *John the Baptist* (1597) and *The Fortune Teller* (1594), and a voluptuous *Romulus and Remus* (1615) by Rubens. In the Cini Gallery is *The Brothers de Wael*, a portrait by Anthony van Dyck

Above *The bronze* Capitoline She-Wolf, *one of the treasures displayed in the Palazzo dei Conservatori*
Opposite *The sculpted hand of Constantine the Great in the courtyard of the Palazzo dei Conservatori*

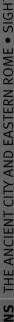

THE ANCIENT CITY AND EASTERN ROME • SIGHTS

REGIONS

painted in Genoa in 1621; a *Self-portrait* by Velázquez, painted in 1650 during his second visit to Rome, also hangs here.

Also on this floor you'll find the Sala del Frontone, part of the Palazzo Caffarelli, which was restored and opened to the public to commemorate the Millennium. It contains fragments from a second-century BC temple.

TABULARIUM

The remains of the Tabularium, an imposing building completed in 78BC, lie underneath the Palazzo Senatorio. In Roman times it was where the archives of the Roman State were kept, bronze *tabulae* containing the state laws and official deeds. It is reached via the underground tunnel that connects the two wings of the museum. For Classical history enthusiasts a visit to this complex is a must, but the attraction for most visitors is the view of the Foro Romano from its arched gallery.

PALAZZO NUOVO

On the north side of the Piazza del Campidoglio stands the Palazzo Nuovo, home to some of Rome's best Classical sculpture. Some of the museum's largest and most exciting pieces are in the lobby and courtyard. A 3m-high (10ft) statue of the goddess Minerva stands against a wall in the lobby. Probably a product of second-century BC Greek craftsmanship and created for a major temple, the statue wears a belted tunic and a helmet—the holes in the belt were used to hang metal ornaments from it. The eyes are hollow, but would have been filled with glittering metal and polished stones.

At the far end of the courtyard is *Marforio*, a sculptural ensemble incorporated into a fountain—typical of the practical High Renaissance approach to ancient works of art, which was to reuse and adapt them. The reclining bearded figure representing a river god dates from the first or second century AD, while the fountain and shells were added in 1594, producing a piece that is an amalgam of ancient and modern. During the Renaissance, *Marforio* was used as a place to leave satirical messages, called *pasquinades*, so the figures of satyrs on either side seem appropriate. Half-man, half-goat, each balances a basket of grapes on his head; they almost certainly once supported roof beams in a loggia, probably located near the Theatre of Pompey.

Below Marforio, *a reclining statue of a river god, in the courtyard of the Palazzo Nuovo*

CLASSICAL SCULPTURE IN PALAZZO NUOVO

Here in the world's oldest public art collection, it is possible to gain a sense of what a museum of the 17th and 18th centuries was like, and scattered among the seemingly endless ranks of statuary in the upstairs rooms of the Palazzo Nuovo are some gems, the city's best Roman copies of Greek sculpture.

Originally, Classical statues were brightly painted and acted as focal points in buildings and public spaces. Renaissance restorers mended, replaced and polished, often substituting arms and even heads if the originals were damaged or missing. The *Discobolos* (discus thrower), in the gallery, is a prime example. The original was sculpted in Greece around 460BC. Many copies were made, including the powerful torso of the figure here; the rest of the statue was reworked (not very satisfactorily) around 1700. Off the gallery, the Sala delle Colombe contains a beautiful Roman copy of a Hellenistic *Young Girl with a Dove*. The avian theme continues in the room's most famous work, the second-century AD *Mosaic of the Doves* from Hadrian's Villa at Tivoli, which depicts doves drinking at a fountain. Both marble and glass were used for the mosaic, and also in the second-century *Mosaic of the Theatrical Masks*. Also off the gallery, in a small polygonal room, is the *Capitoline Venus*, discovered in the late 17th century. Slightly larger than life-size, this is a depiction of Venus-Aphrodite, a popular theme of Classical sculptors. Beautifully modelled, this version dates from the first century BC.

In both the Sala degli Imperatori and the Sala dei Filosofi are numerous portrait busts, some of which have surprisingly modern-looking faces. Beyond here is the Great Hall with, among other full-size pieces, the *Apollo of Omphalos*, a fine Roman copy of the fifth-century BC Greek original. The masterpiece in Sala del Fauno is the *Drunken Faun*, carved in red marble and, although over-restored in the 18th century, a splendid piece, full of *joie de vivre*. Beyond here, the Sala del Gladiatore takes its name from the *Dying Gaul*, one of the most famous and emotive of all Classical statues. Once thought to be a dying gladiator, its true subject is clear from the warrior's weapons, his nudity and his hairstyle—all Celtic attributes.

Above The Dying Gaul, *a Classical marble sculpture, is one of the treasures in the Palazzo Nuovo*

MOSAICS

The processes employed to make the mosaics in the Capitoline are still used today. Large sheets of glass, or thin slabs of marble, are first shattered into tiny pieces to make the mosaic tiles (tesserae). The surface on which the mosaic will be built is covered with a layer of cement, on which the outline of the image is traced. Next comes a thin layer of mortar; on this, a detailed painting of the final design is made. The pieces of glass and marble, set at fractionally different angles to refract the light, are then pressed into the wet mortar, creating an image that can endure for millennia. The smaller the tesserae, and the more varied the hue, the more expensive the mosaics.

MERCATI DI TRAIANO
▷ 152–153.

MUSEI CAPITOLINI
▷ 154–159.

PALATINO
www.archeorm.arti.beniculturali.it

The Palatine Hill offers a lovely walk through gardens and shaded areas, where time seems to have stood still. One of the seven hills of Rome and rich in archaeology, the Palatine is considered the cradle of the city.

Emperors preferred the Palatine for their palaces. Augustus set the trend by enlarging his house after it was damaged by fire; Tiberius followed (his palace is now largely beneath the Farnese Gardens), as did Nero with part of the Golden House (Domus Aurea). But what remains today consists mainly of Domitian's vast imperial palace.

Among the ruins on the hill are temples to Cybele, goddess of fertility, and to Apollo and Victory, and the first-century BC House of Livia. The remains of Domitian's palace include the Domus Flavia (the seat of government), the Domus Augustana (the Emperor's private quarters) and the House of the Griffins, with frescoes depicting those winged mythological beasts. The Palatine museum houses fragments of frescoes, statues, bas-reliefs and objects found in the Palatine buildings.

The Orti Farnesiani (Farnese Gardens) were designed for Cardinal Alessandro Farnese in the mid-16th century and were laid out on the site of the Domus Tiberiana, Emperor Tiberius' first-century palace.

From Via Nova, the Nymphaeum of Rain, with Renaissance frescoes on the walls and vault, is the first building you encounter when you enter the gardens. From here, two staircases with ornamental niches lead to the main gardens. At the top, Rainaldi built two pavilions, known as the Aviaries. On the eastern side is the Nymphaeum of Mirrors with beautiful mosaics on the walls; lilies, a symbol of the

Farnese family, are grown here. The gardens, as planted today, are largely the work of the 19th-century archaeologist Giacomo Boni.

✚ 138 E6 ✉ Entrances on Via dei Fori Imperiali, Via Sacra, Via di San Teodoro and Via di San Gregorio 30 ☎ 06 0608; 06 3996 7700 🕓 Last Sun in Mar to Aug daily 8.30–7.15; Sep 8.30–7; Oct 8.30–6.30; Nov to mid-Feb 8.30–4.30; mid-Feb to mid-Mar 8.30–5; mid-Mar to last Sat in Mar 8.30–5.30 ✋ Adult €12, child €6, EU citizens 18–24 €7.50, EU citizens under 18 and over 65 free. Ticket valid for two days and includes entry to the Colosseum (▷ 143–144) and Foro Romano (▷ 146–151). Tickets can be booked in advance online at www.pierreci.it/it/acquista-il-biglietto/biglietto-on-line.aspx or by phone on 06 0608. If you intend visiting many of the city's ancient sites, it may be worth buying the Roma Archeologica Card (▷ 259) 🚇 Colosseo 🚌 60, 75, 81, 175, 673 to Via di San Gregorio; 60, 84, 85, 87, 117, 175, 810, 850; tram 3 to Via dei Fori Imperiali

PIAZZA DEL CAMPIDOGLIO
www.museicapitolini.org

The Piazza del Campidoglio is one of the most spectacular places in Rome, unmissable for the superb view of the Roman Forum and for Michelangelo's architecture.

Michelangelo designed the square to look out over the city of Rome like an open terrace, and placed on it three magnificent

buildings: the Palazzo Senatorio, Palazzo dei Conservatori and Palazzo Nuovo (Musei Capitolini, ▷ 154–159). Much of the work on the palaces was in fact carried out after Michelangelo's death by other architects. He also designed the Cordonata, a monumental ramp leading up to the square. At the top, on either side, are Roman statues of Castor and Pollux, the twin sons of Jupiter by Leda, standing beside their horses. In the middle of the piazza's beautiful, geometric-patterned paving is a modern copy of the equestrian statue of Marcus Aurelius—the original is in the Palazzo dei Conservatori (▷ 157).

Near the steps leading to the Palazzo Senatorio (Rome's city hall) is a fountain flanked by two enormous bearded statues representing the Nile, shown by a sphinx, and, on the right, the Tiber, with the figures of Romulus and Remus and the she-wolf.

The Palazzo Caffarelli, on the far right of the Cordonata, now hosts temporary exhibitions.

✚ 138 E6 🚇 Colosseo 🚌 44, 46, 84, 715, 716, 780, 781, 810, 916

Above *Statues of Castor and Pollux guard the entrance to the Piazza del Campidoglio*
Opposite *The Palatine Hill, above the Forum, was where the city's rich and powerful chose to live*

SAN CLEMENTE
▷ 162–163.

SANTI COSMA E DAMIANO
The origins of this church are somewhat unusual. It was formed by combining the library of the Temple of Peace, part of Vespasian's Forum (see Fori Imperiali, ▷ 145) and part of the Temple of Romulus in the Roman Forum, the remains of which are still visible inside. The church, the first to reuse a building in the Forum, was consecrated in AD526 by Pope Felix IV and dedicated to twin brothers, miraculous healers from Cilicia (southern Turkey).

The church took on its present form in the 17th century, under Pope Urban VIII Barberini. The original Roman church was hidden in a sort of crypt, and the present facade and the cloister were erected. Paintings in the 17th-century coffered ceiling depict the triumph of the saintly brothers. Decoration also includes the Barberini coat of arms

The sixth-century mosaics in the apse, the church's principal treasure, were highly influential. They portray Christ against a sunset background with the apostles Peter and Paul and the saints Cosma and Damiano. The church also houses a remarkable 18th-century Neapolitan *presepio* (nativity scene).
✚ 138 F6 ✉ Via dei Fori Imperiali 1, 00184 ☎ 06 692 0441 ⊙ Daily 9–1, 3–7 ▣ Free ⊙ Colosseo ▣ 60, 75, 81, 175, 673 to Via di San Gregorio; 84, 85, 87, 60, 117, 175, 810, 850 to Via dei Fori Imperiali ◈ Audioguide €1.50 in Italian, French, English, German, Spanish

SANTA CROCE IN GERUSALEMME
St. Helena, mother of Emperor Constantine, amassed a collection of relics from the Holy Land in her palace in Rome. In the fourth century, part of the palace became the church of the Holy Cross in Jerusalem, built to house the holy relics, which included a fragment of the Holy Cross, a nail from the Cross, thorns from the Crown of Thorns and the original inscription over the Cross. The original 12th-century church was restored and altered in the 18th century.

Emperor Charles V's confessor, Cardinal Francesco Quiñones (d.1540) is buried in the apse; his tomb is by Jacopo Sansovino. The vault here is decorated with a Renaissance fresco depicting the discovery of the True Cross by St. Helena, attributed to Antoniazzo Romano. In the Chapel of St. Helena, reached by descending a 15th-century ramp at the end of the south aisle, are beautiful mosaics by Melozzo da Forlì and a statue of the saint adapted from a Classical statue of Juno. The Holy Relics are kept in the Chapel of the Relics at the end of the north aisle. The church also contains a 12th-century cosmatesque (inlaid marble) floor.
✚ 139 J6 ✉ Piazza di Santa Croce in Gerusalemme 12, 00183 ☎ 06 7061 3053 ⊙ Daily 7–12.45, 3.30–7.30 ▣ Free ⊚ San Giovanni or Manzoni ▣ 117, 186, 218, 649, 650, 850 ▦

SAN GIOVANNI IN LATERANO
▷ 164–165.

SANTI GIOVANNI E PAOLO
This church, one of the oldest Christian places of worship, was built over a Roman house, said to be the home of two Christian martyrs who died during the reign of Julian the Apostate (AD361–363). The church contains magnificent paintings that once embellished the Roman house beneath.

The original church was built in the fourth century by a private citizen named Pammachius. It was rebuilt by Pope Paschal II, who added a campanile and porch in the 12th century. The five arches above the porch, and the gallery, belong to the original building.

The interior mostly dates from the 18th century. Entrance to the original Roman house is down the steps at the end of the aisle. There are several rooms to see, some decorated with wall paintings, most notably a third-century marine fresco in the underground nymphaeum.

The apse is decorated with a frieze by Pomarancio and fourth-century frescoes.
✚ 138 F6 ✉ Piazza dei Santi Giovanni e Paolo 13, 00184 ☎ 06 700 5745 ⊙ Mon–Sat 8.30–12, 3.30–6, Sun 8.30–12.30 ▣ Free ⊚ Circo Massimo ▣ C3, 60, 75, 81, 175, 271, 673 to Via di San Gregorio

INFORMATION

www.basilicasanclemente.com

✠ 139 G6 ✉ Via Labicana 95/Via di San Giovanni in Laterano, 00184 ☎ 06 7740 0201 ⏰ Church and lower levels: Mon–Sat 9–12.30, 3–6, Sun 12–6 ✋ Church: free. Lower levels: Adult €5, under 26 €3.50 Ⓜ Colosseo, San Giovanni 🚌 85, 117, 850 to Via di San Giovanni in Laterano 📖 €3.65, all languages 🎁 Well stocked with guides and souvenirs

Above *The 13th-century gold mosaic in the apse is the highlight of San Clemente's upper basilica*

INTRODUCTION

San Clemente is one of Rome's oldest basilicas, taking its name from St. Clement, a first-century pope. The church is remarkable for its three interior levels, spanning 2,000 years of history: the present 12th-century church, filled with some sublime medieval works of art; the remains of a much older church; and the fragments of a Mithraic temple and other Roman buildings.

Pope Paschal II built the upper church in 1108 after the earlier church was badly damaged in 1084. He followed the original plans as closely as possible. The church on the second level has a similar layout, but is wider. Very little of this original fourth-century building still exists, apart from areas of the north and south walls and other fragments. It was dedicated to the Christian cult in the fifth century. According to legend, St. Cyril brought St. Clement's relics from the Black Sea to Rome, placing them in the church in AD869.

Down on the third level are two first-century Roman buildings, divided by a narrow passage. One is part of a warehouse of the early Flavian era, which is believed to have been the mint of ancient Rome. The second building, probably the home of a rich family, can be dated to AD92–6. Later, it was converted to the worship of the Persian god Mithras, a religion widespread in the Roman Empire. Farther down, archaeologists have found buildings that were probably destroyed in the fire of AD64.

WHAT TO SEE
THE THIRD LEVEL

The best way to see the whole church is to start from the third, underground level. Down here is a temple of Mithras (mithraeum) and what may have been a school for initiates into Mithraism, with remains of stuccowork and frescoes.

The mithraeum, the focal point of the Mithraic cult, had benches down both sides for ritual banquets and was in use until the fourth century, when the Christians probably destroyed it. The altar of Mithras is still there: On one side it shows the god cutting a bull's throat during initiation rites, and on the other a snake representing regeneration. Ironically, filling in the mithraeum to make the foundations of the first Christian church helped to preserve it. A narrow passage that was once an alley open to the sky leads to various rooms, one of which contains a source of spring water (not drinkable) that once fed an underground watercourse.

THE LOWER BASILICA

Above the temple is the apse of the lower basilica, consisting of a nave and two aisles. There are fragments of its once fine mosaic floor and some eighth-century frescoes, including one in a niche in the north wall that shows the Virgin as queen of heaven with saints. The frescoes decorating the nave show the legend of Sisinius, Prefect of Rome. Sisinius went to arrest his wife, who was attending a secret Mass held by Pope Clement. He was struck blind in the presence of the holy man, as were his servants, who carried out a column instead of the woman. What makes the Sisinius frescoes so unusual is that the accompanying inscription is written in a very early form of Italian. In the 11th–12th century, pilasters were added to reinforce earlier columns. These were decorated with frescoes showing scenes from the life and death of St. Clement and the legend of St. Alexis.

THE UPPER BASILICA

A few decades later, work began on the upper basilica. The church preserved the plan of the previous structure: one nave and two aisles either side leading up to a triumphal arch and a semi-domed apse, a quiet courtyard, a four-sided portico with Ionic columns and architraves, and a belfry. Just before the arch is the marble-walled medieval choir, the largely 13th-century *schola cantorum*, including some elements that survived from the lower basilica.

It is the apse, however, that is the highlight of the upper basilica, decorated with a beautiful 13th-century gold mosaic portraying the Triumph of the Cross, with the crucifixion at its centre. Twelve doves symbolizing the Apostles adorn the Cross; the Virgin and St. John stand at the side, and God's hand descends from heaven bearing a crown for His son. The people arriving to drink from the waters of life at the foot of the Cross represent followers of Christ coming for baptism. The cosmatesque (inlaid marble) floor is one of the best-preserved floors of its kind in Rome. Note, too, the beautiful marble wall, containing, among other things, the monogram of Pope Giovanni II, which dates from the seventh century.

At the beginning of the 18th century, a radical restoration project began. New windows were added, together with the plain baroque facade, and the upper walls of the nave and ceiling were frescoed.

The church contains several more major works, including the 15th-century Monument to Cardinal Bartolomeo Roverella, who died in 1476, located on the right wall at the far end of the right (south) nave. The church's most outstanding art, however, are the frescoes in the Cappella di Santa Caterina, on the left (north) aisle, just to the right of the church's side entrance. The paintings are mostly the work of Masolino da Panicale, and probably date from 1428–31. It is thought Masolino may have been helped by Masaccio, one of the greatest innovators of the early Renaissance, with whom he also worked on the influential frescoes in the Cappella Brancacci in Florence. Few works by either artist survive, making this one of the most important fresco cycles of its age in Rome. Among the scenes portrayed are the Crucifixion (rear wall), episodes from the life of St. Ambrogio (right wall) and stories from the life of St. Catherine of Alessandria.

Above *The church's plain baroque facade was an 18th-century addition*

INFORMATION

www.vatican.va

🚌 139 G7 ✉ Piazza di San Giovanni in Laterano 4, 00185 ☎ Church: 06 6988 6433. Scala Santa: 06 772 6641. Vatican History Museum: 06 6988 6376 🕐 Basilica: Apr–Sep daily 7–7; Oct–Mar 7–6. Cloister: daily 9–6 (occasionally 6.30). Baptistery: daily 7.30–12.30, 4–6. Scala Santa: daily 6.15–12, 3–6. Cappella Sancta Santorum: Apr–Sep Mon–Tue, Thu–Sat 10.30–11.30, 3.30–6.30, Wed 3.30–6.30; Oct–Mar closes daily 6pm. Vatican History Museum: daily 10–5.30. All hours may vary 💰 Basilica, Scala Santa and baptistery: free. Cloister: €2. Cappella Sancta Santorum: €3.50. Vatican History Museum: €4 🚇 San Giovanni 🚌 16, 85, 87, 117, 186, 218, 650, 850 to Piazza di San Giovanni in Laterano 🎧 Audiotours: basilica and cloister €5.50 📖 Guidebook in English €3.30 🏪 Souvenir shop inside the basilica (open 9–6)

Above The church's imposing 18th-century baroque facade

INTRODUCTION

San Giovanni in Laterano is the cathedral church of Rome—not St. Peter's, which is in Vatican City, a separate state. Solemn and peaceful, it was originally dedicated to Christ the Saviour, and only later to St. John the Evangelist and St. John the Baptist. It dates from the fourth century, and the time of Constantine, the first Christian emperor, who, following his victory over Maxentius in AD312 and the establishment of Christianity as the Imperial religion, built a basilica here on the site of his rival's guard's barracks.

In AD314 Pope Sylvester I took up residence in the group of Lateran buildings, which included a palace, a basilica and a baptistery. This became the official papal residence until the popes moved to Avignon in France in the 14th century. After various repairs and much rebuilding, the church was radically restored in the baroque style in the 17th and 18th centuries.

The church is best approached from the splendid piazza, named—like San Giovanni itself—after the Laterani family, who once owned this land. Before entering, note the statues on the roof, which represent Christ, St. John the Baptist, St. John the Evangelist and the 12 Doctors of the Church. Inside, take time to appreciate the church's overall scale before focusing on the individual treasures. The baptistery is near the exit on the left and you can access the cloister from the left aisle. The Scala Santa entrance is outside.

WHAT TO SEE

EXTERIOR

The severe baroque east facade built by Alessandro Galilei in 1735 supports a balustrade with 15 gigantic statues representing Christ, the two St. Johns, and the Doctors of the Church. The portico in front of the church, inspired by that of St. Peter's (▷ 210–215), has antique bronze doors from the Senate House in the Foro Romano (▷ 146–151) and a huge statue of Constantine, discovered in the Baths of Constantine on the Quirinale. The last door on the right is the Holy Door, opened most recently in 2000 by Pope John Paul II to mark the start of a Holy Year, a once-every-25-years occurrence.

THE NAVE

The present interior of the church was commissioned by Pope Innocent X in 1646 and is mainly the work of Francesco Borromini. He's responsible for the nave and four aisles, while the ornate ceiling is probably by Piero Ligorio. Statues of the 12 Apostles flank the nave, each in its own separate niche and surmounted by bas-reliefs depicting stories from the Bible. On the left-hand pillar in the right aisle, its fragility protected by glass, is a restored fragment of a Giotto fresco of Boniface VIII declaring the Holy Year of 1300, while the Corsini Chapel, designed by Alessandro Galilei, is on the left.

THE TRANSEPT AND APSE

In contrast to the nave, the transept, a fine example of Mannerist decoration, is elaborately detailed in style. Nebbia, Pomarancio and Cavaliere d'Arpino were responsible for the frescoes; the ornate ceiling, showing Clement VIII's coat of arms, is by Taddeo Landini.

The apse mosaic is a 19th-century restoration of Jacopo Torriti's 13th-century masterpiece. Torriti added figures of the Virgin, Pope Nicholas IV and major saints. The small figure of St. Francis on the left was probably included because Torriti was a Franciscan monk.

THE PAPAL ALTAR

At the heart of the basilica is the Papal Altar, at which only the Pope may officiate; it contains a wooden table said to have been used by St. Peter, although it probably dates from the fourth century. Above rises a fine 14th-century Gothic canopy, made of marble and decorated with mosaics. Here, too, are copies of the 15th-century reliquaries containing the relics of St. Peter and St. Paul, housed in a tabernacle frescoed with the Good Shepherd, the Crucifixion, the Virgin and various saints. Beneath the altar of the Confessio (the crypt below the Papal Altar) is the tomb slab of Pope Martin V (d.1431).

THE CLOISTERS

The exquisite cloisters, built between 1215 and 1232, are the work of Jacopo and Pietro Vassalletto, famous artists of the cosmatesque style of mosaic. The sparkling, multi-hued, twisted and plain columns have splendid capitals, and the marble mosaic frieze is decorated with bizarre birds and beasts; stand by the ninth-century well in the middle of the garden for the best view. Fragments of the medieval basilica are displayed around the cloister walls.

THE SCALA SANTA

The Scala Santa (Holy Staircase) is supposedly from the house of Pontius Pilate in Jerusalem, ascended by Christ before his Crucifixion. The 28 marble steps—which believers climb on their knees—have covers to protect stains said to be traces of Christ's blood. The staircase leads to the Sancta Santorum, once the popes' private chapel and adorned with fine mosaics.

THE BAPTISTERY

The Battistero Lateranense is located to the rear right of the church, on its north side. Created by Emperor Constantine at the same time as the church, it was built on the site of a first-century bathhouse. In the 16th and 17th centuries it was extended and modified. Its octagonal plan would be the blueprint for similar baptisteries across Italy and beyond, notably in Florence. The green basalt urn at the centre is the baptismal font.

The baptistery contains four chapels, two of which contain early (but restored) mosaics: the Cappella di Santa Rufina, with panels from the sixth century (plus architectural fragments from the baptistery's original entrance, including pieces of Roman architrave); and the Cappella di Venanzio, built by Pope John IV in AD640 and adorned with mosaics from the seventh century.

TIPS

» Be sure to arrive by 11am to see the Scala Santa before the crowds arrive.
» If you visit in the morning, take time to check out Via Sannio, scene of one of Rome's best-known markets (▷ 178).

POST-MORTEM TRIAL

The ninth century saw a strange trial held in the basilica, that of the dead Pope Formosus. His corpse, dressed in papal finery, was set in front of the judge, Pope Stephen VI, who found him guilty of giving the Emperor's crown to the barbarian Arnoul, the last of the Carolingians. Formosus' body was then mutilated and thrown into the Tiber.

THE ANCIENT CITY AND EASTERN ROME • SIGHTS

REGIONS

Below *The octagonal baptistery, dating from the fourth century, inspired similar structures across Italy*

SAN GREGORIO MAGNO

Not far from the Colosseo is the majestic church of San Gregorio Magno, set on the beautiful, quiet Caelian Hill and surrounded by tranquil gardens.

The church stands on the site of St. Andrew's monastery, founded in AD575 by St. Gregory. It was restored in 1633 for Cardinal Scipione Borghese—the eagle and dragon of his coat of arms are visible above the lower arches. A spectacular staircase and broad portico take you inside, where there are three chapels built in the 17th century by Cardinal Cesare Baronio.

In St. Barbara's Chapel is a marble table believed to have been used by St. Gregory to feed the poor. St. Sylvia's Chapel, dedicated to Gregory's mother, has a fresco by Guido Reni in the apse showing a concert of angels. The chapel of St. Andrew has frescoes of the *Flagellation of St. Andrew* by Domenichino and *St. Andrew's Matryrdom* also by Reni.

In the chapel at the end of the right aisle stands the altar of St. Gregory the Great, decorated with bas-reliefs illustrating events in his life. To the right, in the cell of St. Gregory, are the relics of the saint, his marble throne and the stone he used as a pillow.

✚ 138 F7 ✉ Piazza di San Gregorio 1, 00184 ☎ 06 700 8227 ◷ Daily 9–1, 3.30–7 (hours subject to change) ✋ Free Ⓜ Circo Massimo 🚌 C3, 60, 75, 81, 175, 271, 673 to Via di San Gregorio

SANTA MARIA IN ARACOELI

There has been a church on this site since at least the sixth century, and in the eighth century it was part of a monastery. However, much of what you see today dates from the end of the 13th century.

Inside, the badly worn tomb of Archdeacon Giovanni Crivelli, carved by the Florentine sculptor Donatello in 1432, stands to the right of the entrance. Another tomb (1465), that of Cardinal d'Albret, is one of Andrea Bregno's best works. The decorative frescoes

in the chapel of St. Bernardino of Siena are by Pinturricchio and depict the life and death of the saint. The left transept leads to a little chapel dedicated to the Santo Bambino (Holy Child). The jewelled wooden statue of the Christ Child is a modern replica of the 15th-century original—said to have been carved out of olive wood from the Garden of Gethsemane—which was stolen in the 1990s.

From the top of the Scalinata d'Aracoeli on the Capitolino (Capitoline Hill) there is a great view of the city. Allow time to take this in before passing behind the austere brick facade.

✚ 138 E5 ✉ Piazza d'Aracoeli, 00186 ☎ 06 6976 3839 ◷ May–Sep daily 9–12.30, 3–6.30; Oct–Apr 9–12.30, 2.30–5.20 ✋ Free Ⓜ Colosseo 🚌 44, 46, 84, 715, 716, 780, 781, 810, 916 to Piazza Venezia

SANTA MARIA IN COSMEDIN

The church of Santa Maria in Cosmedin is best known for the Bocca della Verità (Mouth of Truth) and its associated superstition, rather than for anything inside. Although if you venture in, you'll find a rare Roman medieval church that has been stripped of its later baroque additions.

There were Classical temples on the site of the present church, and in the sixth century a deaconry was established here to provide aid for the poor. The church that existed by the eighth century was given to Greek refugees from Byzantium, which was when the word Cosmedin (from the Greek for 'decorated') became part of its name. The church retains its Greek connections; a Greek Orthodox Mass is celebrated here every week.

Inside, the 12th-century cosmatesque floors are very good, and the frescoes in the apse and mosaic fragment in the sacristy are worth a look. The Corinthian columns probably came from the preceding pagan temple.

The Bocca della Verità, a large stone disc carved with the face of a man, is just inside the church porch. According to medieval tradition, a liar risks having his hand bitten off if he dares to put it in the mouth of the image. In reality, the stone was probably nothing more sinister than a Roman drain cover, but the popular myth has endured.

✚ 138 E6 ✉ Piazza Bocca della Verità 18, 00184 ☎ 06 678 7759 ◷ May–Oct daily 9.30–6; Nov–Apr 9.30–5 ✋ Free Ⓜ Circo Massimo 🚌 81, 160, 628, 715

Below *Views of the city from the steps outside Santa Maria in Aracoeli are superb*

Above *Byzantine mosaics in Santa Prassede's Cappella di San Zeno*

SANTA MARIA IN DOMNICA

Its setting, near Villa Celimontana, makes the church of Santa Maria in Domnica a popular choice for weddings. It is also known as Santa Maria della Navicella ('little boat'), after the 16th-century fountain incorporating a Roman stone boat which stands on the piazza in front of the church.

The church was built in the ninth century by Pope Paschal I on the site of an earlier house of worship called a *dominicum*. Pope Leo X restored it in the 16th century, and you can see his lion emblem on the keystones.

The interior of Santa Maria in Domnica remains much as it was in the ninth century, with a nave and two aisles separated by ancient granite columns. Beautiful Byzantine mosaics decorate the triumphal arch and apse, depicting religious scenes with great realism: Look in particular at the angels' clothes, which appear to be stirring in a breeze. A mosaic at the middle of the vault shows Pope Paschal kneeling before the Virgin; note the square halo, known as a nimbus, indicating that the Pope was still alive at the time.

✚ 138 F7 ✉ Via della Navicella 10, 00184 ☎ 06 7720 2685 🕒 Apr–Oct daily 9–12, 3.30–7; Nov–Mar 9–12, 3.30–6 🖐 Free 🚇 Circo Massimo 🚌 81, 117, 673 to Via della Navicella

SANTA MARIA MAGGIORE

▷ 168–169.

SAN PIETRO IN VINCOLI

The name of this church, St. Peter in Chains, gives a clue to one of its treasures: the chains that bound St. Peter in prison, which can be seen in a gilt bronze urn under the high altar.

The ceiling of the church is decorated with a fresco showing the miracle of the chains. According to the legend, two sets of chains that were used to bind St. Peter—in Jerusalem and in the Mamertine prison in Rome—miraculously fused together when placed side by side.

The church's main attraction, however, is Michelangelo's statue of Moses, which was one of the 40 figures that were intended to adorn the mausoleum of Pope Julius II in St. Peter's Basilica. The original project was abandoned after Julius' death. The huge seated figure of Moses is sculpted from Carrara marble, and the figures in the niches are Jacob's wives, Leah and Rachel.

✚ 138 F5 ✉ Piazza San Pietro in Vincoli 4A, 00184 ☎ 06 9784 4950 🕒 Apr–Sep daily 8–12.30, 3.30–7; Oct–Mar 8–12.30, 3–6. Closed to visitors during Mass (Sun 8–11). Hours subject to change 🖐 Free 🚇 Cavour 🚌 75, 84, 117 to Via Cavour 🎧 Audioguide €1 in English, French, German, Spanish and Italian

SANTA PRASSEDE

An unimposing entrance through an arch supported by pillars leads into the atrium of the church of St. Prassede, worth visiting for its Byzantine mosaics, notably those in the Cappella di San Zeno, the most important examples in Rome.

A house of worship has stood on this spot since AD489. The present building was built in AD822 by Pope Paschal I, who enlarged it to store relics of martyrs from the catacombs. It has been rebuilt and restored many times since.

In the right aisle is the tomb of Bishop Giovanni Battista Santoni, the first work by Gian Lorenzo Bernini. Remarkable ninth-century

mosaics embellish the apse and the triumphal arch. The coffered ceiling is a 19th-century addition.

The Chapel of St. Zeno in the right aisle contains beautiful mosaics depicting Christ, saints and the Virgin Mary, all on a brilliant gold background. It also has an excellent ornamental pavement in polychrome marble. In a room to the right of the entrance is a fragment of a column brought from Jerusalem in 1223; according to tradition, it is where Jesus was scourged.

✚ 139 G5 ✉ Via di Santa Prassede 9/A, 00184 ☎ 06 488 2456 🕒 Mon–Sat 7.30–12, 4–6.30, Sun 8–12, 4–6.30 🖐 Free 🚇 Cavour, Termini or Vittorio Emanuele 🚌 C3, 16, 70, 71, 360, 590, 649, 714 to Piazza Santa Maria Maggiore or Via Merulana

SANTI QUATTRO CORONATI

Like all the churches built on the Caelian Hill, Santi Quattro Coronati (Four Crowned Saints), at the end of a steep, quiet road, is a little gem.

This picturesque church and the adjoining convent are dedicated to four Christian Roman soldiers (or possibly sculptors), martyred because they refused to worship (or make a statue of) the Greek demigod of healing, Esculapio. An earlier church was completely demolished during the sack of Rome of 1084, and 20 years later a new, fortified church was built on the site by Pope Paschal II. This had a larger central nave and a spacious courtyard at the entrance; the aisles were pulled down to make way for the lovely cloister and a dining hall.

Above the entrance is a tower-like belfry. Inside, there is an unusual *matroneum*, or women's gallery. The large apse is decorated with baroque frescoes illustrating the lives of the Quattro Coronati. The adjoining cloister and the crypt are also well worth a look.

✚ 139 G6 ✉ Via dei Santi Quattro Coronati 20, 00184 ☎ 06 7047 5427 🕒 Basilica: daily 9.30–12, 4.30–6. Cloister: Mon–Sat 10–12, 4.30–6, Sun 4.30–6 🖐 Free 🚇 San Giovanni 🚌 85, 117, 850 to Via di San Giovanni in Laterano

SANTA MARIA MAGGIORE

INFORMATION

www.vatican.va

✚ 139 G5 ✉ Piazza Santa Maria Maggiore 00184 ☎ 06 6988 6800 ◐ Basilica: daily 7–7. Cappella Sforza: Mon–Fri 9–5. Museum: daily 8.30–6.30. Sacristy: daily 7–12.30, 3–6.30. Guided tours of the loggia Mar–Oct daily 9–6.30; Nov–Feb 9–1 ♿ Basilica and Cappella Sforza: free. Museum: Adult €4, child (under 18) €2. Loggia: €3 ⓜ Cavour, Termini or Vittorio Emanuele 🚌 16, 70, 71, 75, 105, 204, 360, 590, 649, 714 ➔ Guided tours of Loggia delle Benedizioni (€2.60) and Presepe di Arnolfo di Cambio (€1.50). Ask in the museum. Audiotours: €5 📷 €3.50 in English, Italian, German, Spanish 📖 Bookshop inside basilica

INTRODUCTION

Legend, sadly now disproved, associates the founding of this magnificent basilica with Pope Liberius in the fourth century. He dreamed the Virgin instructed him to build it wherever snow fell that night—5 August, the height of summer. In the morning, snow dusted the Esquiline Hill, and so the church was duly built here.

Pope Sixtus III built much of the present church between AD432 and AD440, though considerable changes were made in the 12th and 13th centuries, and the chapels were added in the 16th century. The present facade, with its triple-arched loggia, was designed around the original mosaics by Ferdinando Fuga in 1746.

Pause to admire the 18th-century facade of the basilica, with Rome's tallest campanile rising behind. You may then want to visit the Museum of the Patriarcale Basilica di Santa Maria Maggiore, next to the basilica. If timings are right, visit the Loggia delle Benedizione for the view over the piazza and the 13th-century mosaics by Filippo Rusuti. Pass through the portico, with a bronze statue of Philip IV and the great Holy Door, and, once inside, spend a few moments absorbing everything before starting your tour.

WHAT TO SEE

THE NAVE AND AISLES CHANCEL

The interior of this immense church is dominated by the long nave, flanked with 40 ancient Roman columns. Above, 36 fifth-century mosaic panels tell Old Testament stories; they're high and hard to see, but perseverance pays off. Higher still, the superb Renaissance coffered ceiling is said to be decorated with the first gold to have been brought from the New World—a gift from Ferdinand and Isabella of Spain. The coats of arms are those of popes Calixtus III and Alexander V. Beneath your feet stretches a beautiful cosmatesque marble pavement, dating from the 12th century.

Above The church's bell tower, the tallest in the city, rises high over the 18th-century facade

THE CHANCEL AND APSE

The fifth-century Byzantine-style mosaics glitter from the triumphal arch, whose four sections depict the Annunciation, the Epiphany and other scenes from the early life of Christ. The apse mosaic is later, created in 1295 by Jacopo Torriti; it shows the Coronation of the Virgin, attended by Pope Nicholas IV and Cardinal Iacopo Colonna.

The *baldacchino* (altar canopy) made up of porphyry columns with bronze foliage, is by Ferdinando Fuga. It stands above the *confessio*, the most sacred spot in the basilica, which contains a silver urn by Giuseppe Valadier supposedly containing fragments of the Christ child's wooden crib.

THE CHAPELS

The Cappella Sistina, to the right of the nave, was commissioned by Pope Sixtus V and built by Domenico Fontana (1585) on a Greek-cross plan, reusing marble from a Classical Roman building. The chapel, with its dome, frescoes, marbles and monumental tombs, is as large as many churches. Beneath it are the remnants of the *presepio* (Nativity scene), with exquisite figures by sculptor Arnolfo di Cambio that once accompanied the holy crib (see above).

The Cappella Paolina, just off the north aisle, mirrors the Sistine Chapel, and is perhaps even more beautiful, with mosaics by Cavaliere d'Arpino, frescoes by Guido Reni and an incredibly sumptuous bejewelled altar. It is also known as the Borghese Chapel after the family name of the commissioning Pope Paul V. Nearby, off the left aisle, the Cappella Sforza was probably built by Giacomo della Porta from drawings by Michelangelo.

On the right wall at the end of the nave is the magnificent inlaid marble tomb of Cardinal Consalvo Rodriguez (d.1299), a contrast to the simple, humble tomb of the Bernini family nearby.

THE BAPTISTERY

The baptistery is baroque, the work of Flaminio Ponzio. The font, made from porphyry, was decorated by Giuseppe Valadier; the high-relief *Assumption* on the altar is by Pietro Bernini, father of the famous Gian Lorenzo.

TIPS

» If you want to see everything properly, call in advance to book a guided tour.
» The area near the basilica, around Termini station, is not one of the safest; watch your belongings.
» Bring binoculars if you're really interested in seeing the mosaics or join one of the guided tours that offer a close-up view of the mosaics in the loggia.

Below *The 13th-century apse mosaic depicts the Coronation of the Virgin*

SANTA SABINA

The basilica of Santa Sabina, on the Aventine Hill, has kept its original fifth-century early-Christian plan almost intact. Next to the church is a beautiful medieval cloister.

A church dedicated to the martyred Roman matron St. Sabina has stood on this spot on the Aventine Hill since AD425. The basilica has seen many changes over the centuries: It was turned into a fortress in the 10th century, incongruously restored in the 16th century by Domenico Fontana, and restored again in the 19th century, when all its baroque elements were removed and the church was returned to its original plan.

At the entrance, behind a front portico, is one of the church's main treasures. The entrance doors are divided into wooden panels, many of them survivors from the fifth-century church, carved with scenes from the Old and New testaments. The Crucifixion can be seen high up on the left.

The church is well proportioned, with light entering through the beautiful ninth-century windows.
✛ 138 E7 ✉ Via di Santa Sabina 2, 00158 ☎ 06 5794 0660; 06 579 401 🕐 Daily 8.15–12.30, 3.30–6. Ask sacristan to visit Pope Pius V's room and St. Dominic's cell ✋ Free. Medieval cloister: €1 🚇 Circo Massimo 🚌 60, 73, 75, 118, 175, 715; tram 3 to Viale Aventino

SANTO STEFANO ROTONDO

Santo Stefano, set in a private park on the Caelian Hill, is one of the oldest and largest round churches anywhere, and has plenty to interest lovers of both art and history.

The church was built in the late fifth century by Pope Simplicius and dedicated to St. Stephen, the first Christian martyr, whose relics are here, and later also to St. Stephen of Hungary.

The walls are frescoed with 34 scenes of Christian martyrs painted by Pomarancio and Antonio Tempesta in the 16th century. The harrowing scenes have inscriptions explaining the action and giving

the names of the emperors who ordered the executions.

The opulent mosaics and marble decorations date from AD523–530. One mosaic shows two fourth-century martyrs, Primus and Felician, with a jewelled cross. Their relics were brought here by Pope Theodore I in the seventh century.

Long before the Christian church was built, there was a pagan sanctuary on this site dedicated to the god Mithras (see San Clemente, ▷ 162–163). This was discovered below the church during recent excavations. For safety reasons, it is currently closed to the public.
✛ 139 G7 ✉ Via di Santo Stefano Rotondo 7, 00184 ☎ 06 421 199 🕐 Apr–Sep Tue–Sat 9.30–12.30, 3–6, Sun 9.30–12.30; Oct–Mar Tue–Sat 9.30–12.30, 2–5, Sun 9.30–12.30 ✋ Free 🚇 Colosseo, San Giovanni 🚌 81, 117, 673, 714, 850

TEATRO DI MARCELLO

The Teatro di Marcello is one of Rome's more evocative sights, with medieval and other houses woven into the surviving arches and columns of the original Roman theatre. Begun by Julius Caesar, the theatre was second only to the nearby Teatro di Pompeo, with a capacity of 13,000.

Originally the exterior would have had three levels, with Ionic, Doric and Corinthian columns and capitals (just like the Colosseum). Only the lower two survive (the Doric and Ionic), the third having been sacrificed first in the 16th century to build a fortress on the site for the Savelli family, and subsequently in the 18th century to build the Palazzo Orsini (now subdivided into appartments) for the powerful Orsini dynasty.

The theatre was abandoned in the sixth century, and the lower level ransacked, its stone taken to build churches and other buildings. As a result, just 12 of the original arches survive. The adjacent archaeological area contains, among other things, three marble columns from the Tempio di Apollo Sosiano, built in 431BC and restored in 179BC.

✛ 138 E6 ✉ Via del Teatro di Marcello 🚇 Colosseo 🚌 All services to Piazza Venezia

TERME DI CARACALLA

www.archeorm.arti.beniculturali.it
The Baths of Caracalla were the most luxurious of the Imperial baths, and are among the most impressive monumental complexes to have survived from ancient Rome. Designed not only for the care of the body but as a cultural and local meeting place, they also had flourishing gardens.

The baths were opened in AD217 under Emperor Caracalla, but were completed by his successors Elegabalus and Alexander Severus. They remained in use until the wars with the Goths, when soldiers destroyed part of the aqueducts supplying water to the baths in AD537 as part of their strategy to conquer Rome.

The complex included pools, rooms for cold, hot and warm baths, porticoes, gymnasiums, halls, fine statues, libraries and even a stadium. There was room for 600 people at a time to bathe here. All the rooms were decorated with alabaster and granite, with superb ceilings and wall mosaics, many of them still intact.

Excavations have uncovered an underground mithraeum, a temple dedicated to the cult of the pagan god Mithras.
✛ 138 F7 ✉ Viale delle Terme di Caracalla 52, 00153 ☎ Information and advance tickets: 06 3996 7700 🕐 Apr–Aug Tue–Sun 9–7.15, Mon 9–2; Sep Tue–Sun 9–7, Mon 9–2; Oct Tue–Sun 9–6.30, Mon 9–2; Nov to mid-Feb Tue–Sun 9–4.30, Mon 9–2; mid-Feb to mid-Mar Tue–Sun 9–5, Mon 9–2; mid-Mar to end Mar Tue–Sun 9–5.30, Mon 9–2 ✋ Adult €6, EU citizens 18–24 €3, EU citizens under 18 and over 65 free. Tickets can be bought online at www.pierreci.it. If you intend visiting many of the city's ancient sites, it may be worth buying the Roma Archeologica Card (▷ 259) 🚇 Circo Massimo 🚌 67, 90, 118, 160, 613, 714, 715 🚐

Opposite *The evocative ruins of the Teatro di Marcello*

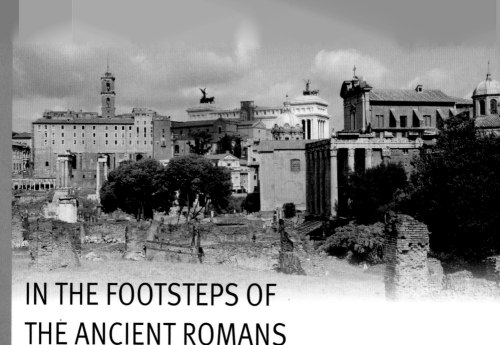

IN THE FOOTSTEPS OF THE ANCIENT ROMANS

From Michelangelo's Piazza del Campidoglio, you plunge down into the pedestrian lanes of the Foro Romano and take a step back in time as you explore the ancient ruins of Imperial Rome.

THE WALK

Distance: 2km (1.2 miles)
Allow: 2 hours
Start at: Piazza del Campidoglio
End at: Piazza del Campidoglio

HOW TO GET THERE

For Piazza del Campidoglio, the nearest metro station is Colosseo. Alternatively, several buses will take you nearby: Nos. 44, 46, 84, 715, 716, 780, 781, 810 and 916.

★ From Piazza del Campidoglio take the lane to the left of Palazzo Senatorio, the middle palace. Look up at the corner of the building to see a statue of the she-wolf with Romulus and Remus, founders of Rome. At the back of the building, the Foro Romano (▷ 146–151) opens up in front of you. Take in the view from this elevated position before descending the steps to the Forum. Before passing through the Arco di Settimio Severo (▷ 150), look to your right.

❶ The columns here belong to the Tempio di Saturno, one of the oldest buildings in the Forum, dating from 479BC, although what remains today is from reconstructions in 42BC and AD284. As the god of agriculture, Saturn was extremely important. Saturnalia, a festival in his honour that took place in December, lasted a whole week.

Pass through the Arch of Septimius Severus, with the austere, red-brick Curia (▷ 149–150) on your left.

❷ The Curia was home to the Senate and during the Republic was the most politically important place in the Roman world, where policies were shaped.

Continue along the Via Sacra, the main route through the Forum, passing the Basilica Aemilia on your left, until you come to the area covered by a green roof. This is the Tempio di Cesare.

❸ Despite laws banning burials in the Forum, Mark Antony appealed to the Romans to allow Caesar's body to be cremated here. Augustus built a temple in Caesar's honour in 29BC; a column marks the place where he was cremated.

With the temple on your left, look straight ahead. What you see is the temple of the twin brothers of Helen of Troy, Castor and Pollux, the Dioscuri, whose statues stand just below the Piazza del Campidoglio. To the left of the temple is the Basilica Giulia. Although very little remains, it is clear that this was a large and important building. It was built as a courthouse and a meeting place for the city's civic tribunals.

Rejoin the Via Sacra. The next building on your left, which remains surprisingly intact, is the Tempio di Antonino e Faustina.

❹ Built by Emperor Antoninus Pius in AD141, the temple was dedicated to his wife Faustina, in honour of her virtue—something of an irony as she was reputed to have had numerous affairs. The building was converted to a church in the 11th century, which ensured its survival.

Next to the temple is the sixth-century church of Santi Cosma e Damiano (▷ 161), whose entrance is on Via dei Fori Imperiali.

5 The church, the first to reuse a building in the Forum, was consecrated in AD526. The small, round building on the Forum side of the church is the fourth-century AD Tempio de Divo Romolo, dedicated to the son of Emperor Maxentius.

With your back to the temple, the large complex ahead of you is the Atrium Vestae, the house of the Vestal Virgins (▷ 148–149).

6 The ruins of the circular white temple are composed of fragments dating from AD191, although a temple dedicated to Vesta had stood here from the earliest of times. The site was reconstructed in the 1930s.

Continue along the Via Sacra; the vast, triple-arched building on the left is the Basilica di Massenzio.

7 The basilica was begun during the reign of Maxentius in AD306 and continued by his successor, Constantine. The building was designed as a hub for business and justice. Maxentius designed the building to be entered from the right-hand, shorter side, with a nave and aisles running its 100m (330ft) length. Constantine moved the entrance to the longer side (facing you), which produced three shorter (65m/215ft), broader aisles, each ending in the barrel-vaulted room that is seen today.
    The next building along the Via Sacra is the Tempio di Venere e Roma. There is no public access,

but you get a good view of the building as you leave the Forum.

Walk through the Arco di Tito (▷ 151), and leave the Forum along the last stretch of the Via Sacra. At the end is the Meta Sudans, the remains of a large fountain built at the same time as the Colosseo.

8 Turn right to walk around the Arco di Costantino (▷ 141), then go around the outside of the Colosseo (▷ 142–144; the entrance is on the northwest side of the amphitheatre).

Walk up Via dei Fori Imperiali towards the Fori Imperiali (▷ 145). Turn right onto the traffic-free Via del Foro di Traiano.

9 On the right are the remains of the Foro di Augusto. On the left, on the opposite side of Via dei Fori Imperiali, is the Foro di Cesare, the first to be built outside the old Forum. The greater part of these fora is buried under Via dei Fori Imperiali, built by Mussolini in 1932.

At the end of the traffic-free street, turn right, and then left onto Via

Alessandrina. This road leads you to the Mercati di Traiano (▷ 152–153, entrance on Via Quattro Novembre) on the right and, on the left, Foro Traiano.

10 The broken columns do little to suggest that the Foro Traiano was once one of the city's finest monuments, but the exquisite Colonna Traiana (▷ 145), at the top of the site, remains largely intact.

Follow the road around to the left to arrive at Piazza Venezia, around the corner from Piazza del Campidoglio.

WHEN TO GO
Any time is suitable, but in summer the outside of the Colosseo is floodlit after dark. The fora close at dusk.

WHERE TO EAT
Although there is nowhere to eat within the Forum itself, there are many places nearby.

BAR CAPITOLINA
▷ 180.

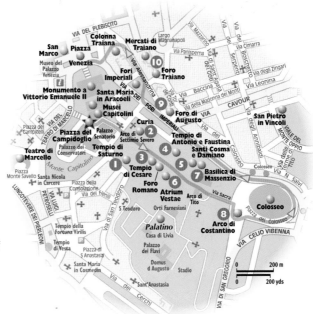

REGIONS THE ANCIENT CITY AND EASTERN ROME • WALK

ROME'S CHURCHES

Standing in busy squares redolent of history, or dreaming peacefully in quiet, romantic little streets, the churches that punctuate this walk offer both interest and variety.

THE WALK

Distance: 2km (1.2 miles)
Allow: 2.5 hours
Start at: Piazza di Santa Maria Maggiore
End at: Piazza di Santa Maria Maggiore

HOW TO GET THERE

The nearest metro stations for Piazza di Santa Maria Maggiore are Cavour (line B) and Vittorio Emanuele (line A). Bus Nos. 16, 70, 71, 360 and 649 also stop nearby.

★ Begin on Piazza di Santa Maria Maggiore. With your back to the basilica of Santa Maria Maggiore (▷ 168–169), take Via Merulana, a major thoroughfare on the right. Take the first narrow street on the right to visit the church of Santa Prassede (▷ 167).

❶ Santa Prassede is renowned for its beautiful Byzantine mosaics.

Follow the road around to the left to rejoin Via Merulana, which is lined with lively shops. Cross Viale Manzoni and climb up to Piazza di Porta San Giovanni.

❷ The entrance to the church of San Giovanni in Laterano (▷ 164–165) is on the opposite side of the building from here. Take time to admire the basilica, the Lateran Palace, and the Egyptian obelisk, which was originally erected in Thebes during the 15th century BC.

Almost opposite the entrance to San Giovanni is the Scala Santa.

❸ This Holy Staircase is said to be the steps from Pilate's palace in Jerusalem climbed by Jesus at his trial. They were brought to Rome by St. Helena, mother of the Emperor Constantine. Wood now protects the marble steps, and glass panels show what are claimed to be Christ's bloodstains. The devout climb the steps on their knees to earn indulgences (remission from temporal sins).

After returning to the square, leave by Via di San Giovanni in Laterano, then take the road on the left, Via di Santo Stefano Rotondo, which runs alongside the Ospedale San Giovanni. Almost at the end of the road on your left is the church of Santo Stefano Rotondo (▷ 170).

❹ Dating from the late fifth century, Santo Stefano Rotondo is built to a beautiful circular plan. It is one of the oldest and largest round churches in the world.

Above *The beautiful interior of the church of Santi Quattro Coronati*

At the end of the road, turn right onto Via della Navicella, right again to Piazza Celimontana past the Ospedale del Celio, and then another sharp right onto Via Annia. Go straight ahead, turning left near the end onto Via dei Querceti. Walk down the steps and you'll see the back of the church of Santi Quattro Coronati (▷ 167). The entrance is in the next street, the charming and quiet Via dei Santi Quattro Coronati.

5 Santi Quattro Coronati is named after four early Christians, possibly soldiers, who refused to worship pagan idols. They were killed by having an iron crown *(corona)* driven into their heads.

At the end of Via dei Querceti, bear left onto Via di San Giovanni in Laterano; the basilica of San Clemente (▷ 162–163) is in front of you.

6 This 12th-century church hides a much older history: It was built over a fourth-century AD church and a much earlier pagan temple.

Just past the basilica, turn right onto Via Celimontana. At the junction with Via Labicana, cross the road

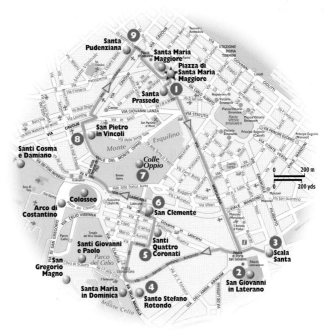

Below The imposing facade of San Giovanni in Laterano

and turn left, heading towards the Colosseo. Keeping on the right-hand side of the road, climb up to Via Nicola Salvi, which leads to the Colle Oppio. Turn right onto Via delle Terme di Tito, left onto Largo della Polveriera, then right and left onto Via Eudossiana, passing the entrance gate to Colle Oppio.

7 Colle Oppio, on the slopes of the Esquiline Hill, is a charming mix of grass, trees and archaeological ruins. It is popular with Romans, but should be avoided after dark.

Follow Via Eudossiana down past the University School of Engineering until you reach Piazza San Pietro in Vincoli.

8 Allow time to visit the church of San Pietro in Vincoli (▷ 167), which contains Michelangelo's mighty sculpture of Moses.

Facing the church, there is a tiny passageway on your left; go down the steps and you'll find yourself on Via Cavour. Head towards the right,

then, at Largo Visconti Venosta, take Via Urbana, which leads to the church of Santa Pudenziana (▷ 78).

9 Fourth-century Santa Pudenziana is one of the oldest sites of Christian worship in Rome.

At the end of the road, turn right and cross Piazza d'Esquilino to return to Santa Maria Maggiore.

WHEN TO GO
Morning is best, as many churches close in the afternoon. Try to get to San Giovanni in Laterano by 11am, to visit the Scala Santa before it shuts at noon. Avoid Colle Oppio after dark.

WHERE TO EAT
There are plenty of places to eat along Via Cavour and Via di San Giovanni in Laterano.

PLACE TO VISIT
SCALA SANTA
✉ Piazza di San Giovanni in Laterano 14, 00185 ☎ 06 772 6641 🕐 Daily 6.15–12, 3–6

SHOPPING

ARCHIVIA

For a profusion of beautiful glass and furnishings head to Archivia. You'll find reasonably priced gifts, from signed handmade glasses to vases, Italian pottery, unusually framed mirrors, rugs, cushions and gorgeous curtains in natural materials in a vast array of hues. It will come as no surprise that the owner is an interior designer.

✚ 184 F5 ✉ Via del Boschetto 15a, 00184 ☎ 06 474 1503 🕐 Sep–Jul Tue–Sun 10–7.30, Mon 3.30–7.30 🚇 Repubblica 🚌 40, 64, 71, 75, 117

AVENATI

Like most delicatessens in Rome, this one is satisfyingly old-fashioned and guaranteed to make your mouth water. It is packed with first-rate, traditional Italian foods including quality salamis, virgin olive oils from Tuscany, Umbria and Puglia, special pastas, wines and cheeses, including handmade buffalo-milk mozzarella.

✚ 184 F5 ✉ Via Milano 44, 00184 ☎ 06 488 2681 🕐 Sep to mid-Aug Mon–Sat 8–8 🚇 Repubblica 🚌 40, 64, 71, 75, 117

BORSE SCULTURA

www.claudiosano.it

Exquisitely handcrafted bags adorned with spirals, lips, and feminine curves and shapes. Briefcases with a keyhole or mouth shape cut out of one side stand cheek by jowl with bags of more classic form: As good to look at on the arm as off. Prices start at €110.

✚ 185 H5 ✉ Largo degli Osci 67a, 00185 ☎ 06 446 9284 🕐 Mon–Sat 10–1, 4–8 🚌 71, 492 to stop nearest Largo degli Osci; tram 3, 19

LA BOTTEGA DEL CIOCCOLATO

www.labottegadelcioccolato.it

Most goodies sold at this blissful little Italian chocolate shop are produced from a 19th-century Piedmont recipe; others are 'secrets of old masters'. A large mirror reflects the chocolate creations along the walls and in jars behind the counter. The pralines are made on site, and a selection of special chocolates for all festive occasions is sold. Prices start from €10 per 100g (4oz).

✚ 184 F5 ✉ Via Leonina 82, 00184 ☎ 06 482 1473 🕐 Sep to mid-Jun Mon–Sat 9.30–7.30 🚇 Cavour 🚌 117

LA CICOGNA

Just along from San Giovanni in Laterano, this shop is part of a chain dealing exclusively in clothes and fancy dress for children up to the age of 14. The clothes are well made and the prices moderate. They also have a good selection of toddlers' shoes. There are other outlets, including the central store near the Spanish Steps at Via Frattina 138 (tel 06 679 1921).

✚ 185 H7 ✉ Piazzale Appio 2, 00183 ☎ 06 7049 2554 🕐 Tue–Sat 9.30–1, 4–7.30, Mon 4–8.30 🚇 San Giovanni

COIN

www.coin.it

One of Rome's most popular department stores is close to San Giovanni in Laterano. Inside the modern, bright, mainly glass building you will find an array of cosmetics, home furnishings, kitchenware, toys and fashions. The top floor is dedicated to home exhibitions. Prices here are higher than in the average store. There is a snack bar on the fourth floor.

✚ 185 H7 ✉ Piazzale Appio 7, 00183 ☎ 06 708 0020 🕐 Mon–Fri 9.30–8, Sat 9.30–8.30, Sun 10.30–8.30 🚇 San Giovanni

LE GALLINELLE

This tiny boutique was once a butcher's shop. It now takes vintage, ethnic and contemporary fabrics and transforms them into inspired retro clothing with a modern twist. There is also a great selection of vintage accessories and garments. Prices are reasonable. There is a small men's section.

✚ 184 F5 ✉ Via del Boschetto 76, 00184 ☎ 06 488 1017 🕐 Mon–Sat 10.30–2.30, 3.30–8 🚍 H, 40, 60, 64, 70, 117, 170

IL GIARDINO DEL TÈ

www.ilgiardinodelte.it

Despite the name there is no garden here, but there are more than 100 teas from all over the world. Soothing Classical music helps you select from a staggering collection, neatly packaged in cellophane bags with instructions attached. The teas conjure up whole other worlds, with names such as Jasmine Dragon Eyes. Biscuits, jams and spiced coffees are also on sale. Tea starts at €3.50 per 100g (4oz).

✚ 184 F5 ✉ Via del Boschetto 107, 00184 ☎ 06 8953 5176 🕐 Jun–Aug Mon–Fri 10.30–2.30, 4.30–8; Sep–May Tue–Fri 10.30–2.30, 4–7.30, Sat 10–1.30, 4–7.30, Mon 4–7.30 🚇 Cavour 🚍 117

LEAM

www.leam.com

Near San Giovanni in Laterano, Leam has two stores within a few doors of each other, selling top designer fashion and accessories for both sexes. It has the best of Italian design: Armani, Gucci, Prada, Dolce & Gabbana and even Philippe Starck dresses. Shop assistants can be overattentive, which is a common complaint in Rome. There is a roof terrace and bar in the women's store. The Babyleam store is close by at Via Appia Nuova 33–37.

✚ 185 H7 ✉ Via Appia Nuova 26 and 32, 00183 ☎ 06 7720 7204 🕐 Tue–Sat 9.30–7.30, Mon 3.30–7.30 🚇 San Giovanni 🚍 87, 360

LEI

The name on the shop window is understated in small letters, but it's well known to young Rome-based socialites and women of fashion. They come here for their D&G staples, Romeo Gigli ready-to-wear, and a dazzling selection of party dresses and delicate slip-on shoes by French designers such as Stephane Kélian.

✚ 184 F5 ✉ Via Nazionale 88, 00184 ☎ 06 482 1700 🕐 Tue–Sat 10–1, 2.30–7.30, Mon 3.30–7.30 🚍 H, 40, 60, 64, 70, 117, 170

MAS

Rome's first department store opened its doors in 1882. Its five floors are filled floor to ceiling with clothing, shoes and houseware. The discounted branded goods help to compensate for the lack of glamour.

✚ 185 G5 ✉ Via dello Statuto 11, 00185 ☎ 06 446 8078 🕐 Daily 9–1, 4–8 🚇 Vittorio

PANELLA

For over a century, Panella has sold dozens of varieties of bread and cakes, and it has the largest selection of home-made *grissini* (breadsticks) in Rome. The three back rooms are packed with hard-to-find ingredients and spices, plus organic pastas, flours, honeys, jams and pulses.

✚ 185 G5 ✉ Via Merulana 54–55, 00185 ☎ 06 487 2435 🕐 Mon–Thu 8am–11pm, Fri–Sat 8am–midnight, Sun 8–4 🚇 Vittorio Emanuele 🚍 16, 204, 714, 850; tram 3

PIAZZA VITTORIO

The former Piazza Vittorio market has moved indoors, and has been officially renamed Nuovo Mercato Esquilino, but most still refer to it by its old name. The move has not dented the market's popularity and it continues to attract thousands of people every day. The area has a large Asian population, which is reflected in the produce sold. You'll find everything from exotic fruits to clothing and suitcases—all for prices at least a third less expensive than anywhere else in the city. Credit cards are not accepted.

✚ 185 G5 ✉ Via Principe Amadeo, 00185 🕐 Mon–Thu 7–3, Fri–Sat 7–4 🚇 Vittorio

SOCRATE

www.socrate.co.it

A kaleidoscope of brightly coloured shirts, sweaters and ties catches your eye in this men's shop. High fashion is represented by many designer names and the clothes are made of beautiful fabrics. Inside you will find more sombre suits as well as the dazzling collection of sportswear. Helpful assistants speak English, too.

✚ 184 F5 ✉ Via Nazionale 89, 00187 ☎ 06 484530 🕐 Tue–Sat 9.30–1, 3.30–7.30, Mon 3.30–7.30 🚇 Repubblica 🚍 H, 40, 60, 64, 70, 170, 117

Opposite *An array of breads at Panella*
Right *Fresh fish on sale at the Nuovo Mercato Esquilino (Piazza Vittorio)*

VIA SANNIO

This market, based in one street and with an indoor section, starts at the side of the Coin department store. Saturday has the most stalls and the best atmosphere. All sorts of clothes, new and second-hand, in a wide range of styles are on sale. Credit cards are not accepted.

🚹 185 H7 ✉ Via Sannio, 00183
🕐 Mon–Fri 8am–2pm, Sat 8am–5pm
🚇 San Giovanni

ENTERTAINMENT AND NIGHTLIFE

AKAB – CAVE

www.akabcave.it
This is one of Rome's oldest nightclubs, but still very much in style. The theme changes during the week to cover electronica, hip hop, R&B, pop and house. It hosts renowned DJs and bands, plus occasional cabaret acts. There are two floors and a courtyard. Credit cards are not accepted.

🚹 184 D8 ✉ Via di Monte Testaccio 69, 00153 ☎ 06 5725 0585 🕐 Tue–Sat 11pm–4.30am 🖐 From €10 🚇 Piramide
🚌 75, 280

AL VINO AL VINO

During the day, Al Vino al Vino operates as a wine store, but in the evening is open as a wine bar, serving Sicilian-influenced food and a choice of 500 different wines by the bottle and 25 by the glass. It also has an excellent selection of grappa, whisky and other Italian and foreign spirits. There's a good chance of finding space here when other places closer to the Colosseo and Foro Romano are full.

🚹 184 F5 ✉ Via dei Serpenti 19, 00184 ☎ 06 485 803 🕐 Wine bar: Sep–Jul daily 5.30pm–1am. Shop: Sep–Jul 10.30am–2.30am. 🚇 Colosseo 🚌 40, 60, 64 and all services to Via Nazionale or Via Cavour

AMBRA JOVINELLI

Once Rome's foremost variety venue, Ambra Jovinelli was entirely renovated in 2001 following a period of decline and now attracts some of Italy's finest comic actors, and also puts on some of the best comic plays and one-man shows in the city. Jazz concerts are also staged here.

🚹 185 H5 ✉ Via Guglielmo Pepe 43–7, 00185 ☎ 06 4434 0262 🕐 Sep–May, with one-off events in Jun and Jul. Box office: Oct–Jun Tue–Sat 10–7, Sun 3–7; Jul, Sep Mon–Sat 10–1, 2–6 🖐 €15–€30 🚇 Termini 🚌 70, 71; tram 5, 14

BEBA DO SAMBA

www.bebadosamba.it
African and Central American sounds predominate at this popular two-room venue in the studenty San Lorenzo district, but there is room for anything as long as it's not mainstream. There are sofas and cushions in one room, and a stage and bar in the other.

🚹 185 H5 ✉ Via Messapi 8, 00185
☎ 39 339 878 5214 🕐 Daily 9pm–2.30am
🖐 Compulsory annual membership €5
🚌 71, 491; tram 3, 19

CAFFÈ EMPORIO

At this spacious bar comfy sofas and armchairs are arranged around tables in the chic surroundings. Renowned for its aperitifs, the bar is very busy, especially towards the end of the week. Happy hour is 6.30–7.30pm.

🚹 184 D7 ✉ Piazza dell'Emporio 1, 00153 ☎ 06 575 4532 🕐 Daily 6pm–2am
🚇 Piramide 🚌 23, 30, 75, 716; tram 3

CAFFÈ LETTERARIO

www.caffeletterarioroma.it
The Ostiense district is becoming increasingly trendy, thanks in part to the Centrale Montemartini museum and the knock-on effect from the established club scene in Testaccio to the north. This designer, book-filled bar is at the heart of a media complex (with galleries and a TV studio), and hosts book launches and other cultural events.

🚹 Off map 184 E8 ✉ Via Ostiense 95, 00154 ☎ 06 5730 2842 🕐 Mon–Fri 10am–2am, Sat–Sun 3pm–2am. Closed for a period in Aug 🖐 Free 🚇 Ostiense

CAVOUR 313

www.cavour313.it
This unpretentious and easy-going wine bar at the southern end of Via Cavour (convenient for the Roman Forum) has been open for many years, offering a range of more than 1,200 wines and simple, fairly priced snacks and light meals.

🚹 184 F5 ✉ Via Cavour 313, 00184
☎ 06 678 5496 🕐 Daily 12.30–2.45, 7.30–12.30 🖐 Free 🚌 75, 84, 117 to Via Cavour or 84, 85, 87, 175 and other services to Via dei Fori Imperiali

CHARITY CAFÉ

www.charitycafe.it
In the afternoon, this bar acts as a tea room, offering 25 different types of herbal tea. At night it becomes an intimate venue for jazz and blues. Settle in to enjoy the music and choose from the selection of wines, cheeses and salamis on offer. Happy hour is 4–10pm. Membership is required (free).

🚹 184 F5 ✉ Via Panisperna 68, 00184
☎ 06 4782 5881 🕐 Mon–Sat 3pm–1am
🖐 Free 🚇 Colosseo

CIRCOLO DEGLI ARTISTI

This large venue is more of a meeting place than a nightclub. There are two dance floors plus a large outdoor area, including bars, food stands, and even a cinema. Live music ranges from acid jazz and funk to reggae-rap. Friday is gay night. Credit cards are not accepted.

🚹 Off map 185 J6 ✉ Via Casilina Vecchia 42, 00182 ☎ 06 7030 5684
🕐 Tue–Thu 8pm–2am, Fri–Sat 8pm–4am, Sun 7pm–2am 🖐 From €10 🚌 105

COMING OUT

www.comingout.it
Look for the rainbow flag over the door and the crowds spilling out into the street. Coming Out is central Rome's most happening gay bar, with a warm orange interior, good bar food and a variety of theme nights from Tuesday to Thursday.

🚹 185 G6 ✉ Via di San Giovanni in Laterano 8, 00184 ☎ 06 700 9871 🕐 Daily 10am–2am; events from 10.30pm 🖐 Lunch €25, Dinner €35, Wine €12 🚇 Colosseo
🚌 60, 75, 87, 117, 175; tram 3

CONCERTI DEL TEMPIETTO

www.tempietto.it

In winter, the Associazione Musicale 'Il Tempietto' stages concerts at the nearby Sala Baldini in Piazza del Campitelli and in the Basilica di San Nicola. In summer, the music is performed alfresco in the stunning, ancient Teatro di Marcello.

➕ 184 E6 ✉ Teatro di Marcello, Via del Teatro di Marcello 44, 00186. Box office: Via Rodolfo Morandi 3, 00139 ☎ 06 8713 1590 🕐 Season: Jun–Sep 🖐 €21 🚇 Teatro di Marcello, Sala Baldini and Basilica di San Nicola: 81, 160, 204, 628 to Via del Teatro di Marcello, or 40, 64, 87, 628 to Piazza Venezia, then walk

HANGAR

www.hangaronline.it

Rome's oldest gay bar is an American-style pick-up bar for men. It is long, narrow and crowded, with music videos playing on either side of a central corridor. Credit cards are not accepted.

➕ 184 F5 ✉ Via in Selci 69A, 00184 ☎ 06 488 1397 🕐 Sep–Jul Wed–Mon 10.30pm–2.30am 🖐 Free 🚇 Colosseo 🚌 75, 84 to Via Cavour

LOCANDA ATLANTIDE

www.locandaatlantide.it

The San Lorenzo district east of Termini station is off the tourist trail, but is at the heart of the university district, and good, inexpensive restaurants, bars and clubs abound. This no-nonsense venue is typical, offering a range of inexpensive concerts, dance nights and other cultural events.

➕ 185 H5 ✉ Via dei Lucani 22/B, 00185 ☎ 06 4470 4540 🕐 Daily 9pm–2am 🖐 Free; €10 on concert nights 🚌 71, 491

MICCA CLUB

www.miccaclub.com

A good bet if you are staying near Termini railway station, thanks to one of the city's most vibrant and free-ranging music policies and the vast size of this underground dance floor and club.

➕ 185 H6 ✉ Via Pietro Micca 7/A, 00121 ☎ 06 8744 0079 🕐 Mon–Tue, Thu–Sat 7pm–4am, Sun 6pm–1am 🖐 Sun–Tue, Thu

Above *Wines are sold by the glass or by the bottle*

free, Fri–Sat €10 pre-booked on website or €15 on the door 🚇 Manzoni 🚌 70, 71 to Via Filippo Turati

L'OASI DELLA BIRRA

Testaccio's 'Oasis of Beer' lives up to its name, offering hundreds of different beers, along with a good selection of wines and a range of snacks and full meals. In summer you can eat and drink outdoors.

➕ 184 E8 ✉ Piazza Testaccio 40, 00153 ☎ 06 574 6122 🕐 Daily 7pm–1am. Closed for a period in Aug 🖐 Free 🚇 Ostiense 🚌 23, 44, 280 to Lungarno Ripa-Via Marmorata

OPPIO CAFFÈ

www.oppiocaffe.it

High-tech meets ancient history here: glass and steel bar fixtures, Plexiglas seats and plasma video screens, all underneath Roman brickwork. There is an amazing view of the Colosseo from the terrace and DJs or live music most nights.

➕ 184 F6 ✉ Via delle Terme di Tito 72, 00184 ☎ 06 474 5262 🕐 Daily 7am–2am 🖐 Free 🚇 Colosseo

TEATRO COLOSSEO

www.teatrocolosseo.it

In the shadow of the mighty Colosseum, this venue is a rarity for Rome—a theatre staging English-language plays. It is a good showcase for young directors and actors, and the small stage suits one-man shows.

➕ 184 F6 ✉ Via Capo d'Africa 5, 00184 ☎ 06 700 4932 🕐 Sep–Jun Mon–Sat 10–1, 3–7 🖐 €10–€20 🚇 Colosseo 🚌 30

SPORTS AND ACTIVITIES
ROME CITY MARATHON

www.maratonadiroma.it

Each spring runners flock to participate in this event, which is slowly achieving the status of the marathons in London and New York. The race starts and finishes on the Via dei Fori Imperiali in front of the Colosseum, and the route passes all the city's major sites.

➕ 184 F6 ✉ Via dei Fori Imperiali, 00186 ☎ 06 406 5064 🕐 3rd Sun in Mar 🚇 Colosseo 🚌 60, 75, 85, 117, 175, 186, 271, 571, 810, 850

PRICES AND SYMBOLS

The restaurants are listed alphabetically (excluding La, Il, Le and I). The prices given are the average for a two-course lunch (L) and a three-course dinner (D) for one person, without drinks. The wine price is for the least expensive bottle. All the restaurants listed accept credit cards unless otherwise stated.

For a key to the symbols, ▷ 2.

AGATA E ROMEO

www.agataeromeo.it

Enjoy Roman and southern Italian dishes in this intimate and elegant restaurant. *Baccalà* (salt cod), smoked and cooked with an orange sauce, is just one of the delights on the menu, and is best accompanied by an Italian wine from their great wine list. Reservations are essential. ✚ 185 G5 ✉ Via Carlo Alberto 45, 00185 ☎ 06 446 6115 🕐 Mon–Fri 12.30–2.30, 7.30–10.30. Closed Aug and 2 weeks in Jan ✋ L €100, D €160, Tasting menu €124, Wine €25 🚇 Vittorio Emanuele 🚌 4, 70, 71, 614

ANTICA LOCANDA

www.antica-locanda.com

Brick walls, oak beams and candlelight make this a delightful place in which to sample fine wines from all over Italy. It's just a 10-minute walk from the Forum in one of the city's oldest quarters. There's a limited but good selection of food: pasta, mixed vegetables and daily specials. Two good Chardonnays to try are the Tenuta Santa Anna and the Prinè Chardonnay Barrique. For reds, try the Cabernet Bosco del Merlo. Wines are sold by the glass or bottle. ✚ 184 F5 ✉ Via del Boschetto 85, 00184 ☎ 06 4788 1729 🕐 Wed–Mon 12–12 ✋ L €15, D €30, Wine €12 🚇 Cavour 🚌 117, or any bus to Via Nazionale

BAR CAPITOLINA

Many people don't realize that you can access Bar Capitolina, the bar of the Musei Capitolini, without actually visiting the museum. It's well worth having a drink or lunch here because, apart from reasonable prices, it has a large terrace with stunning views of the Tarpeian Rock and ancient Rome. Guests with disabilities should ask for elevator access, as it is quite a climb up. The way in to the bar is via the museum exit on Piazzale Caffarelli (look carefully as there are no signs outside). ✚ 184 E6 ✉ Piazzale Caffarelli 4, 00186 ☎ 06 6919 0564 🕐 Tue–Sun 9–7.30 ✋ Sandwich and salad €15 (terrace €20), Wine €7.75, Coffee €1.30 (terrace €4) 🚌 40, 64, 87, 628 to Piazza Venezia, or 40, 62, 63, 64, 492, 571, 628, 916 to Teatro di Marcello 🚇 Spagna 🚌 30, 40, 64, 70

LA BARRIQUE

This wine bar, particularly loved by theatregoers, lies just off Via Nazionale. It is ideal for a light but sophisticated dinner; for a romantic evening, reserve the tiny mezzanine floor. Cooking is creative, with every dish designed to complement a perfectly matched wine. Desserts change daily, but the mousses are always mouth-watering. The ample wine list includes a good choice of wine by the glass. ✚ 184 F5 ✉ Via del Boschetto 41b, 00184 ☎ 06 4782 5953 🕐 Mon–Fri 11–3.30, 6.30–1.30, Sat 6pm–2am ✋ L €15, D €25, Wine €4 (by the glass) 🚇 Repubblica or Cavour 🚌 30x, 64

I BUONI AMICI

www.ibuoniamici.it

This traditional trattoria near San Giovanni in Laterano is one of the best-value restaurants in Rome, despite its celebrity clientele. The interior is traditional in design, with red-and-white checked tablecloths. Delicious *antipasti* include aubergines (eggplant), courgettes (zucchini), spinach and squid salad. Try the fresh pasta with lobster and some chargrilled fish to follow, or the succulent roast lamb. Leave room for the home-made tiramisù and pannacotta. The Cannonau red from Sardinia is a bargain at around €14 a bottle.

Opposite *Traditional Roman dishes are on offer in many of the city's restaurants*

🕂 185 G6 ✉ Via Aleardo Aleardi 4, 00185 ☎ 06 7049 1993 🕐 Mon–Sat 12.30–3, 7.30–11 ✋ L €11, D €25, Wine €7 🚇 Manzoni 🚌 16, 81, 87, 117, 714

CAFÉ CAFÉ
www.cafecafebistrot.it
Escape the tourist traps encircling the Colosseum and relax in bohemian elegance at this café/restaurant. The Swedish owner serves up coffee, cakes, fresh juice, home-made ice cream and light Italian fare. Expect hand-lettered menus, bright walls and soft jazz. It fills up quickly for Sunday brunch: a €6 buffet of crunchy salads, *bruschette*, cheese and prosciutto. Highly recommended for vegetarians and vegans, plus visitors on their own, who will delight in the big pile of newspapers.
🕂 184 F6 ✉ Via dei Santissimi Quattro 44, 00184 ☎ 06 700 8743 🕐 Daily 10am–1.30am ✋ L €4, D €10, Wine €13 🚇 Colosseo

CHARLY'S SAUCIÈRE
This well-established restaurant specializes in French and Swiss cuisine, which is served by attentive staff. As you might expect, French wine is prominent on the carefully selected wine list.
🕂 185 G6 ✉ Via di San Giovanni in Laterano 270, 00184 ☎ 06 7049 5666 🕐 Tue–Fri 12.45–2.15, 8–12, Sat 8pm–midnight, Mon 12.45–2.15. Closed 2 weeks in Aug ✋ L €18, D €35, Wine €12 🚇 Mazzini 🚌 85, 117, 850

NERONE
This small, friendly trattoria, close to the Colosseum, is famous for its Abruzzese cooking—the *antipasti* buffet is particularly good. In warm weather there are tables outside, opposite the Colle Oppio.
🕂 184 F6 ✉ Via delle Terme di Tito 96, 00184 ☎ 06 481 7952 🕐 Sep–Jul Mon–Sat 12–3, 7–11 ✋ L €15, D €30, Wine €8 🚌 30b, 75, 85, 87, 117, 175, 196 to Piazza del Colosseo 🚇 Colosseo

OSTERIA DEL CAMPIDOGLIO
This small trattoria tucked between the Palatine and Capitoline hills, just a few minutes' walk from the Foro Romano, has tables outside in the summer overlooking the baroque facade of Santa Maria della Consolazione. It offers Roman and Tuscan cuisine, with a range of fish and meat dishes, home-made *dolci* and good house wine.
🕂 184 E6 ✉ Via dei Fienili 56, 00186 ☎ 06 678 0250 🕐 Mon–Sat 11.30–3.30, 7.30–11.30 ✋ L €25, D €35, Wine €6 🚌 81, 85, 170, 628 (bus stop on Via Petroselli)

PASQUALINO AL COLOSSEO
This trattoria is on a quiet side street in view of the Colosseum. It has dining on two levels. Downstairs is wonderfully 1960s, with mock-wood walls and huge ceiling fans, while the upper level is more classic in style. The cuisine is essentially Mediterranean (fresh fish daily) with a touch of Sicilian. Pasta with mushrooms, peas and sausage, and *carpaccio* of sea bass and tuna are both exceptional. The swordfish steak with capers and olives is nicely original and the tiramisù is first class.
🕂 184 F6 ✉ Via dei Santissimi Quattro 66, 00184 ☎ 06 700 4576 🕐 Tue–Sun 12–3, 7–11 ✋ L €25, D €40, Wine €11 🚇 Colosseo 🚌 85, 87, 117; tram 3

PIZZA FORUM
www.pizzaforum.it
Pizza Forum is a large pizzeria behind the Colosseo. An entrance hall with Roman cobblestones brings you alongside the pizza ovens and invites you to enter the spacious dining room, which is furnished with stained glass. It's possibly the best pizzeria in Rome serving proper Neapolitan pizza (thicker than Roman pizza). There's a choice of over 35 pizzas from €8. Service is neat and friendly.
🕂 184 F6 ✉ Via di San Giovanni in Laterano 34–38, 00184 ☎ 06 7759 1158 🕐 Thu–Tue 12–3, 7–midnight ✋ L €8, D €12, Wine €9 🚇 Colosseo 🚌 85, 87, 117; tram 3

RISTORANTE CONSOLINI
www.systemfree.net/ristoranteconsolini
This elegant restaurant lies at the foot of the Aventine Hill overlooking ancient Roman warehouses near the Tiber. The attractive, spacious terrace, split between two levels, offers wonderful views and makes an ideal setting for a romantic meal. The wide range of *antipasti* is delightful, and the menu is varied, with delicate risotto and fish dishes as well as more robust traditional Roman fare.
🕂 184 D7 ✉ Via Marmorata 28, 00153 ☎ 06 5730 0148 🕐 Tue–Sun 12.30–3, 7.30–11 ✋ L €35, D €50, Wine €9 🚌 44, 75, 95; tram 3

SAN CLEMENTE
This bar/pizzeria/pub is a great place to take a break between the Colosseum and the Basilica of San Giovanni in Laterano. It has three vaulted rooms and a terrace, 15 different beers from which to choose and serves decent food. The good-value tourist menu is available at both lunch and dinner. It consists of cannelloni to start, followed by roast chicken and potatoes, with wine or beer, plus coffee, and all for around €14.
🕂 185 G6 ✉ Via di San Giovanni in Laterano 124, 00184 ☎ 06 7045 0944 🕐 Mon–Sat 7am–2am, Sun 8am–2am ✋ L €10, D €25, Wine €10 🚇 Colosseo or San Giovanni 🚌 85, 87, 117; tram 3

SILVIO ALLA SUBURRA
This traditional trattoria, serving delicious home-made pasta and robust, tasty meat dishes simmered with wine and herbs, is the sort of place you would expect to find in one of the outlying villages in the hills surrounding the city rather than in central Rome. It is a simple and timeless place, where nothing ever seems to happen in a hurry. Just come and enjoy the good food and house wine. There are just a few tables outside on the narrow street during the summer.
🕂 184 F5 ✉ Via Urbana 67–69, 00184 ☎ 06 486 531 🕐 Tue–Sun 12.30–3, 7–11 ✋ L €20, D €35, Wine €7 🚇 Cavour

PRICES AND SYMBOLS

Prices are the lowest and highest for a double room for one night. Breakfast is included unless noted otherwise. All the hotels listed accept credit cards unless otherwise stated. Note that rates vary widely throughout the year.

For a key to the symbols, ▷ 2.

ANNE AND MARY

www.anne-mary.com

This welcoming bed-and-breakfast occupies an elegant 19th-century building near the Colosseo. Rooms are simple but dramatic, with clean lines and swooping curtains. Each has a small private bathroom with enclosed shower, and a TV and safe in the bedroom. The wood parquetry on the hall floors is especially handsome. Via Cavour is a large, somewhat frantic artery, but the convenience for sights and shops is worth the muted noise.

✚ 184 F5 ⊠ Via Cavour 325, 00184 ☎ 06 6994 1187 ✋ €100–€150 ① 6 ⑤ ⑤ ⑤ Cavour 🚌 75, 81, 85, 87, 116, 117

ANTICA LOCANDA

www.antica-locanda.com

In the oldest part of Rome, not far from the Colosseo, is this quaint and inexpensive family-run hotel. Check in at the 15th-century wine bar of the same name next door. There is no elevator up to the four floors, but a porter service is provided. Rooms have beamed ceilings, wooden floors with rugs, and Italian reproduction furniture, plus TV, minibar, shower and hairdryer. There is a large flower-filled roof terrace (and on request the use of a barbecue) overlooking this medieval part of the city. The Continental breakfast is served in the wine bar.

✚ 184 F5 ⊠ Via del Boschetto 84, 00185 ☎ 06 484 894 ✋ €80–€150 ① 10 ⑤ ⑤ Cavour 🚌 117, or any bus to Via Nazionale

CAPO D'AFRICA

www.hotelcapodafrica.com

This hotel is housed in a handsome 19th-century building close to the Colosseo in a fashionable district. It is a fusion of contemporary and classic, with a hint of Japanese design. The beautiful rooms are in warm ochre and saffron tones, and the fitted bathrooms are in marble and wood. The buffet breakfast is served on the roof with views of the Colosseo. There is also a large, well-equipped gym and solarium.

✚ 185 G6 ⊠ Via Capo d'Africa 54, 00184 ☎ 06 772801 ✋ €380–€540 ① 65 ⑤ ⑤ ⑤ Colosseo 🚌 81, 85, 87, 117; tram 3

FORTYSEVEN

www.fortysevenhotel.com

A team of young designers has created a cool minimalist hotel within ancient Rome, overlooking the Temple of Vesta. A spectacular roof terrace restaurant offers magnificent views, while the hotel is equipped with the latest technology, with WiFi access in every room. There is also an inside courtyard and a fitness centre with a sauna. The staff are friendly and helpful.

✚ 184 E6 ⊠ Via Luigi Petroselli 47, 00186 ☎ 06 678 7816 ✋ €180–€270 ① 61 ⑤ ⑤ Circo Massimo 🚌 H, 30, 44, 63, 81, 95, 170

Opposite and below Many of the city's hotels offer style as well as comfort

HOTEL CELIO
www.hotelcelio.com
The simple facade of this elegant 19th-century hotel, just a short walk from the Colosseo, belies its stunning interior. All bedrooms have frescoes, inspired by Renaissance painters, plus modern amenities such as air conditioning, WiFi and satellite TV. Rooms on the upper floors have jacuzzis.
✚ 184 F6 ✉ Via dei Santissimi Quattro 35c, 00184 ☎ 06 7049 5333 ♨ €180–€330 ⓘ 14 🕭 📺 ⓠ Colosseo 🚌 116, 117

HOTEL NERVA
www.hotelnerva.com
Tucked behind the walls of the Fori Imperiali, this hotel is in a quiet street and could hardly be more central. It is furnished to a comfortable standard, with modern bathrooms, fully equipped soundproofed rooms and a garage. Staff are very friendly and helpful, and breakfast is served in the frescoed bar downstairs.
✚ 184 F5 ✉ Via Tor de'Conti 3–4a, 00184 ☎ 06 678 1835 ♨ €120–€220 ⓘ 19 🕭 ⓠ Cavour 🚌 60, 75, 84, 85, 87, 175, 186, 271

LANCELOT
www.lancelothotel.com
The Lancelot is a welcoming, family-run hotel just around the corner from the Colosseum. The entrance hall and restaurant are furnished with elegant period furniture. Other public spaces are the bar, the library and a delightful courtyard. Guest rooms are spacious, and most have wooden floors, pastel walls and individual charm. All have modern conveniences such as a safe, satellite TV and a bathroom with shower. Some guest rooms have their own terraces, but there's also a lovely roof terrace.
✚ 185 G6 ✉ Via Capo d'Africa 47, 00184 ☎ 06 7045 0615 ♨ €155–€260 ⓘ 60 🕭 ⓠ Colosseo or Manzoni 🚌 81, 85, 87, 117; tram 3

MERCURE HOTEL DELTA COLOSSEO
www.mercurehotels.com
One of the last developments (1975) allowed in this part of the old city, the Mercure is in view of the Colosseo and beside Nero's Domus Aurea (Golden House). It has a beautifully marbled, spacious reception with internet access, a high-tech minimalist bar and a piano bar. The medium-sized rooms are equipped with marble bath, comfortable sofas, satellite and pay TV, safe and minibar. There is also a bar on the roof with a 360-degree view of the city.
✚ 185 G6 ✉ Via Labicana 144, 00184 ☎ 06 770 021 ♨ €270–€300 ⓘ 160 🕭 ♒ Outdoor ⓠ Colosseo or Manzoni 🚌 87, 117; tram 3

ORAZIA
www.hotelorazia.it
The Orazia is on the fifth floor of a building on the Colle Esquilino, just one street away from the Colosseo. Guest rooms are furnished in classic Italian 19th-century style, including marble floors. All have private bath or shower, hairdryer, telephone, minibar and satellite TV. The same Italian style is found in the breakfast room, where evening meals can be served on request.
✚ 185 G5 ✉ Via Buonarroti 51, 00185 ☎ 06 446 7202 ♨ €60–€180, excluding breakfast and air conditioning ⓘ 38 🕭 ⓠ Vittorio Emanuele 🚌 70, 360

RESIDENCE PALAZZO AL VELABRO
www.velabro.it
Surrounded by ancient monuments and just across from the Tiber, this is self-sufficiency in a dream setting. The apartments are light and very spacious, with a living/dining room with folding door concealing a gallery kitchen, plus bedroom and bathroom. Lemon walls, satellite TV and comfortable sofa beds all make for a relaxed atmosphere. There is a bar and two terraces for enjoying the stunning views. Ideal for families.
✚ 184 E6 ✉ Via del Velabro 16, 00186 ☎ 06 679 2758 ♨ From €175–€400, excluding breakfast ⓘ 35 🕭 🚌 81, 160, 204, 628, then 15-min walk

SANTA PRASSEDE
www.hotelsantaprassede.it
The street and hotel take their name from the church of Santa Prassede, known for its early Christian mosaics; Santa Maria Maggiore is just around the corner. The 25 quiet guest rooms, all in typically Roman shades and with dark wooden floors, have private bathrooms, central heating and safe deposit boxes. There is a bar and a TV lounge as part of the communal areas. Laundry service is available.
✚ 185 G5 ✉ Via di Santa Prassede 25, 00184 ☎ 06 481 4850 ♨ €120–€160, excluding breakfast ⓘ 25 🕭 ⓠ Termini or Cavour 🚌 64, 70, 71

San Lorenzo in Lucina
Palazzo Barberini
Galleria dell' Accademia di San Luca
Repubblica Teatro Opera
Via XX SETTEMBRE
Ministero di Difesa

LUNG TOR DI NONA
S Simeone
S Salvatore in Lauro
Palazzo Altemps
Palazzo dei Prefetti
Piazza S Silvestro V
Palazzo di Montecitorio
Palazzo Chigi
Colonna di Marco Aurelio
Fontana di Trevi
Palazzo della Stamperia
Museo Nazionale delle Paste Alimentari
Giardino del Quirinale
San Carlo alle Quattro Fontane
Monte Quirinale

VIA DEL TRITONE

Sant' Agostino
Palazzo della Cancelleria
Piazza Montecitorio
Piazza Colonna
Palazzo della Dataria
Scuderie del Quirinale
Villa Colonna
Palazzo del Quirinale
Sant' Andrea al Quirinale

Chiesa Nuova
Santa Maria della Pace
Sant' Agnese
Sant' Ivo alla Sapienza
Pantheon
Santa Maria sopra Minerva
Sant' Ignazio di Loyola
Palazzo Odescalchi
Santi Apostoli
Palazzo Colonna
La Barrique
Monte Viminale

Silvio alla Suburra
Antica Locanda
Colonna Traiana
Mercati di Traiano
Hotel Nerva
Anne and Mary
San Pietro in Vincoli
Nerone
Domu

CORSO VITTORIO EMANUELE II
Il Gesù
Fori Imperiali
Santa Maria in Aracoeli
Musei Capitolini
Arco di Settimio Severo
Santi Cosma e Damiano

GHETTO
Bar Capitolina
Teatro di Marcello
Palazzo dei Conservatori
Osteria del Campidoglio
Palazzo Senatorio
Foro Romano
Arco di Tito
S Teodoro
Orti Farnesiani
Colosseo
Hotel Celio
Pizza Forum

Santa Nicola in Carcere
Fortyseven
Tempio di Vesta
Residence Palazzo al Velabro
Santa Maria in Cosmedin
Palatino
Casa di Livia
Palazzo dei Flavi
Domus d'Augusto
Stadio
Parco del Celio
Tempio del Divo Claudio
Santi Giovanni e Paolo
Pasqu al Co

Santa Maria in Trastevere
San Crisogono
San Bartolomeo all' Isola
PONTE PALATINO
Bocca della Verità
S Anastasia
Circo Massimo
VIA DEI CERCHI
VIA DI SAN GREGORIO
San Gregorio Magno
S Tommaso
Santa Maria in Domnica
Monte Celio

AVENTINO
Monte Aventino
S Sabina
S Alessio
S Prisca
Obelisco di Axum
Circo Massimo
Villa Celimor

Ristorante Consolini
S Anselmo
Parco di Porta Capena
Santa Balbina
Terme di Caracalla

TESTACCIO
VIA MARMORATA
Marmorata (Vanvitelli)
Parco della Resistenza dell'8 Settembre
S Saba
Terme di Caracalla

MACRO Testaccio
Parco Monte Testaccio
Cimitero Acattolico
Cimitero Inglese di Guerra
Piramide
ROMA PORTA S PAOLO
Porta S Paolo
Viale di Porta Ardeatina

Piazzale dei Partigiani
Collegio Verbo Divino
STAZIONE ROMA OSTIENSE F S

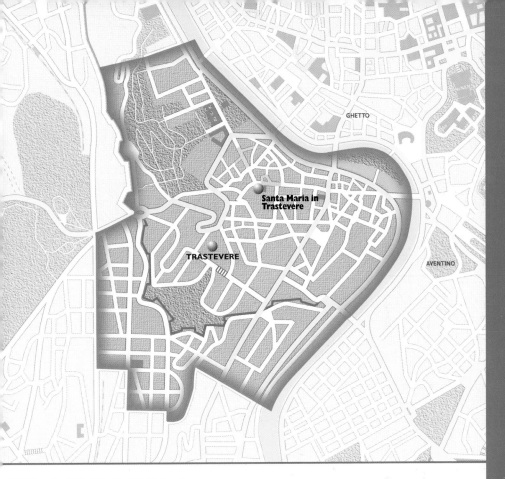

TRASTEVERE

While much of central Rome is a patchwork of sights, streets and monuments from different eras, Trastevere—meaning 'across the Tevere'—is a distinctive and self-contained residential quarter. Largely enclosed in a bend of the Tiber on the river's west bank, it has long been the city's working-class district, and even today its streets and squares, not to mention its inhabitants, feel different to their counterparts across the water.

Trastevere's backstreets are as picturesque as any in the heart of the city, but here the narrow lanes seem quieter and calmer: Laundry drying above the cobbles, cats lazing in the sun and geraniums tumbling from window-boxes recall an older, more traditional Italy. At the same time, the area is becoming more gentrified, and many, though not all, of the neighbourhood shops, markets and old-fashioned bars and trattorias have given way to establishments aimed at visitors.

Many of these visitors come in the evening, for this is one of the key dining areas of the city (and is also pretty to wander around come sundown), but there are also some key sights to see by day, notably the great church of Santa Maria in Trastevere, in the area's main square, and the less well-known Santa Cecilia in Trastevere. There are also the Villa Farnesina and Palazzo Corsini, two relatively unvisited galleries, both of which are gems, as well as the peaceful Orto Botanico (Botanical Garden), which spreads over the slopes of the Gianicolo, a panoramic belvedere above Trastevere's pretty huddle of streets.

STAZIONE ROMA S PIETRO

Maria Addolorata

5

Col Monte de Gallo

VIA INNOCENZO III

Via D Silveri

Via D

VIA DELLE FORNACI

Viale delle Mura

VIA STAZIONE DI SAN PIETRO

VIA NUOVA DELLE FORNACI

Aurelie

del

Gianicolo

Piazzale G Garibaldi

Gianicolo

S Onofrio

Via degli Orti d'Alibert

Via delle Mantellate

della

Via di San Francesco di Sales

Via del Riari

Orto Botanico

LUNGOTEVERE GIANICOLENSE

Ponte Mazzini

Largo Lorenzo Perosi

S Eligio

Mon

LUNGOTEVERE

LUNGOTEVERE DELLA FARN

Lungara

Teve

Palazzo Corsini

Villa Farnesina

Palazzo Torlonia

VIA GARIBALDI

VIA DELLA SCALA

Santa Maria della Scala

Vicolo de Cedr

S E

6

VIA AURELIA ANTICA

Villa Abamelek

Porta S Pancrazio

Piazzale Aurelio

Via di Porta San Pancrazio

Via A Masina

San Pietro in Montorio

VIA GARIBALDI

Via Lu

Via Goffredo Mameli

Via G Sacchi

250 m
250 yds

VIA DI SAN PANCRAZIO

Via G Bruzzesi

Via A Algardi

Via del Vascello

Via F Bonnet

VIALE DELLE MURA GIANICOLENSI

Via P Roselli

Via Giacomo Medici

Via Trenta Aprile

Via Nicola Fabrizi

Via Calandrelli

TRASTEVERE

VIALE GLO

Via F Casini

7

VIA VITELLIA

Bricci

Pamphili

Via F Bolognesi

Via A Busiri Vici

Via Basilio

Via Ludovico di Monreale

Villa

Via O Regnoli

VIALE DE QUATTRO VENTI

VIA GIACINTO CARINI

Via G Rossetti

Via Giovagnoli

Via M Quadrio

POERIO

Villa Sciarra

Via Dandolo

Viale Aurelio Saffi

Bernardin da Feltr

VIA

8

VIA INNOCENZO X

VIA FONTEIANA

Viale

Via San Calepodio

VIALE ANTON GIULIO BARRILI

Via A Cesari

S Maria Reg Pacis

Via A Colautti

Via G B Niccolini

Via F Torre

Via Felice Cavallotti

Via Fr D Guerrazzi

VIA ALESSANDRO

Via F Bandiera

Viale Aurelio Saffi

Via Francesco dell'Ongaro

VIA DI TRASTEVERE

Piazza Ippolito Nievo

Via N Parbor

Via A Ba

188

S Maria d Prov

B

Istituto d Laurentana

C

CORSO
VITTORIO
EMANUELE II

Palazzo della
Cancelleria

Via dei
Pellegrino

Via dei Cappellari

Via Baullari

Sant'Andrea
della Valle

del Sudario

Campo
dei Fiori

Piazza
Farnese

Teatro
Pompeo

Palazzo
Farnese

Palazzo
Spada

Via Pettinari

Via dei Giubbonari

Via delle Zoccolette

GHETTO

Ministero Grazia
Giustizia

Ministero
G Giustizia

Ponte
Sisto

LUNGOTEVERE DEI VALLATI

Via d Cestari

Via di Torre Argentina

CORSO VITTORIO EMANUELE II

Teatro
Argentina

Templi
Repubblicani

Argentina

Via delle Botteghe Oscure

Crypta
Balbi

Via dei Funari

Via del Delfini

Fontana delle
Tartarughe

Via Portico d'Ottavia

Via Catalana

Sinagoga

LUNGOTEVERE DEI CENCI

Teatro di
Marcello

Piazza
Monte Savello

Via del Gesù

Via del Plebiscito

Palazzo
Altieri

Palazzo
Venezia

VIA DEL PLEBISCITO

San Marco

Il Gesù

Museo del
Palazzo
Venezia

Piazza
Venezia

Monumento a Vittorio
Emanuele II

Santa Maria
in Aracoeli

Musei
Capitolini

Piazza del
Campitelli

VIA DEL TEATRO DI MARCELLO

Piazza del
Campidoglio

Palazzo
dei Conservatori

Palazzo
Senatorio

Monte Capitolino

Piazza dei Santi
Apostoli

Piazza
dei Santi
Apostoli

Colonna
Traiana

VIA DEI FORI IMPERIALI

Fori
Imperiali

Arco di
Settimio
Severo

Via di Consolazione

Santa Nicola
in Carcere

Piazza della
Consolazione

Via dei F/enili

Via di San Teodoro

S Teodoro

PONTE
GARIBALDI

LUNGOT DEI SANZIO

Via della Renella

Piazza
G G Belli

LUNGOT DELL' ANGUILLARA

Isola
Tiberina

San Bartolomeo
all' Isola

LUNGOTEVERE DEI PIERLEONI

VIA LUIGI PETROSELLI

Tempio della
Fortuna Virilis

Tempio
di Vesta

Piazza di
S Anastasia

PONTE
PALATINO

Lungaretta

Belli
della

Piazza
di S Maria
in Trastevere

a Maria
astevere

San Crisogono

Piazza
Sidney
Sonnino

Via dei Salumi

Via dei Genovesi

LUNGOTEVERE RIPA

Piazza Bocca
della Verità

Santa Maria
in Cosmedin

Sant'Anastasia

Via dei Cerchi

Via del Cinque

Via dei
e' Renzi

Moro

Via della

ara

Via di San Francesco a Ripa

Via N d Grande

a Maria
astevere

Trastevere
(Mastai)

Piazza
Mastai

Via della Luce

Anicia

Santa Cecilia
in Trastevere

Via S M In Cappella

Via del
Porto

AVENTINO

Circo
Massimo

VIA DEL CIRCO MASSIMO

Morosini

P

Induno

TRASTEVERE

VIA G INDUNO

Trastevere
(M P Istruzione)

Viale delle Mura Portuensi

San Francesco
a Ripa

Via di San Michele

Porta
Portese

PORTO DI RIPA GRANDE

Piazza
Porta
Portese

PONTE
SUBLICIO

Tevere

LUNGOTEVERE AVENTINO

Santa
Sabina

Sabina

Santa

Sabina

S Alessio

Via di San Domenico

Via di Porta Lavernale

Monte

di

S Anselmo

Via di Santa Prisca

S Prisca

Clivo

Pubblici

Aventino

Piazza
Tempio
Diana

V Fonte di Fauno

Via Licinia

AVENTINO

Aventino /
Albania

Via di S Saba

Emporio

Marmorata /
Vanvitelli

Via

sant'

Melania

Via di sant' Alessio

Via Iclio

Via di sant' Anselmo

Via Marcella

Via dei Decii

Piazza
Albania

zza San
simato

PORTUENSE

Lungotevere

Portuense

TESTACCIO

Via Amerigo Vespucci

Via Rubattino

Via Giovanni

Branca

Via Florio

Via B Franklin

V Torricelli

Via Luigi Vanvitelli

Via Mastro Giorgio

Via Bodoni

Via Giovan Battista

Via Aldo Manuzio

Via Nicola Zabaglia

MARMORATA

VIA

Via A Volta

Via Galvani

S M
Liberatrice

VIALE MANLIO GELSOMINI

Parco della
Resistenza
dell'8 Settembre

VIA DELLA P CESTIA

Via Annia Faustina

S Saba

Piazza G L
Bernini

GIANICOLO

Although not one of Rome's original seven hills, the best view of Rome and its monuments has to be from the Janiculum Hill, especially at sunset. Its terrace is the city's largest, but there are spectacular views all the way up from the Passeggiata del Gianicolo, a fine avenue that runs all around the hill, beginning at Ponte Amedeo di Savoia. To save time and energy, take a bus to the top and return to Ponte Amedeo di Savoia on foot.

On the terrace is a huge equestrian monument to Giuseppe Garibaldi, who in 1849 fought a battle nearby to defend the Roman Republic. Eighty busts displayed along the promenade represent famous artists and heroes from Garibaldi's campaign.

The church of Sant'Onofrio has beautiful frescoes by Antoniazzo Romano and Baldassare Peruzzi, together with the remains of the 16th-century Italian poet Torquato Tasso. The adjoining convent, where Tasso spent his last years, has frescoes by Domenichino.

✚ 188 C6 ✉ Passeggiata del Gianicolo
🚌 870

ISOLA TIBERINA

This small island in the Tiber, with its medieval buildings and Roman bridges, feels like a safe harbour, protected from the chaos of the city.

The island is erected on a volcanic rock and its shape resembles that of a ship. There are several legends about its origin, one of which concerns Esculapio, the Greek god of medicine: During the third century BC, the Romans sent a boat to Epidaurus in Greece to discover a cure for the plague. On the return journey, Esculapio left the ship in the shape of a serpent and swam to the island, indicating that a temple to the god of healing should be built there (the church of San Bartolomeo now stands where the sanctuary was erected). In the first century BC, the Romans reshaped the island with slabs of travertine to form a 'prow' and

Above *Ponte Fabricio, one of two bridges linking Isola Tiberina to the riverbanks*
Opposite *There are fine views of the city from Gianicolo*

'stern', and erected an obelisk as a mast, to commemorate Esculapio's ship. The island's tradition of healing and medicine has continued over the centuries, enhanced by the belief that the water on the island is particularly healthy. There is still a large hospital there.

Two bridges join Isola Tiberina to the riverbanks: Ponte Cestio dates back to the first century BC, and leads to Trastevere; while Ponte Fabricio, built in 62BC, and the only Roman bridge to survive intact, joins the island to the Ghetto. The latter used to be called Ponte dei Giudei, which means the Bridge of the Jews. On the north side of the island is Ponte Rotto (Broken Bridge), the remains of a Roman wooden bridge built in 179BC.

✚ 189 D6 🚌 23, 63, 280; tram 8

ORTO BOTANICO

In a tranquil corner of Trastevere (▷ 195) lies the Orto Botanico (Botanical Garden), a great place to escape from the noisy bustle of the area. It was the garden of the imposing Palazzo Corsini (▷ 192) until 1883, and now contains a vast collection of plants, which began with the medicinal plants cultivated

in the Vatican by Pope Nicholas III in the 13th century.

As you enter the gardens, a central path leads to the Tritons Fountain, built in 1570 by architect Ferdinando Fuga and surrounded by the garden's famous palms. Farther up, on the hill, the rose garden contains species that have been cultivated in Rome since the 17th and 18th centuries. There are wonderful views of the city from the Japanese garden. Descending the slope, you will see a 400-year-old plane tree—one of the oldest in Rome—some spectacular Mediterranean conifers, pine trees, oaks, huge sequoia trees and a *Ginkgo biloba* (maidenhair tree). The garden of medicinal herbs, cultivated since the 15th century, is of particular interest. There is an aromatic herb garden specially planted for visitors with visual impairments, and in the various greenhouses there are collections of orchids and tropical plants.

✚ 188 C6 ✉ Largo Cristina di Svezia 24, 00153 ☎ 06 4991 2436 🕐 Apr–Oct Tue–Sat 9–6; Nov–Mar 9.30–5.30 (also Sun–Mon during exhibitions). Closed public hols 🎫 Adult €4, child (under 12) €2 🚌 H, 23, 280; tram 8

PALAZZO CORSINI

www.galleriaborghese.it

This majestic 15th-century palace opposite Villa Farnesina opens onto the flourishing botanical gardens (Orto Botanico, ▷ 191). It contains part of the Galleria Nazionale d'Arte Antica (the rest is in the Palazzo Barberini, ▷ 71) in the form of a rich collection of 16th- to 17th-century art, both Italian and international, collected since the 18th century and acquired by the Italian state in 1883. Paintings worthy of note include a triptych by Fra Angelico, a portrait of Philip II of Spain by Titian, the *Madonna della Paglia* by Van Dyck, Rubens' *St. Sebastian* and *St. John the Baptist in the Desert* by Caravaggio. Of particular interest is the room of Queen Christina of Sweden, who died in the palace in 1689.

✚ 188 C6 ✉ Via della Lungara 10, 00165 ☎ 06 6880 2323 ◷ Tue–Sun 8.30–7.30 ♿ Adult €4, child (under 18) free 🚌 23, 44, 60, 65, 170, 280 🎫

SANTA CECILIA IN TRASTEVERE

You enter the church through a delightful courtyard, with a portico supported by old granite columns and a lily garden with a fountain in the centre. Next, you pass an exquisite facade designed by Ferdinando Fuga in 1741.

According to legend, Cecilia, her fiancé Valeriano and his brother were persecuted and killed in AD303 because of their Christian faith. In the fifth century, a church was built over Cecilia's house, and 400 years later Pope Paschal I built a basilica on the site. In the 12th century, a Romanesque campanile and a portico were added.

A remarkable statue of St. Cecilia by Stefano Maderno is under the high altar. The sculptor was present at the opening of the saint's tomb in 1599 and made sketches of her uncorrupted body.
Splendid ninth-century apse mosaics depicting Jesus with saints Paul, Agata, Peter, Paschal, Valeriano and Cecilia are among

Above *The Gothic altar canopy in Santa Cecilia in Trastevere is the work of di Cambio*

Santa Cecilia's treasures. Another is the beautiful fresco *Last Judgement* (1293) by Pietro Cavallini, the remains of a medieval masterpiece that once covered the walls of the central nave. The fresco was moved to the nuns' choir of the adjoining convent, where it can be seen.

✚ 189 D6 ✉ Piazza di Santa Cecilia 22, 00153 ☎ 06 589 9289 ◷ Church: Mon–Sat 9.30–1, 4–6.30, Sun 11.30–12.30, 4–6.30. Cavallini frescoes: Mon–Sat 10.15–12.15, Sun 11.30–12.30. Excavations: daily 9.30–12.30, 4–6.30 ♿ Church: free. Frescoes: €2.50. Excavations: €2.50 🚌 23, 44, 65, 170, 280; tram 8 🎧 Audioguide in Italian, German, Spanish, French, English €1

SAN CRISOGONO

The simple facade of medieval San Crisogono reveals little of its history and its hidden treasures.

The original church was founded in the fifth century, and a new church was built between 1123 and 1129 over the old building. The bell tower, together with the nave, the aisles and 22 granite columns, are all that remain of the 12th-century church. Inside, there is a very fine 13th-century inlaid marble floor, and a late 13th-century mosaic in the vault of the apse, depicting the

Virgin and Child with St. James and St. Crisogono, which is attributed to the school of Pietro Cavallini. The Cappella del Santissimo Sacramento is thought to have been designed by Bernini.

The overall appearance of this church, half Mannerist, half baroque, is the work of the architect Giambattista Soria, who restored the church between 1620 and 1626 on the orders of Cardinal Scipione Borghese. Soria kept the ancient pillars, rebuilding their capitals in stucco, opened up windows in the nave to let more light in, and installed a coffered ceiling with the coat of arms of Cardinal Borghese. The baldachin is also his work.

In 1907, archaeologists discovered traces of the original fifth-century Christian church 6m (20ft) below the floor. The remains, which can also be visited, include a later relic chamber with eighth-century frescoes.

✚ 189 D6 ✉ Piazza Sidney Sonnino 44, 00153 ☎ 06 581 0076 ◷ Church: Mon–Sat 7–11.30, 4–7.30, Sun 8–1, 4–7.30. Early Christian basement: Mon–Sat 7.30–11.30, 4–7, Sun 8–1, 4–7 ♿ Church: free. Early Christian basement: €2 🚌 H, 23, 44, 60, 170; tram 8 to Viale di Trastevere

SAN FRANCESCO A RIPA

The church of San Francesco a Ripa, founded in the 13th century but made thoroughly baroque 400 years later, is in the heart of Trastevere. Its two treasures are the monastic cell where St. Francis of Assisi lived when he was in Rome and Gian Lorenzo Bernini's dramatic statue, the *Blessed Ludovica Albertoni*.

To see Bernini's masterpiece, go down the left aisle to the Albertoni chapel. Bernini captures perfectly Ludovica's transformation from her final agony to the ecstasy of her union with God. The paintings of St. Anne and the Virgin Mary, behind the statue, are by Baciccio.

St. Francis' cell is reached from the sacristy. It contains his marble pillow and a walnut baldachin. In the convent garden is a bitter orange tree, which, according to tradition, was planted by St. Francis.

✚ 189 D7 ✉ Piazza San Francesco d'Assisi 88, 00153 ☎ 06 588 1331 ⏰ Daily 7–12, 4–7.30 ✋ Free 🚌 H, 23, 44, 60, 170; tram 8 to Viale di Trastevere

SANTA MARIA IN TRASTEVERE
▷ 194.

Below right *The ornate Villa Farnesina*
Below *Steep steps leading to Gianicolo Hill*

SAN PIETRO IN MONTORIO AND TEMPIETTO DEL BRAMANTE

In a quiet corner on the Janiculum Hill stands the church of San Pietro in Montorio, with a splendid view over the city. It is best known for the Tempietto, a tiny circular building in the adjoining cloister.

Although there may have been an earlier church on this site, the present building dates from the late 15th century, when the Catholic Monarchs of Spain, Ferdinand and Isabella, commissioned Baccio Pontelli to build it. It was dedicated to St. Peter, who, it was believed, was crucified here.

The church is essentially Renaissance, but has a remarkable Gothic rose window in the facade. The Peruzzi Chapel, the second on the left, was designed by Bernini.

In the middle of the cloister adjoining the church, on what was once thought to be the exact spot of St. Peter's crucifixion, stands the beautiful Renaissance Tempietto, designed by Donato Bramante in around 1500. Its style and perfect proportions hark back to Classical temples such as the Temple of Vesta at Tivoli (▷ 241).

✚ 188 C6 ✉ Church: Piazza di San Pietro in Montorio 2, 00153. Tempietto: Via Garibaldi 33, 00153 ☎ Church: 06 581 3940. Tempietto: 06 581 2806 ⏰ Church: Mon–Fri 8.30–12, 3–4, Sat–Sun 8.30–12. Tempietto: Tue–Sat 9.30–12.30, 2–4.30 ✋ Free 🚌 870

TRASTEVERE
▷ 195.

VILLA FARNESINA

www.villafarnesina.it
www.lincei.it

If you are in Trastevere during the morning, it is well worth visiting the beautiful Renaissance Villa Farnesina for its lovely interior or for a walk in the gardens.

In 1508, Agostino Chigi, a wealthy banker from Siena, commissioned Baldassare Peruzzi to build him a suburban villa. Here, Chigi entertained artists, princes and cardinals. His banquets were memorable: After the meal, Chigi would have the gold and silver dishes thrown into the Tiber to impress his guests with his wealth. In 1580, the villa was bought by the Farnese family, and it has been known as Villa Farnesina ever since.

On the ground floor are the Loggia of Galatea, with a much admired fresco by Raphael of the *Triumph of Galatea*, and the Loggia of Cupid and Psyche, frescoed to Raphael's designs by some of his pupils. On the upper floor is the beautiful Salone delle Prospettive, with a fresco by Baldassare Peruzzi of a *trompe l'oeil* colonnade through which can be seen rural landscapes, villages and a town.

✚ 188 C6 ✉ Via della Lungara 230, 00186 ☎ 06 6802 7397 ⏰ Mon–Sat 9–1 ✋ Adult €5, child (14–18) €4 🚌 23, 271, 280, 870 to Lungotevere Sanzio

INFORMATION

✚ 189 D6 ✉ Piazza di Santa Maria in Trastevere, 00153 ☎ 06 581 9443 🕐 Daily 7.30am–8 or 9pm, but may close 12.30–3.30 🚌 H, 23, 65, 170, 280, 630, 780 to Viale di Trastevere 📖 *Pilgrims in the Heart of Rome: a Journey to Trastevere*, published by the nearby Community of Sant'Egidio, €13.50 🎫 Small bookshop selling general guides (open 9–5)

TIP

» Visit in the evening, then have a drink in one of the outdoor cafés, from where you can appreciate the beautifully lit piazza and basilica.

SANTA MARIA IN TRASTEVERE

At the heart of Trastevere you'll find the beautiful church of Santa Maria in Trastevere. Dedicated to the Virgin Mary, it is one of the finest medieval churches in Rome. It remains a local church, attended by the inhabitants of the quarter.

BUILDING THE CHURCH

Legend has it that in 38BC (or according to an alternative tradition, on the day of Jesus' birth) a fountain of oil suddenly started flowing to announce the coming of God's son. Pope Calixtus (AD217–222) built a sanctuary on this spot, called the Taberna Meritoria, to commemorate the miracle and encourage the worship of the Virgin Mary. The present basilica was built in the 12th century during the pontificate of Innocent II, using material from the Baths of Caracalla.

THE APSE MOSAICS

The apse mosaics, which date from the 12th century, illustrate St. Calixtus and Pope Innocent II offering his church to Mary. The Virgin, adorned with gold, is shown in the Byzantine style with a certain oriental rigidity. At the top of the mosaic is *Paradise*, showing the hand of God crowning Jesus. The city of Jerusalem and town of Bethlehem are shown, and the lambs represent the 12 Apostles.

Another set of mosaics between the windows, a masterpiece by Pietro Cavallini, represents scenes from the life of the Virgin, including her birth, the Annunciation, the Nativity, the Epiphany, the Presentation in the Temple and the Dormition. The medallion above the throne shows the Virgin and Child between saints Peter and Paul, along with Cardinal Bertoldo Stefaneschi, who commissioned the work in 1290.

THE ALTEMPS CHAPEL

The Altemps Chapel contains the sixth-century Byzantine painting of *Our Lady of Mercy*, one of the oldest images of the Virgin in existence. The late 16th-century mosaics in this chapel demonstrate the re-emerging interest in religious art during the Counter-Reformation. To the left of the nave is the Avila Chapel, with a cupola by Antonio Gherardi decorated in a baroque *trompe l'oeil* effect.

EXTERIOR

The 12th-century bell tower has a 17th-century mosaic of the *Virgin and Child*, while on the facade there is a beautiful 12th- to 13th-century mosaic showing the Virgin Mary enthroned, with processions of women approaching from both sides. The statues of saints above the porch on the balustrade in front of the facade have stood there since the 17th century.

Above *Columns from ancient monuments have been used in the church to divide the nave from the aisles*

TRASTEVERE

The nicest way into the area is on the pedestrian-only Ponte Cisto, which takes you to Piazza Trilussa and the start of the warren of pretty streets that characterizes the quarter. Otherwise, the main bridge from Rome proper into Trastevere is the Ponte Garibaldi, which runs into the Viale di Trastevere, the main street that divides the area neatly into east and west zones. Use this road to keep your bearings while you explore the whole of Trastevere; in particular, don't miss the superb church of Santa Maria in Trastevere (▷ 194). Allow half a day for the visit, and aim on eating lunch or dinner at one of the excellent trattorias here.

SOUTH OF VIALE DI TRASTEVERE

The Torre del'Anguillara, opposite the Isola Tiberina, is a medieval tower, the sole survivor of the many family-owned fortress-towers that once crowded Trastevere. Alongside is a fountain with a statue of Gioacchino Belli, a popular Roman dialect poet in the 19th century.

Il Chiostro dei Genovesi (Genoan Cloister) stands next to the church of Santa Maria dell'Orto. This flower-filled cloister, with its central well, was part of a 15th-century hospice for Genoan sailors.

NORTH OF VIALE DI TRASTEVERE

The Gianicolo (▷ 191) has breathtaking views over the whole city and is home to the Orto Botanico (▷ 191).

The Via della Lungara, which runs parallel to the river, was built by Sixtus V to link Trastevere with the Vatican City. Halfway along stands the imposing Regina Coeli prison, named after a church that once stood here. At the end of the street, coming back towards Trastevere, is the sumptuous Renaissance Villa Farnesina (▷ 193), decorated with frescoes by Raphael and Giulio Romano, among others.

The Porta Settimiana takes you to Via della Scala, with its wine bars, pubs and cafés, leading up to the heart of the area. The Casa della Fornarina stands just inside the Porta Settimiana, at Via di Santa Dorotea 20. This 15th-century house is believed to have been the home of Margherita, the great love of Raphael's life, and subject of his painting *La Fornarina*. Piazza San Callisto has an ancient arch, and is a popular meeting place in the evening.

The Fontana della Botte stands at the corner of Piazza San Callisto and Via della Cisterna. Built in 1927, this curious fountain shows a barrel between two wine measures in celebration of the many popular *osterie* (inns) of the area. The Museo di Roma in Trastevere is in the former monastery of Sant'Egidio. The Municipality of Rome acquired the building in 1875, and it now holds a collection of paintings and drawings of Roman life in the 18th and 19th centuries, along with items that belonged to the Roman dialect poet Trilussa (Carlo Salustri, d.1950).

INFORMATION

✚ 188 C7 🚌 H, 8, 780 to Viale di Trastevere or 23, 125, 280 to Lungotevere Anguillara

REGIONS TRASTEVERE • SIGHTS

Above *The beautiful 12th- to 13th-century mosaic depicting the Virgin Mary enthroned, on the facade of Santa Maria in Trastevere*

GHETTO TO TRASTEVERE

This walk passes through two of the city's less explored areas, the Ghetto—the heart of Rome's Jewish community—and Isola Tiberina, before crossing the Tiber to the popular Trastevere quarter.

THE WALK

Distance: 4.25km (2.5 miles)
Allow: 3 hours minimum
Start at: Piazza del Campidoglio
End at: Campo dei Fiori

HOW TO GET THERE

For Piazza del Campidoglio, the nearest metro station is Colosseo (line B). Alternatively, several buses will take you nearby: Nos. 44, 46, 84, 715, 716, 780, 781, 810 and 916.

★ From Piazza del Campidoglio, with the Palazzo Senatorio straight in front of you, take the lane on the right-hand side, leading towards the Foro Romano, but stay on Via di Monte Tarpei. At the bottom, turn right onto Via della Consolazione, cross the piazza and turn down Via di San Giovanni Decollato, turning left into Via del Velabro to find San Giorgio in Velabro.

❶ San Giorgio in Velabro is named after the area where the city's founders, Romulus and Remus, were discovered. The interior of the church is beautifully simple, and reuses marble and granite columns from ancient buildings. The facade of the church was severely damaged in a bomb blast in 1993, but sympathetic renovation has restored it to its former glory.

Retrace your steps past two ancient arches: Arco degli Argentari (Arch of the Moneychangers) adjoins the church, while the second, Arco di Giano, is on the opposite side of the road. Continue to the large Piazza Bocca della Verità. On your right, look for two surprisingly well-preserved second-century BC temples, the circular Tempio di Vesta and the rectangular Tempio di Fortuna Virilis.

❷ Across the piazza on the left-hand side is the 12th-century church of Santa Maria in Cosmedin (▷ 166). The church is best known for the Bocca della Verità (Mouth of Truth), a large stone disc carved with a man's face, in the porch. According to legend, the mouth clamps shut on the hands of liars.

With your back to the church, walk straight across the square, up the stepped ramp, and then right to join Lungotevere dei Pierleoni. Pass through Piazza Monte Savello, where the road becomes Lungotevere dei Cenci. Just ahead of you is the synagogue. Turn right onto Via Portico d'Ottavia, leading to the Portico d'Ottavia.

❸ The Portico d'Ottavia is a fragment of a Roman building begun in 146bc and dedicated to Octavia, Augustus' sister. It now forms part of the 12th-century Sant'Angelo in Pescheria (Angel of the Fishmarket), a reminder of the area's long fishing history in the nearby river.

Above *The Ponte Fabricio, which joins Isola Tiberina to the Ghetto, was built in 62BC*

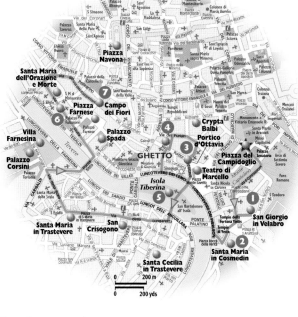

dell'Orazione e Morte, ghoulishly decorated with skulls.

As Via Giulia opens out onto a piazza, turn right onto Vicolo della Moretta, which soon leads on to Via del Pellegrino. Take the first right onto Via dei Cappellari, with its traditional artisans' workshops.

❼ At the end of the street is Campo dei Fiori (▷ 104–105).

WHEN TO GO
Any time, but remember that churches will often be closed during the afternoon.

WHERE TO EAT
There are many restaurants and cafés in Trastevere and Campo dei Fiori.

GIGGETTO AL PORTICO D'OTTAVIA
▷ 129.

PLACE TO VISIT
SAN GIORGIO IN VELABRO
✉ Via del Velabro 19, 00186 ☎ 06 6979 7536 🕐 Tue, Fri–Sat 10–12.30, 4–6.30 (hours subject to change)

Below The elegant Via Giulia once formed the main approach to St. Peter's

Turn left at the top of the street, onto Via dei Funari, which leads to Piazza Mattei and the heart of the old Ghetto (▷ 106).

❹ Although the walls have long been demolished, many Jewish families and businesses are still based in the Ghetto area. The piazza is best known for the charming Fontana delle Tartarughe (Fountain of the Tortoises).

Turn left onto Via della Reginella, which leads back to Via Portico d'Ottavia. Turn right then left through Piazza delle Cinque Scole to rejoin Lungotevere dei Cenci. Turn left, passing the synagogue, then right onto the Ponte Fabricio, Rome's oldest bridge, which crosses the Tiber to the Isola Tiberina (▷ 191).

❺ The island has a tradition of healing, begun in 291BC when a temple was dedicated to Esculapio, the god of healing, and today much of it is given over to a hospital.

Leave the island, on the opposite side, by Ponte Cestio. The bridge

leads you directly into the bustling Trastevere district. Cross the busy Lungotevere dell'Anguillara and continue straight ahead on to Piazza in Piscinula. Turn right onto Via della Lungaretta. Continue straight on until you come to Piazza di Santa Maria in Trastevere and the 12th-century church of the same name (▷ 194). Facing the church, take the right-hand road out of the piazza: Via della Paglia. Continue on to Piazza di San Egidio, then turn right across the piazza and take the left-hand road, Via della Scala. When you reach the junction with Via Garibaldi, turn right onto Via di San Dorotea, which leads to Piazza Trilussa, a small piazza right beside the Tiber. From here, cross the river by the traffic-free Ponte Sisto. Turn left, and follow the right fork into Via Giulia, through an attractive archway draped with vines.

❻ Via Giulia, one of Rome's most elegant streets, was laid out for Pope Julius II in 1508 and formed the main approach to St. Peter's. There are now many interesting buildings lining this street, including the church of Santa Maria

SHOPPING
ALMOST CORNER BOOKSHOP
This small bookshop stocks an interesting selection of competitively priced books, with more than 5,000 titles on display. It is particularly good on biography and history, with an emphasis on Rome and Italy. It has an extensive children's section and can arrange special orders. The owner is helpful and knowledgeable.

🕀 205 D6 ✉ Via del Moro 45, 00153 ☎ 06 583 6942 🕘 Sep–Jul Mon–Sat 10–1.30, 3.30–8, Sun 11–1.30, 3.30–8; Aug Mon–Sat 10–1.30, 3.30–8 🚌 H, 8, 23, 280 to Trastevere; tram 8

ANTICA CACIARA
www.caciara.it

Antica Caciara, a Trastevere institution, is the quintessential old-fashioned Roman delicatessen. Hams and salamis hang from the ceiling, most supplied by trusted producers around Lazio, and there are breads and cheeses, including pecorino and ricotta made by the owner's uncle.

🕀 205 D6 ✉ Via di San Francesco a Ripa 140/A, 00158 ☎ 06 581 2815 🕘 Mon–Sat 7–2, 4–8 🚌 H, 23, 44, 56, 75 and other services to Viale di Trastevere

FIOR DI LUNA
www.fiordiluna.com

Fior di Luna produces sublime chocolates and ice cream to take away. Carefully sourced cocoas are used to make the former, using 16th-century recipes, plus raw cane sugar and no added butter or fat. Ice creams use fresh organic milk and wonderful ingredients such as pistachios from Sicily and hazelnuts from Piedmont. Fruit ices contain only fruit, water and cane sugar.

🕀 205 D6 ✉ Via della Lungaretta 96, 00153 ☎ 06 6456 1314 🕘 Tue–Sun noon–1am 🚌 H, 23, 44, 56, 75 and other services to Viale di Trastevere

INNOCENZI
An old-fashioned store in a street known for its food, Innocenzi sells sweets in open jars, and rice and pulses from overflowing sacks on the floor. It also stocks some of Italy's best regional items, such as breads from Sardinia and delicious honey biscuits from Calabria, as well as organic products. Credit cards are not accepted.

🕀 205 D6 ✉ Via Natale del Grande 31, 00153 ☎ 06 581 2725 🕘 Mon–Wed, Fri–Sat 7–1.30, 2.30–8, Thu 7–1.30 🚌 H, 780; tram 8

Above *For fresh produce head to the lively market in Piazza San Cosimato*

IVANO LANGELLA– LABORATORIO ARTIGIANO
Ivano Langella makes intricate jewellery, fashioning silver, gold and bronze with pearl, horn and even plants to create eye-catching rings and necklaces. Custom-made pieces will be ready in 3–5 days. Credit cards are not accepted.

🕀 205 D6 ✉ Via di Ponte Sisto 73a, 00153 🕘 Sep–Jun Mon–Sat 10.30–1, 4–8; Jul–Aug Mon–Sat 7pm–midnight 🚌 H, 780; tram 8

LUMIÈRES
If an interesting lamp from the French art deco or Italian Liberty periods is what you're after, this is the place to come. Choose from dozens of antique lamps, all fully restored. Or bring your own lamp to be restored by an artisan.

🕀 205 D6 ✉ Vicolo del Cinque 48, 00153 ☎ 06 580 3614 🕘 Tue–Sat 10–1, 3–8, Mon 3–8 🚌 H, 780; tram 8

MATHERIA FARNESE
www.farnese.it

This is the showroom of a renowned group of architects and artisans who create stunning ceramic floor tiles inspired by Roman villas and 18th-century patrician houses. They also restore antique tiles, plates and jugs. This kind of craftsmanship comes at a price, however.

✚ 204 C6 ✉ Via G. Garibaldi 53–55a, 00153 ☎ 06 581 7566 ⏰ Mon–Fri 9.30–2, 3–7, Sat–Sun by appointment only 🚌 23, 280

OPEN DOOR BOOKSHOP
www.books-in-italy.com
This eccentric little bookshop is a real find. The building dates from the 16th century, while the shop opened in 1965. The American owner stocks mainly second-hand books, including rare and out-of-print volumes. He also publishes his own satirical political review on current events, which is well worth browsing through.

✚ 205 D6 ✉ Via della Lungaretta 23, 00153 ☎ 06 589 6478 ⏰ Tue–Sat 10.30–2, 4.30–8, Mon 4.30–8 🚋 Tram 8

PIAZZA SAN COSIMATO
Trastevere's liveliest food and produce market, which, despite the area's appeal to tourists, is still mainly visited by local people. All types of produce are on sale but the cheeses are especially good.

✚ 205 D6 ✉ Piazza San Cosimato ⏰ Mon–Sat 7–1 🚌 H, 23, 280, 780; tram 8

PORTA PORTESE
Rome's most famous flea market is home to nearly 2km (1 mile) of bargains, from fashionable clothes to antiques and downright junk. The whole of Via Portuense from the Porta Portese to Trastevere station is flanked by stands and teeming with people—and there's more in the side streets. Be early for the best buys and beware of pickpockets. Credit cards are not accepted.

✚ 205 D7 ✉ Piazza Porta Portese and around, 00153 ⏰ Sun 6.30–1 🚌 Porta Portese 🚋 Tram 3

LA RENELLA
The wonderfully fresh bread and pizza all day, every day, ensure

La Renella is crowded. Try freshly baked, thick, unctuous slices of simple *pizza bianca*, topped with olive oil and rosemary, or opt for a number of different fresh toppings. They also make excellent cakes.

✚ 205 D6 ✉ Via del Moro 15, 00153 ☎ 06 581 7265 ⏰ Daily 7am–10pm 🚌 H, 780; tram 8

ROMA STORE
Despite the unpromising name, this Trastevere shop stocks an incredibly tantalizing selection of hard-to-find and sophisticated British and French perfumes, including L'Artisan Parfumeur, Creed, Etro, Penhaligon's, L'Occitane and Comptoir Sud Pacifique. Creams and imported US and UK brands of soap and toothpaste complete the almost infinite stock.

✚ 205 D6 ✉ Via della Lungaretta 63, 00153 ☎ 06 581 8789 ⏰ Sep–Jun daily 10–8; Jul–Aug 10–1.30, 4–8 🚌 H, 780; tram 8

VALZANI
Going strong since the mid-1920s, this *pasticceria* (pastry shop) is an institution in the Trastevere district. One of the best German-style cakes, *torrone* (a kind of nougat), chocolates and spicy Roman *pangiallo* fruitcake (called *panpepato* when covered in chocolate) are all made on the premises. *Diavoletti al peperoncino*, chocolates laced with chilli, will make your tongue tingle. Credit cards are not accepted.

✚ 205 D6 ✉ Via del Moro 37b, 00153 ☎ 06 580 3792 ⏰ Sep–Jun Wed–Sun 10–7, Mon–Tue 2–7 🚌 H, 630; tram 8

ENTERTAINMENT AND NIGHTLIFE
ALCAZAR
This cinema is one of the first in the city to show blockbusters in their original language (screenings are usually on Mondays). It's frequented by students and expatriates. The bar sells coffee and popcorn.

✚ 205 D6 ✉ Via Cardinale Merry del Val 14, 00153 ☎ 06 588 0099 ⏰ Daily 💶 From €7 🚌 H, 23, 44, 56, 75, 280 to Viale di Trastevere; tram 8

BIG MAMA
www.bigmama.it
Local and international bands play in the cavernous underground room of this celebrated Trastevere jazz joint. The audience sits close to the band and dancing on tabletops is not uncommon.

✚ 205 D7 ✉ Vicolo San Francesco a Ripa 18, 00158 ☎ 06 581 2551 ⏰ Nov–Jun Tue–Sat 9pm–1.30am 💶 Free with membership (€14 annual, €8 monthly), but extra admission for big-name acts 🚌 H, 23, 44, 56, 75, 280 to Viale di Trastevere, or any bus to Piazza Mastai; tram 8

BIR & FUD
The name may be contrived, but it accurately describes the appeal of this place close to the river off Piazza Trilussa. It is a popular spot, thanks to its well-prepared salads, pizzas and other light meals, and its excellent range of beers.

✚ 205 D6 ✉ Via Benedetta 23, 00153 ☎ 06 589 4016 ⏰ Daily 5.30–midnight 💶 Dinner €40, Wine €12 🚌 23, 271, 280 and other services to Lungotevere della Farnesina

ENOTECA TRASTEVERE
Enjoy more than 900 wines, in addition to salads, soups and home-made desserts at this tavern-like wine bar. During weekends, a pianist plays soft jazz and swing. There are outdoor tables in summer.

✚ 205 D6 ✉ Via della Lungaretta 86, 00153 ☎ 06 588 5659 ⏰ Mon, Tue, Thu–Sat 6pm–2am, Sun 5pm–1am. Closed 3 weeks in Jan 💶 Entry free; Dinner €20, Wine €15 🚌 H, 175; tram 8 to Piazza Sidney Sonnino

FRENI E FRIZIONI

www.freniefrizioni.com

One of the many bars and cafés around Trastevere's Piazza Trilussa, Freni e Frizioni attracts a crowd of summer customers that spills out onto the square and street, too big for this converted former garage and mechanics' workshop (hence its name, which means 'Brakes and Clutches'). It's nothing special, but it is very popular for evening *aperitivi*.

✚ 205 D6 ✉ Via del Politeama 4–6, 00153 ☎ 06 4549 7499 ◷ Daily 10am–2am ✋ Free 🚌 23, 125, 271, 280 to Lungotevere Sanzio-Piazza Trilussa

INTRASTEVERE

Housed in a 17th-century building, this is Rome's most celebrated independent cinema.

✚ 204 D6 ✉ Vicolo Moroni 3a, 00153 ☎ 06 588 4230 ◷ Daily, 3 screenings ✋ From €7 🚌 H, 23, 44, 56, 75, 280 to Viale di Trastevere; tram 8

LETTERE CAFFÈ

www.letterecaffe.org

Virtually next door to the Big Mama (▷ 199), the Lettere Caffè offers nightlife with a literary edge, complete with poetry readings and other cultural events. Its schedule of live concerts is eclectic, featuring anything from jazz to rockabilly.

✚ 205 D7 ✉ Vicolo San Francesco a Ripa 100–101, 00153 ☎ 06 9727 0991 ◷ Sep–Jul daily 5pm–2am 🚌 H, 8, 780 to Viale di Trastevere

NUOVO SACHER

www.sacherfilm.eu

Owned by iconic Italian film director Nanni Moretti, this Trastevere cinema screens independent films from abroad. Films are shown in their original language on Mondays. In the summer, there is also an open-air screen. There is a large snack bar with drinks and food.

✚ 205 D7 ✉ Largo Ascianghi 1, 00153 ☎ 06 581 8116 ◷ Daily ✋ From €7 🚌 H, 23, 44, 56, 75, 280 to Viale di Trastevere; tram 8

Right *A group of children enjoy a puppet show on Gianicolo*

OMBRE ROSSE

www.ombrerossecaffe.it

Ombre Rosse is a central Trastevere institution, serving everything from full breakfast to afternoon tea, and from aperitifs to nightcaps. There is live jazz or blues on Thursday or Sunday nights.

✚ 204 D6 ✉ Piazza Sant'Egidio 12, 00153 ☎ 06 588 4155 ◷ Daily 8am–2am ✋ Free 🚌 H, 23, 44, 56, 75, 280 to Viale di Trastevere; tram 8 to Piazza Sidney Sonnino

RIPARTE CAFE

This cocktail bar, with two stylish, high-tech rooms, has a lively, bubbly atmosphere. The live music on Friday and Saturday evenings should not be missed.

✚ 205 D7 ✉ Via Degli Orti Di Trastevere 1, 00153 ☎ 06 58611 ◷ Mon–Thu 7pm–1am, Fri and Sat 7pm–2am 🚌 H; tram 8

TEATRO VASCELLO

www.teatrovascello.it

On the edge of Trastevere, this is a small but good venue for experimental dance and classical ballet. It also organizes workshops and conferences dedicated to the arts.

✚ 204 C7 ✉ Via Giacinto Carini 72, 00165 ☎ 06 588 1021 ◷ Box office: Tue–Fri 9.30–9, Sat 3–9, Sun 3–7, Mon 9.30–8 ✋ From €15 🚌 44, 75, 115, 710, 870

GIANICOLO

Join families and lovers strolling the ridge overlooking Rome (▷ 191). There is a bar, carousel, puppet show and summer evening theatre, plus miniature pony rides on weekends. The nearby Villa Doria Pamphilj is the city's largest park.

✚ 204 C6 ✉ Piazzale Aurelio, 00152 ✋ Free 🚌 44 to corner Via Giacinto Carini and Via Fratelli Bonnet, or 31, 791, 982

VILLA DORIA PAMPHILJ

One of the most beautiful parks in Rome has villas, ponds and shady green woods. There are workout stations for stretching and muscle toning.

✚ Off map 204 B6 ✉ Villa Doria Pamphilj, 00152 ◷ Daily dawn–dusk ✋ Free 🚌 Tram 8

HEALTH AND BEAUTY
ELLEFFE HAIR

www.elleffehair.com

For beauty treatments such as manicure, pedicure, peeling, waxing and massage head to this hair salon just off the main square in Trastevere. Up-to-the-minute cuts, colour and styling are also available.

✚ 205 D6 ✉ Via di San Calisto 6–6a, 00153 ☎ 06 5833 3875 ◷ Tue–Wed, Fri–Sat 10–7, Thu 10am–11pm 🚌 H, 23, 44, 75, 280; tram 8

PRICES AND SYMBOLS

The restaurants are listed alphabetically (excluding La, Il, Le and I). The prices given are the average for a two-course lunch (L) and a three-course dinner (D) for one person, without drinks. The wine price is for the least expensive bottle. All the restaurants listed accept credit cards unless otherwise stated.

For a key to the symbols, ▷ 2.

ANTICO ARCO

www.anticoarco.it

Sample modern cuisine inside an 18th-century palazzo on the Gianicolo Hill. Antico Arco attracts international accolades for dishes such as pheasant breast with truffles on a potato tart, spaghetti with cheese, pepper and courgette (zucchini) flowers, and Sicilian *cassata* made from ricotta cheese. The wine list is extensive.

✚ 204 C6 ✉ Piazzale Aurelio 7, 00152 ☎ 06 581 5274 ⏰ Mon–Sat 6pm–midnight. Closed 2 weeks in Aug ✋ D €50, Wine €15 🚌 15, 870

ASINO COTTO

Chef Giuliano Brenna takes pride in running a restaurant that combines the best of traditional Roman cooking with a lighter touch for the 21st century. The menu is dictated by the season, with *primi* such as pappardelle with cuttlefish and its ink, a smooth white-bean soup or wholemeal vegetable lasagne, and main courses of venison, rabbit, sea bass or beef fillet. Desserts combine beautiful presentation with rich, imaginative ingredients.

✚ 205 D6 ✉ Via dei Vascellari 48, 00153 ☎ 06 589 8985 ⏰ Tue–Sat 12–2.30, 7.30–11, Sun 7.30–11, Mon 12–2.30 ✋ L €40, D €55, Wine €15 🚌 23, 44, 280; tram 8

BAR GIANICOLO

This coffee shop is a Roman institution. Families flock here after weekend excursions on the Gianicolo hill. At night, young people buzz in and out, but visitors may feel more welcome in the afternoon than later on in the evening. The menu includes fresh apple and carrot juice, small pizzas and light sandwiches. Opt for bar service if you're in a hurry. Credit cards are not accepted.

✚ 204 C6 ✉ Piazzale Aurelio 5, 00152 ☎ 06 580 6275 ⏰ Tue–Sun 6am–1am ✋ Espresso €0.90 at the bar, fresh juice €2.50 🚌 44

BAR SAN CALISTO

Join the rowdy night-time crowd in Piazza San Calisto and sample Bar San Calisto's famous *affogato* (ice cream drizzled with liqueur). The vodka-lemon sorbet is especially sought after. The scene is calmer during the day. The bar, nicknamed Marcello's, serves inexpensive coffee, beer and ice cream from cramped, utilitarian premises. It's glamorous in a gritty way: a true slice of old Trastevere. Credit cards are not accepted.

✚ 205 D6 ✉ Piazza San Calisto 3, 00153 ☎ 06 583 5869 ⏰ Mon–Sat 7am–2am ✋ Coffee €0.90, ice cream €1–€2 🚌 H, 63, 75

BIBLI

www.bibli.it

This Trastevere bookshop-cum-cafeteria is popular for Sunday brunch. A selection of pastas, quiches and other vegetarian dishes are served buffet-style. Among the home-made cakes, poppy seed is very popular. The wine list is limited, but the choice of teas and herbal infusions is so vast as to make this

Above *Trastevere's many restaurants make it a popular destination in the evening*

a perfect place for an afternoon reviver. There is also a tiny courtyard for summer nights.

✚ 205 D6 ✉ Via dei Fienaroli 28, 00153 ☎ 06 581 4534 🕐 Tue–Sun 11am–midnight; Mon buffet-style dinner 5.30–midnight 🍴 Brunch €15, D €30, tea €2 🚌 H, 23, 44, 56, 75, 280; tram 8 to Viale di Trastevere or Piazza Sidney Sonnino

IL BOOM
www.ilboom.it

An original jukebox and photos of *la dolce vita* celebrities hanging on the walls evoke an Italian 1960s atmosphere in this Trastevere *ristorante*. The *granmisto* is a selection of different starters, from fried vegetables to creative *bruschette* (toasted bread). *Gnocchetti sardi pasta* with rocket (arugula) and ricotta is a specialty. The wine list focuses on southern Italy, but there are also Passiti and Malvasie to complement the home-made desserts.

✚ 205 D6 ✉ Via dei Fienaroli 30a, 00153 ☎ 06 589 7196 🕐 Daily 7.30pm–midnight 🍴 D €35, Wine €14 🚌 H, 44, 780; tram 3, 8

CAFÉ DELL'ARANCIA

There's a good reason this café/*gelateria*/cocktail bar is called the Café of Oranges: Sitting out under the canopy, you are surrounded by baskets of the fruit. It's the perfect place to idle away an hour or so in the Piazza di Santa Maria in Trastevere. Try the house special, a Campari citrus cocktail served in a giant crystal flute. A range of citrus cocktails, as well as coffee and ice cream are also served. Credit cards are not accepted.

✚ 205 D6 ✉ Piazza Santa Maria in Trastevere 2, 00153 ☎ 338 110 8064 🕐 Jun–Sep daily 10.30am–1.30am; Oct–Nov, Feb–May Fri–Wed 10.30–8.30 🍴 Cocktails €8, ice cream €8 🚌 23; tram 8

CAFÉ DI MARZIO

Sip exquisite coffee or hot chocolate facing the golden facade of Santa Maria in Trastevere. Of course, a seat at one of the see-and-be-seen outdoor tables is expensive; visitors

on a budget should head inside and enjoy an espresso at the bar, then linger on the fountain steps to soak up the view. Di Marzio is also popular enough to be able to accept large notes (bills), which can be a lifesaver here in the land of correct change.

✚ 205 D6 ✉ Piazza Santa Maria in Trastevere 15, 00153 ☎ 06 581 6095 🕐 Apr–Sep daily 7am–2am; Oct–Mar Wed–Mon 7am–2am 🍴 Coffee from €0.90 inside (€2.50 outside) 🚌 H, 63, 75 to Viale di Trastevere

CASETTA DE' TRASTEVERE

Enter this ordinary-looking restaurant on a quiet little piazza and inside is another piazza bright with red-and-white checked tablecloths and laundry hanging from lines—a life-size re-creation of a Roman square. It's on two levels—you can sit in the house balconies and watch the piazza below. An unsurprising but remarkably inexpensive menu is served here: *Rigatoni della casetta* is nicely *al dente* and incorporates porcini mushrooms, sausage and cheese. Vegetarian dishes are available. There are tables outside on the real piazza, too.

✚ 205 D6 ✉ Piazza de' Renzi 31a–32, 00153 ☎ 06 580 0158 🕐 Daily 12–3, 7–12 🍴 L €15, D €30, Wine €9 🚌 H, 23, 280, 780 to Lungotevere Ponte Sisto; tram 8

DA AGUSTO

This is what cheap and cheerful Roman dining is all about. Sit outside in summer at folding wooden tables with paper tablecloths, on which your bill will be scribbled at the end of the evening. The inside is rather cramped and a little chilly in winter. Spontaneous singing often breaks out and a carafe of the house wine aids appreciation. The *pasta e fagioli* (thick borlotti bean soup with pasta) and gnocchi are delicious. Credit cards are not accepted.

✚ 205 D6 ✉ Piazza de' Renzi 15, 00153 ☎ 06 580 3798 🕐 Mid-Sep to mid-Aug Mon–Fri 12.30–3, 8–11, Sat 12.30–3 🍴 L €14, D €25, Wine €9 🚌 H, 23, 280, 780 to Lungotevere Ponte Sisto; tram 8

DA PARIS
www.ristoranteparis.com

This great restaurant serving Jewish food near Santa Maria in Trastevere is known for its fish and pasta, and particularly for the traditional Roman dish of *trippa alla romana* (tripe in the Roman style). All this is accompanied by an excellent wine list. There is a small terrace in front, where meals are served in warm weather. Reservations are essential.

✚ 205 D6 ✉ Piazza San Callisto 7a, 00153 ☎ 06 581 5378 🕐 Tue–Sat 1–3, 7.30–11, Sun 12–3 🍴 L €35, D €55, Wine €14 🚌 75; tram 8

DA VITTORIO

This pizzeria serves endearing heart-shaped and incredibly tasty Neapolitan pizzas. Start with the mixed antipasti and oil-drenched crust called *pizza bianca*. Many dishes have this as a base, sprinkled only with mozzarella, but Vittorio will also indulge customers craving a sauce, and offer additional toppings such as a bouquet of rocket (arugula) and cherry tomatoes on the pizza Margherita. Reservations are crucial. Credit cards are not accepted.

✚ 205 D6 ✉ Via di San Cosimato 14, 00153 ☎ 06 580 0353 🕐 Daily 12.30–11.30 🍴 L €14, D €14, Wine €8 🚌 H, 63, 75

FRIENDS ART CAFÉ

This is a great place near the Tiber for a good-value *aperitivo*. Snacks set out on the counter are included in the price of a drink. Behind the bar there's a dining area decorated with modern paintings where you can enjoy salads, vegetable pies and a small selection of pastas and meat dishes, plus desserts.

✚ 205 D6 ✉ Piazza Trilussa 34, 00154 ☎ 06 581 6111 🕐 Mon–Sat 7.30am–2am, Sun 7pm–1.30am 🍴 L €15, D €21, cocktails €6 🚌 23; tram 8

GLASS
www.glasshosteria.it

Glass offers a dramatic contrast to the traditional, slightly staid, Trastevere trattoria. It has distinctive

contemporary interiors and serves equally innovative—and mostly successful—modern Italian cooking.
✚ 205 D6 ✉ Vicolo del Cinque 58, 00153 ☎ 06 5833 5903 🕔 Tue–Sun 8am–11.30pm ✋ L €30, D €50, Wine €12 🚌 23, 125 and 280 to Piazza Trilussa-Lungotevere Raffaello Sanzio

IVO A TRASTEVERE
The classic pizza at this Roman institution is always good, but the owners also come up with interesting and unusual toppings. It's busy and bustling, so arrive early or be prepared to wait for a table. However, the turnover is quick and the service efficient.
✚ 205 D6 ✉ Via di San Francesco a Ripa 158 ☎ 06 581 7082 🕔 Wed–Mon 12.30–2.30, 7.30–11.30 ✋ Pizza €12, Wine €8 🚌 8, 44, 75, 780 to Viale di Trastevere

LUMIÈRE DI SICILIA
Enjoy the best Sicilian cuisine north of Palermo at this popular local restaurant. Start with the mixed *antipasti* or *caponata*, an aromatic mélange of aubergine (eggplant), bell pepper, basil and pine nuts. First courses include mouth-watering pistachio pesto, ravioli crammed with orange and ricotta, and squid-ink risotto. The staff are courteous, humorous and warm, even if your children get underfoot. Worth straying off the beaten track for (it's out towards Villa Doria Pamphilj).
✚ 204 C7 ✉ Via Fratelli Bonnet 41, 00152 ☎ 06 581 3287 🕔 Tue–Sun 8pm–11pm, Fri–Sun also 1pm–3pm ✋ D €40, Wine €11 🚌 44

OUZERIE
This restaurant/club in Trastevere is practically the only place in Rome where you can find Greek food and be spontaneously entertained. In an authentic taverna setting with fishing nets and bouzoukis enjoy favourites such as taramasalata, calamari, Greek salads, prawns baked with feta cheese and tomato, delicious kebabs, baklava, and yogurts with a variety of toppings. Live entertainment Friday and Saturday (reservations essential at weekends). A nominal membership (€1.50) is payable on your first visit. Credit cards are not accepted.
✚ 205 E6 ✉ Via dei Salumi 2, 00153 ☎ 06 581 6378 🕔 Mon–Sat 8.30pm–2am. Closed 2 weeks in Aug ✋ D €30, Wine €10 🚌 H to Viale di Trastevere or Piazza Mastai; tram 3, 8

PANATTONI (I MARMI)
Huge marble-slab tables earn this popular Trastevere pizzeria two nicknames: *I Marmi* (The Marbles) and the less appetizing *l'Obitorio* (The Morgue). Vast pizzas and chilled Peroni beer are de rigueur. It's stark but still endearing. Credit cards are not accepted.
✚ 205 D6 ✉ Viale di Trastevere 53–59, 00153 ☎ 06 580 0919 🕔 Thu–Tue 6.30pm–2.30am. Closed 2 weeks in Aug ✋ D €12, Wine €11.50 🚌 H, 63, 75

PIZZERIA POPI POPI
On one of the little alleys that join Viale di Trastevere to the basilica of Santa Maria in Trastevere, Popi Popi is excellent for both its pizzas and its prices. Very popular with young Romans, especially in summer, when you can sit outside and enjoy Trastevere's bustle. There's a selection of traditional dishes in addition to pizzas.
✚ 205 D6 ✉ Via delle Fratte di Trastevere 45, 00153 ☎ 06 589 5167 🕔 Fri–Wed 7pm–1am ✋ Pizza €8, D €15, Wine €5 🚌 H, 23, 44, 56, 75, 280 to Viale di Trastevere; tram 8

ROMOLO 'NEL GIARDINO DI RAFFAELLO E DELLA FORNARINA'
www.ristorantefornarina.it
Next to the ancient gateway of Settimiano, this was the home of Raphael's lover, subject of his famous painting *La Fornarina*. It is also where the poet Trilussa used to wine and dine. The restaurant is divided into four dining rooms, and has oak-beamed ceilings, stone floors and an original fireplace. The lovely garden, however, is the place to be. Try the fried mozzarella rolled with Parma ham and a hint of anchovy to start, followed by chicken breast with mozzarella and Parma ham, artichoke and a delicious creamy tomato sauce.
✚ 204 C6 ✉ Via di Porta Settimiana 8, 00153 ☎ 06 581 8284 🕔 Sep–Jul Tue–Sun 12.30–3, 7–11 ✋ L €25, D €40, Wine €13 🚌 23 to Ponte Sisto or Viale di Trastevere; tram 8

SORA LELLA
www.soralella.com
This family-run restaurant on Isola Tiberina was established in 1943 by the sister of actor Aldo Fabrizi. Roman cuisine is at its best here, and if you're lucky enough to sit near the window, you'll have a river view. All the typical dishes are on offer, from oxtail with cinnamon, cloves, raisins and pine nuts to some memorable *carciofi alla giudia* (Jewish artichokes). Reservations are recommended.
✚ 205 E6 ✉ Via di Ponte Quattro Capi 16, 00153 ☎ 06 686 1601 🕔 Sep–Jul Mon–Sat 12.30–2.30, 7.30–11 ✋ L €40, D €65, Wine €16 🚌 23; tram 8

TAVERNA DE'MERCANTI
There is a medieval atmosphere to this pizzeria tucked away in a tiny piazza near Porta Portese as you climb the torch-lit staircase to the dining area on the first floor. The large room with wooden beams and the bustle of activity make this informal venue popular with Romans looking for a simple, affordable meal. There is a choice of grilled meats as well as pizza.
✚ 205 D7 ✉ Piazza de'Mercanti 3a, 00153 ☎ 06 588 1693 🕔 Tue–Sun 7pm–10.30pm ✋ Pizza €10, D €35, Wine €12 🚌 Tram 3

IL TULIPANO NERO
www.tulipanonero.biz
This small pizzeria is a rarity in Rome, as it serves gluten-free pizza for gluten-intolerants as well as a variety of tasty pasta and main dishes. It also has a good choice of salads and home-made *dolci*. It is a friendly spot and not expensive.
✚ 205 D6 ✉ Via Roma Libera 15, 00153 ☎ 06 581 8309 🕔 Tue–Sun 12.30–3, 7.30–11.30 ✋ L €12, D €25 🚌 44, 175; tram 3 or 8

C di Monte del Gallo
VIA INNOCENZO III
Via D Silveri
VIA DELLE FORNACI
S Onofrio
LUNGOTEVERE GIANICOLENSE
Ponte Mazzini
Largo Lorenzo Perosi
S Monse
S Eligio
LUNGOTEVERE
Tevere

VIA STAZIONE DI SAN PIETRO
Via degli Orti d'Alibert
Via delle Mantellate
della
Lungara
LUNGOTEVERE DELLA FARNE

STAZIONE ROMA S PIETRO
Via di San Francesco di Sales
Villa Farnesina

5 Maria Addolorata

VIA NUOVA DELLE FORNACI
Via dei Riari
Palazzo Corsini
Romolo 'Nel Giardino di Raffaello e della Fornarina
Palazzo Torlonia

Gianicolo
Orto Botanico
VIA DELLA SCALA
Santa Maria della Scala
Vicolo del Cedro
S Egid

250 m
250 yds

Piazzale G Garibaldi
del Gianicolo
Via di Porta San Pancrazio
San Pietro in Montorio
VIA GARIBALDI

6

VIA AURELIA
Porta S Pancrazio
Piazzale Aurelio
VIA GARIBALDI
Via A Masina
Via Coffredo Mameli
VIA Luc
Via G Sacchi

Villa Abamelek
ANTICA
Antico Arco
Bar Gianicolo
VIALE DELLE MURA GIANICOLENSI
Via Giacomo Medici
Via Trenta Aprile
Via Nicola Fabrizi
Via P Roselli
TRASTEVERE

VIA DI SAN PANCRAZIO
Via G Bruzzesi
VIA CARINI
Via Calandrelli
VIALE GLORI

Via A Algardi
Via F Bonnet
Via del Vascello
Lumière di Sicilia

Bricci
VIA VENTI
VIA GIACINTO
Villa Sciarra
Via F Casini
Via G Sacchi

7
VIA VITELLIA
Via F Bolognesi
Via O Regnoli

Via Basilio
Via A Busiri Vici
Via G Rossetti
Dandolo
VIALE Aurelio Saffi
Bernardino da Feltre
VIALE

Pamphili
Via Villa d
VIA QUATTRO
VIA M Quadrio
POERIO
VIA ALESSANDRO
Via U Bassi

VIA Innocenzo X
Via Ludovico di Monreale
Via Giovagnoli
S Maria Reg Pacis
Via F Torre
Viale Aurelio Saffi
Via Francesco dell' Ongaro
Piazza Ippolito Nievo
Via N Parboni

Via San Calepodio
VIALE DE
Via A Colautti
Via F Cavallotti
Via AURELIO Saffi
VIA Francesco dell' Ongaro
VIA DI TRASTEVERE

8
S Maria d Prov
B
Istituto d Laurentana
VIA ANTON GIULIO BARRILI
Via A Cesari
Via G B Niccolini
Via Felice
Via G B
Via Fr D Guerrazzi
VIA F Bandiera
C
Via I Nievo

CORSO VITTORIO EMANUELE II

Palazzo della Cancelleria

Pellegrino

Via del Cappellari

Via Baullari

Campo dei Fiori

Sant'Andrea della Valle

del Sudario

Via del Monte della Farina

Teatro Pompeo

Piazza Farnese

Palazzo Farnese

Teatro Argentina

Palazzo Spada

Via Giubbonari

Via Pettinari

Palazzo Spada

Via delle Zoccolette

Ministero Grazia Giustizia

GHETTO

Ministero G Giustizia

Via Catalana

Sinagoga

Via del Torre Argentina

Via d'cestari

Palazzo Altieri

Il Gesù

CORSO VITTORIO EMANUELE II

Argentina

Via delle Botteghe Oscure

Crypta Balbi

del delfini

Templi Repubblicani

Palazzo Venezia

Museo del Palazzo Venezia

San Marco

Piazza Venezia

Via del PLEBISCITO

Piazza dei Santi Apostoli

Colonna Traiana

VIA DEI FORI IMPERIALI

Monumento a Vittorio Emanuele II

Santa Maria in Aracoeli

Musei Capitolini

Fori Imperiali

Fontana delle Tartarughe

Via Portico d'Ottavia

Piazza del Campitelli

Piazza del Campidoglio

Palazzo Senatorio

Palazzo dei Conservatori

Arco di Settimio Severo

Via dei Funari

LUNGOTEVERE DEI VALLATI

LUNGOTEVERE DEI CENCI

Teatro di Marcello

Monte Capitolino

Santa Nicola in Carcere

Via d Consolazione

S Teodoro

Cairoli

Ponte Sisto

Friends Art Café

Casetta de' Trastevere

Café dell'Arancia

Santa Maria

Café di Marzio

San Sisto

Ivo a Trastevere

Vittorio

Tulipano Nero

LUNGOT DEI SANZIO

Piazza G G Belli

Via della Renella

Belli della

Da Paris

San Crisogono

Il Boom

Bibli

Pizzeria Popi Popi

Panattoni (I Marmi)

Trastevere (Mastai)

Piazza Mastai

Via N d Grande

zza San simato

Morosini

Induno

Trastevere (Min P Istruzione)

Isola Tiberina

Sora Lella

San Bartolomeo all'Isola

LUNGOT DELL' ANGUILLARA

Lungaretta

Piazza Sidney Sonnino

Via dei Salumi

Via dei Genovesi

Santa Cecilia in Trastevere

Piazza Mastai

Via della Luce

Ouzerie

Asino Cotto

Taverna de'Mercanti

Via del Porto

San Francesco a Ripa

VIA G INDUNO

Porta Portese

Viale delle Mura Portuensi

Piazza Porta Portese

PONTE GARIBALDI

PONTE PALATINO

PONTE SUBLICIO

LUNGOTEVERE DEI PIERLEONI

VIA LUIGI PETROSELLI

LUNGOTEVERE RIPA

Tempio della Fortuna Virilis

Tempio di Vesta

Piazza Bocca della Verità

Santa Maria in Cosmedin

Piazza di S Anastasia

Casa di Livia

Palatino

Sant'Anastasia

Via di San Teodoro

Via dei Fienili

Piazza della Consolazione

AVENTINO

PORTO DI RIPA GRANDE

LUNGOTEVERE AVENTINO

Clivo

VIA DEL CIRCO MASSIMO

Circo Massimo

Via dei Cerchi

Emporio

TESTACCIO

Tevere

PORTUENSE

Santa Sabina

S Alessio

S Anselmo

Marmorata / Vanvitelli

Via di Porta Lavernale

S Anselmo

Monte di Aventino

Via di San Domenico

Via di Santa Sabina

Via di Santa Prisca

S Prisca

Piazza Templo Diana

Via Marcella

Piazza Albania

Aventino / Albania

Via di S Saba

S Saba

Via B Franklin

Via Amerigo Vespucci

Via Rubattino

Via Giovanni Branca

Via Luigi Vanvitelli

Via Mastro Giorgio

Via Bodoni

Via Nicola Zabaglia

Via A Volta

Via Galvani

S M Liberatrice

VIALE MANLIO GELSOMINI

Parco della Resistenza dell'8 Settembre

Viale delle Terme Deciane

VIA DI S SABA

Piazza G L Bernini

Via Annia Faustina

VIA DELLA P CESTIA

MARMORATA

PORTUENSE

LUNGOTEVERE

D

E

TRIONFALE

Musei
Vaticani

CITTÀ DEL
VATICANO

Basilica di
San Pietro

Castel
Sant'Angelo

AURELIO

GHETTO

VATICAN CITY AND AROUND

There are no barriers, and no customs posts, but when you step into the great square in front of Basilica di San Pietro, you are entering Vatican City, a separate state, forged in 1929, following an agreement between Mussolini and the papacy.

Although much of this state within a state is devoted to papal affairs and as such is out of bounds to visitors, two of Rome's greatest sights lie within its confines: the basilica itself and the Musei Vaticani, home to, among other things, the famed Cappella Sistina (Sistine Chapel). St. Peter's is the spiritual heart of Roman Catholicism, built over the tomb of the Apostle St. Peter, who according to tradition was crucified close by. A colossal church, deliberately overbearing inside and out, it dates mostly from the 16th century, when it replaced an earlier basilica that had stood on the site for more than 1,000 years.

Immediately alongside the church is part of the immense Vatican palace, built for the popes over the centuries, and now home, in part, to the sprawling Musei Vaticani, a series of interconnected museums and galleries containing some of the countless artefacts acquired by the papacy over almost 2,000 years. Also here are former papal apartments and private chapels, many beautifully decorated, the most famous of which are the Cappella Sistina and Stanze di Raffaello (Raphael Rooms).

Beyond St. Peter's and the Vatican, the small area on this western bank of the Tiber is of relatively little interest, the streets to the north mostly dating from the 19th and 20th centuries, when much of the area was razed and redeveloped. The great exception is the Castel Sant'Angelo, on the banks of the Tiber, originally built as a mausoleum for Emperor Hadrian in the second century, but later a papal fortress and now a fascinating museum with wonderful city views.

2

Città
Giudiziaria

Piazzale
Clodio

VIALE

VIALE

VIA SABOTINE

V Monte Santo

VIALE

GIUSEPPE

MAZZINI

GIUSEPPE

MAZZINI

V A Balamonti

Via A Amato

Olivo di Cima

Platone

Via Trionfale

Via Premuda

Via Cunfida

VIA

DELLA

GIULIANA

Via Emilio Faà di Bruno

Via Racchia

Via R G Lante

Via T Gulli

VIALE ANGELICO

VIA S PELLICO

Via P Borsieri

DELL

TRIONFALE

Via Rodi

Via C Morin

Via G de Saint Bon

Bettolo

Via G Buccari

Via A Labriola

Via S

Via C Passaglia

CIRCONVALLAZIONE TRIONFALE

S Giusep

Via G Bovio

Via B G Telesio

Savonarola

Trionfale

Bruno

Campanella

Via C Camozzi

Milizie
(Distretto
Militare)

VIALE

Milizie
(Angelico)

3

Via U Bartolomei

Via Tommaso d'Aquino

VIA

ANDREA

DORIA

Piazzale
degli Eroi

Via Tommaso

Via V Pisani

Piazza di
S Maria
delle Grazie

Via Ruggero
di Lauria

Campanella

Santamaura

Via Tolemaide

Via Famagosta

Via Orlando

Ottaviano
San Pietro

Ottaviano S Pietro-
Musei Vaticani

VIALE

BARLETTA

Via Simone

Rizzo

Via Piero Zian

Scalia

Cipro

Cipro

VIA

LEONE

IV

Via Vespasiano

VIA OTTAVIANO

S S
Rosario

VIA

degli

Scipioni

Via

Germanico

Via Fabio Mas

VIA

GIULIO

Via F Albenzio

CIPRO

Via Luigi

Via Sebastiano

VIA

Santa Maria
delle Grazie

Via della Meloria

La Goletta

CANDIA

Tunisi

Via Sebastiano Veniero

Viale

Vaticano

Via

VIA

COLA

Via G Vitell

4

Via Marcantonio

Giorgio

Fiore

Bragadin

Via D Milleire

VIA ANGELO EMO

S M
Mediatrice

Vaticano

Viale

Vaticano

Giardini
Vaticani

Museo
Gregoriano

Musei
Vaticani

Casino di
Pio IV

VIALE B DI

MICHELANGELO

Piazza del
Risorgimento

Piazza del
Risorgimento

VIALE

VIA DI PORTA ANGELICA

Borgo
Angelico

Via del Mascherino

Via S Porcari

Borgo

Piazza
Amerigo
Capponi

Bastioni

Vittor

VIA

Via del

Falco

Borgo

Plauto

Pio

Borgo

Santa

Santa

in Traspo

Via del Corridori

AURELIA

VIA ANGELO EMO

Viale

CITTA DEL
VATICANO

Palazzo del
Governatorato

Cappella
Sistina

Basilica di
San Pietro

Piazza

San Pietro

Piazza
Pio XII

Palazzo
Torlonia

VIA DELLA CONCILIAZIC

5

Via di Villa Alberici

Via di S Maria Mediatrice

Campi
Sportivi

Via del Cottolengo

VIA

Viale

Vaticano

Via Nicolo V

STAZIONE
VATICANO

AURELIA

Palazzo del
Sant'Uffizio

Aula delle
Udienze

VIA PAOLO VI

S Michele

Porta
Cavalleggeri

Borgo

Santo Spir

Santo
Santa Sp
in Sassia

Porta
S Spirito

Via Penitenzieri

VIA DI PORTA CAVALLEGGERI

P

VIA GREGORIO VII

Clivo di Monte

Via di Monte

VIA DEL CROCIFISSO

VIA INNOCENZO III

VIA STAZIONE DI SAN PIETRO

Via A de Gasperi

VIA

DELLE

FORNACI

Via del Gianicolo

P

VIA DELLE

Palaz
Salvia

Monte
di
Gallo

VIA GREGORIO VII

S Maria
alle Fornaci

STAZIONE
ROMA S PIETRO

Maria
Addolorata

Mura

Aurelie

V del

0 ————— 250 m

0 ————— 250 yds

Via

A AURELIO

B

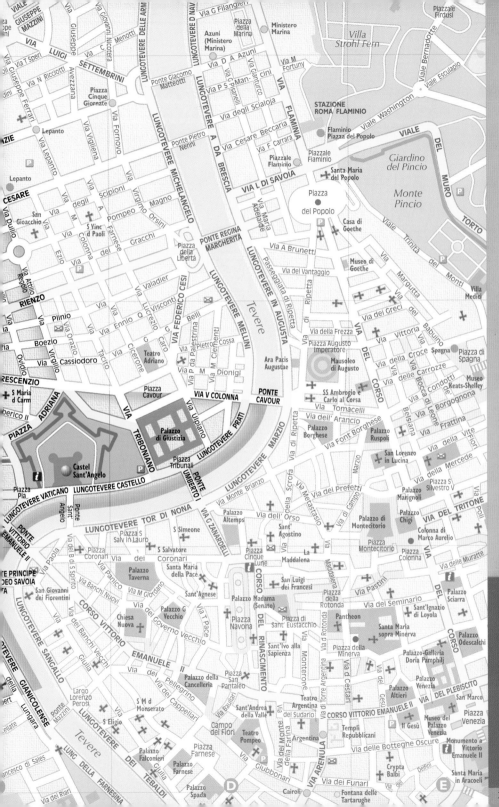

INTRODUCTION

Emperor Constantine built the first basilica on the present site of St. Peter's in AD324, probably over a pagan cemetery, the traditional burial place of the Apostle Peter. Sumptuously decorated with marble, mosaics and gold, it was pillaged during the barbarian invasions, but remained the central church of Christendom for over 1,000 years. Reconstruction was planned in the 1450s, and in 1503 Pope Julius II commissioned the architect Bramante to rebuild the church. It was planned on a Greek-cross layout surmounted by a high dome, and involved the demolition of much of the original basilica.

After Bramante's death in 1514, work on the basilica ceased, and the next 30 years saw no progress as arguments raged over the revised layout. In 1547 Michelangelo, then aged 72, was appointed architect. Despite later changes, today's basilica, and particularly the ground plan and dome, is largely inspired by Michelangelo's designs.

In 1606, with building underway, the nave was lengthened again and the facade altered by Carlo Maderno. Pope Urban VIII consecrated the new basilica in 1626. Much of the Mannerist and baroque decoration is the work of Bernini, who succeeded in unifying the various internal elements. St. Peter's is the world's most important Catholic church: Mass is celebrated here daily and it is where the Church's most important official religious ceremonies are held.

The best approach to St. Peter's is by way of Via della Conciliazione. You cross into the Vatican State on entering Piazza San Pietro. It is a good idea to pause frequently while exploring the basilica and its surroundings: Everything is on a huge scale, but the proportions are so perfect that you need time to appreciate the actual size. Once inside, the best way to see the church is to start by making a circuit of the entire basilica and its artworks, then to visit the Treasury, followed by the crypt. Most visitors leave the ascent to the roof and cupola until the end of their visit.

WHAT TO SEE

PIAZZA SAN PIETRO AND THE COLONNADE

Few buildings are approached through such a superb space as that in front of St. Peter's. The elliptical piazza, folded within the curving wings of the colonnade, is considered Gian Lorenzo Bernini's architectural masterpiece. It was conceived and built between 1655 and 1667, during the pontificate of Pope Alexander VII.

The obelisk in the middle is the oldest monument. It was brought to Rome from Egypt in AD36 by the Emperor Caligula and moved to its present site in 1586; it acts as a sundial, the obelisk's shadow marking noon as it touches the white marble disc. Two beautiful fountains flank the obelisk. That on the right is the work of Carlo Maderno, dating from 1613, while the left-hand fountain, by Carlo Fontana, was erected in 1677.

Between the fountains and the obelisk are two stone slabs set in the paving; stand on either one of these to see the colonnade's four rows of columns merge into one. There are 284 columns in four rows, their proportions calculated to enhance the height of the basilica's facade. Bernini designed the colonnade to enable coaches to drive through it, while the side aisles were for people on foot. The main entrance to the Vatican Palace is reached through the right-hand end of the colonnade, via the Portone di Bronzo. Look through here to get a glimpse of Bernini's famous *trompe l'oeil* Scala Regia, where columns of diminishing size are used to add greatness to what is in reality a steep and irregular staircase.

INFORMATION

www.vatican.va

208 B4 ✉ Piazza San Pietro, 00120
☎ 06 6998 3731 ⊙ Basilica: Apr–Sep daily 7–7; Oct–Mar 7–6.30. Cupola: Apr–Sep daily 8–6; Oct–Mar 8–4.45; if visiting 1 hour before closing, entrance is via elevator only. Treasury Museum: Apr–Sep daily 8–7; Oct–Mar 8–6.15. Crypt: Apr–Sep daily 7–6; Oct–Mar 7–5. Closed during major religious ceremonies. Papal audiences usually take place on Wed at 10.30am (free). Book tickets at least 2 days (but no more than one month) ahead by post (Prefettura della Casa Ponteficia, 00121 Città del Vaticano), by fax (06 6988 5863) or at the north side of the piazza, Mon–Tue 9–1. Application forms are available online at www.vatican.va/various/perfettura/en/biglietti_en.html. Confirm reservations and dress modestly
✋ Basilica: free. Cupola: €7 with elevator, €5 on foot. Treasury Museum: €6. Crypt: free. Necropoli (Scavi) tour €12 🚇 Ottaviano-San Pietro 🚌 34, 46, 64, 98, 881, 916, 982 ☛ The Necropoli (Scavi) can only be visited by guided tour (€12), which must be booked at least 3 days in advance. Email scavi@fsp.va, stating preferred dates, number of people and which language. Tours take 2 hours (Mon–Sat 9–5) 📖 Wide selection of official guidebooks from Vatican bookshop in over 12 languages €5; unofficial guidebooks from souvenir stands and religious shops on Via della Conciliazione 🏪 Shop inside tourist information point. Also official Vatican shop well stocked with guidebooks, postcards, religious souvenirs, posters, videos, CDs, cassettes, slides, candles, religious statues and church furnishings; multilingual assistants; wide range of prices to cater for pilgrims from all over the world, but quality immensely variable, ranging from top-of-the-range to cheap and tacky. Vatican post office is behind the right-hand colonnade for Vatican stamps and albums (open Mon–Sat 8.30–6.30)

Opposite *Bernini's great altar canopy, beneath St. Peter's magnificent dome*

St. Peter's is a working church and the dress code is strict: no shorts or bare upper arms and shoulders.

» A tour of the Scavi—the pagan necropolis and the excavations under the High Altar—adds an interesting contrast.

» The Pope normally gives weekly Mass audiences in the Aula Paolo VI behind the left-hand colonnade. For information on tickets, ▷ 211. Tickets are also available in advance through your local Roman Catholic church.

THE BALDACCHINO, CONFESSIO AND CATTEDRA

The interior of St. Peter's is dominated by Bernini's great altar canopy, the baldachin, which stands directly above the traditional site of the tomb of St. Peter the Apostle, with the Cattedra, the great papal throne, behind. The baldachin's twisted bronze columns and massive lantern rise above the high altar, where only the pope may celebrate Mass. Standing 29m (95ft) high, it took over 10 years to erect and was inaugurated in 1633 by Pope Urban VIII, a member of the Barberini family—bees, their heraldic symbol, swarm among the foliage of the decoration. The baldachin's construction coined a famous lampoon—*quod non fecerunt barbari, fecerunt barberini* ('what the barbarians failed to do, the Barberini did')—as Urban was said to have used bronze taken from the portico of the Pantheon for the columns.

In front of the baldachin is Carlo Maderno's sunken U-shaped Confessio—a crypt beneath the high altar—with 99 perpetually burning lamps along the balustrade and two flights of curving stairs. The kneeling statue of Pope Pius VI (1820), who is buried beneath, is by Antonio Canova. In front of this, directly beneath the papal altar and behind a grille, is the sixth-century Niche of the Pallia, a surviving relic of the first basilica and said to have given access directly to St. Peter's tomb. Excavations in the 1940s strengthened the hypothesis that there is a very early Christian tomb here, which could, indeed, be that of the saint.

Behind the baldachin, and designed to be viewed through it, is the extraordinary set piece known as the Cattedra. The Cattedra itself is an ancient wooden chair, said to have been St. Peter's when he was bishop of Rome, which is enclosed in a bronze throne designed by Bernini in the 1660s. This is raised above the altar of the central apse and surrounded by bronze statues of the Fathers of the Latin and Greek churches. Above this rises a great gilded metallic structure of angels, clouds and rays of light, all illuminated by the sunlight that streams through the central window in which is depicted a dove representing the Holy Spirit.

Below *Bernini's Piazza San Pietro, enclosed by the two vast semicircular colonnades, creates a spectacular approach to the basilica*

FACTS AND FIGURES

The basilica is 218m (715ft) long (externally) and the height to the top of the cross on the dome is 137m (450ft); it contains 778 columns, 395 statues, 44 altars and 135 mosaics.

MICHELANGELO'S PIETÀ

Behind glass, in the first chapel in the right-hand aisle, gleams Michelangelo's white marble *Pietà*, a representation of the Virgin holding her dead son across her knees. It is the only work the artist ever signed and the most famous of all the treasures in St. Peter's.

This portrayal of the Virgin as a young, grieving woman is both spiritually moving and artistically groundbreaking. The young sculptor had mastered anatomy and the handling of marble drapery perfectly; he also solved the compositional problem of the two figures, one upright and one horizontal, by creating a pyramidal shape rising from the horizontal figure of Christ on his mother's lap to the Virgin's head at the apex. After the unveiling, Rome was astounded, and there was talk that so young a man could never have produced such a work. Michelangelo, furious, carved his name on the band across the Virgin's breast, and added an 'M' in the folds of her right hand. This *pietà* is the first of four that Michelangelo was to sculpt during his long life.

Clockwise from above left
Michelangelo's Pietà, *one of the basilica's treasures; the monument to Pius VII, which stands over the door to the sacristy; the 12th-century bronze* St. Peter Enthroned *is much revered—the figure's right foot has been worn smooth by pilgrims kissing it*

BRONZE STATUE OF ST. PETER

At the base of the last pillar on the right of the nave before the transept is enthroned a bronze statue of St. Peter holding the keys to the Kingdom of Heaven in his left hand. For many years believed to be a fifth-century work, it is now known to date from the late 1200s and is attributed to Arnolfo di Cambio, the original designer of the Duomo (cathedral) in Florence. It is an austere and beautiful work, its simplicity emphasized by its baroque setting. Much of the statue's right foot has been worn away by the touch of the faithful down the centuries, as kissing it traditionally gains an indulgence— time deducted from the waiting time in Purgatory before admittance to Heaven. On major feast days the statue is bedecked with lavish, gold-encrusted robes and a tiara; you can see these in the Treasury.

Above *A member of the Swiss Guard*
Right *The distinctive silhouette of*
St. Peter's at dusk

ERECTING THE OBELISK

The obelisk in the piazza was moved to its present site in 1586. The task was immense: forty-four windlasses were erected and 900 men and 140 horses put to work. After four months, the crucial moment arrived and the obelisk was gradually pulled upright. It rose, only to halt as the ropes started to give way. The story goes that the Pope ordered complete silence, but a voice called out 'water on the ropes!' A Genoese sailor knew that adding water would shrink and tighten the ropes, and the day was saved. In gratitude, the Pope rewarded the man's family and hometown.

DAILY MASS

For Catholic priests visiting Rome, the opportunity to celebrate Mass in St. Peter's is a lifetime's dream. Every morning, from around 7, priests from all over the world occupy the altars of the chapels within the basilica, saying Mass in dozens of languages. Confessions are heard in many languages; a red light over a confessional indicates that it is 'open for business', and a sign informs the penitents which languages the priest speaks.

THE CUPOLA AND ROOF

A gallery, 330 steps up from the roof, encloses the base of the interior of the dome, the perfect place for a bird's-eye view. At a height of 53m (174ft) above the floor of the basilica, it is from here more than anywhere else that you can appreciate the sheer size of St. Peter's; figures below appear minuscule. Up here you are close to the vast mosaics of Christ and the apostles, popes and saints, and angels holding the instruments of the Passion—the crown of thorns, the scourge and the nails. Designed by Cavaliere d'Arpino and executed between 1589 and 1612, the mosaics are remarkable for their size (St. Mark's pen is 1.5m/5ft long) but are hardly great works of art.

Outside, the undulating roof and breezy air make it seem as though you are on a ship at sea. Views down to the piazza below appear between the huge statues, and all around you are domes and cupolas. The main dome, with its paired columns and garlands, is true to Michelangelo's design, though probably higher than he intended. Climb the exterior of this masterpiece to its crowning lantern for breathtaking panoramas over the city.

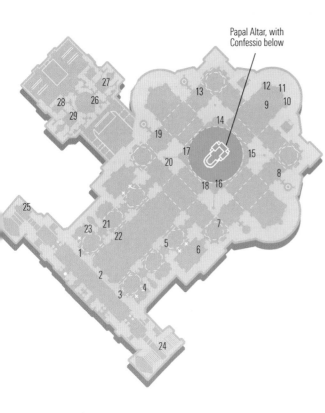

Papal Altar, with Confessio below

FLOOR PLAN

1 Door of the Dead, by Manzù
2 Main door, by Filarete
3 Porta Santa, by Consorti
4 Pietà, by Michelangelo
5 Monument to Christina of Sweden
6 Chapel of the Blessed Sacrament, by Borromini
7 Gregorian Chapel
8 Monument to Clement XIII, by Canova
9 Nave of the Cattedra
10 Monument to Urban VIII, by Bernini
11 Cattedra
12 Monument to Paul III, by della Porta
13 Monument to Alexander VII, by Bernini
14 Statue of St. Veronica, by Bernini
15 Statue of St. Helen, by Bernini
16 Statue of St. Longinus, by Bernini
17 Statue of St. Andrew, by Bernini
18 Bronze statue of St. Peter
19 Monument to Pius VII
20 Altar of the Transfiguration
21 Monument to Maria Clementina-Sobieski
22 Stuart Monument, by Canova
23 Baptistery
24 Equestrian statue of Constantine
25 Equestrian statue of Charlemagne
26 Sacristy
27 Treasury
28 Chapter
29 Canons' Sacristy

Below *The obelisk, Piazza San Pietro*

INFORMATION

www.castelsantangelo.beniculturali.it
✠ 209 C4 ✉ Lungotevere Castello
50, 00165 ☎ 06 681 9111 🕐 Tue–Sun
9–7.30 💶 Adult €8.50, EU citizens 18–25
€6, EU citzens under 18 and over 65
free. Guided visits €4 🚇 Ottaviano San
Pietro 🚌 23, 34, 40, 62, 64, 280, 982,
stopping at Lungotevere Castello 📖 At
tourist information point inside, in several
languages 🍴 Café/restaurant inside 📷

Above and opposite *Stone angels,*
replicas of Bernini's original stautes,
line Ponte Sant'Angelo on the approach
to Castel Sant'Angelo

CASTEL SANT'ANGELO

Emperor Hadrian chose this secluded spot away from the main city as the
site for his tomb. Fortifications were later added, converting the building into
a fortress. Today, Castel Sant'Angelo houses part of the Museo Nazionale
Romano, with an excellent collection of ceramics, weapons and Renaissance
paintings. From the top of the squat structure is one of the finest views over
Rome, looking out across the Tiber.

FROM MAUSOLEUM TO FORTRESS

The mausoleum remained the burial place of the Imperial family up to the
reign of Caracalla in AD217. Aurelian later incorporated the mausoleum
into the city's fortifications and surrounded it with thick walls and vers,
converting it into an imposing fortress.

In AD590 Rome was stricken with the plague, and Pope Gregory he Great
organized a procession to pray for the city's release (▷ 35). As a result of the
miracle, the building was renamed Castel Sant'Angelo. In the ninth century,
Leo IV linked Castel Sant'Angelo to the nearby Vatican by building a high
defensive wall. The *passetto*, a later covered walkway built above the wall, was
used by Clement VII in 1527 to escape from Emperor Charles V's troops.

WHAT TO SEE

The spiral ramp inside the castle dates back to the time of Hadrian's
mausoleum and a part of it can still be climbed to the main courtyard, where
the statue of the Archangel Michael, carved by Raffaello da Montelupo in
1544, stands. Another Archangel Michael, a huge 18th-century statue in
bronze, stands at the top of the terrace along with the Bell of Mercy, which in
the past pealed to announce executions. The moats and gardens are a 20th-
century addition. Inside, along the spiral staircase leading to the upper floors,
are the remains of some decorative mosaics.

IN·FLAGELLA
PARATVS·SVM

INFORMATION

www.vatican.va

✛ 208 B4 ✉ Viale Vaticano 100, 00165
☎ 06 698 846 76; 06 698 3145; 06 6988
4676 ⊙ Apr–Oct Mon–Sat 9–6; Nov–
Mar 9–4. Last Sun of the month 9–1.45.
Closed on public holidays and religious
festivals ✋ Adult €15, child (under 15)
€8, under 6 free; free entrance on last Sun
of month 9–1.45 ⊙ Cipro Musei Vaticani,
Ottaviano-Vaticano ⊟ 19, 32, 49, 81,
98 ⬛ Two-hour guided tour €31; book
by fax on 06 6988 4019 or at museum
information point. Audiotours available
in Italian, English, French, German,
Spanish, Japanese; €5.50. Two-hour tour
of gardens Mar–Oct Tue, Thu and Sat
at 10am; €31 (book by telephone on 06
6988 3145 or email visiteguidatesingoli.
musei@scv.va) 📖 Official guidebook to
museum and Vatican State available in
Italian, English, French, German, Spanish,
Japanese; €8 ☕ Café and pizzeria
inside museum. Expensive, but fine for a
quick refill and rest 🏠 Several shops at
different points in museum well stocked
with guidebooks, postcards, religious
souvenirs, Vatican stamps and museum
reproductions

Above The bronze Sphere within Sphere
by Arnaldo Pomodoro (1990) in the
Cortile della Pigna

INTRODUCTION

The Musei Vaticani showcase the wealth of artistic treasures accumulated by
the papacy over the centuries, as well as other major attractions such as the
Sistine Chapel and the frescoes of the Raphael Rooms. The vast building in
which the museums are housed dates from the time of Innocent III (1179–80),
who made an existing palace, near the basilica of St. Peter, into the permanent
seat of the papacy. Major work was carried out under Nicolas V in the mid-
15th century, and in the 1470s Sixtus IV started to construct what would
become the Sistine Chapel.

Although these areas and the rest of the palace were primarily intended
for the pontiff's own use, the works of art here became the greatest of the
Vatican's treasures. It was not until the 18th century, however, that work
began on arranging the papal collections as a museum, with proper galleries
being built to house sculpture, paintings and objets d'art, a process that
continued into the 20th century.

The museums are extremely popular; it's likely that you will have to wait
in line to buy tickets and undergo security checks irrespective of what
time of year you visit. The sheer size of the complex is in itself confusing
and exhausting, so spend time planning and be aware that it is impossible
to see everything in one visit. Various official routes taking in all the main
attractions are suggested on leaflets available at the entrance, but these can
be very crowded, so it is a good idea to plan your own itinerary. Focus on the
highlights (see below), perhaps taking in one or two other collections; just
walking between these will give glimpses of lots more.

WHAT TO SEE

CAPPELLA SISTINA

The Sistine Chapel was built by Pope Sixtus IV between 1473 and 1481 to
serve as both the pontiff's private chapel and as a venue for the gathering of
cardinals who elect each new pope—a function that it still fulfils. It is a huge
structure, with a beautiful cosmatesque mosaic floor and a marble screen
by Mino da Fiesole. But it is the frescoes, entirely covering the walls and
ceiling, that attract up to 20,000 visitors a day. While the chapel was being
built, Sixtus planned its decoration, settling on scenes from the Old and New

estaments as the subject matter, with the emphasis on the parallels between he lives of Moses and Christ. From Florence, he summoned Sandro Botticelli, ogether with Domenico Ghirlandaio, Cosimo Rosselli and Perugian artist erugino. These artists, joined by Pinturicchio, Luca Signorelli and Piero di osimo, worked on the walls for 11 months, producing a series of glowing works that should attract thousands of visitors in their own right. The two most important scenes are Perugino's *Christ Giving the Keys to Peter* and otticelli's *The Punishment of Korah*, each showing the Arch of Constantine in the background.

These earlier masterpieces, however, tend to be overshadowed by Michelangelo's frescoes on the ceiling and altar wall, arguably Western art's nest achievement and certainly the largest work of painting ever planned nd carried out by one man. Julius II commissioned the ceiling in 1508, and Michelangelo completed it in 1512, an artistic tour de force with narrative cenes, architectural *trompe l'oeil* effects and statuesque figures of great beauty. The nine key panels, running along the central length of the ceiling, ecount events from the Book of Genesis, and are further divided into three roups of three, though some panels depict more than one event.

The first panel shows God creating light and dark. The contorted figure of God is a display of Michaelangelo's technical virtuosity. The next panel ortrays two events, with God depicted twice, first in the act of creating the un and the moon (God's outstretched arms are a deliberate echo of the Crucifixion, a motif repeated elsewhere on the ceiling), the second creating arth, here symbolized by a simple piece of foliage. The third panel in this rilogy of Creation portrays God creating the sea and its creatures.

TIPS

» It's a 10-minute walk round the walls from St. Peter's to the museum entrance; to avoid this, take a bus or taxi to Piazza del Risorgimento, or the metro.

» Entrance to the Vatican Museums is free on the last Sunday of the month, but this means the crowds are at their greatest and waiting time can be over two hours.

» Unlike most Rome museums, the Vatican museums are open on Monday.

» Labelling is very poor; pick up a museum guidebook or an audioguide.

» Bring a pair of binoculars to see the glorious detail in Michelangelo's ceiling frescoes in the Sistine Chapel.

» You can usually backtrack to the Cortile della Pigna and the courtyard outside the Pinacoteca where there are benches and water fountains.

» Guided tours of the Vatican Gardens are available; book at least one week ahead on 06 6988 3145 or email visiteguidatesingoli.musei@scv.va.

» Wheelchairs are available free of charge by pre-booking at accoglienza.musei@ scv.va or by calling at the Special Permits desk in the entrance hall; you will need a valid identity document.

Above *The museum's impressive 1930s spiral staircase*
Left *A member of the Swiss Guard, the Pope's official bodyguards*

The second trilogy contains the Sistine Chapel's most celebrated images, notably the creation of Adam with God's famous outstretched finger: Notice the face of Eve, one of the characters under God's robes, looking towards Adam. The fifth panel shows the creation of Eve and the sixth—which has two scenes—the Temptation (note the dead tree, another recurring motif) and the Expulsion from Eden.

The third trilogy depicts events from the life of Noah, including the flood; the sacrifice of Noah; and the Drunkenness of Noah, a symbol of how far Man has fallen from his state of grace, something emphasized by Noah's aged body and collapsed pose, a deliberate parody on the part of Michelangelo of Adam's pose in the fourth panel.

Years later, in 1535, Michelangelo was again summoned to the chapel, this time by Paul III, to fresco the altar wall with scenes of the Last Judgement, a huge task that occupied him until 1541. The *Last Judgement* is essentially a celebration of the human body, full of power, potency and movement. Even before it was finished the amount of nudity had offended many, not least the Pope's master of ceremonies. Furious, Michelangelo depicted him in the bottom right-hand corner of Hell as Minos, the doorkeeper, complete with ass' ears and entwined in a serpent. Later, Pius IV objected to the nudity to such an extent he commissioned Daniele da Volterra to clothe the genitals—an exercise that earned him the nickname 'trouser-maker'. This overpainting was removed during the extensive restoration of the ceiling and *Last Judgement* during the 1980s and 1990s, a project said to have cost over $3 million.

STANZE DI RAFFAELLO

Not content with the painting of the Sistine Chapel, in 1508 Julius II embarked on a major decorative scheme in the four nearby rooms of his private apartments, today known as the Stanze di Raffaello (Raphael Rooms). The Stanza della Segnatura, the Pope's study, was Raphael's first major Roman commission, painted between 1508 and 1511. The frescoes are allegories representing the humanist ideals of theology, philosophy, poetry and justice. The *School of Athens* stresses truth acquired through reason, with the great Classical thinkers all represented, the central figures of Plato—probably a portrait of Leonardo da Vinci—and Aristotle dominating the scene. The figure on the left is said to be Michelangelo, added after Raphael had a sneak preview of his work in the Sistine Chapel. Opposite is the *Disputation of the Holy Sacrament*, while the side walls show *Parnassus*, home to the Muses, and the *Cardinal Virtues*.

Above left *The giant bronze pine cone in Cortile della Pigna*

Above right *The Galleria delle Carte Geografiche, decorated with 16th-century map frescoes*

Chronologically, the next room to be painted was the Stanza di Eliodoro, with its energy-charged *Expulsion of Heliodorus* and serene *Miracle of Bolsena*. The latter tells the story of the medieval miracle that occurred in

ɔ

Bolsena, when a priest who doubted the doctrine of transubstantiation (the transformation of the Eucharistic bread and wine into the actual body and blood of Christ) saw the wafer bleed during Mass. The window wall has a superb night scene, showing the *Deliverance of St. Peter from Prison*. The two final rooms were painted to Raphael's designs by his pupils after his death.

PINACOTECA VATICANA

The Pinacoteca, founded in 1816 by Pius VI, occupies a separate building, erected in 1932, within the museum complex. It is widely considered to be Rome's best picture gallery, with works from the early and High Renaissance to the 19th century. Among these are some of the most remarkable early paintings in Rome, notably Giotto's *Stefaneschi Triptych* (room II). Painted in the early 1300s for the altar of the Confessio in old St. Peter's, it shows the *Martyrdom of SS. Peter and Paul*. The deaths of both saints are shown, with St. Peter crucified upside-down, at his own request, as he felt unworthy to die the same way as Christ. Cardinal Stefaneschi, the donor, is shown on either side of the triptych. The next rooms are devoted to 15th-century Italian art. Look for Fra Angelico's *Madonna and Child with Saints* in room III and the serene Umbrian pictures in room VII, especially Perugino's *Madonna and Child*.

The next room (VIII) is the Pinacoteca's high point, a stunning collection of Raphael's work, including the tapestries that once hung in the Sistine Chapel, woven in Brussels from Raphael's cartoons. Dominating the room is the *Transfiguration*, a sublime work that was unfinished at the artist's death and hung above his coffin at his funeral; his pupils later completed it. The triumphant figure of the ascending Christ pulses with energy amid piercing light and lowering cloud formations, a superb contrast to the artist's *Coronation of the Virgin*, painted when he was only 20 and his first major composition. The gentle *Madonna of Foligno* was commissioned in 1512 as a votive offering, in gratitude for a lucky escape during a siege.

Leonardo da Vinci is represented in room IX by the unfinished and curiously monochrome *St. Jerome*, one of his few works where the authorship has never been disputed. Look here, too, for the exquisite *Pietà*, by the Venetian painter Giovanni Bellini; the dead Christ lying across his mother's knees was a popular subject for Venetian artists. Venetian painting features again in room X in the shape of two canvases by Titian: a glowing *Madonna with Saints* and the subtle *Portrait of Doge Nicolò Marcello*. There are further psychological insights in Caravaggio's dramatically despairing *Deposition* in room XII, all muted tones and intense *chiaroscuro* (light and shade).

FRESCO

Fresco painting is a medium in which the pigment becomes permanently part of the wall it covers, thus producing, in the right conditions, an extremely long-lasting image. The artist first draws the scene on paper, then, using a graph, expands the drawing to the desired size to make the working cartoon. The outline of the principal figures and background are then pricked out with tiny holes and the cartoon is attached to the wall surface. Renaissance artists then blew charcoal dust through the holes, leaving the outline of the picture on the wall when the cartoon was removed. As fresco pigments need to be applied to fresh, wet plaster, the artist had to assess the area he would cover that day. Once the plaster was applied, he would follow the charcoal outlines with pigment—a method still used. As the plaster dries, a chemical reaction occurs, binding the pigment and plaster and leaving a permanent image.

Below *Michelangelo's frescoes on the Sistine Chapel, an artistic tour de force*

MUSEO PIO CLEMENTINO

To see the cream of the Vatican's Classical sculpture collection, head for the Museo Pio Clementino and its octagonal Court of the Belvedere. The court still contains the two statues that influenced Renaissance sculptors more than any others, both acquired by Julius II: the *Laocöon* and the *Apollo Belvedere*. The *Laocöon* created a sensation on its discovery in 1506 near Nero's Golden House, when it was immediately identified from the description of the first-century Roman scholar Pliny. A Greek second-century BC group from Rhodes, it shows a Trojan priest who, having warned of the dangers of the famous wooden horse, was crushed, along with his sons, by sea serpents sent by Apollo. The *Apollo Belvedere*, a Roman copy of a fourth-century BC Greek statue, more than holds its own next to Canova's *Perseus*. Inside the museum, highlights include a beautiful Hellenistic *Sleeping Ariadne*, superb second-century AD candelabra from Hadrian's Villa at Tivoli, and fine Roman portrait busts, including a splendid one of Julius Caesar.

THE VATICAN GARDENS

The Vatican Gardens date back to the early days of the Christian Church and reflect design trends through the centuries. Few visitors get to view them, but anyone can enjoy glimpses of the beautifully planted gardens from the windows of the Vatican Museums. The overall style is very much in the Italian tradition of formal rectangular parterres, with box hedges, cedars and stone pines, underplanted with roses and bedding plants. There are several of these parterres, linked by shady paths, with shrubs framing views of the dome of St. Peter's. Succeeding popes embellished the gardens, adding summer houses and elaborate fountains.

Above Apollo Belvedere, *part of the Vatican's Classical sculpture display,* in *the Museo Pio Clementino*
Below *The Vatican Gardens*

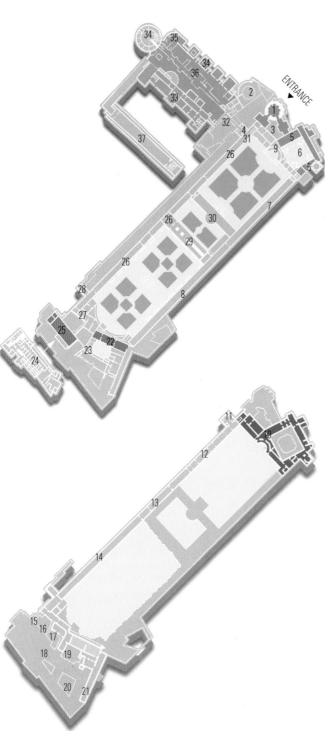

FLOOR PLAN

Lower floor

1 Entrance
2 Staircase
3 Escalators
4 Atrio dei Quattro Cancelli
5 Museo Pio Clementino
6 Octagonal Courtyard
7 Museo Chiaramonti
8 Galleria Lapidaria
9 Museo Gregoriano Egizio
22 Appartamento Borgia
23 Salette Borgia
24 Collection of modern religious art
25 Cappella Sistina
26 Biblioteca Vaticana
27 Museo Sacro
28 Sala delle Nozze Aldobrandine
29 Salone Sistino
30 Braccio Nuovo
31 Museo Profano della Biblioteca
32 Courtyard of the Pinacoteca
33 Pinacoteca
34 Museo Gregoriano Profano
35 Museo Pio Cristiano
36 Museo Missionario-Etnologico
37 Museo Storico Vaticano

Upper floor

10 Museo Gregoriano Etrusco
11 Sala della Biga
12 Galleria dei Candelabri
13 Galleria degli Arazzi
14 Galleria delle Carte Geografiche
15 Cappella di Pio V
16 Sala Sobieski
17 Sala dell'Immacolata
18 Cappella di Urbano VIII
19 Stanze di Raffaello
20 Cappella di Nicolò V
21 Loggia di Raffaello

ENTRANCE ▶

PIAZZA DI SPAGNA TO PIAZZA SAN PIETRO

Some of Rome's best shopping streets form the route to the breathtaking Piazza San Pietro and the vast, awe-inspiring Basilica di San Pietro, one of the city's main attractions.

THE WALK

Distance: 2.5km (1.5 miles)
Allow: 3 hours
Start at: Piazza di Spagna
End at: Piazza San Pietro

HOW TO GET THERE

For Piazza di Spagna, take the metro to Spagna.

★ Spend time in the grid of streets surrounding Piazza di Spagna (▷ 74–75), exploring the exclusive designer shops.

Take Via Frattina (to the left if you have your back to the Spanish Steps). This is a great place to shop for designer labels. On emerging onto Via del Corso, cross the road into Piazza San Lorenzo in Lucina, a charming, peaceful square with outdoor cafés, and a beautiful church of the same name.

❶ San Lorenzo in Lucina is one of Rome's earliest churches, but was rebuilt in 1112. The columns in its facade were recycled from ancient buildings. Inside is a 19th-century memorial to the French painter Nicolas Poussin (d.1665), who is buried in the church.

Cross the square and take Via del Leone on the right. This leads to Largo Fontanella Borghese.

❷ On the right is Palazzo Borghese, once the city residence of the Borghese, one of Rome's most powerful families. Both Cardinal Scipione Borghese, whose art collection is housed in the Museo e Galleria Borghese, and Napoleon's sister Paolina Borghese, the subject of one of the museum's best-known sculptures, lived here. The palace is closed to the public, but a glance into the courtyard gives an idea of its elegance.

Cross the square, and leave it by Via del Clementino, passing through Piazza Nicosia and along Via di Monte Brianzo. Take the last small lane on your left, Via dei Soldati, then go left onto Via dell'Orso, lined with charming shops. Turn right at the church of Sant'Antonio dei Portoghesi onto Via dei Pianellari, which leads to Piazza Sant'Apollinare, where you will see the Palazzo Altemps (▷ 108–109).

❸ The collection at the Palazzo Altemps, part of the Museo Nazionale Romano, includes some of the city's finest Roman sculpture.

With your back to the museum, the elliptical Piazza Navona (▷ 111) is straight ahead.

❹ Laid out in the mid-17th century on the ruins of Domitian's stadium (AD86), the piazza has retained the stadium's original shape.

Above *Castel Sant'Angelo and Ponte Sant'Angelo*

Midway down, on the right-hand side, take Via di Sant'Agnese in Agone. On the corner of Via della Pace is Antico Caffè della Pace, a great place for a drink. Turn right to find Santa Maria della Pace.

⑤ Legend has it that, during a 15th-century war with Florence, a painting of the Virgin bled when it was pierced by a soldier's sword. Pope Sixtus IV vowed that he would build a church if the Virgin interceded to bring peace. Santa Maria della Pace was duly begun around 1480. Frescoes in the Cappella Chigi are by Raphael, and the adjacent cloister is by Bramante—his first work in Rome.

Return to Via di Sant Agnese in Agone, turn right and then continue along Vicolo delle Vacche and Vicolo della Vetrina. From Vicolo della Vetrina turn left onto Via dei Coronari, where there are many antique and furniture shops.

⑥ The church of San Salvatore in Lauro is on your right.

Continue straight on, down the small Vicolo del Curato, as far as Via del Banco di Santo Spirito. Turn right and head straight for Ponte Sant'Angelo.

⑦ There has been a bridge here since AD134, when it was built to connect with Hadrian's mausoleum (now within the Castel Sant'Angelo). Replicas of Bernini's stone angels line the bridge, watching over the traditional pilgrims' route to San Pietro. With their flowing robes and outstretched wings, they appear to be struggling to keep their balance in the wind, which has earned them the nickname 'Breezy Maniacs'.

Cross the bridge to Castel Sant'Angelo (▷ 216).

⑧ Castel Sant'Angelo houses part of the Museo Nazionale Romano.

Turn left onto Via della Conciliazione, which leads you straight to Piazza San Pietro. Facing the basilica, follow the right-hand colonnade to Via di Porta Angelica, which leads up to Piazza del Risorgimento. From here frequent buses run back to the city centre.

WHEN TO GO
Go in either the morning or late afternoon to catch the churches open. Sunset from Ponte Sant' Angelo is a spectacular sight.

Right *The church of Trinità dei Monti, above Piazza di Spagna*

WHERE TO EAT
ANTICO CAFFÈ DELLA PACE
▷ 126.

IL CAPRICCIO
▷ 127.

DA FRANCESCO
▷ 128.

PLACES TO VISIT
SAN LORENZO IN LUCINA
✉ Via in Lucina 16a, 00186 ☎ 06 687 1494 🕐 Daily 8–8; cloister Tue–Sun 10–7

SANTA MARIA DELLA PACE
✉ Vicolo dell'Arco della Pace 5, 00186 ☎ 06 686 1156 🕐 Mon, Wed and Sat 9–noon

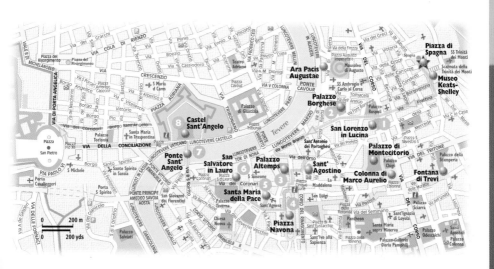

REGIONS · VATICAN CITY AND AROUND · WALK

225

SHOPPING
CASTRONI
www.castroni.com

This deli brings a slice of the 1950s—the date the shop first started trading—to modern-day Rome. It's a treat for the eyes and palate, with a beautiful wood-panelled interior stocked from floor to ceiling with goodies. The assistants in red jackets are ready to lend a hand. An espresso bar is also on site.

✚ 230 B4 ✉ Via Cola di Renzo 106, 00192 ☎ 06 687 4383 🕙 Mon–Sat 7.30am–8pm 🚌 70, 81, 492

ENTERTAINMENT AND NIGHTLIFE
ALEXANDERPLATZ
www.alexanderplatz.it

One of Rome's longest-established jazz clubs is located two blocks north of the Vatican Museums and offers live music most nights performed by well-known Italian and international artists.

✚ 230 B3 ✉ Via Ostia 9, corner of Via Santa Maura, 00165 ☎ 06 3974 2171 🕙 Oct–May daily 8pm–1.30am 🖐 €10 membership plus admission 🚌 19, 32, 49, 81, 98

AUDITORIUM CONCILIAZIONE
www.audotoriumconciliazione.it

This venue, formerly the Auditorio Pio, holds a range of classical concerts and operas.

✚ 230 C4 ✉ Via della Conciliazione 4, 00186 ☎ Box office: 06 684 391 🕙 Oct–Jun daily 10.30–1.30, 3–6 🖐 €10–€50 🚌 23, 40, 62, 64

FONCLEA
www.fonclea.it

This is a restaurant and pub that also hosts a mixture of funk, Latin and other live music acts. The food and drink (including 200 different cocktails) are great. This audience is always ready to move to the music.

✚ 230 C4 ✉ Via Crescenzio 82a, 00197 ☎ 06 689 6302 🕙 Daily 12–3, 8.30pm–2am 🖐 From €5, but often free 🚇 Ottaviano 🚌 23, 271, 280, 492, 990

THE PLACE
www.theplace.it

Just behind Castel Sant'Angelo is this jazz club, hosting performances from acclaimed Italian and international artists. It's open throughout the year, though closes sporadically during the summer months. You can enjoy typical Italian cuisine before you settle down to some excellent music.

✚ 231 C4 ✉ Via Alberico II 27/29, 00193 ☎ 06 6830 7137 🕙 Oct–May daily from 8pm for buffet supper, music 10.30pm–2.30am; summer times vary 🖐 €10–€30 🚇 Lepanto 🚌 81, 492

TEATRO GHIONE
www.teatroghione.it

Close to Piazza San Pietro, Teatro Ghione is dedicated to up-and-coming stars, big-name pianists and other soloists. The lively audience gives the place a more relaxed feel.

✚ 230 B5 ✉ Via delle Fornaci 37, 00186 ☎ 06 637 2294 🕙 Box offfice: daily 10–1, 4–7 🖐 €10–€22 🚌 46, 64, 571, 916

HEALTH AND BEAUTY
GRAND HOTEL TIBERIO
www.ghtiberio.com

If you're a guest at this 4-star hotel, you can relax in its sauna or tone up your muscles in its gym. It's within walking distance of Vatican City.

✚ Off map 230 A3 ✉ Via Lattanzio 51, 00136 ☎ 06 399629 🕙 Daily 7.30am–9.30pm 🖐 Guest use only, free 🚇 Proba Petronia-Appiano

Above *Live jazz at Alexanderplatz*

EATING

PRICES AND SYMBOLS

The restaurants are listed alphabetically (excluding La, Il, Le and I). The prices given are the average for a two-course lunch (L) and a three-course dinner (D) for one person, without drinks. The wine price is for the least expensive bottle. All the restaurants listed accept credit cards unless otherwise stated.

For a key to the symbols, ▷ 2.

BORGO NUOVO

This place is ideal if you have just visited St. Peter's or the Vatican Museums and need a quiet break and some tasty, freshly prepared Italian food. The portions are generous, and the service friendly and efficient. It's open all day, and there's a good range of vegetarian, meat and fish options.

✚ 230 B4 ✉ Borgo Pio 104, 00197 ☎ 06 689 2852 ◷ Apr–Oct daily 10–9; Nov–Mar Wed–Mon 10–9 ✋ L €16, D €30, Wine €10 ⓜ Ottaviano (Piazza del Risorgimento) 🚌 81

DA GIOVANNI

Prices at this tiny artists' hang-out on the edge of Trastevere are unbelievably low and the cooking is good, plain Roman fare. The menu changes daily but *fettuccine al sugo* (pasta with tomato sauce) is always there. Try the pasta with chickpeas or borlotti beans if you can. House wine doesn't cost much more than bottled water. No reservations.

✚ 231 C5 ✉ Via della Lungara 41a, 00165 ☎ 06 686 1514 ◷ Sep–Jul Mon–Sat 12–3, 7–10 ✋ L €10, D €15, Wine €8 🚌 23, 280 to Ponte Mazzini

DAL TOSCANO

www.ristorantedaltoscano.it

This family-run restaurant serves Tuscan cuisine. It offers efficient service in a pleasant, vaulted room; and a shaded terrace in summer. The pappardelle pasta with wild boar sauce is a Tuscan treat, as are the huge chargrilled Fiorentina steaks or the thinly sliced beef cooked with wine and salad leaves. Accompany it all with a glass of superb Chianti.

✚ 230 B4 ✉ Via Germanico 58, 00192 ☎ 06 3972 5717 ◷ Tue–Sun 12.30–3, 8–11. Closed 2 weeks in Aug ✋ L €20, D €35, Wine €13 ⓜ Ottaviano

RISTORANTE IL MATRICIANO

The family-run Il Matriciano, not far from St. Peter's, has a devoted following. The food is uncomplicated country fare. Try the classic *bucatini matriciana*, flavoured with bacon, tomatoes and basil, or opt for the ricotta ravioli, vegetable soup or the *abbacchio* (suckling lamb) *al forno*. In the summer there are tables under a shady canopy outside.

✚ 230 C4 ✉ Via dei Gracchi 55, 00192 ☎ 06 321 2327 ◷ Sep–Jul Thu–Tue 12.30–3, 8–11.30 ✋ L €25, D €40, Wine €9 ⓜ Ottaviano 🚌 81

RISTORANTE-PIZZERIA PIACERE MOLISE

www.piaceremolise.net

Fresh flowers, damask linen and pale walls create an intimate setting for this elegant family-run restaurant, in a shopping street just minutes away from the Musei Vaticani. Pasta with aubergines (eggplant), tomatoes and olives, and roast lamb cutlets with rosemary potatoes are dishes to savour. There's a good selection of fresh fish and decent house wine.

✚ 230 B3 ✉ Via Candia 60, 00195 ☎ 06 3974 3553 ◷ Fri–Wed 12.30–3, 7–12 ✋ L €18, D €30, Wine €12 ⓜ Cipro Musei Vaticani 🚌 23, 70, 99, 492

ROOF GARDEN 'LES ETOILES'

www.atlantehotels.com

For unparalleled views of St. Peter's, and food to match, this roof-terrace restaurant is a must if you can afford it—the dining room is one level down. It offers candlelit tables, sumptuous Mediterranean cuisine, an imaginative wine list and views of St. Peter's illuminated beyond.

✚ 230 C4 ✉ Via Bastioni 1, 00193 ☎ 06 687 3233 ◷ Daily 12.30–2.30, 7.30–10.30 ✋ L €40, D €85, Wine €15 ⓜ Ottaviano 🚌 70, 492

SICILIAINBOCCA

www.siciliainboccaweb.com

This Sicilian fish restaurant serves a good array of *antipasti*, including favourites like *maccheroni alla Norma* with aubergines (eggplant) or pasta with sardines, grilled swordfish, stuffed calamari or baked anchovies, and superb desserts. The wine list is predominantly Sicilian.

✚ 230 B3 ✉ Via E Faà di Bruno 26, 00192 ☎ 06 3735 8400 ◷ Mon–Sat 12–2.30, 7–11 ✋ L €30, D €45, Wine €15 ⓜ Ottaviano 🚌 30

TAVERNA ANGELICA

This is the best mid-priced option near the Vatican. The interior is minimalist and the cooking delicate and innovative. Most of the dishes are fish- or seafood-based, and there is a carefully selected wine list. Reservations are essential.

✚ 230 C4 ✉ Piazza Amerigo Capponi 6, 00193 ☎ 06 687 4514 ◷ Mon–Sat 7–midnight, Sun 12.30–2.30, 7.30–12. Closed 2 weeks in Aug ✋ L €15, D €35, Wine €10 🚌 19, 23, 34, 51, 64, 81, 492, 982 ⓜ Ottaviano

ZEN SUSHI

www.zenworld.it

This minimalist, modern Japanese restaurant invites you to sit at the bar and select tempting dishes from a conveyer belt. The colour-coded plates indicate the price. Sashimi is prepared on request, as are hot dishes like tempura and *yakiniku*. Japanese beer, sake and Italian wine are all available. Works by contemporary artists line the walls.

✚ 231 C3 ✉ Via degli Scipioni 243, 00192 ☎ 06 321 3420 ◷ Mid-Sep to Jul Tue–Fri 1–3, 8.30–11, Sat–Sun 8.30–11 ✋ L €26, D €45 ⓜ Lepanto 🚌 30

PRICES AND SYMBOLS

Prices are the lowest and highest for a double room for one night. Breakfast is included unless noted otherwise. All the hotels listed accept credit cards unless otherwise stated. Note that rates vary widely throughout the year.

For a key to the symbols, ▷ 2.

ADRIATIC

www.adriatichotel.com

Rooms at this family-run hotel, just three blocks from St. Peter's, are moderately spacious with patterned carpets and reproduction furniture. Not all guest rooms have private bathrooms, but they do have satellite TV and air conditioning (€10 extra per day).

✚ 230 C4 ✉ Via G. Vitelleschi 25, 00193 ☎ 06 6880 8080 ✋ €80–€130, excluding breakfast ❶ 42 ⬆ 🚇 Ottaviano San Pietro 🚌 40, 62, 64, 81

ALIMANDI

www.alimandi.it

This superior 3-star, family-run hotel is very good value for money. The 19th-century building, close to the Vatican Museums, retains some original features, including elegant Venetian stuccowork. Rooms are spacious, with modern furnishings; all have satellite and pay TV, and roomy bathrooms. There is an internet computer point for guests to use, and a free airport shuttle, plus parking. The Continental buffet breakfast is served on the roof terrace or in the dining room.

✚ 230 B4 ✉ Via Tunisi, 00192 ☎ 06 3972 3941 🚫 Closed 8 Jan–10 Feb ✋ €170–€190 ❶ 35 ⬆ 🚇 Cipro Musei Vaticani or Ottaviano San Pietro 🚌 81, 492, 495

ATLANTE STAR

www.atlantehotels.com

This luxury hotel between Vatican City and the Castel Sant'Angelo exudes class and elegance, with richly upholstered sofas, heavy drapes, stuccoed ceilings and plush carpets, plus antiques and 18th-century paintings. Rooms are spacious; half have whirlpool baths. There is a bar and a renowned restaurant, plus a free airport shuttle. There are excellent views of St. Peter's from the breakfast room.

✚ 230 C4 ✉ Via G. Vitelleschi 34, 00193 ☎ 06 686638 ✋ €410–€530 ❶ 61 ⬆ 🚇 Ottaviano San Pietro 🚌 32, 81, 492

BBROMA

www.bbroma.com

Choose online from a range of bed-and-breakfast options, some of which are near the Vatican. Rooms are generally spacious and nicely furnished, mostly in a late 19th-century style. All have a telephone, a TV and a bathroom. The organization also arranges stays in rooms in houses with communal kitchens and in apartments. Check the website for conditions. Reservations are handled centrally by Signora Erminia Pascucci. Credit cards are not accepted.

✚ 230 B4 ☎ 06 6821 0776; 06 4547 2549 ✋ €75–€90 ❶ Around 12 properties, including properties in Trastevere and St. Peter's 🚇 Cipro Musei Vaticani 🚌 19, 23, 70, 492, 495

BRAMANTE

www.hotelbramante.com

The polished, mid-range Bramante, in a cobbled alley two blocks east of Piazza San Pietro, is shielded from the bustle around St. Peter's. The building dates from the 16th century and has been an inn since 1873. The rooms vary, but all are modern and tastefully decorated, with plasma TVs. Room 13, although small, is a good choice, thanks to its original beamed ceilings.

✚ 230 C4 ✉ Vicolo delle Pallini 24–25, 00193 ☎ 06 6880 6426 ✋ €140–€240 ❶ 19 🚇 Ottaviano 🚌 40, 64 and other services to Piazza San Pietro

NOVA DOMUS

www.novadomushotel.it

In a quiet location near St. Peter's, this 4-star hotel has good-sized, traditionally furnished rooms, all with satellite TV and private bathroom. The good restaurant compensates for a notable lack of eating places in the surrounding area. The friendly staff are welcoming and knowledgeable. Private city guides are provided at a modest price.

✚ 230 B3 ✉ Via G. Savonarola 38, 00195 ☎ 06 399511 ✋ €130–€280 ❶ 88 ⬆ 🚇 Cipro Musei Vaticani 🚌 492

Opposite *A view along the Tiber and of San Carlo al Corso church*
Left *A hotel sign points the way*

2

Città
Giudiziaria

Piazzale
Clodio

P

V Monte Santo

V SABOTINO

VIALE
GIUSEPPE

VIALE
GIUSEPPE

MAZZINI

MAZZINI

V Mte Santo

Via A Balamonti

Via A Labriola

TRIONFALE

Via di Cirina

Platone

Trionfale

Via Amato

Clivo di

Via
Fedro

Via
Cornelio
Nepote

Via U Bartolomei

Via
Cornelio

Via C Passaglia

Siciliainbocca

VIA

Via Racchia

VIA DELLA

VIA S PELLICO

DELL

Via Emilio Faa di Bruno

VIALE ANGELICO

Via G Camozzi

3

Via Premuda

Via Cunfida

Via R S G Lante

Via de Saint Bon

VIA
GIULIANA

Milizie
(Distretto
Militare)

Via Rodi

Via C Morin

Via Buccari

Trionfale

Via G

Via B G Telesio

VIALE

S Giusep

Nova
Domus

Campanella

Bruno

Saint Bon

Milizie
(Angelico)

Ottaviano
San Pietro

Via P Borsieri

Tommaso d'Aquino

CIRCONVALLAZIONE TRIONFALE

Savonarola

Via Tommaso

VIA
ANDREA
DORIA

VIA
LEONE
IV

VIA BARLETTA

Ottaviano S Pietro-
Musei Vaticani

GIULIO

VIA

degli
Scipioni

Piazzale
degli Eroi

Via Ruggero
di Laura

Via B G

VIA
CIPRO

Cipro

Via F Albenzio

Cipro

Via
Sebastiano

Via Giorgio

VIA della Fiore

Marcantonio

Bragadin

Via Santamaura

VIA
CANDIA

Mocenigo

Tunisi

Via Sebastiano Veniero

Via Famagosta

Via Orvieto

Via Tolemaide

Alimandi

Santa Maria
delle Grazie

Ristorante-Pizzeria
Piacere Molise

Bbroma

Via Vaticano

Piazza di
S Maria
delle Grazie

Viale

Via Vaticano

Dal Toscano

Vespasiano

VIA OTTAVIANO

S S
Rosario

Ristorante
Il Matriciano

Via Fabio Ma

Germanico

Via degli Gracchi

COLA

VIA

Piazza del
Risorgimento

Piazza del
Risorgimento

Museo
Gregoriano

Via S Porcari

Taverna
Angelica

Roof Ga
'les Eto

S M
Mediatrice

Via Angelo Emo

VIA ANGELO EMO

Giardini
Vaticani

Musei
Vaticani

Casino di
Pio IV

VIA DI PORTA ANGELICA

VIALE DI MICHELANGELO

Borgo
Angelico

Borgo
Nuovo

Falco

Piazza
Amerigo
Capponi

Atlante
Star

Bramante

Borgo Pio

Borgo Pio

Vittorio

Ad

Bastioni

Santa

CITTÀ DEL
VATICANO

Cappella
Sistina

Borgo
Vittorio

Via del Mascherino

Plauto

Palazzo del
Governatorato

Basilica di
San Pietro

Palazzo
Torlonia

in Traspo

Via dei Corridori

Borgo Santa

VIA DELLA CONCILIAZIC

Palazzo
Pio XII

Piazza
San Pietro

Santo Sp

Santo Spir

STAZIONE
VATICANO

Viale
Vaticano

Palazzo del
Sant'Uffizio

Palazzo del
Sant'Uffizio

VIA PAOLO VI

Borgo

S Michele

Via Penitenzieri

Santo Sp
in Sassia

Aula delle
Udienze

Porta
Cavalleggeri

Porta
S Spirito

AURELIA

Viale
Vaticano

Via Nicolò V

VIA
AURELIA

VIA DI PORTA CAVALLEGGERI

Via del Gianicolo

P

P

Palaz
Salvia

Via di Villa Alberici

Via di S Maria Mediatrice

VIA DEL CROCEFISSO

Stazione di San Pietro

Via A de Gasperi

VIA
DELLE
FORNACI

S di S Onofrio

S Onofrio

Clivo di Monte

Via Paolo II

Via Nicolò Pietro

Via
VIA

Campi
Sportivi

Via del Cottolengo

VIA GREGORIO VII

Via
delle

S Maria
alle Fornaci

VIA INNOCENZO III

VIA STAZIONE DI SAN PIETRO

del Gallo

0   250 m
0   250 yds

VIA GREGORIO VII

Via San Damaso

Via
Evaristo

della Cava

Via A Ceriani

Via San Silverio

P

Monte
di
Gallo

della
Mura

Aurelie

Via D Silveri

STAZIONE
ROMA S PIETRO

Maria
Addolorata

V deg

A   AURELIO

B

AURELIO

230

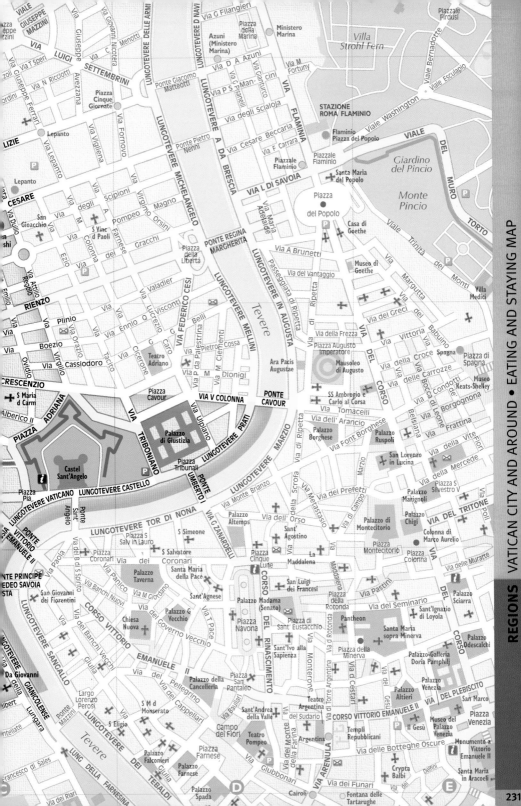

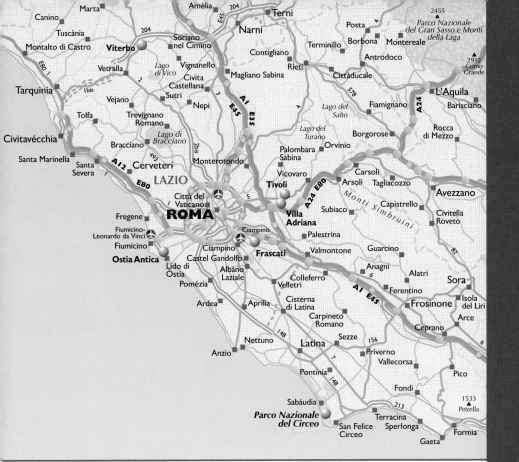

EXCURSIONS

Rome has enough to occupy several lifetimes, but if you want a break from the city, or have time to spare on a longer visit, then it is well placed for short and easily accomplished excursions to a handful of varied attractions.

Two of these outlying attractions are Roman sites as impressive as any in the city itself. The first is Ostia Antica, ancient Rome's principal port, a sprawling area of ruins set in evocative and largely rural surroundings. The second is Villa Adriana, a vast complex created by Emperor Hadrian in the second century AD, situated in the hills east of the city outside the present-day town of Tivoli.

A visit to Villa Adriana can easily be combined with a trip to Tivoli itself, famous for the Villa d'Este, created by a scion of the powerful Este family in the 16th century and celebrated for its beautiful gardens.

Although Tivoli requires a full day's excursion, you can dash out of Rome to Frascati for the afternoon, boarding a train at Termini and enjoying the pretty ride up into the Alban Hills south of the city. The town, of course, is most famous for its white wine, which you can sample in plenty of local bars and restaurants. But it is also a pleasing town in its own right, with glorious views down over distant Rome, and with enough pretty nooks and corners to keep you occupied for a couple of hours.

Viterbo, north of Rome, has more medieval interest, but it also requires more time and effort to reach, as does the Circeo national park, a tiny enclave rich in flora, fauna and easy walking trails on the coast to the south of Rome.

Viterbo 2

Parco Naturale di Veio

Casáccia

Olgiata

Osteria Nuova

Ísola Farnese

Cascina la Riccia

Santa Maria di Galeria

il Pino

2 bis

Tragliatella

La Storta

Ceri

Cascina Centrone

la Giustignana

il Centro

Tomba di Nerone

Tragliata

Ottavia

Fosso della Caduta

Boccea

S ONÓFRIO

Cascina di Castel Campanile

Rio Maggiore

TORREVÉCCHIA

PRIMAVALLE

Palidoro

Casalotti

CITTÀ DEL VATICANO

Torrimpietra

Arrone

Castel di Guido

Monte Spaccato

Ponte Tre Denari

la Serce

la Monachina

VIA AURELIA

Maccarese

Malagrotta

la Pisana

CORVIALE

Fregene

Castel Malnome

Casa Mattei

TRULLO MAGLIANA

Area Protetta del Litorale Romano

Ponte Galeria

A91

Focene

Tevere

A9

Aeropuerto Intercontinental Leonardo da Vinci

Acilia

Vitinia

Fiumicino

Osteria Malpasso

Cascina di Perna

Isola Sacra

Ostia Antica

Casal Palocco

Castel di Décima

Ostia Antica

Castel Fusano

VIA C COLOMBO

Castel Porziano

Trigória Alta

I 48

Lido del Faro

Caste Roma

Lido di Ostia

Monte di Leva

Cascina Capocotta

Tor Paterno

0   5 km
0   3 miles

C Mal
Borghetto

Tevere

A1

Castelchiodato

Parco Naturale
dei Monti
Lucrétili

VIA SALARIA

4 dir

A1 dir

Monterotondo

Mentana

Sant'Ángelo
Romano

Montecelio

Ris Nat
della
Marcigliana

Romitório

Ris Nat di
Nomentum

Settebagni

Bufalotta

Guidonia

Torre
Lupara

Cascina
d Inviolata

Tivoli

A90

Villanova

Bagni
di Tivoli

TUFELLO

SAN
BASILIO

Villalba

Settecamini

Villa
Adriana

MONTE
SACRO

Torre
Cervare

Aniene

S MARIA D
SOCCORSE

Lunghezza

A24

Osteria
Capannelle

OMA

la Rustica

Fosso dell'Osa

TOR
SAPIENZA

Osteria
dell'Osa

CENTOCELLE

Torrenova

Pantano
Borghese

Santa Maria di
Cavamonte

ARBATELLA

6

Finócchio

Laghetto

CINECITTÀ

Torre
Gáia

l'Annunziatella

A1 dir

Colonna

Parco Reg
Suburbano dell'
Appia Antica

7

ecchignola

Morena

Frascati

Montecompatri

Aeropuerto
Intercontinentale
di Ciampino

7 dir

Ciampino

Camáldoli

Rocca Priora

ranello

Grottaferrata

Castel di Leva

Santa Maria
delle Mole

Marino

Falcognana

Frattócchie

Rocca
di Papa

Mandriola

Lago
Albano

Cascina di
Monte Migliore

Castel Gandolfo

Parco Regionale
dei Castelli
Romani

Pavona

Albano
Laziale

Nemi

Paglian
Casale

Aríccia

7

Lago di
Nemi

Santa
Palomba

207

Genzano
di Roma

Zolforata

Cecchina

Parco Nazionale
del Circeo

Fontana
di Papa

Velletri

INFORMATION

www.aptprovroma.it

ℹ Piazza G. Marconi 1, 00044

☎ 06 942 0331

HOW TO GET THERE

🚆 From Stazione Termini every 15–30 minutes; journey time approximately 30 minutes

🚌 From Anagnina metro station to all the Castelli Romani towns; journey time approximately 30 minutes

🚗 Take S215 south (exit Tuscalano on GRA), then S216 to Frascati; journey time approximately 50 minutes

VILLA ALDOBRANDINI

✉ Via Cardinale Massaia 12, 00044

🕐 Garden only: Apr–Nov Mon–Fri 9–1, 3–6; Oct–Mar 9–1, 3–5

TIPS

» Avoid weekends, when Frascati is packed with Romans out for the day.

» For *cantina* (cellar) visits, ask at the tourist information office or enjoy a tour and tasting at one of the local restaurants.

Below *The volcanic soils of the Colli Albani are ideal for cultivating vines*

FRASCATI

Frascati, the loveliest of the Castelli Romani towns of the Colli Albani hills, is famous for its wine and the majestic Villa Aldobrandini and its gardens. Come in late afternoon for the best views across the Campagna towards Rome.

COLLI ALBANI

South of Rome stretches a ridge of volcanic hills, the Colli Albani, famed for the wines produced from the rich soil. The hills are home to a group of 13 towns, the Castelli Romani, so called because they developed around the feudal castles built by the popes and the Roman aristocracy. Despite the sprawling post-World War II development around them, each has its own charm, with Frascati leading the field.

VILLAS

The grandest of Frascati's villas is the Villa Aldobrandini, designed by Giacomo della Porta in 1598 for Cardinal Aldobrandini, a 'nephew' (a tactful euphemism for an illegitimate son) of Pope Clement VII. The vast palace, all faded majesty, dominates the town, and is surrounded by a superb early baroque garden, laid out between 1598 and 1603. Head first for the terrace with its fabulous views towards Rome, then explore the other terraces, avenues and follies, including the water theatre. The fountains in the gardens are often switched off, so you may not see them when you visit.

The town is scattered with other gently decaying palaces, like the Villa Falconieri and the Villa Mondragone. Villa Torlonia, among the grandest, was destroyed during World War II, but its gardens are now the town's park — don't miss the fountain, designed by Carlo Maderno.

The baroque cathedral is worth a look, as are some of the other churches, particularly Il Gesù, but do leave time to enjoy the wine. Made here since the third century BC, Frascati is a worldwide hot seller, and it's a revelation to drink it in its birthplace. Light, floral and aromatic, it's made from both Trebbiano and Malvasio grapes, varieties that thrive in the porous volcanic soil.

INTRODUCTION

Ancient Rome's port is one of the top three best-preserved Roman towns in Italy, and is a haven of romantic ruins and soothing greenery. Roman legend puts Ostia's founding in the seventh century BC; factual dating of the ruins points to the fourth century BC. From then, a small port and trading community established itself, getting a boost from its military role during the First Punic War. The second century BC was boom time for the town, with the commercial port growing in importance as Rome flourished and Ostia's own population reached half a million. However, the port was soon a victim of its own success, unable to handle the vast quantity of trade generated by the Empire. An initiative by Claudius to ease pressure on Ostia saw the construction of a second port—close to the modern airport—in the first to second centuries AD. This Portus Romae attracted more and more shipping, and Ostia became largely a residential town. By the fifth century and the fall of Rome, it was largely abandoned, the sea retreated and the port silted up. Malaria and pirates did the rest, and by the 17th century, Ostia Antica was all but forgotten.

The size and scale of Ostia are more impressive by far than the capital's Forum, and it gives a far better idea of ancient Roman life.

WHAT TO SEE

Archaeological excavations began at Ostia Antica the early 19th century, and today about half the town has been uncovered, with some low-key excavations still continuing. For visitors to the site, Ostia is a quintessentially romantic Classical ruin, complete with elegant umbrella pines, grassy slopes and spreads of colourful wildflowers. These certainly contribute to its evocative allure, but they make preservation a nightmare, damaging already

INFORMATION

www.ostiaantica.net

✉ Viale dei Romagnoli 717, 00170

☎ 06 5635 8099; 06 5635 0215

🕐 Apr–Sep Tue–Sun 8.30–6; Nov–Feb 8.30–4; Mar, Oct 8.30–5. Castello: Tue–Sun 9–1 ✋ Adult €6.50, child (under 18) free. Includes entry to Museo Ostiense nearby. Castello: free 🖥 🏛 Bookshop with guidebooks (guidebook in English €6.50), maps and plans, postcards and souvenirs, audioguide €4

HOW TO GET THERE

🚇 Metro from Termini to Stazione Ostiense (Piramide metro station); journey time 30 minutes. Then train from Stazione Ostiense to Ostia Antica; journey time 30 minutes.

🚌 35–40 minutes if the traffic's not bad; take Via del Mare (SS8) from Porta San Paolo

Above *Ostia Antica's restored first-century AD amphitheatre*

TIPS

» Allow a whole day for the site; perhaps bring a picnic.

» In summer, take water with you, and rest in the shade during the hottest part of the day.

» To get the most out of a visit, buy a plan of the site when you arrive (available at the museum shop) and plan what you want to see.

WHERE TO EAT

There are plenty of seafood restaurants in Ostia Lido along the Lungomare. Take a train or metro to Ostia Lido C. Colombo (the last stop on the line you arrived on).

RISTORANTE IL MONUMENTO

www.ristorantemonumento.it

At the entrance to the beautiful medieval Borgo you can enjoy reasonably priced local dishes on the veranda here.

✉ Piazza Umberto I 8, 00170 ☎ 06 565 0021 🕐 Tue–Sun 12–3.30, 8–11

fragile walls and foundations: It's the age-old Italian story of too much to preserve and simply not enough money to do it.

DECUMANUS MAXIMUS

Like all Roman towns, Ostia was bisected by a dead-straight main street, the Decumanus Maximus, and its cobbled length is the first thing you see as you enter the site through the Porta Romana. On either side of this there's a confusing jumble of streets and ruins, admittedly evocative, but you'll need a plan to make sense of it all.

A city this size needed civic buildings, temples, administrative offices, entertainment complexes and shops, as well as housing for a population covering the full social spectrum. Some of these you should certainly track down, so head down the Decumanus towards the town. The first big building on the right is the Terme di Nettuno, the public baths, built by Hadrian and wonderfully decorated with mosaics aptly showing Neptune himself and his wife Amphitrite, goddess of the sea. Next to the baths is the amphitheatre, a semicircular building constructed in AD196, which was designed to seat 4,000 spectators. Its tiers of seats have been restored and it is used for summer concerts. Ostian citizens could move through the back of the theatre directly into the Piazzale delle Corporazioni.

PIAZZALE DELLE CORPORAZIONI

The Piazzale delle Corporazioni is the mercantile heart of the city. Here, the shipping agents had their offices, many of them identified by the black and white mosaics in front of their doors—chandlers, grain-merchants, rope-makers and others. Their warehouses, known as *horrea*, are scattered all over the site. To get some idea of the scale of commerce in ancient times, spend a few moments simply taking in the sheer number of these *horrea* and their impressive proportions.

Near the piazzale, there are a couple of private houses you should see: the Casa di Apulius and the Casa di Diana. The former's owner splashed out on an atrium and mosaic-decorated rooms, interior design that was unusual this far north—you're more likely to see it in Pompeii. He was a devotee of the god Mithras, and there's a Mithraic temple next to the house. The owners of the nearby Casa di Diana also worshipped Mithras and had a mithraeum at the back of their grand house, with its central courtyard.

THE INSULAE AND FORUM

Not all Ostians lived in villas, and it is the blocks of workers' flats that really speak to us across the centuries. These *insulae* (islands) rose to four or five floors, had running water, heating and plumbing and often shared a communal garden—the Casa di Giardino is a fine example.

Citizens of all classes flocked to the Forum, with its Capitol, baths and basilicas, but just as many doubtless spent time in the Thermopolium, near the Casa di Diana. This ancient café, with its high counter, outside seats and display shelves, gives a wonderful insight into everyday Roman life.

To flesh out the bones of what you've seen, head for the museum, which is devoted to finds from the site. There's a fine statue of Mithras killing a bull (the god's symbol), sarcophagi from all over the town and wall paintings with touching scenes of everyday life.

THE BORGO

It's worth making a detour across the road to the Borgo, Ostia's medieval village. It is dominated by the Castello, built for Pope Julius II between 1483 and 1486 by Florentine architect Baccio Pontelli. Once the customs house for ships sailing up the Tiber to Rome, the castle lost its usefulness when the river changed course in 1587.

PARCO NAZIONALE DEL CIRCEO

Circeo National Park, south of Rome, is a green oasis with immensely varied scenery and a mixed flora and fauna that's unique in this part of Italy.

In 1928 Mussolini embarked on a massive drainage project, transforming the malaria-ridden and unproductive Pontine Marshes into a productive agricultural area, complete with the new towns of Latina and Sabaudia. Conservationists quickly realized the threat the scheme might pose to this sensitive coastal environment, and in 1934 the Parco Nazionale del Circeo was founded. It's the smallest of Italy's national parks, covering an area of 8,500ha (21,000 acres), but embraces a superb variety of natural environments, ranging from dunes, wetlands, sea caves and beaches to deciduous woods and limestone maquis. Roads, tracks and paths thread through the park and link the different zones, providing excellent access to the area.

WHAT TO SEE

Circeo has superb woods of deciduous oaks, holm and cork oaks, but its dunes, maquis and wetlands are what draws naturalists and birdwatchers to the park. The dunes are backed by four lakes, drawing a wide variety of both resident and migratory birds—more than 230 species have been recorded. Spring and autumn, during the migration, are particularly good times to come. You may see the turned-over earth that signals wild boar, or get a glimpse of fallow and roe deer, foxes or even a pine marten. In spring the maquis—the typical scrubby Mediterranean habitat—is at its best, burgeoning with brilliant cistus, rosemary and broom. The park has man-made attractions, too, in the shape of a rich archaeological heritage—Domitian's Villa is the best known.

EXPLORING THE PARK

Explore the park by heading south from Sabaudia, taking in the dunes and wetlands on the way to Monte Circeo, at 541m (1,775ft) the highest point. The drive south covers the quintessential Mediterranean coastline of the promontory—white-sand beaches, rocky coves and aromatic pines running down to the sea. A road leads to the top of Monte Circeo and from its summit there are fabulous views north over the beaches and lagoons. Monte Circeo is thought to be the legendary island of Circe mentioned in Homer's *Odyssey*, and the whole promontory resembles the sorceress' reclining figure. From the top, the road exits the park into the picturesque, and distinctly trendy, coastal village of San Felice Circeo. In summer, it's crowded with flashy cars and yachts, but any other time should be high on the sightseeing list.

INFORMATION

www.parks.it/parco.nazionale.circeo
www.parcocirceo.it

🛈 Centro d'Informazione Parco Nazionale del Circeo. Main park information centre with exhibitions, audio-visual show, natural history museum and picnic area ✉ Via Carlo Alberto 104, Sabaudia, 04016 ☎ 0773 512240
🛈 Sabaudia, 04014 ☎ 0773 695404
🛈 San Felice Circeo 04014 ☎ 0773 547770

HOW TO GET THERE

🚆 From Laurentina to San Felice Circeo/Sabaudia; journey time 2.25 hours
🚌 Take S148 south via Latina, then follow signs east to Sabaudia; journey time 1.5–2 hours

TIPS

» Spend time at the visitor centre in Sabaudia to learn about the park.
» Take a boat trip around the lagoon from Sabaudia, or up and down the coast or to Circe's grotto from San Felice Circeo.
» If you want to stay the night, try one of the moderately priced hotels in San Felice, which are busy only in high season.

Below *Paola Lake, Sabaudia*

INFORMATION

ℹ️ Piazza Garibaldi, 00011

HOW TO GET THERE

🚆 From Stazione Tiburtina; journey time approximately 35–60 minutes
🚌 From Ponte Mammolo (Via Prenestina) every 15 minutes; journey time 1 hour
🚗 Take A24 northeast, then Tivoli exit; allow about 1 hour

VILLA D'ESTE

www.villadestetivoli.info
✉️ Piazza Trento, 00011 ☎️ 0774 332920. Bookings: 199 766166 or +39 0445 230310 (from outside Italy)
🕐 May–Aug Tue–Sun 8.30–6.45; Sep 8.30–6.15; Oct 8.30–7.30; Nov–Jan 8.30–4; Feb 8.30–4.30; Mar 8.30–5.15; Apr 8.30–6.30 🎫 Adult €8, child (under 18) free 📖 Guidebook €6 and €5
📷 🏛️

Above *The spectacular Organ Fountain at Villa d'Este*
Opposite *A fountain at the Villa d'Este*

INTRODUCTION

A hill town that's home to one of Europe's greatest Renaissance water gardens, a gorge complete with crashing waterfalls, and tempting restaurants for alfresco dining, Tivoli has much to offer visitors. Perched among olive groves on a ridge of the Monti Tiburtini, the town has always provided an escape for Romans from the heat of the city—it's amazing what a bit of height can do to the freshness of the air. In Classical times it was a retirement town and summer retreat for wealthy Romans, including the emperor—Hadrian's enormous Villa Adriana is just outside the town (▷ 242–243). Later, Renaissance nobility built country villas throughout the town and surrounding area. The most famous of these is the Villa d'Este, whose gardens are a symphony of lush greenery and thundering water.

The town is enfolded in an oxbow formed by the River Aniene. It retains its picturesque medieval streets, fine churches and a general air of prosperity, wealth derived from the nearby travertine stone quarries.

THE VILLA D'ESTE

Tivoli's main draw is the Villa d'Este and its stunning landscaped garden, where cascading water is combined with lush cool greenery. The Renaissance villa was converted from a former Benedictine convent by Pirro Ligorio for Cardinal Ippolito d'Este in 1550. The cardinal was the son of Lucrezia Borgia and the Duke of Ferrara, and had grown up in a rich and sophisticated court, a background that is reflected in both the villa and gardens.

Ten rooms on the ground floor of the villa have been restored; these are vividly frescoed with scenes from mythology and the history of Tivoli by Girolamo Muziano and Federico Zuccari. The frescoes were executed between 1550 and 1560. There's a great view over the garden's symmetrical terraces from the loggia.

THE VILLA'S GARDENS

Below the villa stretch the spectacular gardens. They represent the full flowering of Renaissance culture and had a huge influence on garden design throughout Europe. Laid out around a central axis, the design is strictly formal, based on the combination of static lines of greenery, sculpture and statuary with living water. It's this contrast between the sombre planting and the exuberance of the myriad fountains and water features that gives the gardens much of their appeal.

THE FOUNTAINS

Fountain-wise, the stupendous Organ Fountain takes top prize. Fully restored, it sends millions of litres of water thundering into the air against a spectacular decorative stone background. Visitors have always loved the Viale delle Cento Fontane, a wooded walkway flanked by a hundred cooling spouts of water, whose focal point is the splendid Fontana dei Draghi (its builder Pope Gregory XIII's emblem featured a *drago*, or dragon). The Fontana dell'Ovata is fringed with statues and set against a shadowy arcade, and the great Gian Lorenzo Bernini was responsible for the graceful shell-shaped Fontana del Bicchierone. Another stunner is the Fontana della Rometta, little Rome, with reproductions of Rome's main Classical monuments.

These set-pieces are scattered throughout the gardens, but wherever you go you'll be surrounded by the sound of water and find a surprise round every corner. Originally, the surprises included the watery jokes found in every great Renaissance garden—jets that drenched visitors at the touch of a hidden button, benches that flooded when sat upon, curtains of water to trap the unwary, owls that whistled and chirruped during the day. These no longer work, but remember that such conceits were as much part of the gardens as the beauty of the fountains and cascades.

VILLA GREGORIANA

Tivoli's other garden, the Villa Gregoriana, was created much later. The River Aniene was prone to flood the town, and in 1831 Pope Gregory XVI solved the problem by diverting the flow of water over an artificial waterfall, the Cascata Grande. Bernini had a hand in the plan, designing a smaller cascade at the neck of the 60m-deep (200ft) gorge. The park and gorge are a wonderfully luxuriant habitat, overgrown and wild, and a good contrast to the formal style of the Villa d'Este.

THE WATERFALLS

From the deafening vantage point overlooking the Cascata Grande, there is a path, noisy and cool with the rush of water, zigzagging down to the bottom of the gorge. It passes two smaller waterfalls before retracking to the main falls and continuing past two grottoes; water rushes straight down past the Grotto della Sirena, and the Grotta di Nettuno is heavily covered with mineral deposits. The climb back up the other side is steep, but it is well worth it for the views from the top and the close-up of the little Tempio di Vesta. The temple is in the grounds of a restaurant, but you can go in and peer out from the belvedere.

THE TOWN

It's worth a quick wander round the town, particularly along the Via del Duomo, where there's a high percentage of late-medieval houses. Fans of the Romanesque should take in some of the churches: San Pietro alla Carità has a lovely facade and Classical columns. The Duomo, founded in the fifth century, has a Romanesque campanile, though its portico dates from 1650. To see an earlier portico, head for San Silvestro—its columns are Roman, and there are 13th-century frescoes in the apse.

VILLA GREGORIANA

www.villagregoriana.it

✉ Piazza Tempio di Vesta, Largo Sant'Angelo, 00011 ☎ 06 3996 7701

🕓 Apr to mid-Oct Tue–Sun 10–6.30; mid-Oct to Mar 10–2.30. By appointment only Dec–Feb 👤 Adult €5, child (4–12) €2.50 🏛

TIPS

» Allow all day to visit Tivoli, particularly if you're going to visit both the Villa d'Este and the Villa Adriana (▷ 242–243).

» Be prepared to find some fountains at Villa d'Este out of action owing to continuing restoration.

» Don't be tempted to drink the water, or even splash around in it—it's basically sewage from the town above. Some fountains are labelled *acqua potabile*; these are safe.

WHERE TO EAT
IL GROTTINO

Expect simple regional cooking at this rustic trattoria on a pretty piazza. In summer there's also alfresco dining.

✉ Via Paolo D'Egina 12, 00019
☎ 0774 357834 🕓 Tue–Sun 12–3, 7–11

RISTORANTE SIBILLA

The location is enviable, with tables set around the temples of Vesta and Sibilla, overlooking the famous cascades of Villa Gregoriana.

✉ Via della Sibilla 50, 00011 ☎ 0774 335 281 🕓 Tue–Sun 12.30–3, 7.30–10.30

VILLA ADRIANA

INFORMATION

🏠 Piazza Garibaldi, 00011 Tivoli
☎ 0774 311249

VILLA ADRIANA

☎ 0774 530302; 0774 382733; 06 3996
7900 🕐 May–Aug daily 9–7.30; Oct
9–6.30; Nov–Jan 9–5; Feb 9–6; Mar
9–6.30; Apr, Sep 9–7 🖐 Adult €6.50,
child (under 18) free 🔲 🏧

HOW TO GET THERE

🚆 From Stazione Tiburtina to Tivoli;
journey time approximately 30 minutes.
🚌 Cotral bus from Ponte Mammolo (Via
Prenestina) to Tivoli; journey time 1 hour.
From Tivoli, take bus No. 4/4X from Piazza
Garibaldi out to Villa Adriana.
🚗 Take A24 northeast, then Tivoli exit;
Villa Adriana is signed from here. Allow
about 1 hour

Above *The Canopus is the highlight of a
visit to the Villa Adriana*

INTRODUCTION

The epitome of a romantic ruin, the remains of the largest and most elaborate
villa ever constructed during the Roman Empire are set in a peaceful and
beautiful landscape. The Villa Adriana, just outside Tivoli, was built by Hadrian,
emperor from AD118 to AD138. As a provincial, Hadrian was viewed with
suspicion by both the Senate and the aristocracy. It was partly for this reason
that Hadrian made this grandiose villa his main residence when he was in
Rome, rather than taking over one of the existing imperial palaces. He also
kept away from the power struggles in Rome by travelling throughout the
Empire, and probably hoped eventually to make this sumptuous villa his
retirement home. Sadly, ill health forced him south and he only had a few
years to enjoy the completed villa. His travels had played a large part in
the planning; an enthusiastic sight-seer, Hadrian dotted his creation with
reconstructions of buildings that had impressed him throughout the Roman
world—a sort of second-century theme park. Building started in AD125 and
continued for 10 years. Tivoli, with its famous travertine quarries and abundant
water, was an ideal place for such a vast project, as there was plenty of tufa
and lime available to mix the tonnes of cement needed.

The villa eventually covered more than 100ha (250 acres), with over 30
buildings, some of which have still to be excavated. After Hadrian's death, the
complex fell rapidly into disrepair, was plundered and forgotten, until early
Renaissance enthusiasts rediscovered it in 1450.

WHAT TO SEE

You'll need plenty of imagination to visualize the ancient glory of the site; the
upper parts of the buildings no longer exist, making the complex seem much
more open than it would originally have been. What now appear to be open
spaces were originally covered walkways connecting the various buildings,
which were several floors high, embellished with domes and faced with

marble and other precious stones. It must once have looked like an enclosed city—it's worth remembering that the villa covered an area as large as the area of Imperial Rome itself. Archaeologists still haven't discovered the original purpose of many of the site's structures, so it makes sense to concentrate only on the best.

THE PECILE

Begin your explorations at the Pecile, the huge colonnade near the entrance. Once surrounded by gardens, its focal point is the central pool. Hadrian based its design on the Stoa Poikile of Athens, which he admired on his travels. It was probably used as a gymnasium and it is thought that it also served as an after-dinner promenade during the summer. Along the west side you'll see the Cento Camerelle, a warren of small rooms probably used as storage space and slave quarters.

TEATRO MARITTIMO

In the northeast corner of the Pecile there's access through the ruins of a large hall to the Teatro Marittimo, one of the villa's highlights and one of the few places where there's a real impression of the original appearance. An Ionic-columned portico rings a circular canal, once crossed by movable bridges leading to a little round island. This was Hadrian's own retreat, where he withdrew to relax in the miniature *domus* (palace) that stood on the islet.

THE BATHS

Just south of here is a modestly sized set of baths, with a *heliocaminus*, a round pool used for sunbathing where you baked before bravely plunging into the nearby *frigidarium*, the cold-water pool. Far grander is the *terme* proper, a vast bath complex with open-air pools, hot baths heated by an elaborate system and courtyards for relaxing. By contrast to this hedonism, there's a bit of cultural stimulus near here in the shape of the Canopus, modelled on an Egyptian site that had much impressed Hadrian. It's a replica of the Temple of Serapis at Canopus, which was linked to the Nile by a canal; here, an artificial waterway runs down a man-made valley to the temple replica—it is fringed with statues and fragments of columns, including four serene caryatids. It must have been a wonderful backdrop for late-night dining, which was probably its purpose. Have a look at the nearby Pretorio, the barracks, then visit the underground portico where the Emperor took his summertime strolls.

PALAZZO IMPERIALE

Winter would have seen Hadrian making full use of the Palazzo Imperiale itself, a complex that covered 50,000sq m (180,000sq ft) and came complete with an efficient underground heating system. The palace was made up of three complexes set round their own peristyles, which housed both residential and official rooms. The Piazza d'Oro, in the southeast, has yielded some fabulous archaeological treasures; like so much else from here, they're now dispersed to museums in Rome and all over the world. The library building is another thought-provoking area—two originally multi-floor buildings that housed works in Greek and Latin. One side of the library courtyard was occupied by 10 guest rooms, perhaps for visiting scholars, paved with black and white mosaic floors and complete with three sleeping niches in each room.

There's much more besides, best enjoyed as part of the overall scene. There's also an entire underground series of roads, passages and storerooms, from where the infrastructure needed to run this huge palace operated. The small museum exhibits some statues, portraits and mosaics (although all the best are elsewhere). Recent archaeological finds are also sometimes on display here.

TIPS

» The site is enormous and it would be hard to cover everything thoroughly in a day. Buy the large-scale map available at the bookshop and plan what you want to see.

» This is a wonderful place for a picnic; buy provisions before you arrive.

» Visit in the late afternoon to see the site at its most romantic.

WHERE TO EAT
RISTORANTE ADRIANO

Close to the villa entrance, this elegant restaurant, with beautiful gardens, serves local cuisine and good wines.

✉ Via di Villa Adriana 194, 00011
☎ 0774 382235 🕐 Daily 12.30–3, 7–10.30

Below *The perfectly preserved subterranean Cryptoportico below the Peschiera*

INFORMATION

www.viterboonline.com

ℹ Piazza San Carluccio 5, 01100

☎ 0761 304795

HOW TO GET THERE

🚆 Every 20 minutes from Termini, Roma Ostiense or Stazione Flaminio; journey time approximately 1.5–2 hours. The town is a 10- to 15-minute walk

🚌 From Saxa Rubra (Via Flaminia) every 30 minutes; journey time approximately 1.5 hours

🚗 Take A1 (E35) north to GRA, then exit at Orte onto S204 signed to Viterbo (110km/68 miles); journey time 1.5 hours. Villa Lante is 5km (3 miles) east of Viterbo. Bus No. 6 hourly from Piazza Martini dei Ungheria; by car, east of town at Bagnaia, follow signs off S204

INTRODUCTION

There may come a point in your stay when you tire of Rome's endless museums and churches, particularly if you visit during the oppressively hot summer months. The countryside of Lazio and beyond is a refreshing change from the city's heat, and much of it is accessible by public transport, making it an easy day's escape. Whenever possible, avoid visiting on Saturday and Sunday: The Romans enjoy getting out of the city, too, and the popular places will be crowded. Plan your visit for a weekday and you might even have the place to yourself. So why not do as the Romans do: Pack up a picnic and head for *la campagna*.

The largest town in northern Lazio and a quietly prosperous provincial capital, Viterbo has a long history. It's this legacy of the past, in the shape of intact medieval walls, a maze of narrow streets and its stately *palazzi*, that gives the town its appeal today. Viterbo was originally an Etruscan settlement, absorbed by Rome in AD310. Its heyday was the Middle Ages, when a succession of popes scuttled here to live away from trouble in Rome, making it their capital in 1257. It was during this period that the magnificent walls went up, civic buildings and churches were constructed and the town took on its present form.

WHAT TO SEE
THE HEART OF TOWN

After the unattractive approach to the town, it's a relief to see the battlemented walls that encircle the old town. Once inside, spend time getting your bearings in the Piazza del Plebiscito, a fine square surrounded by 15th- and 16th-century palaces. The main, arcaded building is the 15th-century Palazzo dei Priori, decorated, like many others, with lions and palm trees, symbols of Viterbo. The palazzo's council chamber, reached through a lovely courtyard overlooking the river valley, is decorated with a series of murals telling the town's history. From here, head down Via San Lorenzo to the Romanesque church of Santa Maria Nuova—where St. Thomas Aquinas preached for peace in 1266. Then head to the picturesque Quartiere San Pellegrino, Viterbo's oldest area, with its tangle of narrow alleys. Don't miss the walk up Via San Pellegrino to the Piazza San Pellegrino; it's Viterbo's main street and has an example of just about everything that makes the area special.

Clockwise from above The loggia of Viterbo's 13th-century Palazzo Papale; 11th-century Santa Maria Nuova, Viterbo; the gardens at Villa Lante, in the town of Bagnaia, east of Viterbo

PIAZZA SAN LORENZO

Retrack to the Piazza del Plebiscito and head in the opposite direction, towards Piazza San Lorenzo. The square was built on the original Etruscan town and is flanked by the 13th-century Palazzo Papale and the Duomo. The Great Hall in the Papal Palace was once the scene of half a dozen or so papal elections, but for most visitors it's the view from the open Gothic loggia to the green gorge that slices into central Viterbo that's truly memorable. Memorable, too, is the serene beauty of the Romanesque Duomo, with its elegant striped cosmatesque floor and stately campanile.

CHURCHES AND MUSEUMS

Santa Maria Nuova, built in 1080, and the Duomo are the pick of the town's churches, but it's worth tracking down the 19th-century building dedicated to Santa Rosa, at the far end of Corso Italia. Inside a chapel in the south aisle is the saint's body, still dressed in nun's clothing; macabre, but fascinating.

The Museo Nazionale Archeologico, up the hill in Piazza della Rocca, focuses on archaeological finds from the Stone Age to the Middle Ages, with the emphasis on the Etruscan finds from the area around Viterbo. There are more local treasures in the Museo Civico, outside the walls, including Roman sarcophagi found nearby, but it's the paintings on the upper floors that shine.

THE VILLA LANTE

To the east of Viterbo is the small town of Bagnaia, completely dominated by the 16th-century palace of the Villa Lante, whose gardens are considered one of the finest of all the existing Renaissance Mannerist gardens. The villa is easily reached from Viterbo, and you should certainly leave time to visit it.

Spreading over a series of five terraces, the gardens are perfectly proportioned and richly detailed, the planting enhancing the importance of water in the overall design. There are some 16th-century water jokes, which the guide can activate if you ask. It's a lovely place on a hot summer's day.

TIPS

» If you're driving, aim to reach Viterbo in the morning, when everything will be open, then head for the gardens of Villa Lante around lunchtime to escape the oppressive heat.

» Park outside the city walls to avoid having to struggle with narrow streets and congestion.

» There are occasional guided walks around the *centro storico*; ask at the tourist office for more information.

MUSEO NAZIONALE ARCHEOLOGICO

✉ Rocca Albornoz, Piazza della Rocca 21b, 00110 ☎ 0761 325929 🕓 Tue–Sun 8.30–7.30 ✋ Adult €4

MUSEO CIVICO

✉ Piazza F. Crispi 2, 00110 ☎ 0761 340810 🕓 Apr–Oct Tue–Sat 9–7; Nov–Mar Tue–Sat 9–6 ✋ Adult/child €3.50

VILLA LANTE

✉ Via Iacopo Barozzi 71, 00110, Bagnaia ☎ 0761 288008 🕓 16 Apr–15 Sep Tue–Sun 8.30–7.30; 16 Sep–Oct 8.30–6.30; Nov–Feb 8.30–4.30; Mar 8.30–5.30; 1 Apr–15 Apr 8.30–6.30 ✋ Adult €5, child (under 18) and over 65 free

There are many companies who provide organized tours in and around Rome and beyond. Tours range from escorted walks around the city's streets and museums to personalized tours with your own guide. Most operators offer their tours in a number of different languages.

GUIDED WALKS

There are lots of companies offering walking tours of Rome, so you are sure to find something that appeals.

ENJOY ROME

www.enjoyrome.com

Enjoy Rome offers a wide range of city itineraries (in English only), including tours of the Jewish Ghetto, Trastevere or Caravaggio's Rome. The three-hour tours cost €30, or €25 for under-26s. They run every day except Christmas Day and 6 January. The catacombs tour costs €48 for all ages.

✉ Via Marghera 8a, 00185 ☎ 06 445 1843; 06 4938 2724

ROMAN ODYSSEY

www.romanodyssey.com

This company offers group and private tours headed by native-English speakers; itineraries include Rome in a Day, the Ancient City and Vatican Privilege Tour. Prices start at €50.

☎ Contact via website (Skype connection) or tel 328 912 3720

THROUGH ETERNITY

www.througheternity.com

Archaeologists, art historians and other experts on ancient Rome offer the usual popular tours, plus an interactive one, where audience participation is essential. Prices vary according to the length of time, but start at €200 (minimum of five people) for a three-hour tour.

☎ 06 700 9336

BUS TOURS

There are many companies providing a range of bus tours of Rome and beyond.

ATAC

www.atac.roma.it

www.trambusopen.com

Rome's public transport company runs the 110 City Tour, which leaves from Termini station. You can buy a Stop and Go ticket for €20 (children 6–12 €15), which allows you to hop on and off the bus all day. The service runs daily at 15-minute intervals from 9am to 8.30pm (8pm Oct–Mar), and makes 10 stops. You can book in advance at the ticket office, or buy your tickets on the bus or at any of the stops. Trambus Open also offers night tours (€12). The tour (110 Open) departs from Piazza Venezia (Piazza San Marco 52) at 10pm and 11.30pm on Friday and Saturday from April to September.

✉ Via Gaeta 78, 00185 ☎ 06 4695 2252, 800 431784

ATAC also runs **Archeobus**, which departs every hour daily from 9.45am to 4.45pm. It has 16 stops at the treasures of the Via Appia Antica, the fourth-century BC road that linked Rome south to Capua, a distance of 212km (132 miles). The journey takes 2 hours 20 minutes and costs €12 (child 6–12 €8). A joint ticket for the 110 City Tour and Archeobus costs €30 (child 6–12 €20) and lasts 2 days.

Other bus companies run tours around the city and to popular places farther afield, such as Tivoli and Ostia Antica. These include **Appian Line** (Piazza Esquilino 6/7, 00185, tel 06 4878 6601, www. appianline.it); and **Green Line Tours** (Via Farini 5a, 00185, tel 06 483787, www.greenlinetours.com).

Above *Joining an organized tour can help you make the best of your time in the city*

BOAT TOURS

BATTELLI DI ROMA

www.battellidiroma.it

This company runs cruises along the Tiber, with a commentary. Tickets can be bought in advance from the Hotel Reservations desk at Termini station, at the quays at Isola Tiberina and Castel Sant'Angelo or on board the boat. 'Hop on, Hop Off' cruises cost €15 between the Isola Tiberina and Ponte Cavour.

☎ 06 9774 5498

PERSONAL GUIDES

CAST

www.cast-turismo.it

Cast provides guides for groups of up to 20 people. Three-hour group tours cost €115.

✉ Via Cavour 184, 00184 ☎ 06 482 5698

CENTRO GUIDE TURISTICHE DI ROMA

www.centroguideroma.net

www.trambusopen.com

This company offers personal guided tours for up to 20 people. Prices start at €145 for three-hour group tours. Surcharges are payable for groups larger than 20 people.

✉ Via di Santa Maria alle Fornaci 8d, 00165 ☎ 06 639 0409

PRACTICALITIES

Practicalities gives you all the important practical information you will need during your visit, from money matters to emergency phone numbers.

WEATHER
TEMPERATURE

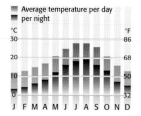

RAINFALL

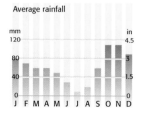

CLIMATE

Rome's weather can be unpredictable. Rainfall can be high, even in the warmer, summer months but, equally, you can experience bright, clear, cold days in winter. The charts above show what you are likely to find, but it is best to pack for all possibilities.

WHEN TO GO

The best time to visit Rome is in spring or autumn, when the temperature should be pleasantly warm. There is less risk of rain than in the winter months, but you might still catch the occasional shower. The downside of visiting at this time of year is that everyone else does too. Easter, especially, is popular, with high numbers of tourists swollen by visiting pilgrims to the Holy City. The summer, particularly July and August, can be oppressively hot, with temperatures of up to 40°C (105°F) broken by sudden and dramatic thunderstorms. Many Romans take their holidays in August, and it is not

unusual for shops and restaurants to be closed for between two weeks and a month. Winters are generally mild and damp, and snow is rare.

WEATHER REPORTS

Weather reports are given during most news bulletins on Italian channels, as well as on English-language channels shown on satellite TV, such as CNN and BBC World. You can also check the website of your local news network station, such as the BBC (www.bbc.co.uk) or CNN (www.cnn.com), or a specialist website like the Weather Channel (www.weather.com).

DOCUMENTS
PASSPORTS

British citizens need a passport to enter Italy. Visitors from other EU countries should contact the Italian embassy in their home country for details of the documentation required. Non-EU visitors will need a passport, which should be valid for at least six months from the date of entry. If you intend to work or study in Italy, make sure your passport is stamped with your date of entry. You will need it to apply for a *Permesso di Soggiorno*.

VISAS

EU, Australian, Canadian, New Zealand and US nationals do not need a visa for stays of up to 90 days. To extend a visit for a further 90 days, you can, one time only, apply at any police station. This extension cannot be used for studying or employment, and you must prove that you can support yourself financially. If you are a citizen of a country not mentioned above, you should contact the Italian embassy in your home country to check visa requirements.

Visa and passport regulations differ depending on your nationality and are subject to change. Check visa requirements prior to a visit and

follow news events that may affect the situation.

DUTY-FREE AND DUTY-PAID GUIDELINES

Anything that is clearly for personal use can be taken into Italy free of duty. However, it is worth carrying receipts for valuable items in case you need to prove on your return that they weren't bought in Italy.

For the latest advice on duty-free and duty-paid allowance, see either the US Department of Homeland Security's website (www.cbp.gov) or that of HM Customs and Excise (www.hmce.gov.uk). Note that you cannot buy goods duty-free if you are journeying within the EU. Whatever your entitlement, you cannot bring home goods for payment (including payment in kind) or for resale. These goods are considered for commercial use, and duty is payable.

TIME ZONES

Italy is on Central European Time (CET), one hour ahead of GMT (Greenwich Mean Time, measured from London) during the winter. At the end of March, the clocks are put forward by one hour, and then put back again at the end of October.

CITY	TIME DIFFERENCE	TIME AT 12 NOON IN ITALY
Amsterdam	0	noon
Auckland	+11	11pm
Berlin	0	noon
Brussels	0	noon
Chicago	-7	5am
Dublin	-1	11am
Johannesburg	+1	1pm
London	-1	11am
Madrid	0	noon
Montréal	-6	6am
New York	-6	6am
Paris	0	noon
Perth, Australia	+7	7pm
San Francisco	-9	3am
Sydney	+9	9pm
Tokyo	+8	8pm

CUSTOMS

Importing wildlife souvenirs from rare or endangered species may be either illegal or require a special permit. Check customs regulations before you buy.

For details of duty-free and duty-paid allowances, see panel below.

HEALTH ISSUES

No vaccinations are necessary, unless you are coming from an infected area. If you have any doubts, contact your doctor before your trip. Make sure your insurance policy is valid for the duration of your visit. Most policies cover cancellation, medical expenses, accident compensation, personal liability, and personal belongings (including money). Your policy should cover the cost of getting you home in a medical emergency. If you have private medical coverage, check your policy, as you may be covered while you are away.

As well as health insurance, European citizens should carry a European Health Insurance Card (EHIC), available from post offices, health centres and social security offices. This entitles you to free or reduced-cost healthcare and covers treatment that health insurance often doesn't. Each person travelling needs their own EHIC, available from their home country.

For up-to-date information, see the Department of Health's website on www.dh.gov.uk (in the UK), or the National Center for Infectious Diseases on www.cdc.gov/travel in the US.

WHAT TO TAKE

La bella figura is alive and well, and living in Rome. Romans tend to dress well at all times, and anyone appearing scruffy is likely to be stared at—although you won't be refused admission to most places.

» Most importantly, bring a pair of comfortable shoes. You will probably do a lot of walking, either through the streets or around museums or archaeological sites—very tiring on the feet.

» Bring clothes that cover your shoulders and knees for visiting churches. A lightweight raincoat is useful for summer showers, as is a folding umbrella.

» A small shoulder bag that can be worn across the body or a money belt are handy for daily use.

» Bring your address book, for emergency contacts or postcards, and photocopies of all important documents, such as your passport and insurance details.

» A torch (flashlight) is useful for viewing works of art in dark churches. You may also find binoculars useful for a closer look.

» Bring a first-aid kit, including plasters (Band Aids), antiseptic cream, painkillers and any prescription medicine.

» Don't forget an Italian phrasebook. Although most people you meet will speak at least some English, any attempt at Italian is always appreciated.

» Earplugs are useful if you are a light sleeper, or if your hotel doesn't have double glazing. Rome is a noisy city.

ITALIAN EMBASSIES ABROAD

AUSTRALIA
12 Grey Street, Deakin,
ACT 2600
Tel 02 6273 3333;
www.ambcanberra.esteri.it

CANADA
275 Slater Street,
21st Floor, Ottawa, Ontario K1P 5H9
Tel 613 232 2401;
www.ambottawa.esteri.it

IRELAND
63/65 Northumberland Road, Dublin 4
Tel 01 660 1744;
www.ambdublino.esteri.it

NEW ZEALAND
34–38 Grant Road,
P. O. Box 463, Thorndon, Wellington
Tel 04 4735 339; www.ambwellington.esteri.it

SOUTH AFRICA
796 George Avenue, Arcadia 0083, Pretoria
Tel 12 423 0000; www.ambpretoria.esteri.it

UK
14 Three Kings Yard, London W1K 4EH
Tel 020 7312 2200; www.amblondra.org.uk

USA
3000 Whitehaven Street NW, Washington DC
Tel 202 612 4400;
www.ambwashingtondc.esteri.it

DUTY-FREE AND DUTY-PAID GUIDELINES

DUTY-PAID GUIDELINES FOR NON-EU CITIZENS

US citizens can bring home up to $800 of duty-paid goods, provided they have been out of the country for at least 48 hours and haven't made another international trip in the past 30 days. This limit applies to all members of the family, regardless of age, and exemptions may be pooled.

» 200 cigarettes; or
» 100 cigarillos; or
» 50 cigars; or
» 250g smoking tobacco
» 1 litre of spirits or strong liquors

» 2 litres of still table wine
» 2 litres of fortified wine, sparkling wine or other liquors
» 60cc/ml of perfume
» 250cc/ml of toilet water (perfume)

DUTY-PAID GUIDELINES FOR EU CITIZENS

European Union citizens can take home unlimited amounts of duty-paid goods, as long as they are for personal use. In the UK, HM Customs and Excise consider anything over the following guidelines as for commercial use:

» 3,200 cigarettes; or
» 400 cigarillos; or
» 200 cigars; or
» 3kg of tobacco
» 110 litres of beer

» 10 litres of spirits
» 90 litres of wine (of which only 60 litres can be sparkling wine)
» 20 litres of fortified wine (such as port or sherry)

MONEY

Italy is one of 17 European countries that have adopted the euro as their official currency. Euro notes and coins were introduced in January 2002, replacing the former currency, the lira.

LOST/STOLEN CREDIT CARDS	
American Express	06 72 282
Diners Club	800 864064
CartaSi, including MasterCard and Visa	
	800 151616
MasterCard	800 819014
Visa	800 819014

BEFORE YOU GO

» It's advisable to use a combination of cash, travellers' cheques and credit cards, rather than relying on one means of payment during your trip.

» Check with your bank and/or credit card company that you can withdraw cash from ATMs. Also check what fee will be charged and what number you should call if your card is lost or stolen.

» Notify your credit card company that you will be using your card abroad. Some place blocks on use overseas for security reasons.

» Remember to keep a separate note of your travellers' cheque numbers, with a note of the number to call if they are stolen.

EXCHANGE RATES

» The euro exchange rate for visitors is subject to daily fluctuation. For up-to-date rates for a wide range of currencies, visit www.oanda.com.

CREDIT CARDS

» Italians have traditionally used cash, but this is changing and credit cards are now more widely accepted, but not for small sums. Look for the credit card symbols in the shop window or check with the staff.

» Food bills are usually paid in cash. Indeed, market traders and many smaller establishments will often only take cash.

TRAVELLERS' CHEQUES

» Travellers' cheques are accepted almost everywhere. For the best exchange rates, take travellers' cheques in euros, pounds sterling or US dollars.

» There is a branch of Thomas Cook at Piazza Barberini, and a branch of American Express in Piazza di Spagna. They will cash travellers'

cheques issued by their company without charging commission.

LOST AND STOLEN CARDS AND TRAVELLERS' CHEQUES

» If your credit card or bank card is stolen, report it to the police and the appropriate emergency number. All are open 24 hours a day and have English-speaking staff.

» If your travellers' cheques are stolen, notify the police, then follow the instructions given with the cheques. You can contact the Rome office of American Express or Thomas Cook, or telephone the following toll-free numbers:
– For American Express travellers' cheques, call 800 872000; 914912
– For Thomas Cook travellers' cheques, call 800 872050

ATMS

» Cash machines, called *Bancomats* in Italy, are plentiful in Rome, and many are accessible 24 hours a day.

» Most ATMs have instructions in English (and other languages) as well as Italian.

» Check with your bank before leaving home that you will be able to access your account from Italy.

BANKS

» There is no shortage of banks in Rome, most of which have cash machines and exchange facilities, although there are often long queues for this as they offer the best rates.

» Banks are usually open from 8.30 until 1 or 1.30, and again for an hour or so in the afternoon. Some now open on Saturdays.

BUREAUX DE CHANGE

» There are bureaux de change (cambio) all over the city, usually open throughout the day until around 7.30. They often offer 'commission-free' exchanges but the exchange rates are not usually as good as those from banks.

DISCOUNTS

» EU citizens who are over 65 can often get free or discounted admission to museums and galleries—use your passport or driver's licence as proof of age.

» Children's admission charges are usually available up to 18 years of age, and reductions on the full adult rate are sometimes made for 18–26 year olds.

» Students sometimes qualify for discounts. You should apply for an International Student Identification Card (ISIC, ▷ 49).

» Sometimes these discounts are available only for European citizens.

WIRING MONEY

» Wiring money is a lengthy process and the bureaucracy involved means that it is probably not worthwhile unless you are planning to be in Rome for a while.

» Ask your bank at home for a list of affiliated banks. You can get money wired to any bank from home, but if your bank already has a connection with certain banks in Italy, it will make the process a lot easier.

» If you have a bank account in Italy and at home, you can transfer money directly if both banks are part of the Swift system of international transfers. Again, it takes about 5–7 days, if not longer.

» Always ask for a separate letter, telex or fax to be sent to Swift, confirming that the money has been sent. It can take up to a week for the money to transfer.

» American Express, Moneygram and Western Union Money Transfers are faster from the US, but more expensive. Citibank has a service where you can transfer money for a flat fee to anywhere in the world.

TAX REFUNDS

» Sales tax, known as IVA, is added to all goods and services in Italy.

» Visitors from non-EU countries are entitled to reimbursement of the tax paid on major purchases.

» The store must provide an invoice (una fattura), itemizing all goods, the price paid for them and the tax charged, as well as the full address of the vendor and the purchaser.

» The goods must be taken out of the EU within three months of the date of purchase.

» When leaving Italy, present the fattura to customs for stamping. You may need to show the goods, so make sure they are easy to reach.

» When you get home, send the stamped receipt to the shop. Your refund will either be made by cheque or directly back to your credit card account.

10 EVERYDAY ITEMS AND HOW MUCH THEY COST	
Takeaway sandwich	€3–€6
Bottle of water	€1
Cup of coffee (at bar/seated)	€1/€4
Beer—half a litre (at bar/seated)	€3.50/€8 plus
Glass of house wine (at bar/seated)	€1/€5
Soft drink	€1
Daily newspaper (Italian)	€1.20
20 cigarettes	€3.60–€4.40
Ice cream (takeaway)	€2.50
Litre of petrol (gasoline)	€1.13–€1.25

TIPPING

Italians do not tip heavily. Service is often included in your hotel or restaurant bill, although a little extra is appreciated. As a general guide:

Pizzerias/trattorias:	round up to the nearest euro
Smart restaurants:	10%
Bar service:	up to €0.25, or 5–10% for table service
Taxis:	round up to nearest €0.50
Porters:	€0.50–€1 per bag
Chambermaids:	€0.50–€1 per day
Cloakroom attendants:	€0.50
Toilets:	€0.25

BANCA DI ROMA

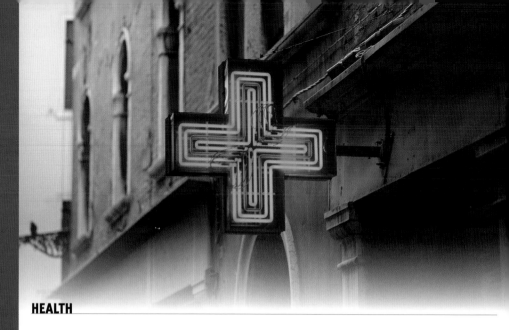

HEALTH

Visitors from many countries are entitled to free or reduced-cost emergency health treatment through Italy's national health system, both from doctors and hospitals.

For an ambulance,

Call 118

BEFORE YOU GO

» No vaccinations are required, but it is a good idea to check when you last had a tetanus injection and, if more than 10 years ago, have a booster before you travel.

» Italy has a standard agreement with other EU countries entitling EU citizens to a certain amount of free health care, including hospital treatment. In the UK, you should obtain a European Health Insurance Card (EHIC) before you leave home (▷ 249).

» If you will need treatment for a pre-existing condition while you are away, such as injections, you should apply to your department of health for an E112.

» Despite this reciprocal health-care arrangement for EU citizens, you are strongly advised to take out travel insurance. For non-EU visitors this is essential.

» Visitors from the US and Canada may find that their existing health policy covers them while they are abroad. Check with your insurance company before you travel, and remember to bring your policy identification card.

» Check with your doctor or pharmacist for the generic chemical name of any prescription drugs you need, in case you have to replace them while you are away. The brand name will often change from country to country.

» It is a good idea to take photocopies of all important documents, such as travel insurance and your EHIC (for EU citizens), which should be kept separate from the originals. You could scan the photocopies, and send them to an email address that can be accessed anywhere in the world.

HOW TO GET A DOCTOR (UN MEDICO)

» To get in touch with a doctor, it's best to ask at your hotel reception.

FOR EMERGENCY TREATMENT

If you need emergency treatment, you can go directly to the *pronto soccorso* (casualty department or emergency room) at the following hospitals:

Bambino Gesù (children's hospital), Piazza San Onofrio 4, tel 06 68591; www.ospedalebambinogesu.it

Fatebenefratelli, Isola Tiberina, tel 06 68371; www.fatebenefratelli-isolatiberina.it

Policlinico Gemelli, Largo Agostino Gemelli 8, tel 06 30151/800 554 455; www.rm.unicatt.it

Policlinico Umberto I, Viale del Policlinico 155, tel 06 49971; www.policlinicoumberto1.it

San Camillo, Circonvallazione Gianicolense 87, tel 06 58701; www.scamilloforlanini.rm.it

San'Eugenio, Piazzale dell'Umanesimo 10 (at EUR), tel 06 51001; 06 5100 2469

San Filippo Neri, Via Martinotti 20. tel 06 33061, www.sanfilipponeri.roma.it

San Giovanni, Via dell'Amba Aradam 9, tel 06 7705 3444; www.hsangiovanni.roma.it

If you prefer to be treated at a private hospital, contact:

Salvator Mundi International Hospital, Viale delle Mura Gianicolensi 66–67, tel 800 402323; www.salvatormundi.it

There is also a group of American doctors practising at Via Ludovisi 36, 00187 (tel 06 488 4143).

HOW TO GET TREATMENT WITH YOUR EHIC

» If you are taken ill while you are away, take your EHIC to the Unità Sanitaria Locale (USL) office (ask your hotel reception or consult the *Pagine Gialle*, *Yellow Pages*; www.paginegialle.it), who will give you a certificate of entitlement. Take this to any doctor or dentist on the USL list for free treatment.

» If you are referred to a hospital, you will be given a certificate that entitles you to free treatment. If you go to a hospital without being referred by a doctor, you should give the EHIC to the hospital.

» If you do not have a USL certificate, you will have to pay for medical treatment and may have difficulty getting the money back afterwards, and then probably only a partial refund.

» If you are charged in full for medicines, keep the receipts—you will not get a refund without them.

» It is advisable to carry a photocopy of your EHIC, as some doctors and hospitals keep the card. If they do, you can request another card when you get home.

» In addition to your EHIC, make sure you have adequate medical cover as part of your travel insurance.

HOW TO GET TREATMENT WITH TRAVEL INSURANCE

» Take copies of your travel insurance documents to the doctor or hospital—they may be able to bill your insurance company direct.

» If you pay for treatment, keep all your receipts as you will need to send them to your insurers to prove that your claim is valid.

DENTISTS *(DENTISTI)*

» For emergency dental treatment with an EHIC, contact the Unità Sanitaria Locale (USL), as above.

» If you do not have an EHIC, you should contact a private dentist (ask at your hotel reception). Again, take a copy of your insurance details, and keep your receipts.

PHARMACIES *(FARMACIE)*

» Pharmacies are easily recognized by a green cross sign. They sell toiletries as well as a wide range of over-the-counter medicines.

» Pharmacists in Italy are well trained and can give advice or deal with minor ailments.

» Most pharmacies open from 8.30 to 1 and 4 until 8, but they operate a rota system so that there is at least one open at all times—there will be a list displayed in the window or published in the newspaper.

» If the pharmacy does not have the medicine that you need, try the pharmacy at the Vatican.

OPTICIANS *(OTTICHI)*

» Opticians can usually carry out minor repairs to your glasses, such as replacing screws, on the spot, for little or no charge.

» If you break one of the lenses in your glasses during your stay, these can often be replaced overnight.

» If you really cannot survive without your glasses or contact lenses, bring a copy of your prescription with you so that you can have replacements made up quickly and easily. Better still, bring spares with you.

ALTERNATIVE TREATMENTS

» You can buy homeopathic remedies at most pharmacies.

» For information on homeopathic doctors and treatments (including acupuncture), contact S. Ano, Via Tacito 7, 00186 Rome, tel 06 3600 0139 (Mon–Fri 9–8, Sat 9–1).

TAP WATER

» Yes, you can drink the water. Rome's tap water is completely safe, as is the water in the city's drinking fountains.

» However, you should look out for signs that say *acqua non potabile* (not drinking water).

SUMMER HAZARDS

» The sun can be strong between May and September, and a high-factor sun block is recommended, particularly if you have very fair skin, as are sun hats and sunglasses.

» There are few biting insects as such in Rome, but if you plan to visit the surrounding area, you might like to take an insect repellent, although insect bites are more irritating than dangerous.

HEALTHY FLYING

» Visitors to Italy from as far as the US, Australia or New Zealand may be concerned about the effect of long-haul flights on their health. The most widely publicized concern is deep vein thrombosis, or DVT. Misleadingly called 'economy class syndrome', DVT is the forming of a blood clot in the body's deep veins, particularly in the legs. The clot can move around the bloodstream and could be fatal.

» Those most at risk include the elderly, pregnant women and those using the contraceptive pill, smokers and the overweight. If you are at increased risk of DVT see your doctor before departing. Flying increases the likelihood of DVT because passengers are often seated in a cramped position for long periods of time and may become dehydrated.

To minimize risk:

Drink water (not alcohol)

Don't stay immobile for hours at a time

Stretch and exercise your legs periodically

Do wear elastic flight socks, which support veins and reduce the chances of a clot forming

Exercises

1. Ankle Rotations Lift feet off the floor. Draw a circle with the toes, moving one foot clockwise and the other counterclockwise.

2. Calf Stretches Start with heels on the floor and point feet upwards as high as you can. Then lift heels high keeping balls of feet on the floor.

3. Knee Lifts Lift leg with knee bent while contracting your thigh muscle. Then straighten leg pressing foot flat to the floor.

BASICS

ELECTRICITY

» The power supply is 240 volts.
» Plugs have two (or sometimes three) round pins. Adaptors are readily available in the city, but it is a good idea to bring one with you.
» Visitors from North America should also bring a transformer for appliances operating on 110/120 volts; again, you can find these in Rome.

LAUNDRY

Most visitors trust their laundry to their hotel, where your clothes are returned to your room and the charge (which is usually high) is added to your bill. However, there are alternatives:
» Rome's old-style cleaners *(tintorie)* are still plentiful in the city. Charges start at around €4, but check the rate for any additional services, such as pressing pleats. A *tintoria* will also provide a dry-cleaning service. There are plenty of modern laundries *(lavanderie)* in the city, too.
» Self-service launderettes are few and far between. One of the most central is Punto Blu at Via Cavour 168, tel 06 481 7857 (daily 8am–9pm).

CONVERSION CHART

FROM	TO	MULTIPLY BY
Inches	Centimetres	2.54
Centimetres	Inches	0.3937
Feet	Metres	0.3048
Metres	Feet	3.2810
Yards	Metres	0.9144
Metres	Yards	1.0940
Miles	Kilometres	1.6090
Kilometres	Miles	0.6214
Acres	Hectares	0.4047
Hectares	Acres	2.4710
Gallons	Litres	4.5460
Litres	Gallons	0.2200
Ounces	Grams	28.35
Grams	Ounces	0.0353
Pounds	Grams	453.6
Grams	Pounds	0.0022
Pounds	Kilograms	0.4536
Kilograms	Pounds	2.205
Tons	Tonnes	1.0160
Tonnes	Tons	0.9842

PLACES OF WORSHIP

Most of Rome's churches are Catholic, and Basilica di San Pietro is the most important. The Catholic churches below have services in English on Sundays. Other religions are also well represented. If your faith is not shown below, the tourist information office can advise you of your nearest place of worship.

Catholic

San Silvestro, Piazza San Silvestro 1, tel 06 679 7775
Santa Susanna, Piazza San Bernardo, tel 06 488 2748; 06 4201 4554

Jewish

Sinagoga (Synagogue), Lungotevere Cenci 9, tel 06 684 0061; www.romaebraica.it

Muslim

Moschea di Roma, Viale della Moschea, tel 06 808 2167

Protestant

St. Paul's Episcopal, Chiesa Americana di San Paolo, Via Napoli 58, tel 06 488 3339; www.stpaulsrome.it
Anglican Church of England, All Saints', Via del Babuino 153b, tel 06 3600 1881; www.allsaintsrome.org
Presbyterian Church of Scotland, Chiesa di Scozia, Via XX Settembre 7, tel 06 482 7627; www.presbyterianchurchrome.org

Orthodox

Chiesa Ortodossa Russa di Santa Caterina, Via del Lago Terrione 77, tel 06 3937 5477; www.santacaterina.org

MEASUREMENTS

» Italy uses the metric system, with all foodstuffs sold by the kilogram or litre. Italians also use the *ettogramme* (hectogram—100g or just under 4oz), usually abbreviated to *etto*.

» Fuel (gas) is sold by the litre.

» Distances are measured in kilometres.

TOILETS

» You will find public toilets at railway stations and in larger museums, but otherwise they are very few and far between. There are toilets in Piazza San Pietro, either side of the square, and others at the Colosseum.

» In other parts of Rome you will need to use the toilet in a bar or café. Although they are obliged to let you use their facilities, staff prefer you to buy something.

» Facilities can be basic. Toilet paper may or may not be provided, and sometimes there is only one toilet for both men and women.

» In some places there will be a dish for gratuities—you should tip around €0.25.

» Where separate facilities exist, make sure you recognize the difference between *signori* (men) and *signore* (women).

SMOKING

» A law prohibits smoking in all public areas—including bars and restaurants. It also covers public transport, airport buildings and public offices, such as post offices and police stations.

» Cigarettes and other tobacco products can legally be sold only in *tabacchi* (tobacconists) and only to those over 16. The stand-alone *tabacchi* are open only during normal shop hours (usually 8–1, 3.30–8), but others are attached to bars, so stay open longer.

LOCAL WAYS

» A few words of Italian will always go down well (▷ 278–283), even if you can only manage to say hello and goodbye.

» Italians tend to use please and thank you less frequently than other nationalities.

» Use *buongiorno* as a greeting, up to midday, and *buonasera* in the afternoon and evening.

» Show respect and dress appropriately when visiting places of worship. Cover your shoulders and knees. St. Peter's in particular has a strict dress and conduct code.

» Don't intrude on religious services unless you wish to take part.

» Always check before taking photographs in churches and museums, and never use a flash on paintings, frescoes or mosaics.

» Italians tend to drink alcohol only with meals, and public drunkenness is frowned upon.

» In cafés, never pay bar prices and then try to use the tables.

» If you only want a one-course meal, eat in a pizzeria. It's considered bad form to eat fewer than two courses in a restaurant.

» Be polite but assertive when waiting to be served: It may look disorganized, but everyone knows who is in front of them (▷ 13).

VISITING ROME WITH CHILDREN

» Children are welcomed at most restaurants. Although children's menus are rare in the city's restaurant's, most places will serve up small portions, and will often produce simple pasta or pizza.

» Disposable nappies (diapers) and baby foods are available in many food shops, but changing facilities are hard to find. Museums and restaurants with the most modern facilities are your best option.

» There is a lack of public toilets, and most will not be as clean as you might like. Always carry tissues or wipes, as some establishments do not supply toilet paper.

» Rome has few attractions specifically aimed at children, many of whom will get bored visiting museums and galleries. As a compromise, look out for things that will interest your child, such as animals in paintings or sculptures.

» Admission to most of Rome's museums and galleries is free for under-18s. Where there is a charge, it is usually reduced for children.

» Children under the age of 10 travel free on Rome's public transport system. Some of Rome's metro stations are not accessible with prams (strollers).

» See page 267 for suggested attractions for children.

VISITORS WITH DISABILITIES

» Wheelchair access in Rome is improving, but very slowly. Check with individual establishments what their access is like. The narrow, cobbled streets and lack of pavements can prove difficult for people with mobility issues.

» All the major hotels, as well as the newer ones, should have wheelchair access. In older buildings, it is not always possible to make the changes needed, and you should contact the individual hotels to ask about your specific needs.

» Facilities on Rome's public transport system have improved, and around half the stations are now accessible by wheelchairs. Most new buses have ramps that can be lowered for access.

» See page 54 for more information.

USEFUL CONTACTS FOR VISITORS WITH DISABILITIES

CO.IN Sociale
www.coinsociale.it (English and Italian)
Useful information on accessible sights. Publishes guides, organizes guided tours; mini-bus available for excursions and transfers.
✉ Via Enrico Giglioli 54a, Rome ☎ 06 2326 9231

SATH (Society for Accessible Travel and Hospitality)
www.sath.org
Lots of tips on how to travel with mobility or visual impairment.
✉ 347 Fifth Avenue, Suite 605, New York NY10016 ☎ 212/447-7284

Tourism for All
www.tourismforall.org.uk
Publications and information on accessibility and tourism.
✉ c/o Vitalise, Shap Road Industrial Estate, Kendal, Cumbria LA9 6NZ ☎ 0845 124 9971

FINDING HELP

PERSONAL SECURITY

Rome is basically a safe city and instances of serious crime against visitors are rare. The main problems for visitors are likely to be pickpockets or bag snatchers. By taking a few sensible precautions, you can minimize the risk of becoming a victim.

» Never carry money or valuables in your back pocket—always keep them secure in a money belt, pouch or something similar.

» Don't flaunt your valuables.

» Never put your camera or bag down on a café table, where it could be snatched.

» Be wary of groups of children who approach you. Often one child will create a diversion while another steals from your pocket or bag.

» Carry bags or cameras on your side that is away from the road, to minimize the risk from bag snatchers on scooters.

» Keep a close eye on your possessions while on crowded buses or metros, particularly in areas popular with visitors.

» Leave valuable jewellery in the hotel safe.

» Wear handbags across your body to prevent them being snatched.

» Don't use your date of birth as the code for a hotel safe. It is on your passport and your hotel registration.

» After dark, avoid parks, the area around Termini train station and the edge of Trastevere.

» You should report any theft to a police station, where you will need to make a statement. Although it is unlikely that you will get your belongings back, you will need the statement *(denuncia)* to make a claim on your insurance.

» The main police station is Questura, Via San Vitale 15 (tel 06 46861).

LOST PROPERTY

» For items lost on public transport or in public places contact the municipal police lost property office, Reparto Oggetti Rinvenuti, at Circonvallazione Ostiense 191

(tel 06 6769 3214). It is open Mon–Fri 8.30–1 in July and August, and Mon–Wed, Fri 8.30–1, Thu 8.30–5 at other times.

» For anything lost on any FS trains, try the office on platform 24 of Termini (daily 7am–midnight, tel 06 4782 5543).

» If you wish to make an insurance claim, you will need to report the loss to the police to get a statement *(denuncia)*.

» If your passport is lost or stolen, report it to the police and your embassy (see below).

» If your credit card or travellers' cheques are lost or stolen, report them to the issuing company immediately (▷ 250).

WHAT TO DO IF YOU ARE ARRESTED

If you are taken into custody by the police, you could be held for up to 48 hours without appearing before a magistrate. You can also be interviewed without a lawyer present. You do, however, have the right to contact your consul, who is based at your country's embassy.

Your consul will not be able to get you released, but they can put you in touch with English-speaking lawyers and interpreters, and contact your family on your behalf.

WHAT TO DO IF YOU LOSE YOUR PASSPORT

If you lose your passport, contact your embassy in Rome. It helps if

you know your passport number, so either keep a note of it or carry a photocopy of the information page separately from your passport. Alternatively, you could scan the page and email it to a web-based account that can be accessed anywhere.

POLICE

There are three branches of the police in Italy, any of whom should be able to help you if you find yourself in difficulty.

» The *carabinieri* are military police, easily recognizable by the white sash they wear across their bodies. They deal with general crime, including drug control.

» The *polizia* is the state police force, who wear blue uniforms. Like the *carabinieri*, they deal with general crime, and if you are unfortunate enough to be robbed (or worse), they are the ones you will need to see.

» The *vigili urbani,* who wear dark blue uniforms and white hats, are traffic police.

EMERGENCY NUMBERS	
Police	113
Carabinieri	112
Ambulance	118
Fire brigade	115
Red Cross	800 166 666
Police HQ (Questura)	06 46861
Samaritans	800 860 022
(English-speaking volunteers available 1–10pm)	

CONTACTING YOUR EMBASSY	
American Embassy	Via Vittorio Veneto 121, 00187, tel 06 46741; www.usis.it or http://rome.usembassy.gov
Australian Embassy	Via Antonio Bosio 5, 00161, tel 06 852721; www.italy.embassy.gov.au
British Embassy	Via XX Settembre 80a, 00187, tel 06 4220 0001; www.fco.gov.uk
Canadian Embassy	Via Salaria 243, 00199 (consular section Via Zara 30, 00198), tel 06 85444 2911; www.canada.it
Irish Embassy	Piazza del Campitelli 3, 00186, tel 06 697 9121; www.embassyofireland.it
New Zealand Embassy	Via Clitunno 4, 00198, tel 06 853 7501; www.nzembassy.com
South African Embassy	Via Tanaro 14, 00198, tel 06 852541; www.sudafrica.it

USEFUL NUMBERS	
Operator	170
Post/telegram enquiries	80 31 60
Time	4161
Italian directory enquiries	12
International directory enquiries	170

COUNTRY CODES FROM ITALY

To call abroad from Italy, first dial 00, followed by your country code (see below), the area code (sometimes minus the first zero) and then the telephone number.

Australia	61
Belgium	32
Canada	1
France	33
Germany	49
Ireland	353
Netherlands	31
New Zealand	64
Spain	34
UK	44
US	1

To call Italy from home, the country code is 39: You need to keep the zero of the code (but drop the zero for Italian mobiles).

COMMUNICATION
TELEPHONES
Call Charges
» There are two call bands for telephone charges. Peak time is Mon–Fri 8am–6.30pm, and Sat 8am–1pm; all other times are off peak. The same call bands now apply for international calls.

PAYING FOR CALLS
Public telephones
» Most public payphones are operated by the partly privatized Telecom Italia, though you may find payphones operated by smaller private companies, particularly at airports and stations. Call charges are usually lower from the payphones of these companies.
» Most payphones now take phonecards, rather than cash. Telecom Italia and other phonecards are sold in denominations of €5 and €10 at tobacconists, news-stands and some bars. Tear off the top right-hand corner of the card before you use it.
» For overseas calls, buy an Interglobal Card 5 (€5), which can be

used with public, private and mobile phones. Like scratch cards, they have a hidden number.

Telefono a scatti
» There are also a number of places around Rome where you can make a metered call from a soundproofed booth, such as Fiumicino airport and Termini station. At the end of the call, you pay the cashier.
» There is no additional charge for this service, but most of these places are not open late enough to take advantage of the cheaper evening rates. The only exception is the Palazzo delle Poste at Piazza San Silvestro, which is open 24 hours.

SPECIAL PREFIXES
» The area code for Rome is 06, and you need to dial this as part of the telephone number, even if you are calling from within Rome.
» Numbers beginning 800 are free, known as *numeri verdi*, and those that start with 840 or 848 will be charged at only one unit.
» Italian mobile phone numbers start with 3, although you might still

see them written as 03, their old format (drop the zero and dial the rest of the number).

MOBILE PHONES
» Italy uses the so-called GSM 900/1800 system for mobile phones (which in Italy are known as *cellulare* or *telefonino*, or 'little telephone'). This is compatible with phones and networks in the rest of Europe, Australia and New Zealand. Note, however, that you may need to unbar your telephone for use overseas. Contact your service provider before leaving home for further details.
» Phones issued in North America use GSM 1900 and will only work in Italy if they are triband, because of the different frequency. The same goes for Japanese phones, which also use a different system.
» It can be very expensive to use your mobile (cell) phone abroad, as you will often be charged to receive calls as well as to make them. If you travel frequently, consider

which may remain open until 6.30pm.

MAIL

» Rome's once notorious postal service has greatly improved. Letters can now be sent by *posta prioritaria,* and take around three days to reach Europe, and four to eight days to reach North America.
» The postage rate for Europe is slightly higher than that for letters sent within Italy.
» You can buy postage stamps *(francobolli)* from post offices, although they are always very busy. You can also buy them from tobacconists, where there will be less of a wait.
» Registered letters or parcels are sent by *Raccomandata.* The cost varies considerably, depending on the size and weight of the package.
» Mailboxes are red and have two slots: *Per la città* is for Rome, and *Tutte le altre destinazione* for everywhere else, including international destinations.
» The Vatican operates its own postal service, which is more efficient than the Roman one. There is a post office outside Basilica di San Pietro, in Piazza San Pietro, where you can buy stamps, and there is a post box outside. Both are on the left as you face the basilica.
» Italian stamps are not valid in Vatican City, and vice versa.

POSTCARDS

» Postcards are classed as low priority post. However, you can send your postcard by *prioritaria.* This faster service should only take around three days in Europe, and four to eight days to non-European destinations, and is similarly priced (see table below). Otherwise delivery can be slow. It helps if you put your postcard in an envelope.

swapping your SIM card for one from an alternative provider—either a network based in Italy or a dedicated provider of international mobile phone services. You can buy these at mobile phone stores before you leave home or when you are in Rome.
» Another alternative is to rent a mobile phone while you are in Rome. Phones can be rented from HLC, Via Bettolo 6, 00195; tel 06 372 0700. The shop is open Mon–Sat 9–6, and rental charges are €10 per day or €65 per week, plus the cost of calls.
» Text messages are often a cheaper alternative to voice calls, but check the charges with your service provider.
» Remember to add the international dialling code to the numbers you wish to call at home. Add 00 and the international country code (▷ 257).

INTERNET ACCESS

» Much of central Rome is covered by WiFi hotspots sponsored by the city council. You will need to register using your mobile phone number, then log on; access is free (www.romawireless.com). In addition, many hotels have built-in dataports, and even budget places will allow you to plug into their phone systems. Download speeds are excellent.

COLLECT OR CREDIT CARD CALLS

» To make collect calls go through the operator on 170. For credit card calls you will need to call the operator in the country you are calling:

Australia (OPTUS)	800 172 611
Australia (TELSTRA)	800 172 601
Canada	800 218 800
Ireland	800 172 256
New Zealand	800 172 641
UK	800 172 442
USA (AT&T)	800 172 444
USA (MCI)	800 905 825
USA (SPRINT)	800 172 405

» There are many internet cafés in the city; try EasyEverything (Via Barberini 2; daily 8am–2am; €2 per hour; 250 terminals). Email accounts such as Hotmail, gmail and Yahoo! are easily accessible in Rome.
» Stations and airports have public internet points, which you can pay for with a normal phonecard.

POST OFFICES

» The main post office is the Ufficio Postale Centrale at Piazza San Silvestro 19, 00187 (tel 80 31 60; www.poste.it). It is open Mon–Fri 9–6 and Sat 9–2.
» The city's other post offices open Mon–Fri 8.25–2 or 2.30 and Sat 8.25–noon. The central post offices also offer a currency exchange,

POSTAGE RATES

Posta Prioritaria	Letter (under 20g)	Letter (20g–50g)	Letter (50–100g)	Delivery time
Europe	€0.52	€0.93	€1.14	3 days
North America, Africa, Asia	€0.65	€1.03	€1.45	4–8 days
Australia, New Zealand, Oceania	€0.62	€1.55	€1.55	4–8 days

OPENING TIMES AND TICKETS

PUBLIC HOLIDAYS

Shops and banks generally close on public holidays, and roads and railways are usually very busy. However, with the exception of Labour Day, Assumption and Christmas Day, most bars and restaurants will still be open. There is a limited public transport service on Labour Day and the afternoon of Christmas Day.

If a public holiday falls on a weekend, it is not celebrated on the next working day. However, if the holiday falls on a Tuesday or Thursday, many people take a day's holiday to create a long weekend.

SHOPS

Traditionally, shops open between 8 and 9, closing for lunch at around 1. They reopen at 3.30 or 4 and close at 8. Most are closed all day Sunday plus Monday morning.

However, Rome's shops are increasingly staying open all day—look for the sign *orario continuato*.

BANKS

These open Mon–Fri 8.30–1.30. Some larger branches might open on Saturday.

POST OFFICES

Post office opening times vary, but they usually open between 8 and 8.30 and close at 2.

DOCTORS AND PHARMACIES

Pharmacies are usually open the same hours as shops, but take it in turns to stay open longer hours. Look for the list posted in the window for the nearest pharmacy that will be open.

MUSEUMS AND GALLERIES

Opening times for museums and galleries vary greatly. Some are open all day, while others close at lunchtime. Many close one day each week, usually Monday. See individual entries or contact the museum or gallery concerned for the most up-to-date information.

CHURCHES

Most churches open early in the morning for Mass, often around 7am. They close at lunchtime, then reopen between 4pm and 7pm. Some of the larger churches are open all day, and some are closed to non-worshippers during services. For the most up-to-date information contact the church to check.

CAFÉS AND BARS

The hours kept by Rome's cafés and bars vary considerably from place to place and according to the season. Some open for breakfast, others in time for lunch and some only in the evenings. Bars usually close at midnight or later.

RESTAURANTS

Restaurants that serve lunch open at around 12.30 and usually close during the afternoon. They reopen, along with those that serve only dinner, sometime after 7 and stay open late. Pizzerias are usually open only in the evening.

Many restaurants close for the whole of August—look for the sign *chiuso per ferie*.

TICKETS

Most churches do not charge admission (although often expect donations). Sometimes a charge is made at churches with a special architectural feature or work of art.

Most establishments operate separately, each charging their own admission fee. The exceptions are the Roma Archeologica Card, which is valid for seven days and gives admission to the Colosseo, Crypta Balbi, Foro Romano and Palatino, Terme di Caracalla, Terme di Diocleziano, Palazzo Altemps, Palazzo Massimo alle Terme, Villa dei Quintili and the tomb of Cecilia Metella, offering considerable reductions on individual prices; and the Museum Card, which is valid for three days and covers Palazzo Altemps, Palazzo Massimo alle Terme, Crypta Balbi and Terme di Diocleziano. The cards cost €27.50 and €23 (concessions €12)

respectively, and are available from any of the participating sights.

Also available is the similar Roma Pass (www.romapass.it). Valid for three days, it allows discounted entry to many museums, and free use of most bus and metro services. The cost is €25.

You can pre-book tickets for key museums and galleries through an agency. These charge a booking fee on top of the admission price.

ROMAN HOLIDAYS	
1 Jan	New Year's Day
6 Jan	Epiphany
Mar/Apr	Easter Monday
25 Apr	Liberation Day
1 May	Labour Day
2 Jun	Republic Day
29 Jun	St. Peter and St. Paul Day (or St. Peter's Day)
15 Aug	Assumption of the Virgin (Ferragosto)
1 Nov	All Saints' Day
8 Dec	Feast of the Immaculate Conception
25 Dec	Christmas Day
26 Dec	Santo Stefano

TICKET AGENCIES
Ticketclic (www.ticketclic.it)
Colosseo
Crypta Balbi
Musei Capitolini
Palazzo Altemps
Palazzo Massimo alle Terme
Terme di Caracalla
Terme di Diocleziano
Villa Adriana (Tivoli)
Ticketeria (www.ticketeria.it)
Cecilia Metella (Via Appia Antica)
Galleria Borghese
Galleria Corsini
Galleria Spada
Museo Etrusco (at Tarquinia)
Museo Nazionale Etrusco
Necropoli dei Monterozzi (at Tarquinia)
Palazzo Barberini
Palazzo Venezia
Strumenti Musicali
Villa Gregoriana (Tivoli)

TOURIST OFFICES

The city's main tourist office is at Via Parigi 5, near Terme di Diocleziano (tel 06 48891; daily 9–7.30). The best contacts for visitor information are the call centre (tel 06 0608) and the official websites (www.060608.it and www.romaturismo.it).

There are smaller information points (daily 9.30–6.30 or 7) in green pagodas dotted around the city, with maps and other information (in English):

» Aeroporto Ciampino (in baggage collection area).
» Aeroporto Leonardo da Vinci (in arrivals, Terminal B).
» Stazione Termini, platform 24.
» Palazzo delle Esposizioni, Via Nazionale.
» Piazza delle Cinque Lune, near Piazza Navona.

» Piazza Pia, near Castel Sant'Angelo.
» Piazza Sonnino, Trastevere.
» Via dell'Olmata, near Santa Maria Maggiore.
» Piazza dei Cinquecento, outside Termini.

» Via Marco Minghetti, near Trevi Fountain.
» Via San Pietro (left-hand side of Basilica's facade, for information on St. Peter's; tel 06 6988 2019).

ITALIAN GOVERNMENT TOURIST OFFICES

AUSTRALIA	UK
Level 4, 46 Market Street, NSW 2000 Sydney, tel 02 9262 1666; www.italiantourism.com.au	1 Princes Street, London W1B 2AY, tel 02 7408 1254; www.enit.it

CANADA	US
175 Bloor Street East, Suite 907 South Tower, Toronto, Ontario M4W 3R8, tel 416 925-4882, fax 416 925-4799; www.italiantourism.com	630 Fifth Avenue, Suite 1565, New York NY 10111, tel 212 245-5618, fax 212 586-9249; www.italiantourism.com Also offices in Chicago and Los Angeles

USEFUL WEBSITES

TOURISM

www.romaturismo.it
The city's official website is packed with information, such as hotel and restaurant listings, itineraries and events. You can also request brochures. In English and Italian.

www.enjoyrome.com
This independent website is great for organized tours, accommodation and information on life in Rome. In English only.

www.vatican.va
Information on the Vatican state. In six languages, including English.

www.romaclick.com
An English-language website good for booking online accommodation.

www.060608.it
Comprehensive, city-run site in English and Italian covering hospitality, transport, sightseeing and entertainment.

www.wantedinrome.com
Site aimed at resident and visiting foreigners with excellent listings, accommodation and restaurant guide and what's on information.

TRANSPORT

www.atac.roma.it
Details of routes, fares and tickets for buses, trams and the metro. In English and Italian.

www.trenitalia.it
Information on getting around the country by Italy's train service. In English and Italian.

www.adr.it
Airport services and flight information for Rome's airports.

NEWS

www.bbc.co.uk
For world, regional and UK news, plus weather reports. You can also listen to BBC radio stations via the website.

KEY SIGHTS QUICK WEBSITE FINDER

SIGHT	WEBSITE	PAGE
Basilica di San Pietro	www.vatican.va	210–215
Casa di Goethe	www.casadigoethe.it	61
Colosseo	www.pierreci.it	142–144
Foro Romano	www.capitolium.org	146–151
Galleria Borghese	www.galleriaborghese.it	64–69
Mercati di Traiano	www.mercatiditraiano.it	152–153
Musei Capitolini	www.museicapitolini.org	154–158
Musei Vaticani	www.vatican.va	218–223
Palazzo Barberini	www.galleriaborghese.it	71
Palazzo Corsini	www.galleriaborghese.it	192
Palazzo-Galleria Doria Pamphilj	www.dopart.it	107
Palazzo del Quirinale	www.quirinale.it	70
Palazzo Spada	www.galleriaborghese.it	110
San Carlo alle Quattro Fontane	www.sancarlino-borromini.it	77
Santa Maria della Concezione	www.cappucciniviaveneto.it	77
Santa Maria sopra Minerva	www.basilicaminerva.it	117
Villa Farnesina	www.villafarnesina.it	193
Villa Medici	www.villamedici.it	79

MEDIA

TELEVISION

» Italy has three state-run television stations (RAI-1, -2 and -3), three stations run by Berlusconi's Mediaset group (Italia Uno, Rete Quattro and Canale Cinque), plus a number of local channels. RAI-3 has an international news programme, which includes an English-language section. It starts at 1.15am.

» Italian television shows are almost always accompanied by scantily-clad women. Moves are underway to change this, with a view to portraying a more respectful image of women, but with the role of 'game show girl' as popular as ever, how successful this will be remains to be seen.

» Most hotels, from mid-range upwards, have satellite television, which means you can keep up to date with the news on BBC World or CNN.

RADIO

» RAI Radio 1, 2 and 3 (89.7FM, 91.7FM and 93.7FM respectively), the state-run stations, have a mixture of light music, chat shows and news—all in Italian.

» Radio Vaticano (93.3FM) broadcasts news in a number of languages. There are English-language broadcasts daily at 5am, 4.15pm and 7.50pm.

» Some of the local radio stations play American and British music, so if you are feeling homesick, tune into Radio Centro Suono (101.3FM), which plays music from the 1960s up to the present day. Radio Antenna 1 (107.1FM) plays American and British hits from the 1970s, 80s and early 90s. For light classical music, try 100.3FM, or if Latin-American rhythms are your thing, tune into Radio Mambo (106.85FM).

» The BBC World Service frequencies for Rome are MHz 6.195, 9.410, 12.095, 15.485 and 17.640. Check online at www.bbc.co.uk/worldservice for schedules. You can also listen to programmes directly via the website.

NEWSPAPERS

English-language Newspapers

» You can often buy major international newspapers on the day of publication, from about 2pm, at larger news-stands. Titles include *The Times*, *The Guardian*, *The Financial Times*, *The New York Times*, *The Wall Street Journal* and the *International Herald Tribune*.

Italian-language Newspapers

» *Il Messaggero* is the local paper, popular with Romans. *La Repubblica*, *Corriere della Sera*, *La Stampa* and *Il Sole/24 Ore* are the main national dailies. *La Repubblica* and *Corriere della Sera* both have local editions for Rome. *La Repubblica* has a good what's-on section on Thursdays and a glossy magazine supplement on Saturdays called *La Repubblica delle Donne*, with excellent articles reflecting all aspects of Italian life and society.

» Two daily sports papers are published in Italy: *La Gazzetta dello Sport* and the *Corriere dello Sport*, both dominated by football and motorsport news. *La Gazzetta dello Sport* also publishes a supplement on Saturdays called *Sport Week*, which tends to cover a wider range of sports, with colour photos and features on the week's events.

MAGAZINES

» English-speakers will see many familiar-looking magazines on the news-stands in the city. Italian versions of well-known publications such as *Vogue* and *Marie Claire* are very popular.

» Many Italian magazines on sale in Rome are adorned with pictures of scantily-clad women, but this isn't necessarily a reflection of their content (although it can be).

» English-language magazines are few and far between, but if you read a little Italian, magazines such as *Panorama* and *L'Espresso* are good for news, while *Sette* (Thursdays) and *Venerdì* (Fridays) are colour supplements with lots of pictures.

» *Roma C'è* (Fridays) has an English-language section. *Wanted in Rome* is aimed at resident English-speakers, but also has what's-on listings (every other Tuesday).

BOOKS, FILMS AND MAPS
BOOKS

There are any number of books dealing with Rome's long and eventful history. By far the most in-depth is Edward Gibbon's 19th-century *The History of the Decline and Fall of the Roman Empire*, published in six volumes (although abridged versions are available from publishers such as Penguin). *The Battle for Rome*, by Robert Katz, recounts the German occupation of Rome and the fall of Mussolini.

For history in novel form, try *I, Claudius*, by Robert Graves, or Irvine Stone's *The Agony and the Ecstasy*. More light-hearted is Lindsey Davis' series of detective stories, based around the Roman Empire, but mostly set in Rome.

Anyone interested in Italian politics should read *The Dark Heart of Italy* by Tobias Jones, which discusses Berlusconi's administration (▷ 18).

John Varriano's *Rome: A Literary Companion* is full of quotes from major writers who spent time in Rome. Another good companion is *City Secrets Rome*, by Robert Kahn, which gives you an insight into how modern-day Romans see their city.

For younger readers, *The Rotten Romans*, part of the popular Horrible Histories series, takes a more light-hearted look at this facinating period of history. The book is aimed at 9–12-year olds.

Above *Second-hand books for sale*
Opposite *Matt Damon and Cate Blanchett in the 1999 film* The Talented Mr. Ripley

FILMS

Mussolini's Cinecittà studios didn't really come into their own until after World War II, when they began to make neo-realist films, like *Ladri di Biciclette (Bicycle Thieves —1948)*. A winner of both a BAFTA and a Golden Globe, it was shot entirely in Rome, using non-actors.

The 1950s saw a resurgence in film-making in Rome, with the acclaimed *Roman Holiday* (1953), starring Audrey Hepburn. You'll recognize many of the landmarks she and Gregory Peck visit, including the Bocca della Verità (▷ 166). *Three Coins in the Fountain* (1954) followed, and although it now seems dated, it's still a great travelogue for Rome. Probably the most famous image of Rome is Anita Ekberg's dip in the Trevi Fountain in *La Dolce Vita* (1960), which was also filmed in Tivoli and Viterbo (▷ 240–241 and 244–245).

The Agony and the Ecstasy (1965) is one of many historical epics set in Rome, with Charlton Heston as a tortured Michelangelo painting the Sistine Chapel's ceiling for Julius II (Rex Harrison).

Roma (1972) is a typical piece of Felliniesque film-making. This plotless film shows Fellini's Rome, which he narrates in the English-language version.

The Talented Mr. Ripley (1999) was filmed all over Italy, including Rome, and *Gladiator* (2000) is set, in part, in Rome. More recently, *Angels and Demons* (2009) and *The American* (2010), starring George Clooney, were shot in Rome.

MAPS

There is a central street map at the back of this guide (▷ Maps section), and a metro and tram map on the inside back cover and in the On the Move section (▷ 47). In Rome, all the tourist information points have free street maps and there are free metro and bus maps available from ATAC kiosks. There is an ATAC kiosk outside Termini, on Piazza dei Cinquecento.

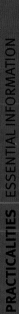

WHAT TO DO

SHOPPING

The Eternal City has plenty of stores to keep even the most ardent shopper busy. More and more shops are now open all day from 9.30am to 8pm. Many are also open on Sunday, often from 11am to 1pm and 4pm to 7.30pm.

OPENING TIMES

Traditionally, shops have closed for lunch and the siesta from 1pm to 4pm, but this is becoming less common. During winter, shops tend to open earlier in the afternoon, while in summer to avoid the heat 5pm is more usual. We have indicated where shops open outside these hours.

August is holiday time in Rome, when many small businesses take their two-week annual break, and almost everything closes around *Ferragosto*, the public holiday on 15 August. Many shops are also closed on Monday mornings, and food stores tend to close on Saturday afternoons in summer and Thursday afternoons in winter.

CREDIT CARDS

Although Italy is traditionally a cash society, credit cards are widely accepted in Rome, with the main exceptions of small grocery shops and delicatessens. You should always get a receipt *(ricevuta fiscale)*, as the law requires all shopkeepers and restaurateurs to provide this, and they (and you) can be fined if they don't. In practice, this is rare, but it's useful if you have bought high-value goods and need proof for customs—or if you need to make an insurance claim.

SMALL IS BEAUTIFUL

Shopping malls and department stores are in their infancy in Rome, although there are exceptions such as the popular La Rinascente (▷ 87). Small, specialized shops are the way to a Roman heart and when in Rome…

Different areas tend to specialize in different goods. The most famous designers have taken over the streets around the Piazza di Spagna, especially along the very chic Via Condotti, where starry names such as Gucci, Bulgari and Prada are clustered. Here the Italian art form of *la bella figura* — presenting yourself in the most stylish, polished way possible—is at its height. Near Piazza Navona, the Via del Governo Vecchio has less expensive independent designer boutiques, while the Via dei Giubbonari, near Campo dei Fiori, has inexpensive fashion. In stylish Rome, even inexpensive clothes tend to be good quality and well cut.

The roads down from Via Condotti have some gorgeous shoes, bags, belts and every other kind of accessory, while Via Nazionale, Via del Tritone and Via del Corso are good places to seek out beautiful, reasonably priced must-haves.

The Via Margutta is full of artists' studios, while Via dei Coronari showcases some of Rome's finest antiques. Trastevere is full of artisan workshops selling handmade jewellery and ceramics.

Near the Vatican, the Via Cola di Rienzo is fashion central, with some of the big names and all the mid-market chains, as well as newcomers from overseas, such as Mango. This is also a good place to visit some of Rome's popular delis, where you'll be in gourmet heaven.

SOUVENIRS

Pasta in every shape and size, the greenest extra virgin olive oil, *funghi porcini* (dried mushrooms), truffle oil and spices all make durable food buys to take home as gifts.

Handmade ceramics, kitchen gadgets, espresso coffee pots and individually designed cups, kettles, salt and pepper grinders—especially those with the Alessi mark—provide Italian style at its best. There is a long tradition of artisan silver- and goldsmithing in Rome. Herbalists and shops specializing in lotions and potions have tempting arrays of fragrant delicacies.

The souvenir shops around the Vatican do a healthy trade in Catholic paraphernalia. Around the tourist sights are plenty of souvenirs, from figures of gladiators to models of the Colosseo.

ENTERTAINMENT AND NIGHTLIFE

Rome is often likened to an outdoor theatre and its 'actors' have an innate sense of style. A night at the opera, a concert or the theatre is a showcase for visual display and it would be almost a sin not to dress suitably for the occasion. So, don your finery in the certainty you will not be overdressed. Whether it's a quiet drink in an atmospheric *enoteca* or dancing until dawn in a club, there's something for everyone in Rome. Choose from lounge, house, retro, electronica, cheesy Euro sounds, hip hop, R&B, speed-dating, high tech, cool sounds with attitude, hot South American, reggae—the list is endless. Most clubs don't get going until around 1am, so a visit to a couple of bars and a late pizza is the Roman way to kick off proceedings. Note that smoking is no longer allowed in any public venue.

CINEMA

Cinema is flourishing in Rome. Although foreign films tend to be dubbed into Italian, increasingly cinemas are showing them in their original version. The Nuovo Olimpia (▷ 88) often dedicates one of its screens to original-language films. The Cineporto has become one of the most popular summer festivals. Generally credit cards are not accepted at cinemas.

CLASSICAL MUSIC

For classical music, the Accademia Nazionale di Santa Cecilia (▷ 87) is the jewel in the crown. Founded in the 16th century, it attracts some of the world's best-known conductors. The winter season is held at the giant Auditorium Parco della Musica (tel 06 8024 2501 or 06 6880 1044; www.auditorium.com), in the Flaminio district of the city.

Other main companies include the Accademia Filarmonica Romana (tel 06 320 1752; www.filarmonicaromana.org), which can claim Verdi, Donizetti, Paganini and Rossini among its founders. Its varied offerings include chamber music, opera, ballet and ancient music. This Accademia uses the Teatro Olimpico (tel 06 326 5991; www.teatroolimpico.it) for Thursday and Sunday performances and also acts as a venue for many of the events in the trendy RomaEuropa Festival (tel 06 4555 3055; www.romaeuropa.net).

In the listings in this book, the opening times refer to the box office and the dates to when the season runs. Credit cards are accepted at most venues; we have stated only when they are not. Smoking is usually allowed at outdoor events.

CONCERTS

The Auditorium Parco della Musica is Rome's main venue for classical, rock and pop concerts. There are also some stunning venues that play host to international stars—such as the Villa Borghese and Ostia Antica's Roman theatre. Most smaller venues do not take credit cards.

THEATRE

The main theatres include Teatro di Roma-Argentina (▷ 125). The little Teatro Valle (▷ 125), in the remains of the Teatro di Pompei, is a theatrical jewel and is managed by the Italian Drama Board—the Ente Teatrale Italiano (ETI; www.enteteatrale.it). Also managed by the ETI, the Teatro Quirino (Via Mario Minghetti, tel 06 679 4585; www.teatroquirino.it) stages productions by well-known playwrights. There are around 80 theatres in and around the city, and there are many experimental performances to see as well as more mainstream and classical offerings.

The Teatro dell'Opera di Roma (▷ 88–89) has almost perfect acoustics. The season runs from November to June, and during the summer at different open-air venues. The resident ballet company, Corpo di Ballo, also performs at the Teatro dell'Opera and in the summer at other venues (www.operaroma.it). For contemporary ballet and modern dance try the Teatro Olimpico, Teatro Vascello (▷ 200) or Teatro

Greco (Via R. Leoncavallo 10–16, tel 06 860 7513; www.teatrogreco.it).

WHAT'S ON

For listings of what's on where, the weekly *Roma C'è* has an English-language section. *Trovaroma* appears on Thursdays (free with *La Repubblica*); it covers the week's cultural events, and has an English-language section. The monthly *WHERE Rome* magazine provides listings and some articles. It is available from many hotels and tourist information points.

TICKETS

The following agencies are useful. They usually charge a commission of about 10 per cent:
» Orbis (Piazza dell'Esquino 37, tel 06 482 7403).
» Hello Ticket (tel 06 4807 8400 or 800 907 080 toll free in Italy; www.helloticket.it).

WHERE TO GO

Campo dei Fiori is the place for posing and pubs, Trastevere bristles with bars, and the university quarter, San Lorenzo, buzzes with cheap bars and pubs. But the heart of Roman nightlife is Testaccio, a hilly area south of the Aventine Hill, out of the *centro storico*. If you're using public transport, there is a *servizio notturno* (night-bus service), identified by the letter N. It covers most of the city from midnight to 5.30am, after which normal daytime service is resumed. Traditionally revellers round off a night on the tiles with a cappuccino and fresh *cornetti caldi* (hot croissants) at one of the bars in Testaccio.

There are plenty of alternative and gay hang-outs—especially in Testaccio. The Alibi was one of the first scene-setters to put Testaccio on the club map and it's still just as popular today.

PRICES

Clubs and discobars can be expensive. In addition to the entrance fee, they often make you pay for a membership card *(tessera)*. Admission often includes one free drink, but from then on you pay full price. Prepare to wait for entry to the hottest clubs. It pays to dress up. Cool clothes, vampire garb, black leather goth style, scanty and flimsy—any number of variations are de rigueur in the hippest spots.

GAY AND LESBIAN

For more on the gay scene, pick up a copy of *Babilonia*, a monthly magazine which has comprehensive listings for the whole of Italy (€5.20 at news-stands), or log on to www.arcigay.it, Italy's foremost gay and lesbian network (Italian and English), or www.mariomieli.org, a Rome-based gay and lesbian group (Italian only).

SPORTS AND ACTIVITIES

Generally Romans prefer to watch sports rather than participate in them, and there are plenty of sporting events taking place all over the city if you want to experience the buzz of watching a live match. Highlights of the Roman sporting calendar include the Rome City Marathon in March and the Italian Open in May, one of Europe's major tennis tournaments. Lazio and Roma, Rome's two Serie A football teams, play at the Stadio Olimpico, and Italy's national rugby team usually plays at the Stadio Flaminio. Although participatory sports are not high on most people's agenda, if you do want to sweat off some of those calories head to Villa Borghese for cycling, boating and in-line skating. The city also has some excellent swimming pools.

FOOTBALL
Italy's great national passion is football, and Rome's two teams, Lazio and Roma, are hero-worshipped. Lazio play in blue and white with an eagle as the mascot, while Roma wear red and yellow with a wolf. One team plays at home almost every Sunday from September until June at the Stadio Olimpico. Tickets for big matches tend to sell out quickly, and you should expect to pay prices up to around €85. Tickets are also available from ticket agencies such as Orbis (tel 06 4620 4310).

OTHER SPORTS
There are few tennis courts in the city, but the Italian Open tennis tournament in May is a very popular, stylish event, held at the Foro Italico.

The International Horse Show comes to town in April and May at the Villa Borghese, and other equestrian events, including flat racing, steeplechases and show jumping, take place at the Ippodromo delle Capanelle (Via Appia Nuova, tel 06 718 8750).

Should you want to experience Rome on horseback you could try the Centro Ippico di Villa Borghese (Vicolo del Galoppatoio 23, tel 06 320 1667) or the Cavalieri dell'Appia Antica (Via dei Cerceni 15, tel 06 780 1214).

OTHER ACTIVITIES
As kitsch as they might sound, a stroll around the edge of the Forum, a cool drink overlooking the Colosseo, or a visit to the Fontana di Trevi, especially at moonlight, can be truly magical experiences. Don't forget to toss two coins over your shoulder to ensure your return to the Eternal City.

FOR CHILDREN

There are few attractions specifically aimed at children in Rome, but there are few other cities in the world where they can act out fantasies of chariot races, clamber over ruins or pretend to be a gladiator. And, if all else fails, there's always a delicious ice cream—the Italians are still the masters of glorious *gelato*.

FOOD
Children's menus don't really exist in Rome, but pizza and pasta are plentiful and, in all but the most expensive establishments, restaurateurs will generally give children a warm welcome; menus are easily adaptable. Rome is also the perfect place for picnics. Stock up on goodies at the Campo dei Fiori and take your picnic to the Villa Borghese gardens; on the northern side is the Bioparco zoo (▷ 83), which is always very popular with children. Alternatively, picnic on the Palatine Hill, the legendary birthplace of Rome. Here the cooler air is refreshing and the views over the Forum and Colosseo are superb.

WHAT TO SEE
The Colosseo is free for under-18s, and is probably the top attraction. Visit the Circo Massimo, the oldest and largest ancient arena where chariot races were held, as seen in *Ben Hur*. The city is positively awash with fountains—there are more than 4,000—always popular with kids. Encourage them to toss a coin into the Trevi Fountain, but don't let them take a dip as this will incur a heavy fine.

Today's celebrations are less extravagant than they were in the days of ancient Rome, but there are still many festivals and exhibitions held in the city throughout the year.

JANUARY

SAN SILVESTRO AND CAPODANNO

Crowds throng to Piazza del Popolo to see out the old year and welcome in the new with a free disco, concert and spectacular firework display. New Year's Day is a public holiday.
☒ Piazza del Popolo ☻ 31 Dec–1 Jan
☻ Flaminio ⊟ 88, 95, 117, 119, 490, 491, 495; tram 2

EPIFANIA–LA BEFANA

The Feast of the Epiphany is celebrated in a Mass said by the Pope at St. Peter's. The Romans know Epiphany better as *La Befana*—the old witch—who, according to legend, gave presents to good children and lumps of coal to bad ones. Piazza Navona is full of market stalls from mid-December to Epiphany; *La Befana* arrives in the piazza late on 5 January.
☻ 6 Jan (public holiday)
Basilica di San Pietro ☒ Piazza San Pietro ☻ Ottaviano ⊟ 46, 64, 98, 916, 982
Piazza Navona ⊟ 23, 30, 62, 64, 70, 81, 87, 116, 280, 492, 628, 810, 916

SANT'EUSEBIO ANIMAL BLESSING

The congregation of the little church of Sant'Eusebio all'Esquilino consists of animals with their doting owners, keen to get them blessed.
☒ Via Napoleone 111 ☻ 17 Jan
☻ Vittorio ⊟ 70, 71, 105; tram 5, 14

FEBRUARY–MARCH

CARNEVALE

There are street celebrations and masked revellers throughout the city during the traditional festival of *Carnevale* ('farewell to meat').
☻ Feb–Mar (the week before Lent)

MARCH

FESTA DI SANTA FRANCESCA ROMANA

Santa Francesca Romana is the patron saint of motorists. Drivers bring their cars to her church to be blessed.
☒ Eastern (Colosseo) end of the Foro Romano ☻ 9 March ☻ Colosseo ⊟ 60, 75, 85, 87, 117, 175, 810, 850

MARCH–APRIL

SETTIMANA SANTA E PASQUA

Holy Week starts with an open-air Mass in St. Peter's Square on the Saturday before Palm Sunday. On Good Friday, the Pope's Stations of the Cross (Via Crucis) and Mass take place at the Colosseum late in the evening. On Easter Sunday there is a papal blessing at St. Peter's. Easter Monday is a public holiday.
☻ Mid-Mar to mid-Apr (date varies)
Piazza del Colosseo ☻ Colosseo ⊟ 60, 75, 85, 87, 117, 175, 810, 850
Vatican ⊟ 34, 46, 64, 98, 881, 916, 982

APRIL

NATALE DI ROMA

Celebrations of Rome's official birthday focus on the torchlit Campidoglio, with spectacular firework displays.
☒ Piazza del Campidoglio ☻ 21 Apr
⊟ 44, 46, 84, 715, 780, 781, 810, 916

APRIL–MAY

FIERA D'ARTE DI VIA MARGUTTA

The street is full of art galleries that burst into life during these two open-air exhibitions.
☒ Via Margutta ☎ 06 812 3340 ☻ Late April–May (also Oct/Nov) ☻ Spagna
⊟ 88, 95, 117, 119, 628, 926; tram 2

MAY
MOSTRA DELL'ANTIQUARIATO

During the two-week-long fair, held in Via dei Coronari—the heart of the antiques trade—the street is lit with candles and shops stay open late.
✉ Via dei Coronari ☎ 06 361 2322; 06 6880 6052 🕐 May (also late Oct) 🚌 30, 40, 46, 70, 81, 87, 116

JUNE
FESTA DI SAN GIOVANNI

The Festival of St. John involves eating snails *(lumache in umido)* and roast suckling pig *(porchetta)*, plus a fair and a fireworks display in the Piazza di San Giovanni in Laterano. A candlelit procession is usually led by the Pope to the church.
✉ San Giovanni in Laterano, Piazza di San Giovanni in Laterano 🕐 24 Jun Ⓜ San Giovanni 🚌 16, 85, 87, 117, 218, 650, 850

JUNE–SEPTEMBER
ESTATE ROMANA

www.estateromana.it
Outdoor film screenings, music, ballet and theatre are among hundreds of events throughout the Roman Summer Festival in venues from parks to palazzi.
🕐 21 Jun–Sep

FESTA DI SANTI PIETRO E PAOLO

This annual festival honours Rome's patron saints, Peter and Paul. At St. Peter's there is a Mass, while at St. Paul's there is an all-night street fair outside the church.
🕐 29 Jun **Basilica di San Pietro**
✉ Piazza San Pietro Ⓜ Ottaviano 🚌 34, 46, 64, 98, 881, 916, 982
San Paolo fuori le Mura ✉ Piazzale San Paolo 1c Ⓜ Basilica di San Paolo 🚌 4, 23, 128, 761, 769, 770

JULY–AUGUST
CINEPORTO

www.cineporto.com
Films shown on two large screens have made this summer festival in the park hugely popular. There are also frequent live concerts.
✉ Parco della Farnesina, north suburbs by the Stadio Olimpico 🕐 Jul–Aug ☎ 329 448 6538

FESTIVAL EUROMEDITERRANEO

The stunning Villa Adriana (▷ 242–243), east of central Rome, is the setting for a wide range of events, from opera to drama and flamenco dancing—all with a Mediterranean character.
✉ Villa Adriana, Via di Villa Adriana ☎ 06 8190 7218 🕐 Jul–Aug 🚌 Cotral bus from metro Ponte Mammolo.

TEATRO ROMANO DI OSTIA ANTICA

Concerts and Greek and Roman classics are performed in this beautifully preserved open-air theatre, southwest of the city. Take a cushion.
✉ Scavi di Ostia Antica, Viale dei Romagnoli 117 ☎ 06 5635 8099 🕐 Mid-Jul to mid-Aug

AUGUST
FESTA DELLA MADONNA DELLA NEVE

To commemorate the legend of snow falling on the Esquiline Hill on 5 August AD352 (▷ 168), petals are showered onto the congregation attending Mass in the basilica of Santa Maria Maggiore.
✉ Basilica di Santa Maria Maggiore, Piazza Santa Maria Maggiore ☎ 06 483 195 🕐 5 Aug 🚌 16, 70, 71, 75, 105, 204, 360, 590, 649, 714; tram 5, 14

FERRAGOSTO

This is the main midsummer holiday, when just about everything in the city closes down.
🕐 15 Aug (public holiday)

SEPTEMBER–NOVEMBER
ROMAEUROPA FESTIVAL

www.romaeuropa.net
This is Rome's major arts festival, with something for every taste offered by performers of international calibre. The venues include some of Rome's most glorious monuments.
✉ Festival Office: Via XX Settembre 3 ☎ 06 422 961 🕐 Sep–Nov

NOVEMBER
OGNISSANTI

All Saints' Day, also known as Day of the Dead, is marked by Romans visiting family graves and a Mass celebrated by the Pope at the Verano cemetery.
✉ Cimitero del Verano, Piazzale del Verano 🕐 1 Nov (public holiday) 🚌 71, 163, 492; tram 3, 19

DECEMBER
FESTA DELL'IMMACOLATA CONCEZIONE

Religious service in the piazza to celebrate the Festival of the Immaculate Conception, where the focal point is the statue of the Madonna, decorated with flowers.
✉ Piazza di Spagna 🕐 8 Dec (public holiday) Ⓜ Spagna 🚌 116, 117, 119, 590

NATALE & SANTO STEFANO

During the Christmas period, ornate cribs/creches *(presepi)* decorate many of Rome's churches—the largest is in St. Peter's Square along with a towering Christmas tree. If you want to attend Midnight Mass in St. Peter's, put your request in months in advance.
✉ Prefettura Office: Piazza San Pietro ☎ 06 6988 3273 🕐 25–26 Dec (public holidays) 🚌 34, 46, 64, 98, 881, 916, 982

EATING

In Rome, prepare yourself for rich, sun-drenched tastes. More than 5,000 eateries cater for every budget and provide every kind of dining experience. The feasts of ancient Rome may have long since disappeared, but eating is so much a social way of life that it is far from uncommon to spend hours over a meal. Traditionally, many establishments are family-run, the owners priding themselves on offering fresh, home-made delicacies.

CUCINA ROMANA

The fertile countryside around Rome is rich in herbs, exquisite vegetables and pungent garlic and onions. Plump globe artichokes, fried whole in olive oil until crispy, are served to perfection by the Romans. Known as *carciofi alla giudia*, this is a typical dish of the Ghetto area, the historic heart of Rome's Jewish community. The Ghetto's long history is reflected in the Roman cuisine, *cucina romana*, and Jewish dishes in the local restaurants.

Fishy delights are plentiful, too, with a bountiful harvest of seafood from the shores just 24km (15 miles) from the city. Many of the city's starriest restaurants are temples to the best of seafood, including Quinzi e Gabrieli (▷ 130).

As in other Italian regions, pasta is still the mainstay of the Roman meal. *Spaghetti alle vongole* (with clams and tomatoes) is one of the best-known Roman pasta dishes, while *spaghetti alla carbonara*, made with cured bacon, egg yolk and cheese, is equally famous and Roman to the core. The ever-popular pizza comes in every variety, from the authentic thin, crisp *pizza romana* to the thicker, puffier Neapolitan version.

Traditional *cucina romana* uses the often discarded parts of animals and originates from the area of Testaccio, near the old slaughterhouse where many locals once worked. The butchers were paid partly in cash, partly in offal—known as the fifth quarter—

including liver, heart, intestines and brains. Slow cooking with herbs and spices transformed these cuts into high-protein, low-cost dishes that can still be found in many of Rome's top restaurants today. *Coda alla vaccinara*, literally 'tail in the style of the slaughterhouse worker', is a famous signature dish of braised oxtail that was created at Rome's oldest and most famous restaurant in Testaccio, Checchino dal 1887.

WHEN TO EAT

If you are eating breakfast in a bar, as many Romans do, you will find that most open at around 7–7.30am for cappuccino and a *cornetto* (croissant). In hotels, breakfast usually starts at 8am, and includes cereal, cold meat and cheeses.

Restaurants open for lunch at 12.30 or 1pm, and serve until around 3pm. Romans generally eat dinner late, so many establishments don't open for evening meals until 8pm, although you will find some that open earlier. Some places, especially cafés and bars, stay open all day.

WHERE TO EAT

Perhaps confusingly, there are several different types of eating establishment in Rome. A *ristorante* tends to be the most expensive, with pristine table linen and equally pristine waiters. The *trattoria* is less formal, less expensive and often still family-run. An *osteria* or *hostaria* can be basic, sometimes with paper tablecloths and no written menu, but can often serve some of the best food in the city. Interestingly, some of Rome's trendiest and most glamorous establishments have adopted the name *osteria*, echoing the shabby-chic fashion. A *rosticceria* or *tavola calda* is a fast-food outlet serving mostly foods that you can eat then and there or take away for a picnic. A take-out pizzeria is advertised as *pizzeria rustica* or *a taglio* (by the slice). If you want to sit down to enjoy your pizza, always look for the sign *pizzeria forno a legno* to make sure that it is traditionally cooked in a wood-fired brick oven.

WHAT'S ON THE MENU

A traditional full meal begins with *antipasti* (starters/hors d'oeuvres). This is followed by a *primo*—a first course of pasta. This could be *spaghetti alle vongole*, which is best on Tuesdays and Fridays when the clams are guaranteed to be fresh, or *gnocchi alla romana*, little dumplings made in the traditional Roman way in different sauces—Thursday is gnocchi day. The second course, *secondo*, is usually a meat, fish or vegetarian dish, accompanied by *contorni*—vegetables, which are served as side dishes. Finally, you come to the *formaggio* (cheese) and/or *dolci* (desserts),

the espresso and perhaps a drink to aid digestion—*digestivo*. If this quantity of food seems daunting, do not despair. Locals rarely eat such gargantuan meals and pick and mix their courses. However, while it may be acceptable to order *antipasti* alone for lunch, it is not the done thing for dinner and, should you skip the pasta course, you may be given a sad-eyed look—not for nothing is it known as *il primo*. Upscale restaurants will sometimes offer a *gourmet menù degustazione*, not to be confused with a *menù turistico*. With the latter you usually pay for quantity rather than quality and it is unlikely to give you an authentic Roman dining experience. If you see yellowing photographs of various dishes displayed outside a restaurant, it is best to just give skip it and find somewhere else!

PRICE MATTERS/IL CONTO

Although in theory restaurants are no longer allowed to add a bread and cover *(pane e coperto)* charge to the bill *(il conto)*, many feign oblivion to this and just charge for the bread anyway, usually between €1–€2 per person. Normally, service is not included, although a minority do still add it as a fixed item to the bill. In everyday establishments, a tip of around 5 per cent is perfectly adequate, but in *ristoranti*, if the service has been good, 10 per cent would be more acceptable.

You should always be given a receipt *(ricevuta fiscale)* after paying the bill as, theoretically, the restaurant could be fined if they don't issue one.

CAFFÈ SOCIETY

Drinking coffee is a ritual in Rome— some would say it is an addiction. It is quite normal to see people at the bar counter at any time of day and night, getting their quick fix of caffeine. It is also normal to drink the heady brew standing up, even in the most famous cafés, such as the Sant'Eustachio Il Caffè (▷ 131), which, many say, serves the best espresso in Rome.

The line between café and bar is blurred, but generally a bar is good for a quick drink, while a café is somewhere you linger while enjoying your coffee, or meal, or long, cool drink—or all three. You will certainly pay at least double if you elect to be waited upon rather than consume your drink at the bar.

The type of coffee you drink is also important. Romans wouldn't dream of drinking a cappuccino after noon, opting instead for an espresso or a caffè macchiato, with just a drop of milk.

Another variation on the theme is the *enoteca*, or wine bar. These are extremely popular and keep popping up all over the city. Some are self-consciously chic, others are dark and atmospheric, while some serve excellent food, but all are united in their love of their carefully selected wine. You can drink by the glass or bottle, usually with cold and hot snacks.

GELATERIE

The *gelato* is an indispensable part of Roman life. Some view it as an art form, such as Il Gelato di San Crispino (▷ 91), just behind the Trevi Fountain, which many regard as the best ice cream maker in town. Here, the choices are distinctively seasonal, ranging from summer raspberry to nougat, *tiramisù* and countless others. Glorious *gelato* is almost a fashion accessory during the evening *passeggiata* and, even if you don't want to take time to sit and enjoy it, there are kiosks at the corner of almost every street. Look out for the sign *produzione artigianale*, meaning that it is home-made, and avoid the most lurid, which probably means it contains synthetic additives. Other variations include a *gratachecca*, a water ice grated by hand and topped with fruit syrup.

For the truly sublime, do try a *tartufo* ice cream. Named after its resemblance to the shape of an exotic truffle, this chocolate-studded ice cream is utterly delicious, expensive and not a little decadent.

MENU READER

Dining in one of Rome's many fine restaurants, or enjoying a simpler meal in one of its family-run *trattoria*, is one of the great pleasures when visiting the city. To appreciate the city's cuisine fully you will need an adventurous spirit and at least a smattering of Italian. If you don't speak the language, menus can be a daunting prospect, but knowledge of a few key words will help you to work out what's on offer, order what you want and avoid any embarrassing blunders. This menu reader is designed to help you translate common words and familiarize yourself with dishes that you are likely to come across on a Roman menu.

PIATTI–COURSES
antipasti .... starters
stuzzichini ....appetizers
primi piatti ....first courses
secondi piatti ....main courses
contorni ......vegetables/side dishes
dolci ....desserts
spuntini .... snacks

CARNE–MEAT
agnello .... lamb
cacciagione .... game
coniglio ....rabbit
cuore ....heart
fegato ....liver
maiale ....pork
manzo ....beef
pancetta .... bacon
pollame ....poultry
pollo ....chicken
prosciutto ....cured ham
prosciutto cotto .... cooked ham
rognoni ....kidneys
salsiccia ....sausage
tacchino .... turkey
vitello ....veal

PESCE–FISH
alici ....anchovies
baccalà .... dried salt cod
branzino .... sea bass
dorate ....bream

fritto misto .... mixed fried fish
merluzzo ....cod
pesce spada .... swordfish
sarde ....sardines
sogliola ....sole
tonno ....tuna
triglia ....mullet
trota ....trout

FRUTTI DI MARE–SEAFOOD
aragoste .... lobster
calamari .... squid
canestrelli .... scallops
cozze .... mussels
gamberetti .... prawns
granceola ....spiny spider crab
molluschi .... shellfish
ostriche ....oysters
seppia ....cuttlefish
vongole ....clams

VERDURE–VEGETABLES
asparagi ....asparagus
carciofo .... artichoke
carote ....carrots
cavolfiore ....cauliflower
cavolo .... cabbage
cetriolino ....gherkin (pickle)
cetriolo ....cucumber
cicoria .... chicory
cipolla ....onion
fagioli ....beans

fagiolini .... green beans
fave .... broad beans
finocchio .... fennel
lattuga ....lettuce
melanzane .... aubergines (eggplant)
patate .... potatoes
peperone .... sweet pepper
(capsicum)
piselli ....peas
pomodori ....tomatoes
spinaci ....spinach
verdure cotte .... cooked greens
zucchini ....courgettes

METODI DI CUCINA–COOKING METHODS
affumicato .... smoked
al forno .... baked
alla griglia .... grilled
arrosto .... roasted
bollito .... boiled
casalingo ....home-made
crudo .... raw
fritto ....fried
frulatto ....whisked
ripieno ....stuffed
stufato ....stewed

LA PASTA–PASTA
cannelloni ....baked meat- or
cheese-filled tubes
conchiglie .... shell shapes

farfalle .... butterfly shapes
fettucine ....wide strips
fusilli .... spiral shapes
lasagne ...... sheets of pasta, layered
with meat sauce
and béchamel sauce
to make lasagne al forno
linguine .... thin strips
pappardelle .... rippled strips
penne .... quill shapes
ravioli ......pasta cushions filled with
meat, cheese or spinach
rigatoni ....short, fat tubes
tagliatelle ....thin ribbons or strips
tortellini ..... little 'hats' with meat or
cheese filling
trenette .... long narrow strips

SALSI/SUGI–SAUCES

amatriciana ....bacon, tomato and
onion
arrabbiata .... tomato and hot chilli
cacciatore .... sauce for meat:
tomato, onion, garlic, wine
carbonara .... smoked bacon, egg,
cream and black pepper
pesto ....basil, garlic, pine nuts, olive
oil and pecorino cheese
puttanesca ....tomato, garlic, hot
chilli, anchovies, capers
ragù .... minced meat,
tomato and garlic
salsa di pomodoro ....tomato
salsa verde .... piquant/vinaigrette

SPECIALITÀ–SPECIAL DISHES

carpaccio ....thin-sliced raw beef
served with a cold vinaigrette
coda alla vaccinara ....oxtail stew
osso bucco .... veal stewed with
tomatoes, onions and garlic
pastiera ....Neapolitan Easter
grain pie, filled with ricotta
and flavoured with orange
peperonata .... sweet pepper
(capsicum) and tomato stew
polpetti ....meatballs
saltimbocca ..... veal escalopes with
ham, sage and white wine
scaloppini ....thinly sliced veal
cooked in white wine
stracotto .... beef stew
timballo .... baked meat and
vegetable pie

CONTORNI–SIDE DISHES

insalata mista ....mixed salad

insalata tricolore .... mozzarella,
tomato and fresh basil
insalata verde ....green salad
pane ....bread
patate fritte .... chips (french fries)
polenta .... maize-meal dish
riso .... rice

ALTRI PIATTI–OTHER DISHES

antipasto misto ....mixed cold
meats: salami, ham etc.
brodetto ....fish soup
brodo ....broth
frittata .... omelette
gnocchi ....small dumplings made
from potato and flour or semolina
minestra ....vegetable soup
risotto ai funghi ....mushroom
risotto
risotto alla Milanese ....risotto with
saffron
strufolone .... rolled pizza
uovo .... egg
zuppa .... soup

DOLCI–CAKES/DESSERTS

cassata ....Sicilian fruit ice cream
cioccolata ....chocolate
crema .... custard
macedonia ....fruit salad
panna .... cream
una pasta .... a cake/pastry
semifreddo ..... chilled dessert made
with ice cream
tiramisù ....chocolate/coffee sponge
dessert
torta ....tart
zabaglione .... egg, sugar and
Marsala dessert
zabaione di Verduzzo .... custard
pudding with Friuli wine
zuccotto .... ice-cream sponge
zuppa inglese .... trifle

FRUTTI—FRUITS

arancia .... orange
fragola .... strawberry
lampone .... raspberry
mela .... apple
melone .... melon
pera .... pear
pesca .... peach
pesca noci .... nectarine
uve .... grapes

FORMAGI—CHEESES

formaggio di capra .. goat's cheese

formaggio dolce ....mild cheese
formaggio nostrano .. local cheese
parmigiano .... Parmesan
pecorino .... Roman hard cheese,
like Parmesan

BEVANDE–DRINKS

acqua minerale ....mineral water
(*gassata*, sparkling; *naturale*, still)
birra ....beer
caffè corretto .... coffee with
liqueur/spirit
caffè freddo .... iced coffee
caffè latte ....milky coffee
caffè lungo ....weak coffee
caffè macchiato .... coffee with a
drop of milk
caffè ristretto ....strong coffee
digestivo ....after-dinner liqueur
dolce ....sweet
ghiaccio .... ice
liquore .... liqueur
porto .... port wine
secco ....dry
spumante ....sparkling wine
succo di arancia .... orange juice
té .... tea
té al latte freddo ....tea with milk
té freddo ....iced tea
vini pregiati ....quality wines
vino bianco ....white wine
vino rosato ....rosé wine
vino rosso .... red wine
vino di tavola ....house wine

CONDIMENTI–SEASONINGS

aceto .... vinegar
aglio .... garlic
aromatiche .... herbs
basilico ....basil
capperi .... capers
pepe ....pepper
peperoncino ....chilli pepper
prezzemolo ....parsley
rosmarino .... rosemary
sale ....salt
salvia ....sage
senape ....mustard
timo .... thyme
zucchero .... sugar

IL CONTO–THE BILL

coperto .... cover charge
IVA ....value-added tax (sales tax)
servizio (non) compreso ....service
charge (not) included

RESTAURANTS BY CUISINE

PRACTICALITIES EATING

Restoration and renovation projects, and changes in the law to coincide with the Jubilee Year celebrations in 2000, left the city an important legacy, with more five-star hotels and more simple and inexpensive bed-and-breakfast options now available. Yet accommodation in Rome can still be expensive, especially in the high season from Easter to September. Rooms in the relatively few hotels in the heart of the historic centre are also pricey.

LOCATION, LOCATION

As in any city, Rome has a wide range of accommodation types, from small, low-budget hotels around Termini to grand, five-star luxury hotels on the Via Vittoria Veneto. What to expect, in terms of price and quality, depends largely on whereabouts your hotel is in the city.

Staying in the *centro storico* means that you are close to all of Rome's sights, but also to its sounds. Rome is a noisy city that goes to bed late and gets up early, and narrow streets and tall buildings tend to amplify sounds. Quiet places can be found, on the edge of the popular areas or in hotels with double or even triple glazing. Some of the more expensive hotels have soundproofing. When booking a hotel, ask for a quiet room, which will either be at the back of the building or overlooking a central courtyard. If you really value your sleep, book a hotel in the quieter Aventino, Celio or Prati districts. The disadvantage here is that you will have to spend time commuting into

the *centro storico*. However, public transport is inexpensive and reliable, and hotels here are often cheaper than similarly rated establishments in the heart of the city.

WHAT YOU GET FOR YOUR EUROS

The familiar star system operates in Italy, with 5 stars denoting the highest standard of comfort, luxury and facilities. A 1-star hotel has few facilities and frequently does not include a private bathroom. Normally both television and telephone will be downstairs in the lobby. These establishments may have an early curfew, often do not accept credit cards and do not have a 24-hour desk service. You should expect to pay up to around €125 for a double room per night, although some are substantially cheaper.

With the advent of online booking, fixed pricing has virtually disappeared as hotel websites constantly update charges to reflect booking levels for individual nights. Booking well ahead may pay

dividends price-wise, but there are often excellent last-minute prices on offer. As a rough guide, prices range from €125 for a basic double room to €450 and up for a de luxe hotel.

Some hotels charge extra for breakfast and, as a general rule of thumb, the more expensive the establishment, the less likely it is that breakfast is included. In the listings in this book, breakfast is included unless stated otherwise. In the more moderately priced hotels, most rooms will have telephones and a mini-bar, and prices here tend to include breakfast, tax and service charges. The smaller boutique hotels are extremely popular and tend to be in lovely, old historic buildings tucked away from the main streets. These do not come cheap, but offer many services and usually include breakfast, tax and service. The larger, luxury hotels usually have full business facilities and access to the internet, as well as spas, gyms and pools. The cost of a stay here is usually exclusive of both breakfast and service.

RESERVATIONS

As Rome is an eternally popular destination, it pays to reserve well in advance, especially if your stay is over the peak periods. January to March and August are the least popular months of the tourist calendar and you should be able to find some good deals at this time. Do consult hotel websites for details of special offers, and remember that specialist tour operators usually have a fixed allocation in some of the best hotels and can include your flights and transfers in a very competitively priced package. If you arrive without a reservation, do ask to see the room first before you commit yourself. Information and accommodation agencies are always a useful resource.

ACCOMMODATION SERVICES

The **APT** (Azienda di Promozione Turistica di Roma) tourist office at Via Parigi 5, Esquilino (tel 06 8205 9127; www.romaturismo.com or www.060608.it) provides an independent list of accommodation, although you are responsible for making your own reservation. The office is open Mon–Sat 9–7, while the phone line is open daily 9–7.30. There is also a branch at Fiumicino airport (tel 06 3600 4399). Also at Rome's Fiumicino airport, the **Hotel Reservation Service** (arrivals halls, Terminals 1, 2 and 3; daily 7.30am– 10.30pm – times vary) has English operators and can provide details of availability of accommodation in every price range. The service also has branches at Ciampino airport and at Termini (by platforms 2–3 and 20). The telephone number for the Hotel Reservation Service is 06 699 1000; www.hotelreservation.it.

Termini – the area around the station – is full of 'officials' who are keen to direct you to a hotel. Some are appointed by the tourist office, others are impostors, so be wary. To avoid any misunderstanding head directly to the tourist information point (PIT – Punti Informativi Turistici, instantly recognizable by the green-painted kiosk) at Termini

(daily 8am–9pm). There are other information points around the city.

A very useful service is run by **Enjoy Rome**, which is a private English-speaking agency that can give helpful advice and also provides a free accommodation booking service. Its main office is just by Termini station (take the north exit from the station at Via Marsala, walk straight along for three blocks and it is on the left) at Via Marghera 8a (tel 06 445 1843; www.enjoyrome.com). It is open Mar–Oct Mon–Fri 8.30–7, Sat 8.30–2; Nov–Feb Mon–Fri 9–6.30, Sat 8.30–2. Credit cards are not accepted.

CAMPING
The Touring Club Italiano
(www.touringclub.it) publishes an annual directory, *Campeggi in Italia*, which covers campsites throughout the country. This book is available online or in bookstores (around €12). Alternatively, visit www.campeggi.it.

BED-AND-BREAKFAST
Bed-and-breakfast is a relatively new concept in Rome, but it is booming. More than a thousand are now registered, from spare bedrooms in out-of-town family flats to rooms in opulent palazzi. Many are furnished in shabby-chic style and some are a great deal more chic than shabby.

The **Bed and Breakfast Italia** agency (Palazzo Sforza Cesarini, Corso Vittorio Emanuele II 282, tel 06 687 8618; www.bbitalia.it) lists around 1,650 properties in 550 locations around Italy, including luxury accommodation in palazzi. Prices start from around €60 per room in the luxury category, descending to around €25 for the least expensive choices.

RENTING AN APARTMENT
If you want to rent an apartment, the best times for availability tend to be in July, August and December, when the owners traditionally take their own holidays. Agencies specializing in apartment and villa rentals include:

Homes International, Via L. Bissolati 20, tel 06 488 1800; www.homeinternational.com. The service covers short- and long-term rentals for apartments and villas, and English is spoken. The office is open Mon–Fri 9–1, 2–7, Sat 9–1.

Rome Property Network, Via dei Gesù e Maria 25 (near Piazza del Popolo), tel 06 321 2341; www.romeproperty.com. English is also spoken at this American-run agency, where they specialize in apartments and villas in the *centro storico* and Trastevere. It is open Mon–Fri 9–6.

Useful websites for property rental include www.flatinrome.com and www.romeguide.it.

Once you have mastered a few basic rules, Italian is an easy language to speak: It is phonetic and, unlike English, particular combinations of letters are always pronounced the same way. The stress is usually on the penultimate syllable, but if the word has an accent, this is where the stress falls.

Vowels are pronounced as follows:

a	casa	as in	mat (short 'a')
e	vero	as in	base
e	sette	as in	vet (short 'e')
i	vino	as in	mean
o	dove	as in	bowl
o	otto	as in	not
u	uva	as in	blue

Consonants as in English except:
**c before i or e becomes ch
as in church
ch before i or e becomes c
as in cat
g before i or e becomes j
as in Julia
gh before i or e becomes g
as in good
gn as in onion
gli as in million
h is rare in Italian words, and is
always silent
r usually rolled
z is pronounced tz when it falls
in the middle of a word**

All Italian nouns are either masculine (usually ending in o when singular or i when plural) or feminine (usually ending in a when singular or e when plural). Some nouns, which may be masculine or feminine, end in e (which changes to i when plural). An adjective's ending changes to match that of the noun.

CONVERSATION
What is the time?
Che ore sono?

When do you open/close?
A che ora apre/chiude?

I don't speak Italian
Non parlo italiano

I only speak a little Italian
Parlo solo un poco italiano

Do you speak English?
Parla inglese?

I don't understand
Non capisco

Please repeat that
Può ripetere?

Please speak more slowly
Può parlare più lentamente?

What does this mean?
Cosa significa questo?

Write that down for me, please
Lo scriva, per piacere

Please spell that
Come si scrive?

I'll look that up
Lo cerco

My name is
Mi chiamo

What's your name?
Come si chiama?

Hello, pleased to meet you
Piacere

This is my friend
Le presento il mio amico/la mia amica

This is my wife/husband/ daughter/son
Le presento mia moglie/mio marito/ mia figlia/mio figlio

Where do you live?
Dove abiti?

I live in...
Vivo in...

I'm here on holiday
Sono qui in vacanza

Good morning
Buongiorno

Good afternoon/evening
Buonasera

Goodbye
Arrivederci

See you later
A più tardi

See you tomorrow
A domani

See you soon
A presto

How are you?
Come sta?

Fine, thank you
Bene, grazie

I'm sorry
Mi dispiace

That's alright
Si figuri

USEFUL WORDS
yes	sì
no	no
please	per piacere/per favore
thank you	grazie
you're welcome	prego
excuse me!	scusi!
where	dove
here	qui
there	là
when	quando
now	adesso
later	più tardi
why	perchè
who	chi
may I/can I	posso

SHOPPING

Could you help me, please?
Può aiutarmi, per favore?

I'm looking for...
Cerco...

Where can I buy...?
Dove posso comprare...?

How much is this/that?
Quanto costa questo/quello?

When does the shop open/close?
Quando apre/chiude il negozio?

I'm just looking, thank you
Sto solo dando un'occhiata

This isn't what I want
Non è quel che cerco

I'll take this
Prendo questo

Do you have anything less expensive/smaller/larger?
Ha qualcosa di meno caro/più piccolo/più grande?

Are the instructions included?
Ci sono anche le istruzioni?

Do you have a bag for this?
Può darmi una busta?

I'm looking for a present
Cerco un regalo

Can you gift-wrap this, please?
Può farmi un pacco regalo?

Do you accept credit cards?
Accettate carte di credito?

I'd like a kilo of...
Vorrei un chilo di...

Do you have shoes to match this?
Ha delle scarpe che vadano con questo?

This is the right size
Questa è la taglia (misura—for shoes) giusta

Can you measure me please?
Può prendermi la misura, per favore?

This doesn't suit me
Questo non mi sta bene

Do you have this in...?
Avete questo in...?

Should this be dry-cleaned?
Questo è da lavare a secco?

Is there a market?
C'è un mercato?

NUMBERS

0	zero
1	uno
2	due
3	tre
4	quattro
5	cinque
6	sei
7	sette
8	otto
9	nove
10	dieci
11	undici
12	dodici
13	tredici
14	quattordici
15	quindici
16	sedici
17	diciassette
18	diciotto
19	diciannove
20	venti
21	ventuno
22	ventidue
30	trenta
40	quaranta
50	cinquanta
60	sessanta
70	settanta
80	ottanta
90	novanta
100	cento
1000	mille
million	milione
quarter	quarto
half	mezza
three quarters	tre quarti

MONEY

Is there a bank/currency exchange office nearby?
C'è una banca/un ufficio di cambio qui vicino?

Can I cash this here?
Posso incassare questo?

I'd like to change sterling/dollars into euros
Vorrei cambiare sterline/dollari in euro

Can I use my credit card to withdraw cash?
Posso usare la mia carta di credito per prelevare contanti?

What is the exchange rate today?
Quant'è il cambio oggi?

I'd like to cash this travellers' cheque
Vorrei incassare questo travellers cheque

POST AND TELEPHONE

Where is the nearest post office/mail box?
Dov'è l'ufficio postale più vicino/la cassetta delle lettere più vicina?

What is the postage to...?
Quando costa spedire una lettera a...?

One stamp, please
Un francobollo, per favore

I'd like to send this by air mail/registered mail
Vorrei spedire questo per posta aerea/posta raccomandata

Can you direct me to a public phone?
Dov'è il telefono pubblico più vicino?

What is the charge per minute?
Quanto si paga al minuto?

Can I dial direct to...?
Posso chiamare... in teleselezione?

Do I need to dial 0 first?
Devo comporre prima lo zero?

Where can I find a phone directory?
Dove posso trovare un elenco telefonico?

Where can I buy a phone card?
Dove posso comprare una carta telefonica?

What is the number for directory enquiries?
Qual è il numero del servizio informazioni?

Please put me through to...
Mi passi...

Have there been any calls for me?
Ci sono state telefonate per me?

Hello, this is...
Pronto, sono...

Who is this speaking please?
Con chi parlo?

I'd like to speak to...
Vorrei parlare con...

Extension...please
Interno...per piacere

Please ask him/her to call me back
Puo dirgli/dirle di richiamarmi?

GETTING AROUND
Where is the train/bus station?
Dov'è la stazione ferroviaria/ degli autobus (dei pullman—long distance)?

Does this train/bus go to...?
È questo il treno/l'autobus (il pullman—long distance) per...?

Does this train/bus stop at...?
Questo treno/autobus (pullman—long distance) ferma a...?

Please stop at the next stop
La prossima fermata, per favore

Where are we?
Dove siamo?

Do I have to get off here?
Devo scendere qui?

Where can I buy a ticket?
Dove si comprano i biglietti?

Is this seat taken?
È occupato?

Where can I reserve a seat?
Dove si prenotano i posti?

Please can I have a single/ return ticket to...
Un biglietto di andata/andata e ritorno per...

When is the first/last bus to...?
Quando c'è il primo/l'ultimo autobus per...?

I would like a standard/first class ticket to...
Un biglietto di seconda/ prima classe per...

Where is the information desk?
Dov'è il banco informazioni?

Where is the timetable?
Dov'è l'orario?

Do you have a subway/bus map?
Ha una piantina della metropolitana/degli autobus?

Where can I find a taxi?
Dove sono i tassì?

Please take me to...
Per favore, mi porti a...

How much is the journey?
Quanto costerà il viaggio?

Please turn on the meter
Accenda il tassametro, per favore

I'd like to get out here, please
Vorrei scendere qui, per favore

Could you wait for me please?
Mi può aspettare, per favore?

Is this the way to...?
È questa la strada per...?

Excuse me, I think I am lost
Mi scusi, penso di essermi perduto/a

SHOPS
baker's..............panetteria or forno
bookshop.........................libreria
butcher's......................macelleria
cake shop.....................pasticceria
clothes shop...........abbigliamento
delicatessen...................salumeria
dry-cleaner's.................lavasecco
fishmonger's...............pescheria
florist...................................fiorista
gift shop...............................regali
grocer's.........................alimentare
hairdresser's.............parrucchiere
jeweller's......................gioielleria
launderette.......lavanderia/Tintoria
lingerie shop......biancheria intima
newsagent's.................giornalaio
perfume shop.............profumeria
photographic shop.......fotografo
shoe shop.....................calzature
sports shop............articoli sportivi
tobacconist's.............tabaccheria

COLOURS
black...nero
brown.............................. marrone
pink...rosa
red..rosso
orange............................. arancia
yellow...................................giallo
green.....................................verde
blue...blu
light blue...........................celeste
sky blue..............................azzurro
purple....................................viola
white.................................. bianco
gold..oro
silver.................................argento
grey....................................grigio
turquoise........................turchese

TIMES/DAYS/MONTHS/ HOLIDAYS
morning............................mattina
afternoon....................pomeriggio
evening................................. sera

night	notte
day	giorno
month	mese
year	anno
today	oggi
yesterday	ieri
tomorrow	domani
Monday	lunedì
Tuesday	martedì
Wednesday	mercoledì
Thursday	giovedì
Friday	venerdì
Saturday	sabato
Sunday	domenica
January	gennaio
February	febbraio
March	marzo
April	aprile
May	maggio
June	giugno
July	luglio
August	agosto
September	settembre
October	ottobre
November	novembre
December	dicembre
spring	primavera
summer	estate
autumn	autunno
winter	inverno
New Year's Day	Capodanno
Epiphany	Epifania
Easter	Pasqua
Assumption	Ferragosto
All Saints' Day	Ognissanti
Christmas	Natale
26 December	Santo Stefano
New Year's Eve	San Silvestro

IN TROUBLE

Help! Aiuto!

Stop, thief! Al ladro!

Can you help me, please?
Può aiutarmi, per favore?

Call the fire brigade/police/an ambulance
Chiami i pompieri/la polizia/un'ambulanza

I have lost my passport/wallet/purse/handbag
Ho perso il passaporto/il portafoglio/il borsellino/la borsa

Is there a lost property office?
C'è un ufficio oggetti smarriti?

Where is the police station?
Dov'è il commissariato?

I have been robbed
Sono stato/a derubato/a

I have had an accident
Ho avuto un incidente

Here is my name and address
Ecco il mio nome e indirizzo

Did you see the accident?
Ho visto l'incidente?

Are you insured?
È assicurato/a?

Can I have your name and address, please?
Mi dà il suo nome e indirizzo?

I need information for my insurance company
Ho bisogno d'informazioni per la mia compagnia d'assicurazione

ILLNESS
I don't feel well
Non mi sento bene

Could you call a doctor please?
Può chiamare un medico, per favore?

Is there a doctor/pharmacist on duty?
C'è un medico/farmacista di turno?

I need to see a doctor/dentist
Ho bisogno di un medico/ dentista

Where is the hospital?
Dov'è l'ospedale?

When is the surgery open?
Quando apre l'ambulatorio

I need to make an emergency appointment
Ho bisogno di un appuntamento di emergenza

Do I need to make an appointment?
Ho bisogno di un appuntamento?

I feel sick
Mi sento male

I am allergic to...
Sono allergico/a a...

I have a heart condition
Ho disturbi cardiaci

I am diabetic
Sono diabetico/a

I'm asthmatic
Ho l'asma

I've been stung by a wasp/bee
Mi ha punto una vespa/un'ape

Can I have a painkiller?
Posso avere un analgesico?

How many tablets a day should I take?
Quante pillole al giorno devo prendere?

How long will I have to stay in bed/hospital?
Per quanto tempo dovrò rimanere a letto/in ospedale?

I have a bad toothache
Mi fanno molto male i denti

I have broken my tooth/crown
Mi sono rotto un dente/una corona

A filling has come out
Ho perso un'otturazione

Can you repair my dentures?
Può ripararmi la dentiera?

RESTAURANTS
Waiter/waitress
Cameriere/cameriera

What time does the restaurant open?
A che ora apre il ristorante?

**I'd like to reserve a table for...
people at...**
Vorrei prenotare un tavolo
per...persone a...

A table for..., please
Un tavolo per..., per favore

We have/haven't booked
Abbiamo/non abbiamo prenotato

Could we sit there?
Possiamo sederci qui?

Is this table taken?
Questa tavola è occupata?

Are there tables outside?
Ci sono tavoli all'aperto?

Where are the toilets?
Dove sono i bagni?

We would like to wait for a table
Aspettiamo che si liberi un tavolo

Could you warm this up for me?
Mi può riscaldare questo, per
piacere?

We'd like something to drink
Vorremo qualcosa da bere

**Could we see the menu/
wine list?**
Possiamo vedere il menù/la lista
dei vini?

**Do you have a menu/wine list
in English?**
Avete un menù/una lista dei vini in
inglese?

What do you recommend?
Cosa consiglia?

Is there a dish of the day?
C'è un piatto del giorno?

What is the house special?
Qual è la specialità della casa?

**I can't eat wheat/sugar/salt/
pork/beef/dairy**
Non posso mangiare grano/
zucchero/sale/maiale/
manzo/latticini

I am a vegetarian
Sono vegetariano/a

I'd like...
Vorrei...

I ordered...
Ho ordinato...

**Could I have bottled still/
sparkling water?**
Vorrei acqua minerale
naturale/gassata

**Could we have some
more bread?**
Può portare ancora pane?

**Could we have some salt
and pepper?**
Può portare del sale e del pepe?

The food is cold
Il cibo è freddo

**The meat is overcooked/
too rare**
La carne è troppo cotta/
non è abbastanza cotta

This is not what I ordered
Non ho ordinato questo

Can I have the bill, please?
Il conto, per favore?

Is service included?
Il servizio è compreso?

The bill is not right
Il conto è sbagliato

We didn't have this
Non abbiamo avuto questo

How much is this dish?
Quanto costa questo piatto?

**I'd like to speak to the
manager, please**
Vorrei parlare con il direttore

The food was excellent
Abbiamo mangiato benissimo

HOTELS
**I have made a reservation
for...nights**
Ho prenotato per...notti

Do you have a room?
Avete camere libere?

How much per night?
Quanto costa una notte?

Double/single room
Camera doppia/singola

Twin room
Camera a due letti

With bath/shower
Con bagno/doccia

May I see the room?
Posso vedere la camera?

I'll take this room
Prendo questa camera

Could I have another room?
Vorrei cambiare camera

Is there a lift in the hotel?
C'è un ascensore nell'albergo?

Is the room air-conditioned/heated?
C'è aria condizionata/riscaldamento nella camera?

Is breakfast included in the price?
La colazione è compreso?

Do you have room service?
C'è servizio in camera?

When is breakfast served?
A che ora è servita la colazione?

I need an alarm call at...
Potete svegliarmi alle...

The room is too hot/too cold/dirty
La camera è troppo calda/troppo fredda/sporca

I am leaving this morning
Parto stamattina

Can I pay my bill, please?
Posso pagare il conto?

Please order a taxi for me
Mi chiama un tassì, per favore

TOURIST INFORMATION
Where is the tourist information office/tourist information desk, please?
Dov'è l'ufficio turistico/il banco informazioni turistiche?

What can we visit in the area?
Che cosa c'è da vedere in questa zona?

Do you have a city map?
Avete una cartina della città?

Can you give me some information about...?
Puo darmi delle informazioni su...?

What sights/hotels/restaurants can you recommend?
Quali monumenti/alberghi/ristoranti mi consiglia?

Please could you point them out on the map?
Me li può indicare sulla cartina?

What is the admission price?
Quant'è il biglietto d'ingresso?

Is there a discount for senior citizens/students?
Ci sono riduzioni per anziani/studenti?

Are there guided tours?
Ci sono visite guidate?

Are there boat trips?
Ci sono gite in barca?

Where do they go?
Dove vanno?

Is there an English-speaking guide?
C'è una guida di lingue inglese?

Are there organized excursions?
Ci sono escursioni organizzate?

Can we make reservations here?
Possiamo prenotare qui?

What time does it open/close?
A che ora apre/chiude?

Is photography allowed?
Si possono fare fotografie?

Do you have a brochure in English?
Avete un opuscolo in inglese?

Where can I find a good nightclub?
Mi può consigliare un buon nightclub?

What time does the show start?
A che ora comincia lo spettacolo?

Could you reserve tickets for me?
Mi può prenotare dei biglietti?

How much is a ticket?
Quanto costa un biglietto?

Should we dress up?
È necessario l'abito da sera?

IN THE TOWN
on/to the right .... a destra
on/to the left .... a sinistra
around the corner .... all'angolo
opposite .... di fronte a...
at the bottom (of) .... in fondo (a)
straight on .... sempre dritto
near .... vicino a
cross over .... attraversi
in front of .... davanti
behind .... dietro
north .... nord
south .... sud
east .... est
west .... ovest
free .... gratis
donation .... donazione
open .... aperto
closed .... chiuso
daily .... giornalmente
cathedral .... cattedrale
church .... chiesa
castle .... castello
museum .... museo
monument .... monumento
palace .... palazzo
gallery .... galleria
old town .... centro storico
boulevard .... corso
square .... piazza
street .... via
avenue .... viale
island ....isola
river ....fiume
lake .... lago
bridge .... ponte
no entry .... vietato l'accesso
push .... spingere
pull ....tirare
entrance .... ingresso
exit .... uscita

toilets — men/women
bagni — uomini/donne

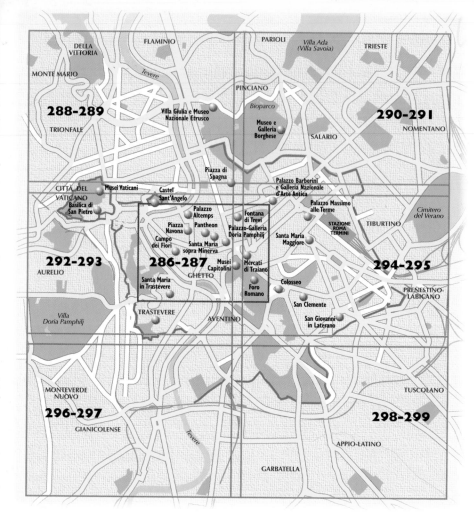

288-289	290-291
TRIONFALE	NOMENTANO
292-293	294-295
AURELIO	PRENESTINO-LABICANO
286-287	
296-297	298-299
GIANICOLENSE	TUSCOLANO

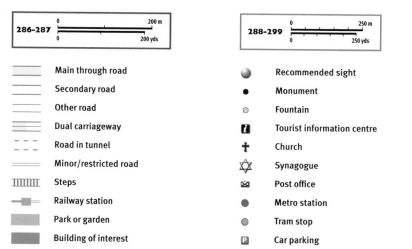

| 286-287 | 0 — 200 m |
| | 0 — 200 yds |

| 288-299 | 0 — 250 m |
| | 0 — 250 yds |

Main through road

Secondary road

Other road

Dual carriageway

Road in tunnel

Minor/restricted road

Steps

Railway station

Park or garden

Building of interest

Recommended sight

Monument

Fountain

Tourist information centre

Church

Synagogue

Post office

Metro station

Tram stop

Car parking

MAPS

Map references for the sights refer to the individual locator maps within the regional chapters. For example, Campo dei Fiori has the reference ✚ 102 D5, indicating the locator map page number (102) and the grid square in which Campo dei Fiori sits (D5). These same grid references can also be used to locate the sights in this section. For example, Campo dei Fiori appears again in grid square D5 within the atlas, on page 286.

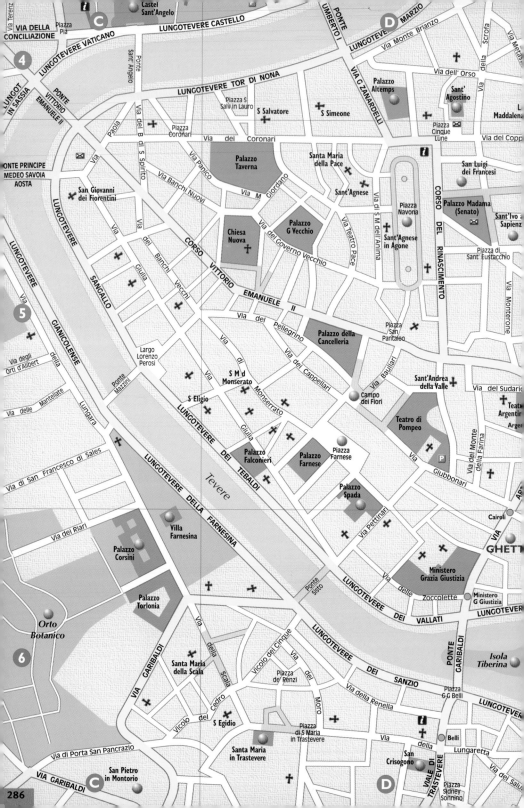

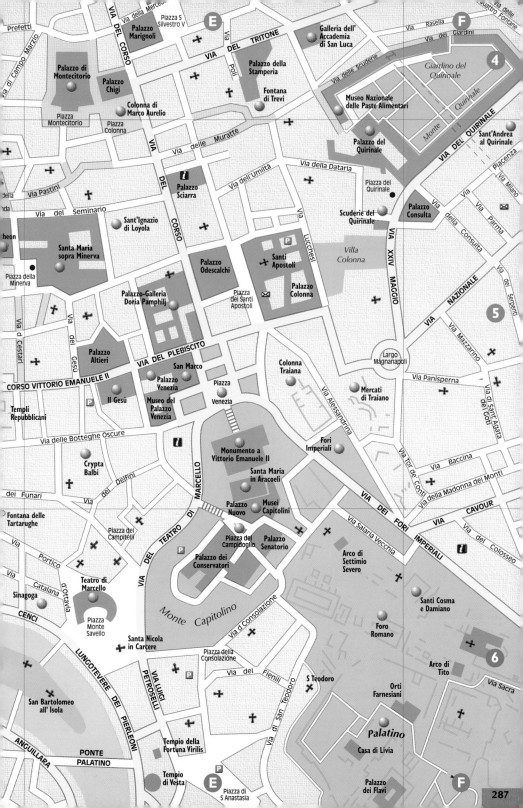

Prefetti

VIA DEL CORSO

VIA della Mercede

Piazza S
Silvestro V

E

Via Poli

VIA DEL TRITONE

Via delle Quattro Fontane

Via Rasella

F

Via dei Giardini

4

Palazzo
Marignoli

Palazzo di
Montecitorio

Palazzo
Chigi

Colonna di
Marco Aurelio

Piazza
Montecitorio

Via di Campo Marzio

Piazza
Colonna

Palazzo della
Stamperia

Fontana
di Trevi

VIA DEL CORSO

Via delle Muratte

VIA delle Scuderie

Galleria dell'
Accademia
di San Luca

Museo Nazionale
delle Paste Alimentari

Monte

Quirinale

Giardino del
Quirinale

Palazzo del
Quirinale

VIA DEL QUIRINALE

Sant'Andrea
al Quirinale

Piazza del
Quirinale

Via della Dataria

Placenza

Via Milano

Via Pastini

Via del Seminario

Palazzo
Sciarra

Sant'Ignazio
di Loyola

Pheon

della

nda

Via del Cestari

Santa Maria
sopra Minerva

Piazza della
Minerva

VIA DEL CORSO

VIA dell'Umiltà

Lucchesi

Palazzo
Odescalchi

Piazza
dei Santi
Apostoli

Santi
Apostoli

Palazzo
Colonna

Villa
Colonna

Scuderie del
Quirinale

Palazzo
Consulta

VIA della Consulta

Via della Parma

Via Milano

VIA XXIV MAGGIO

Largo
Magnanapoli

VIA NAZIONALE

Via dei Serpenti

5

Via del Gesù

Palazzo-Galleria
Doria Pamphilj

Palazzo
Altieri

VIA DEL PLEBISCITO

San Marco

Palazzo
Venezia

Il Gesù

Museo del
Palazzo Venezia

Piazza
Venezia

CORSO VITTORIO EMANUELE II

Templi
Repubblicani

Via delle Botteghe Oscure

Crypta
Balbi

Via dei Delfini

Via dei Funari

Fontana delle
Tartarughe

Piazza del
Campitelli

Via Portico

Via Catalana

d'Ottavia

Sinagoga

CENCI

Teatro di
Marcello

Piazza
Monte
Savello

LUNGOTEVERE DEI PIERLEONI

San Bartolomeo
all' Isola

ANGUILLARA

PONTE
PALATINO

Colonna
Traiana

VIA Alessandrina

Mercati
di Traiano

Via Panisperna

Via Mazzarino

Via di Sant'Agata dei Goti

Via Baccina

Fori
Imperiali

Via Tor de' Conti

Monumento a
Vittorio Emanuele II

Santa Maria
in Aracoeli

Palazzo
Nuovo

Musei
Capitolini

VIA DEL TEATRO DI MARCELLO

Piazza del
Campidoglio

Palazzo
Senatorio

Palazzo dei
Conservatori

Monte Capitolino

Via d Consolazione

Santa Nicola
in Carcere

Piazza della
Consolazione

VIA LUIGI PETROSELLI

Via di San Teodoro

Via dei Fienili

S Teodoro

Orti
Farnesiani

Via Salaria Vecchia

Arco di
Settimio
Severo

Foro
Romano

Santi Cosma
e Damiano

VIA DEI FORI IMPERIALI

VIA CAVOUR

Via del Colosseo

Via della Madonna dei Monti

6

Arco di
Tito

Via Sacra

Tempio della
Fortuna Virilis

Tempio
di Vesta

E

Piazza di
S Anastasia

Palatino

Casa di Livia

Palazzo
dei Flavi

F

287

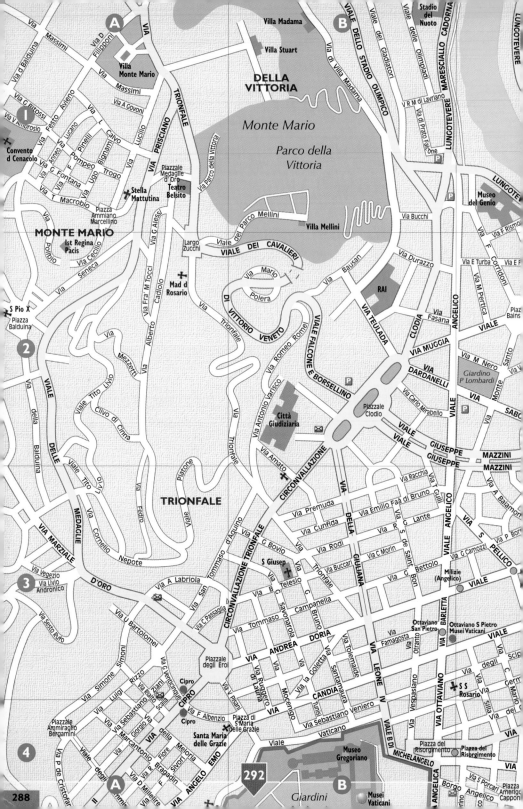

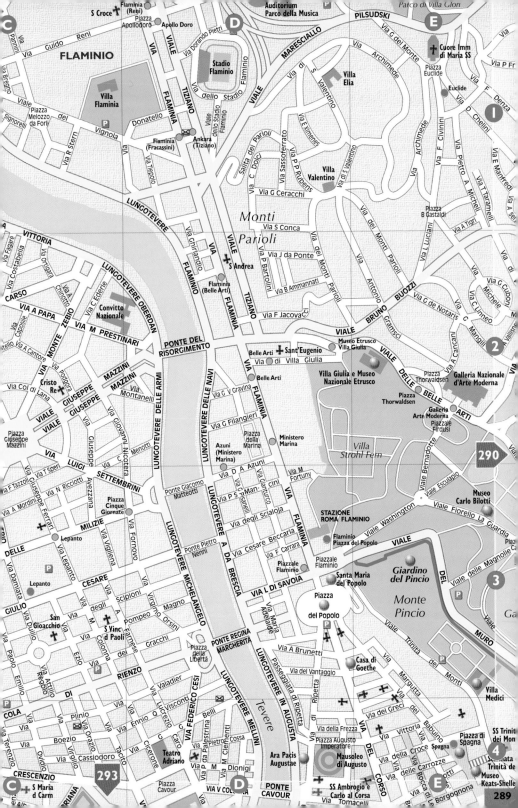

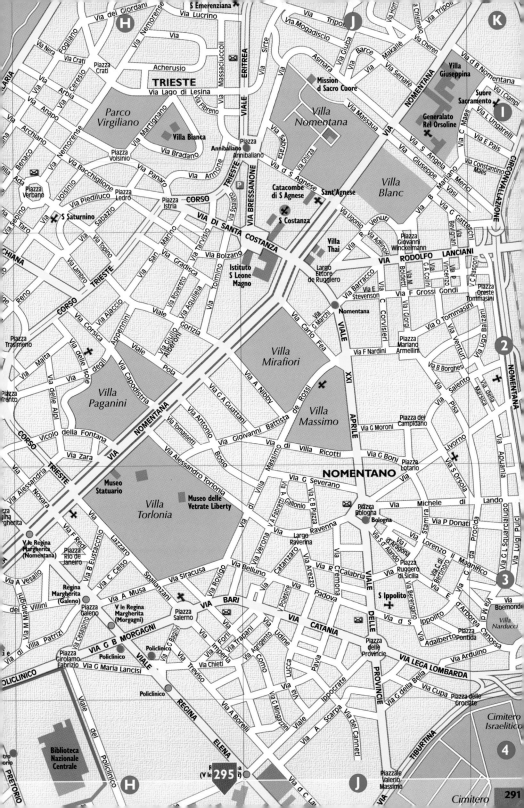

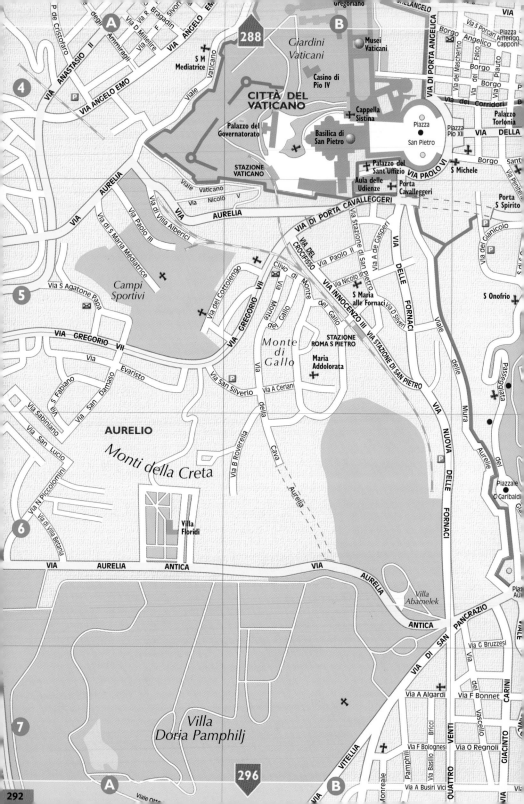

288

Giardini
Vaticani

Musei
Vaticani

P de Cristoforo
degli Ammiragli
Via D Millelire
Via Bragadin
Via D Sivori
VIA ANGELO EMO
ANGELO EM

S M
Mediatrice

Casino di
Pio IV

4

VIA ANASTASIO II

P

VIA ANGELO EMO

CITTÀ DEL
VATICANO

Cappella
Sistina

Piazza
Pio XII

Palazzo
Torlonia

VIA DELLA

VIA DI PORTA ANGELICA

Via S Porcari
Piazza
Amerigo
Capponi

Borgo
Angelico

Via del Mascherino

Borgo
Via del Falco

Borgo

Via
Plauto

VIA dei Corridori

Borgo

Palazzo del
Governatorato

Basilica di
San Pietro

Piazza
San Pietro

Borgo

Sant

STAZIONE
VATICANO

Palazzo del
Sant'Uffizio

Aula delle
Udienze

Porta
Cavalleggeri

S Michele

VIA PAOLO VI

VIA

AURELIA

Viale

Vaticano

Via Nicolo V

VIA

AURELIA

Porta
S Spirito

Porta
S Spirito

Via del Gianicolo

P

5

Via S Agatone Papa

Campi
Sportivi

VIA DI PORTA CAVALLEGGERI

VIA DEL CROCIFISSO

Via di S Maria Mediatrice

Via di Villa Alberici

Via Paolo III

VIA

Via di Villa Alberici

Via del Cottolengo

VIA GREGORIO VII

Clivo di Monte

Via A de Gasperi

Via A de Gasperi

Via Paolo II

VIA INNOCENZO III

Via Nicolo III

S Maria
alle Fornaci

VIA DELLE FORNACI

Via D Silveri

S Onofrio

VIA GREGORIO VII

Via

Evaristo

VIA GREGORIO VII

Via S Damaso

Via San Silverio

Monte
di Gallo

Via del Gallo

STAZIONE
ROMA S PIETRO

Maria
Addolorata

Viale

delle

Mura

VIA STAZIONE DI SAN PIETRO

Via
Fabiano

Via S Fabiano

Via San Damaso

P

Via A Ceriani

della

Cava

VIA NUOVA DELLE

Aurelia

Aurelia

del

AURELIO

Via Sabiniano

Via San Lucio

AURELIO

Monti della Creta

Via B Roverella

Villa
Floridi

Aurelia

Piazzale
G Garibaldi

6

Via N Piccolomini

Via di Villa Betania

VIA

AURELIA

ANTICA

VIA

AURELIA

Villa
Abamelek

ANTICA

PANCRAZIO

FORNACI

Piaz
Auli

VITELLIA

VIA DI SAN

Via G Bruzzesi

Via

CARINI

Via A Algardi

Via F Bonnet

Bricci

del

Vascello

VENTI

GIACINTO

7

*Villa
Doria Pamphilj*

Via F Bolognesi

Via O Regnoli

Pamphili

Via Basilio

Monreale

Via A Busiri Vici

QUATTRO

296

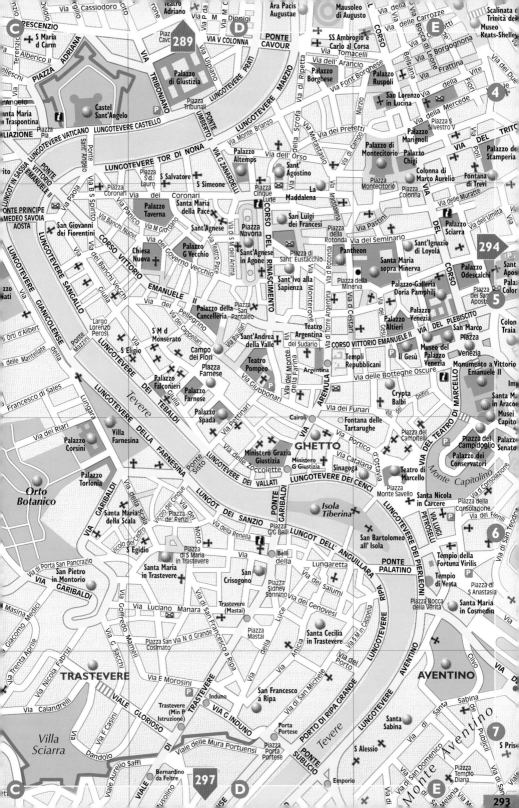

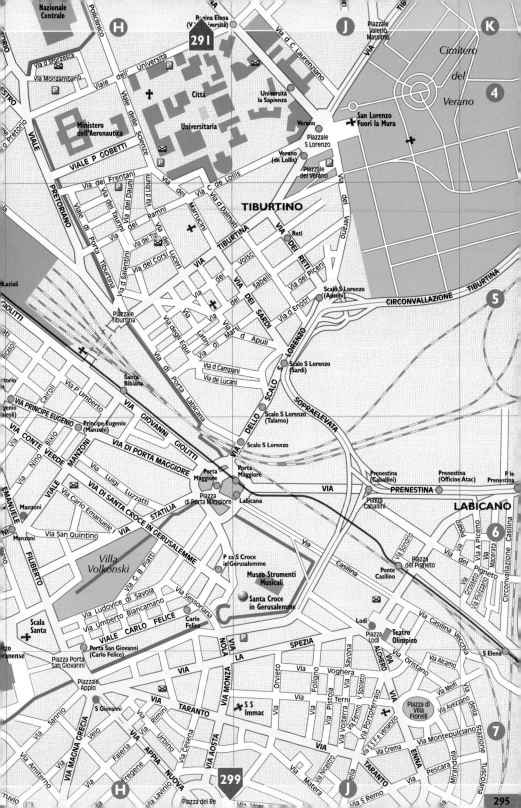

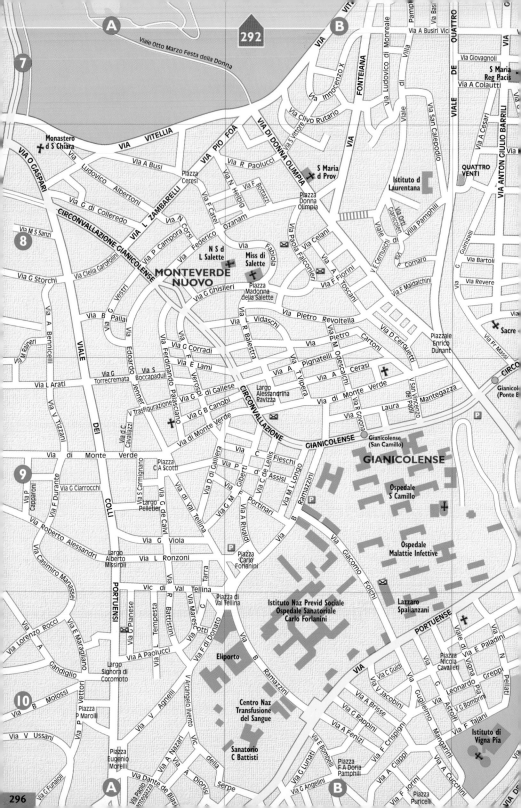

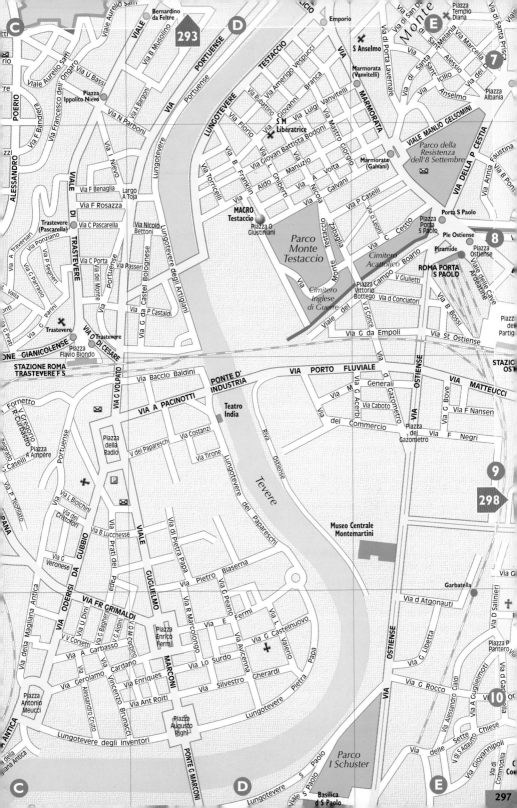

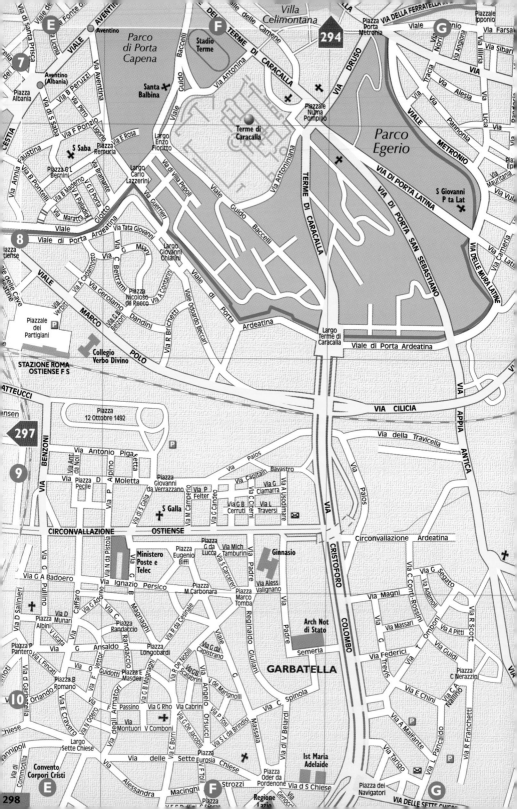

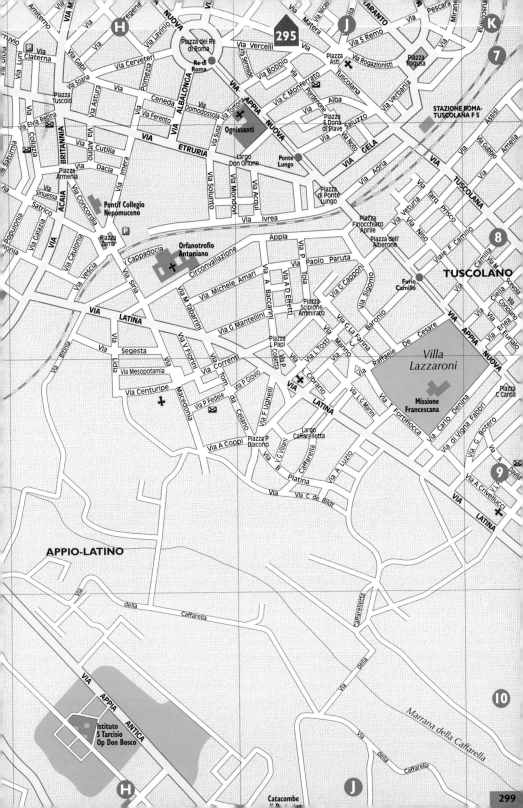

MAPS INDEX

MAPS INDEX

303

INDEX   ROME

313

ARCHITECTURAL GLOSSARY

Aisle: the interior corridors of a church, running either side of the nave

Alabaster: a fine grained limestone, often red and white or yellow and white. Thinly cut, it was used to glaze church windows in the Middle Ages

Allegory: a painting, sculpture or story where the meaning is shown through symbols

Apse: the semi-circular end of a church or chapel

Arcade: a range of arches, supported by pillars

Architrave: a moulded frame around a door or window

Atrium: an inner courtyard, open to the sky

Baldacchino/baldachin: a canopy, usually over a throne or altar

Balustrade: a series of short pillars, or balusters, supporting a rail

Baroque: architectural style popular in 17th-century Rome. It is characterized by its elaborate decoration of convex and concave curves

Basalt: dark volcanic rock

Basilica: originally, in ancient Rome, a public hall, but the building shape and the name were later used for early Christian churches. A basilica has no transepts

Bas-relief: a carving showing a three-dimensional scene, whose surface is relatively shallow

Belvedere: a small tower on the roof of a building

Byzantine: architectural style developed after AD330, when Byzantium became capital of the Eastern Empire. It is characterized by its Eastern influences and highly decorated style

Campanile: a bell tower, often separate from the main building

Cartoon: a full-size preliminary sketch for a painting, mosaic or tapestry

Caryatid: a column, sculpted as a female figure

Casina: literally 'little house', used by 18th-century gentry for dancing, entertainment and gambling

Catacomb: an underground cemetery, usually Christian

Cattedra: the bishop's throne, usually in the apse of the cathedral church

Chancel: the eastern end of a church, where the high altar is found

Chiaroscuro: the treatment of light and shade in painting

Cinerary urn: used to hold ashes after cremation

Circus: in ancient Roman architecture, an elongated rectangular structure with rounded ends used for horse racing; in 18th-century architecture, a row of houses arranged in a circular pattern

Classical: architectural style characterized by its use of elements from ancient Greece or Rome, including finely proportioned, simple shapes, and which has its roots in the fifth century BC. Classicism has seen many revivals from the 15th century to the present day, including Renaissance in the 16th century and neoclassicism, which was popular between the late 18th and early 19th centuries

Cloister: a courtyard, often in a monastic building, surrounded by a covered passageway with an open arcade or colonnade on the interior side

Coffering: ceiling decoration made up from patterns of recessed squares or other shapes

Colonnade: a row of columns supporting a beam

Column: an upright, usually used as a decorative support, but sometimes free-standing as a monument. The design and proportions of columns vary, depending on their order (*see* Orders of columns)

Confessio: an underground area of a church, usually below the altar, which houses relics

Cosmatesque: decorative flooring of marble, glass and stones

Crossing: the area of a church where the transepts, nave and chancel intersect

Cruciform: cross-shaped, usually refers to a church

Crypt: area below the main church, usually for graves

Cupola: a domed roof

Entablature: comprising architrave, frieze and cornice, and resting horizontally on top of Classical columns

Etruscans: a race of people who inhabited Rome from around the eighth century BC. Their architecture was similar in style to that of Greek architecture of the same period

Exedra: in ancient Rome, a recess with raised seating

Fascist era: the extreme right-wing nationalist movement of 1922–43

Flavian era: the period of rule of Emperor Vespasian and his sons, Titus and Domitian, from 69–96AD

Forum: in ancient Rome, a large open space surrounded by public buildings

Fresco: a painting made directly onto damp plaster so that the image becomes permanent

Frieze: a decorated band, often along the top of a wall

Gothic: architectural style popular between the late 12th century and the mid-16th century, characterized by its pointed arches and ribbed vaulting on the ceiling

Greek cross: a church layout, whose ground plan resembles a cross with four equal arms (*see also* Latin cross)

Grotesque: style based on ancient Roman decoration found in underground ruins

Holy Door: a door in a major basilica, which is only opened in a Jubilee Year (every 25 years — the last Jubilee Year was 2000). The devout can earn an indulgence (time deducted from their time in Purgatory) by passing through the door

Imperial age: the age of the emperors, from 27BC to AD284

Lantern: a small, roofed tower with windows all around to provide daylight to the building below

Lapis lazuli: a blue mineral used as a gemstone. In Renaissance Italy, it was ground to make a bright blue pigment

Latin cross: a church layout, whose ground plan resembles a cross with three short arms and one longer one

Loggia: a room or gallery that is open on one or more sides

Malachite: a bright green mineral, often used as a gemstone

Mannerism: an architectural style, popular between 1530 and 1590, characterized by breaking the rules of Classicism and using Classical forms in a way other than is traditionally acceptable

Medallion: a round decorative panel

Medieval period: between 1000 and 1453

Nave: the long arm of a Latin cross church; the opposite end to the apse

Nymphaeum: in ancient Rome, a temple of the nymphs (semi-divine female river spirits)

Oculus: a circular opening, usually in a wall, but also at the top of a dome

Orders of columns: the style of the column. In Classical architecture there are four main orders of column: Doric, Tuscan, Ionic and Corinthian. All have a base, a shaft (the main part of the column) and a capital (the decorative top part). Doric columns have fluted shafts and a simple two-part capital. Tuscan columns are similar, but with a smooth shaft. Ionic columns are usually slimmer and taller, and their capitals have two large curls (sometimes two on each face), called volutes. Corinthian columns are slimmer again, with a very elaborate capital, decorated with leaves and curls. A final order, the Composite column, has a capital similar to a Corinthian one, but topped with the volutes of an Ionic capital

Papal altar: an altar at which only the pope can say Mass

Pediment: in Classical architecture, a low gable and entableture forming a triangular shape. Usually on the outside of a building, but also above doorways and fireplaces

Peristyle: columns ranged around a building or courtyard

Pier: a supporting pillar; the solid wall between two windows or other openings; or certain types of Gothic column that appear to be made of many shafts (when viewed in cross section)

Pilaster: a decorative column, protruding only slightly from a wall. It will always correspond to one of the orders of column (see left)

Porphyry: a hard rock, flecked with white or red crystals

Portico: a roofed area, usually the focus of a building's facade, supported by columns and topped with a pediment (see left)

Reliquary: an elaborate container holding part of a deceased holy person's body

Renaissance (High Renaissance): a period of Classical revival, popular in 16th-century Italy, where it is sometimes called the Rinascimento

Republican age: from the declaration of the Republic in 509BC to 27BC

Rococo: architectural style popular in the 18th century, characterized by low-relief decoration, usually in white and gold

Romanesque: an architectural style popular in the 11th–12th centuries, combining Classicism with influences from Byzantium and Islam

Rose window: large, circular window, usually in a church

Sacristy: a room in a church, where the vestments and sacred vessels are kept

Sarcophagus: a stone coffin

Satyr: a mythological woodland god with an animal's ears and tail

Sepulchre: a tomb cut from rock, or built from stone or brick

Stucco/stuccowork: a slow setting plaster, used to form intricate decoration

Tabernacle: in a church, an ornamental container for the consecrated host

Tempietto: literally, a small temple

Tesserae: small squares of glass, marble or stone, used to make mosaics

Transept: the short arms of a Latin cross church

Travertine stone: a white or light calcium carbonate-based rock, used for building

Triptych: a picture or carving on three panels, often used as an altarpiece

Trompe l'oeil: paintings that appear to show a room or landscape by use of perspective

Tufa: a porous rock found around mineral springs

Tympanum: between the lintel over a door and the arch above it. Also used to describe the flat area inside a pediment (see left)

Vaulting: an arched ceiling or roof

Villa: in Renaissance architecture, a country residence. Sometimes used to describe the parkland surrounding such a residence

PICTURES

The Automobile Association would like to thank the following photographers, companies and picture libraries for their assistance in the preparation of this book.

Abbreviations for the picture credits are as follows – (t) top; (b) bottom; (c) centre; (l) left; (r) right; (AA) AA World Travel Library.

4 AA/S McBride;
5 AA/A Kouprianoff;
6 AA/A Kouprianoff;
7 AA/P Wilson;
8 AA/A Mockford & N Bonetti;
9t AA/A Mockford & N Bonetti;
9b AA/C Sawyer;
10 AA/A Mockford & N Bonetti;
11 AA/A Mockford & N Bonetti;
12 AA/A Mockford & N Bonetti;
13t AA/C Sawyer;
13b AA/J Holmes;
14 Sipa Press/Rex Features;
15t Arturo Mari-Pool/Getty Images;
15b Action Press/Rex Features;
16 AA/A Mockford & N Bonetti;
17l AA/C Sawyer;
17r AA/A Mockford & N Bonetti;
18 AA/A Mockford & N Bonetti;
19t AA/A Mockford & N Bonetti;
19b Alberto Pizzoli/AFP/Getty Images;
20 AA/A Mockford & N Bonetti;
21l AA/S McBride;
21r AA/C Sawyer;
22 Miramax/Dimension Films/The Kobal Collection/Mario Tursi;
23t Pierluigi/Rex Features;
23b Rex Features;
24 AA/A Mockford & N Bonetti;
25 AA/S McBride;
26 AA/J Holmes;
27l AA/S McBride;
27r AA/P Wilson;
28 AA/A Mockford & N Bonetti;
29t Mary Evans Picture Library;
29b AA;
30 Musée des Augustins, Toulouse, France/The Bridgeman Art Library;
31t Mary Evans Picture Library;
31b AA;
32 AA;
33t AA/A Mockford & N Bonetti;
33b AA/J Holmes;
34 AA/J Holmes;
35t AA;
35b Mary Evans Picture Library;
36 AA/S McBride;
37l AA;
37r AA;

38 Mary Evans Picture Library;
39t AA/J Holmes;
39b AA/A Mockford & N Bonetti;
40l Hulton Archive/Getty Images;
40r Hulton Archive/Getty Images;
41 AA/A Mockford & N Bonetti;
42 Digitalvision;
44 AA/A Mockford & N Bonetti;
45 AA/A Mockford & N Bonetti;
46 AA/A Mockford & N Bonetti;
50 AA/A Mockford & N Bonetti;
51 AA/A Mockford & N Bonetti;
52 AA/A Mockford & N Bonetti;
53 AA/S McBride;
54 AA/A Mockford & N Bonetti;
55 AA/A Mockford & N Bonetti;
56 AA/S McBride;
60 AA/D Miterdiri;
61 AA/A Mockford & N Bonetti;
62 AA/A Mockford & N Bonetti;
63 MACRO – copyright Luigi Filetici – ODBC;
64 AA/D Miterdiri;
65 AA/D Miterdiri;
66l Galleria Borghese, Rome/Lauros/ Giraudon/The Bridgeman Art Library;
66r Galleria Borghese, Rome/The Bridgeman Art Library;
67 Galleria Borghese, Rome/The Bridgeman Art Library;
68 Galleria Borghese, Rome/The Bridgeman Art Library;
69 AA/D Miterdiri;
70 World Pictures/Photoshop;
71 AA/P Wilson;
72 AA/A Mockford & N Bonetti;
73 AA/A Mockford & N Bonetti;
74 AA/A Mockford & N Bonetti;
76 AA/A Kouprianoff;
77 AA/A Mockford & N Bonetti;
78 AA/D Miterdiri;
79 AA/P Wilson;
80 AA/A Mockford & N Bonetti;
81 AA/A Mockford & N Bonetti;
82 AA/A Mockford & N Bonetti;
83 AA/J Holmes;
84 AA/C Sawyer;
86 AA/S McBride;
87 AA/C Sawyer;
88 Digitalvision;

90 AA/A Mockford & N Bonetti;
94 AA/C Sawyer;
96 AA/C Sawyer;
100 AA/A Mockford & N Bonetti;
104 AA/C Sawyer;
106 AA/A Mockford & N Bonetti;
107 AA/P Wilson;
108 AA/S McBride;
109l AA/A Mockford & N Bonetti;
109r AA/A Mockford & N Bonetti;
110l AA/S McBride;
110r AA/A Mockford & N Bonetti;
111 AA/C Sawyer;
112 AA/A Mockford & N Bonetti;
113 AA/S McBride;
114 AA/A Mockford & N Bonetti;
115 Roma Turismo;
116l AA/A Mockford & N Bonetti;
116r AA/A Kouprianoff;
117 AA/C Sawyer;
118 AA/A Mockford & N Bonetti;
119 AA/A Mockford & N Bonetti;
120 AA/C Sawyer;
121 AA/C Sawyer;
123 AA/C Sawyer;
124 Digitalvision;
125 AA/C Sawyer;
126 AA/C Sawyer;
132 AA/A Mockford & N Bonetti;
136 AA/S McBride;
140 AA/A Mockford & N Bonetti;
141t AA/A Mockford & N Bonetti;
141b AA/A Mockford & N Bonetti;
142 AA/A Mockford & N Bonetti;
144 AA/A Mockford & N Bonetti;
145 AA/J Holmes
146 AA/A Mockford & N Bonetti;
147 AA/A Mockford & N Bonetti;
148 AA/A Mockford & N Bonetti;
149 AA/A Mockford & N Bonetti;
150 AA/S McBride;
151l AA/A Mockford & N Bonetti;
151r AA/A Mockford & N Bonetti;
152 imagebroker/Alamy
153 AA/A Mockford & N Bonetti
154 AA/C Sawyer;
155l AA/C Sawyer;
155r AA/C Sawyer
156 AA/J Holmes
157 AA/C Sawyer

158 AA/C Sawyer;
159 AA/C Sawyer;
160 AA/A Mockford & N Bonetti;
161 AA/A Kouprianoff;
162 AA/A Mockford & N Bonetti;
163 AA/S McBride;
164 AA/S McBride;
165 AA/S McBride;
166 AA/A Mockford & N Bonetti;
167 AA/D Miterdiri;
168 AA/A Mockford & N Bonetti;
169 AA/A Mockford & N Bonetti;
171 AA/A Mockford & N Bonetti;
172 AA/A Mockford & N Bonetti;
174 AA/A Mockford & N Bonetti;
175l AA/S McBride;
175r AA/D Miterdiri;
176 AA/C Sawyer;
177 AA/C Sawyer;
179 AA/C Sawyer;
180 AA/A Mockford & N Bonetti;
182 AA/A Mockford & N Bonetti;
183 AA/K Blackwell;
186 AA/A Mockford & N Bonetti;
190 AA/A Mockford & N Bonetti;
191 AA/A Mockford & N Bonetti;
192 AA/J Holmes;
193l AA/A Mockford & N Bonetti;
193r AA/J Holmes;
194 AA/S McBride;
195 AA/A Mockford & N Bonetti;
196 AA/J Holmes;
197 AA/J Holmes;

198 AA/C Sawyer;
199 AA/J Holmes;
200 AA/A Mockford & N Bonetti;
201 AA/A Mockford & N Bonetti;
206 AA/A Mockford & N Bonetti;
210 AA/T Souter;
212 AA/S McBride;
213tl AA/P Wilson;
213tr AA/S McBride;
213b AA/D Miterdiri;
214l AA/C Sawyer;
214r AA/C Sawyer;
215 AA/A Mockford & N Bonetti;
216 AA/A Mockford & N Bonetti;
217 AA/A Mockford & N Bonetti;
218 AA/J Holmes;
219t AA/J Holmes;
219b AA/S McBride;
220l AA/S McBride;
220r AA/S McBride;
221 AA/S McBride;
222t Corbis;
222b AA/A Mockford & N Bonetti;
224 AA/A Mockford & N Bonetti;
225 AA/A Mockford & N Bonetti;
226 Digitalvision;
228 AA/A Mockford & N Bonetti;
229 AA/A Mockford & N Bonetti;
232 AA/S McBride;
236 Photolibrary Group;
237 AA/A Mockford & N Bonetti;
239 Cubo Images/Robert Harding;
240 AA/A Mockford & N Bonetti;

241 AA/C Sawyer;
242 AA/A Mockford & N Bonetti;
243 AA/S McBride;
244 Photolibrary Group;
245l Photolibrary Group;
245r Photolibrary Group;
246 AA/J Holmes;
247 AA/A Mockford & N Bonetti;
250 AA/C Sawyer;
251 AA/C Sawyer;
252 AA/C Sawyer;
254 AA/A Mockford & N Bonetti;
257 AA/A Mockford & N Bonetti;
258 AA/A Kouprianoff;
261 AA/A Mockford & N Bonetti;
262l AA/A Mockford & N Bonetti;
262r AA/C Sawyer;
263 Paramount/Miramax/The Kobal
Collection/Phil Bray;
264 AA/A Mockford & N Bonetti;
265 Digitalvision;
266 AA/A Mockford & N Bonetti;
267 AA/A Mockford & N Bonetti;
268 AA/A Mockford & N Bonetti;
269 Roma Europa Festival;
270 AA/C Sawyer;
272 AA/A Mockford & N Bonetti;
274 AA/A Mockford & N Bonetti;
275 AA/C Sawyer;
276 AA/A Mockford & N Bonetti;
277 AA/C Sawyer;
282 AA/S McBride;
285 AA/J Holmes.

CREDITS

Series editor
Sheila Hawkins

Project editor
Laura Linder

Design
Bookwork Creative Associates Ltd

Cover design
Chie Ushio

Picture research
Wilf Matos

Image retouching and repro
Sarah Montgomery

Mapping
Maps produced by the Mapping Services Department
of AA Publishing

Text updated by Sally Roy

Indexer
Marie Lorimer

Production
Lorraine Taylor

See It Rome
ISBN 978-0-87637-138-1
Fifth Edition

Published in the United States by Fodor's Travel and simultaneously in Canada by Random House of Canada Limited, Toronto.
Published in the United Kingdom by AA Publishing.
Fodor's is a registered trademark of Random House, Inc., and Fodor's See It is a trademark of Random House, Inc.
Fodor's Travel is a division of Random House, Inc.

All rights reserved. Distributed by Random House, Inc., New York.
No maps, illustrations, or other portions of this book may be reproduced in any form without written permission from the publishers.

© AA Media Limited 2012

Color separation by AA Digital Department
Printed and bound by Leo Paper Products, China
10 9 8 7 6 5 4 3 2 1

Special Sales: This book is available for special discounts for bulk purchases for sales promotions or premiums. Special editions, including
personalized covers, excerpts of existing books, and corporate imprints, can be created in large quantities for special needs.
For more information, write to Special Markets/Premium Sales, 1745 Broadway, MD 3-1, New York, NY 10019
or e-mail specialmarkets@randomhouse.com
Important Note: Time inevitably brings changes, so always confirm prices, travel facts, and other perishable information when it matters.
Although Fodor's cannot accept responsibility for errors, you can use this guide in the confidence that we have taken every care to ensure
its accuracy.

A04723
Maps in this title produced from mapping © MAIRDUMONT/Falk Verlag 2012
Regional map produced from mapping © ISTITUTO GEOGRAFICO DE AGOSTINI S.p.A, Novara – 2009
Transport map © Communicarta Ltd, UK
Weather chart statistics supplied by Weatherbase © Copyright 2003 Canty and Associates, LLC

Unleash the Possibilities of Travel With Fodor's

Read before you get there, navigate your picks while you're there – make your trip unforgettable with Fodor's guidebooks. Fodor's offers the assurance of our expertise, the guarantee of selectivity, and the choice details that truly define a destination. Our books are written by local authors, so it's like having a friend wherever you travel.

With more than 10 different types of guidebooks to more than 150 destinations around the world, Fodor's has choices to meet every traveler's needs.

Visit **www.fodors.com** to find the guidebooks and connect with a like-minded community of selective travelers – living, learning, and traveling on their terms.

Fodor's For Choice Travel Experiences